CAMBRIDGE IBERIAN AND LATIN AMERICAN STUDIES

GENERAL EDITOR
P. E. RUSSELL F.B.A.
Emeritus Professor of Spanish Studies
University of Oxford

ASSOCIATE EDITORS
E. PUPO-WALKER
Director, Center for Latin American and Iberian Studies
Vanderbilt University
A. R. D. PAGDEN
Lecturer in History, University of Cambridge

Response to Revolution

CAMBRIDGE IBERIAN AND LATIN AMERICAN STUDIES

HISTORY AND SOCIAL THEORY

ROBERT I. BURNS: *Muslims, Christians, and Jews in the Crusader Kingdom of Valencia*

MICHAEL P. COSTELOE: *Response to Revolution: Imperial Spain and the Spanish American revolutions, 1810–1840*

HEATH DILLARD: *Daughters of the Reconquest: Women in Castilian town society, 1100–1300*

JOHN EDWARDS: *Christian Córdoba: the city and its region in the late Middle Ages*

JUAN LOPEZ-MORILLAS: *The Krausist Movement and Ideological Change in Spain, 1854–1874*

LINDA MARTZ: *Poverty and Welfare in Habsburg Spain: the example of Toledo*

ANTHONY PAGDEN: *The Fall of Natural Man: the American Indian and the origins of comparative ethnology*

EVELYN S. PROCTER: *Curia and Cortes in León and Castile, 1072–1295*

A. C. DE G. M. SAUNDERS: *A Social History of Black Slaves and Freedmen in Portugal, 1441–1555*

DAVID E. VASSBERG: *Land and Society in Golden-Age Castile*

LITERATURE AND LITERARY THEORY

STEVEN BOLDY: *The Novels of Julio Cortázar*

ANTHONY CASCARDI: *The Limits of Illusion: a critical study of Calderón*

MAURICE HEMINGWAY: *Emilia Pardo Bazán: the making of a novelist*

B. W. IFE: *Reading and Fiction in Golden-Age Spain: a Platonist critique and some picaresque replies*

JOHN LYON: *The Theatre of Valle-Inclán*

JULIÁN OLIVARES: *The Love Poetry of Francisco de Quevedo: an aesthetic and existential study*

FRANCISCO RICO: *The Spanish Picaresque Novel and the Point of View*

HENRY W. SULLIVAN: *Calderón in the German Lands and the Low Countries: his reception and influence, 1654–1980*

DIANE F. UREY: *Galdós and the Irony of Language*

Response to Revolution

Imperial Spain and the Spanish American revolutions, 1810–1840

MICHAEL P. COSTELOE

Professor of Hispanic and Latin American Studies
University of Bristol

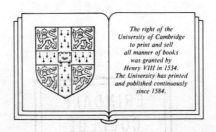

The right of the
University of Cambridge
to print and sell
all manner of books
was granted by
Henry VIII in 1534.
The University has printed
and published continuously
since 1584.

CAMBRIDGE UNIVERSITY PRESS

CAMBRIDGE
LONDON   NEW YORK   NEW ROCHELLE
MELBOURNE   SYDNEY

Published by the Press Syndicate of the University of Cambridge
The Pitt Building, Trumpington Street, Cambridge CB2 1RP
32 East 57th Street, New York, NY 10022, USA
10 Stamford Road, Oakleigh, Melbourne 3166, Australia

© Cambridge University Press 1986

First published 1986

Printed in Great Britain at
the University Press, Cambridge

British Library Cataloguing in Publication Data
Costeloe, Michael P.
Response to revolution: imperial Spain and the
Spanish American revolutions 1810–1840.
1. Spain – Foreign relations – 19th century
2. Spain – Foreign relations – Latin America
3. Latin America – Foreign relations – Spain
I. Title
327.4608   DP86.L29

Library of Congress Cataloguing in Publication Data
Costeloe, Michael P.
Response to revolution.
(Cambridge Iberian and Latin American studies)
Bibliography: p.
1. South America – History – Wars of Independence,
1806–1830 – Foreign public opinion, Spanish.
2. Public opinion – Spain – History – 19th century.
3. South America – Foreign relations – Spain. 4. Spain –
Foreign relations – South America. I. Title.
II. Series.
F2235.C67   1986   980'.02   85–21253

ISBN 0 521 32083 6

SE

For Eleanor

Contents

Preface	*page*	ix
Acknowledgements		xiii
1	An introduction	1
2	Revolution: the view from Spain	20
3	The military solution	52
4	The logistics of reconquest	101
5	Economic and commercial reform	117
6	The aftermath of imperial decline	150
7	A new relationship	171
8	The diplomatic initiative	193
	Epilogue	218
	Notes	231
	Sources and works cited	257
	Index	267

Preface

This book is about the Spanish American revolutions for independence as seen by Spaniards in Spain. It arose from a desire to know what Spaniards thought about the revolutions and how they responded to the threat and then the actual loss of their centuries-old empire in the New World. Having read many general histories and scholarly monographs on myriad aspects of the separatist movements, it was obvious that the peninsular Spanish viewpoint was not well represented in the standard bibliography. History has for the most part concentrated attention on the heroic careers of the great liberators of America and the campaigns for freedom from colonial oppression which they led, but what did Spaniards living in the metropolis think of Simón Bolívar and his fellow revolutionaries? What was the Spanish interpretation of events in America, what policies were adopted, what were the effects on Spanish trade and the merchants who conducted it, what actions did Spain take to meet American demands or to suppress them? In short, how did Spaniards respond to revolution and how in retrospect did they see the end of their nation's long role as a major imperial power?

It is with these and related questions that this study is concerned. I have chosen to adopt a topical approach mainly because the Spanish response was not determined or even significantly affected by the radical shifts of political control in the Mother Country which occurred during the reign of Ferdinand VII. Although an age of ideological ferment in Spain, liberals and conservatives, absolute monarchists and supporters of popular sovereignty, all shared a more or less common attitude towards the revolutions and even though their proposed solutions to the imperial crisis differed in detail and in emphasis, in substance their attitudes and response were the same. Their interpretation of events, the conclusions reached and the policies advocated when the first news of the revolutions arrived in

Cádiz in the summer of 1810 remained basically unchanged some twenty years later and in some respects well into the nineteenth century. Indeed, as discussed in the introductory chapter, there was a notable consistency and continuity in the Spanish response, all the more surprising perhaps in view of the political instability at home and the fundamental changes occurring within and without the Iberian peninsula. Secondly, the dates given for the period of this study, 1810–40, are approximate only. The latter date in particular is somewhat arbitrary for I have sought to illustrate in several chapters the retrospective views of some Spaniards who looked back from the 1830s onwards at the events of their own time in what may be conveniently termed the imperial post-mortem. Again, despite the passage of time and the advantage of hindsight, few Spaniards changed their initial attitudes and these seem to have been inherited by subsequent generations of the nineteenth century. Of course, Spanish attitudes and policy were largely determined by their knowledge and understanding of what was going on in America, what had caused the revolutions and who was involved. These matters are among those examined in the first chapter and then, following a more or less chronological narrative within each section, I have divided the work into those areas of military, economic, political and diplomatic action and opinion which, taken together, are intended to illustrate the principal aspects of the Spanish response to colonial revolution. Finally, among the many dilemmas faced by Spaniards who lived through and witnessed the loss of their American empire was how to respond to the birth of the new republics in America. It was to take much of the nineteenth century for them to reconcile themselves to defeat and in the epilogue I have included some of the reasoning used by successive generations to explain their unwillingness to accept that their empire was gone forever.

Clearly, a nation's response to its imperial decline is a subject of infinite dimensions and for practical reasons as well as of historical interpretation, restrictions must be imposed. I have included nothing of what those *afrancesado* Spaniards who supported the intrusive Napoleonic régime from 1808 to 1814 felt about the situation in America, nor of those Spanish exiles, for example, Blanco White, who lived elsewhere in Europe. Similarly, I have excluded those Spaniards who remained in America throughout the years of war and, except in a few cases, have given little attention to the ideas, always treated with suspicion by Spaniards, of Americans living in the metropolis. I have been concerned only with those Spaniards in Spain who were directly affected by or who participated in the Spanish response. It must also be emphasized that this is in no sense a study of the movements for independence and there is little reference to the course of events in America. This is because specific incidents, for example, a major victory or defeat on the battlefields, appear to have had minimal impact on Spanish thought or action with developments across the length and breadth of the American continent proceeding almost independently of the Spanish response. This was partly because there was so much contradictory information pouring into government offices that there is a good case for arguing that Spaniards were never fully aware of what was happening or certainly never believed that they had an accurate and complete picture. Their response was more the product of an accumulation of information, opinion and their own pre-existing prejudices towards Americans. While histories of the revolutions rightly emphasize the victory of the royalist forces and the apparent restoration of Spanish dominion in most provinces by approximately 1816, it was never thought by the politicians and others in Madrid that the insurgents were defeated. They knew that the spirit of rebellion was profound and spreading and some had even concluded that the loss of the whole empire was by then inevitable.

The fluctuating scene in America was not reflected, therefore, in any substantial changes of attitude or policy in Spain. Regardless of the fortunes of their cause in the New World, Spaniards knew from 1811 onwards that their empire was under grave and constant threat of disintegration. It also appears, although to a lesser extent, that political and other developments throughout Ferdinand's long and eventful reign bore little direct relation to the Spanish response to events in America. Hence, while I have necessarily included an outline of the major political and constitutional changes in Spain, I have only infrequently referred to those activities of either the liberal régimes or those of Ferdinand which pertain almost exclusively to peninsular affairs. On the other hand, it must be emphasized that in some respects, especially economic matters, internal affairs did intrude significantly on those of the empire and there were vital political considerations affecting the domestic scene which no government could ignore when deciding its American policy; these factors have been explained and incorporated where appropriate.

A subject of infinite dimensions has, of course, for all practical purposes an infinite quantity and range of sources. Much of the information used has been derived from several national Spanish archives and, to obtain a limited provincial view, some local ones have also been consulted. There is in addition a mass of contemporary printed material including newspapers, memoirs and unlimited pamphlets and this has been referred to extensively. My initial impression when embarking on the research was that little had been written on the subject, but it was quickly apparent that I was mistaken. Prominent incidents, for example, the ill-fated Buenos Aires expedition of 1819, have been well investigated and Spanish policy towards some areas in America, again most notably the River Plate, has received considerable attention from, it seems, mostly Latin American historians. Also, there are a number of unpublished doctoral dissertations on one or more aspects of the subject and Spain's economic relationship with America particularly in the final decades of the *ancien régime* has in recent years attracted important scholarly attention. It is nevertheless true, however, that there are still relatively few studies restricted to the Spanish response or which offer more than a limited analysis of some of its multiple aspects. Among those which do attempt a wider view, Professor Anna's book *Spain and the loss of America* has been a useful reference for the largely political matters with which it is concerned, although I have many disagreements with his interpretation; for example, his view that 'the real failure of empire . . . and most of the real debate over American policy' took place after 1814 (p.xiv). Equally useful are the published works of Fernández Almagro, Delgado, Friede, Mariluz Urquijo and the doctoral dissertations and articles of Woodward, Rhodes and Resnick. None of these works, nor any of the other mass of secondary literature which has been consulted, has proved as helpful as the prodigiously researched book by E. A. Heredia entitled *Planes españoles para reconquistar Hispanoamérica*. For the years which he investigated, Professor Heredia located and utilized an enormous amount of manuscript material and his narrative summaries of the documents have proved invaluable for my own research.

Acknowledgements

Grateful acknowledgement is made to the many scholars and the staff of archives and libraries in Spain, Great Britain and the United States, without whose generous assistance and cooperation the research for this book would not have been possible. I am particularly indebted to Dr Rosario Parra, Director of the Archivo de Indias in Seville, for help in locating and filming a large number of manuscripts. My thanks are due also to Carmen Martín Acebes and Julián García Valverde for hospitality in Madrid, and to the following for obtaining copies of books and documents: Mr and Mrs Robert Mills (Madrid), Jane Garner (Texas), Pedro Grases (Caracas), Antoni Turull (Barcelona). Jean Heelis and Rosemary Jenkins willingly and efficiently did the typing and both the British Academy and the University of Bristol provided essential financial support.

M.P.C.

I

An introduction

On 2 February 1944 the distinguished scholar, Melchor Fernández Almagro, began his inaugural lecture to the Spanish Royal Academy of History with the following hypothesis. If one was to stop passers-by in the streets of Spain and ask, 'When did Spain lose its American Empire?', the answer from most people would be 1898, the year when in fact Spain lost the islands of Cuba, Puerto Rico and the Philippines which were no more than the final, comparatively insignificant remnants of the once great American empire. Some people, he added, might perhaps reply with an earlier date but few would be precise, and it would be rare indeed to find anyone who knew of the battle of Ayacucho of 1824 which effectively marked the end of Spanish rule on the American continent. Why then, Fernández Almagro wondered, has the loss of Spanish America left so slight an impression in the collective Spanish memory? The answer, he suggested, lay in the fact that the wars of emancipation in America left little or no impression on the generation of Spaniards who lived through and witnessed Spain's humiliation and defeat. Hence with the first impression faint, memories faded quickly and the disaster of Ayacucho and all that it implied was soon forgotten.[1]

I would venture to suggest that if one conducted a similar opinion poll in Spain today, the answers would still be as Fernández Almagro predicted. The loss of America does appear to have had little impact on general Spanish public opinion at the time when it occurred, despite the relative rapidity with which the monolithic imperial structure disintegrated. The empire, arguably the greatest the world had ever seen, was lost between 1810 and 1824. In those few years, revolution spread throughout the colonies from Chile in the south to Mexico in the north. The continent and its sixteen million people, colonized and governed by generation after generation of Spaniards for more than three hundred years, rejected all Spanish authority.

The once great viceroyalties were replaced by new republics and the political, economic and strategic map of the world was radically altered. Yet, at first sight, most Spaniards do indeed seem to have had little or no interest in these momentous events and at best were indifferent towards the fate of their empire. There is no sign of any public expression or sense of national disaster, or willingness to make sacrifices for the sake of preserving the imperial heritage.[2] Government attempts to levy special taxes for the war effort in America were met with the usual evasive tactics that often greeted taxation. For example, a small surcharge was added to theatre tickets throughout Spain, but the theatre owners refused to collect it. A similar levy was put on tickets for the bullfights, but the *aficionados* also refused to pay. Retail businesses were required to pay an insignificant amount in additional taxation, but again the shopkeepers refused to cooperate. Attempts to raise loans for the war effort from the wealthy sectors of society met with the same resistance and hostility. Volunteers to fight in the colonies were few, and of those who were voluntarily or otherwise enlisted in the expeditionary armies, many promptly deserted in America, some unwilling to risk their lives in war but others to join the rebel forces.[3]

In the decades which followed the battle of Ayacucho, there is also an intriguing absence of comment or reference to America where one might expect to find at least some observation, if not a profound reaction and inquisition into what had gone wrong. There are histories of the reign of Ferdinand VII who ruled, albeit intermittently, from 1808–33, written in the 1830s onwards, which scarcely mention America. There are memoirs by men who, in the 1860s, looking back over their lives provide detailed, informative accounts of the events of their time and yet, in some of these, there is no reference at all to America.[4] For such well-known observers of the public scene as Mesonero Romanos and Mariano Larra, the latter writing his myriad articles in the 1830s and 1840s, the empire already seems to have been forgotten and not a matter of any concern. Spain's great novelist, Pérez Galdós, author of a series of historical novels covering the years from 1808 onwards, and known to be diligent in his pursuit of sources and historical accuracy, makes only passing and superficial reference to the wars in America, and permits his characters almost no opinions on what Spaniards felt about the loss of their empire.[5] One modern literary historian, surveying the thousands of novels published in the nineteenth century as a whole, states, 'It is a fact that the independence of America is not reflected in, nor did it inspire, any important novel in the nineteenth century.'[6] Similarly, no Romantic dramatist or poet in Spain seems to have found any inspiration in the heroic or tragic aspects of the emancipation movements, the frequently used symbols of liberty struggling against tyranny, nor in the colourful and larger-than-life images of Simón Bolívar and the other great liberators of their nations.

There are several possible explanations for this absence of wide-spread public reaction, or faint impression, as Fernández Almagro put it. The most likely is the historical context in which the revolutions in America took place and the relative significance which the imperial problem assumed for Spaniards when seen against other events of their age. For many, there were other issues of fundamental and, clearly for some, greater significance in the evolution of peninsular Spain. The Napoleonic invasion of 1808 and the subsequent war of Spanish independence obviously preoccupied people and politicians until the final expulsion of the French armies in 1814. Those years of war also heralded the emergence of liberal reformers who sought to dismantle the institutions and practices of absolutism and to replace them with their vision of a progressive, secular society based on constitutional monarchy. Prolonged conflict with the reactionary forces of the *ancien régime* was inevitable and although some of the issues were resolved either by war or by time, the pattern of chronic instability, fiscal crisis and military intervention in civil affairs was established.

Not surprisingly, therefore, given the constant ideological, economic and social ferment, their more immediate difficulties were paramount in the minds of Spaniards and the problems of their distant empire did not intrude directly into their lives. To some extent, it is also true to say that for the great majority of Spaniards, the empire had never been of any obvious or tangible importance. Throughout the 300-year-old-union, the material links between Spain and America were the concern of only a small minority. In addition to the upper levels of the colonial bureaucracy and ecclesiastical hierarchy which had always been largely staffed by officials sent from the peninsula, the only social group closely involved in the affairs of the empire was the merchant community. Spanish policy since the sixteenth century, however, had consistently been to restrict the transatlantic trade to a comparatively small group of privileged ports and merchants. Even after the liberalization of the commercial code in the second half of the eighteenth century, approximately 90 per cent of all Spanish trade with America was conducted through the port of Cádiz.[7] Other ports traded with the colonies but only as a negligible proportion of their total foreign trade, whereas Cádiz was wholly dependent on the colonial trade for its affluence and, indeed, its survival as a major city-port. It was there that the merchant companies, shipowners, insurance brokers and many ancillary professions had earned their fortunes and made their city into the most prosperous in the peninsula. But, the main beneficiaries of colonial commerce in the good times were also the first victims in the bad and, when the wars in America brought about the collapse of trade, Cádiz rapidly declined into poverty and stagnation. Much of the impetus and the money for the war effort against the dissidents was to come from Cádiz, but often its pleas for greater urgency and action by central government met with no response and even outright hostility, precisely, as was frequently stated at the time, because they came from a minority and obviously vested interest group. The Cádiz merchants had been a privileged minority for too long and their contemporaries both knew and resented it. Hence among fellow merchants in other areas of Spain who traded with but were not dependent on America for their livelihoods, there was little sympathy for their plight. Rafael Catalá, a young Barcelona-based merchant whose family firm occasionally traded with the colonies, expressed this quite succinctly. In 1813, in a private letter, he wrote: 'I could not care less if we separated from that damned rabble; anyone who saves his skin in the present circumstances will be lucky.'[8]

For most Spaniards, therefore, for the rural peasants, the urban workers, the majority of the middle and upper classes, America was detached and seemingly unrelated to their daily lives and from which they personally derived no immediate benefit. Even though the legal imports of colonial produce which such people consumed – sugar, coffee, cocoa, etc. – declined, the little evidence we have seems to suggest that there was no significant scarcity or prolonged price rise in these commodities.[9] Alternative sources of supply and the contraband trade probably provided the balance.[10] It is clear within this context of national and personal priorities that there was, to use Vilar's phrase, no 'outburst of collective passion' by the Spanish people when they were confronted with the possibility of the loss of their American empire. Yet this picture of apathy or indifference displayed by the majority of the Spanish people does not tell the whole story. Slight though the reaction was of the general public, at least as far as we can deduce, it would be wrong to assert that the passing of Spanish rule on the American continent went unnoticed by Spaniards or that all Spaniards were indifferent to or unaware of the immeasurable consequences for their nation of the loss of its imperial power. On the contrary, from the monarch and his ministers to politicians, clergy, bureaucrats, merchants, shipowners and those ordinary Spaniards who had business or family ties with the colonies, all desperately sought every means open to them to reconcile the dissident Americans and to restore imperial harmony. Of course, it was in the realm of politics and in the corridors of power where the decisions had to be taken and where the consequences of failure for Spain were most discussed. Some historians have been misled by the apparent public apathy into believing that the American issue always remained on the fringe of political affairs, overshadowed by the more immediate domestic conflicts in the peninsula. This is only partly the case, for the 'pacification' of America, as it became known, was constantly in the minds of governments throughout the reign of Ferdinand VII and vast amounts of time and resources, both human and material, were expended in vain attempts to achieve it. Although irreconcilable differences of opinion over the future nature of the political, social and economic evolution of the monarchy dominated the public scene, the views of men of all shades of the political spectrum from radical progressive to extreme reactionary were almost uniform with regard to the subject of American independence. Spain's position rested on a single, consistent policy; recognition of independence would not be granted. That fundamental position was maintained throughout the reign of Ferdinand VII irrespective of whether the country was governed as a constitutional monarchy under the control of liberals or by Ferdinand in full possession of his powers as an absolute monarch. It provided possibly the only point of consensus in the ideological ferment of the age and the attitude of the liberals at Cádiz and Madrid during the two periods of constitutional government (1810–14; 1820–3) differed little, if anything, in substance from that prevailing during the years of absolutist rule by Ferdinand (1814–20; 1823–33). There were clearly individual exceptions and varying degrees of flexibility, but, whereas it might be, and indeed, was expected by Americans and foreign interests at the time that the liberals would be more inclined to compromise than the absolutists of the *ancien régime*, this proved not to be the case. The traditional labels – conservatives, liberals, progressives, reactionaries, constitutionalists, absolutists etc. – tell us nothing in respect of men's attitudes towards the colonial wars. Men who were wholly committed to the defence, for example, of popular sovereignty and the right of a people to self-government refused to extend their sacred principles to America, while others who declined to countenance any significant change in Spanish society were willing to be at least pragmatic when it came to seeking ways and means of resolving the imperial crisis.

The overall objective of retaining the empire, even if in a new form, was, therefore, shared by men of all political persuasions. The constitutionalist and absolutist régimes were willing to consider any measure which offered the hope of achieving this objective and the policies actually adopted by both were the same in most cases. For example, the belief, followed by the practice, that using military force to suppress the insurgents offered the best hope of success originated in the Regency and liberal-dominated Cortes at Cádiz in 1811. It was actively pursued during the remaining years of the first constitutional period and when Ferdinand was restored to full regal power in 1814, he and his advisers did not change the policy except to prosecute it in a stronger form. During the second constitutional era of 1820–3, the hope that military force was still a credible option was not abandoned and there were still those who campaigned for it, even though the practicalities of the situation were by then such that little military action was in fact undertaken. Nevertheless, despite the all too evident reality of the nation's military and financial impotence, Ferdinand and his advisers continued throughout the 1820s to plot and dream of reconquest, even to the extent of authorizing a futile and humiliating attack on Mexico in 1829. The same continuity of ideas and policy applied in most areas. Mediation by Britain or another foreign power was first discussed at Cádiz and the possibility was investigated on many occasions throughout the absolutist years until at least 1819. Direct negotiations with the rebels, peace envoys, the offer of concessions and myriad other proposed avenues that were explored were almost all initiated at Cádiz and remained within the global policy options of all Spanish governments until Ferdinand's demise.

There was a widespread and often expressed feeling that national honour was at stake and that to acquiesce in the separation of the colonies and thereby admit military defeat was dishonourable, even years after the military phase of the revolutions was over. For politicians, merchants, journalists, diplomats and others, a persistent belief, or perhaps hope, endured that the wars in America were not being fought with the aim of complete independence but rather to achieve an improved relationship with the Mother Country. Spaniards found it difficult to accept that the people of America, especially the white creole population as a whole, sharing as they did a common language and above all, religion, were really seeking to break all the ties of kinship and cultural heritage which bound them in so many ways to the peninsula. It was this belief that underlined and encouraged many of the reforms that were devised and offered to the insurgents and the policy of responding, for the most part positively if belatedly, to any and all American demands, always short of full independence. Furthermore, the attitude of Spaniards and their reactions were to a considerable extent determined by their interpretation of what had caused the revolutions in the first place. There was no agreement on any one or more causes, but it is significant that the array of explanations put forward in Cádiz from 1810 to 1812 was much the same as those advanced by Ferdinand's advisers and again by the liberals in the 1820s. One important exception is evident in the analysis of causes, but it again illustrates the widely held assumption common to both liberals and conservatives that a negotiated solution to restore imperial unity was always possible. The liberals often attributed the emancipation movements to the system of government, that is absolute monarchism, under which the overseas provinces had been ruled for so long. The construction of a liberal, constitutional monarchy with all that that implied in terms of individual rights and liberties was for the reformers a sure way of reattracting the loyalty of Americans, since they would at least in theory be treated in the future on equal terms with peninsular Spaniards. Hence the new constitution was paraded as the panacea to resolve all imperial difficulties, both in 1812 and in 1820. At the same time, however, the absolutists were convinced that it was precisely the collapse of the existing system of government in Spain, brought about by the French invasion and the bourgeois revolution, which had caused the rebellion of the Americas. Thus at Cádiz they thought, once the French usurpers were expelled, the liberal experiment dismantled and the *ancien régime* headed by Ferdinand restored, so the colonial subjects of the Crown would loyally return to the imperial fold. They held the same view a decade later, blaming the reintroduction of the 1812 constitution for stimulating the fresh outbreak of revolt in colonies which had seemed to be pacified.

Such attitudes explain in part the continuity of Spain's consistent refusal to recognize American independence and the persistence of the same general solutions to the problem regardless of the ideology of the government in office. There were clearly variations in emphasis, particularly in the debate over the effectiveness or otherwise of military force, but the differences rarely represented any basic change of attitude. Usually they were reactions to the fluctuating circumstances of the time within the political and financial situation in the peninsula and even more so to the changing fortunes of the royal armies on the fields of battle. Yet, although the reunification of the empire remained the common aim, there was no agreement over how to achieve it. Indeed, for some contemporary participants assessing the events in retrospect, it was the disagreement over means that prevented the realization of the agreed end and prevented the adoption of any coherent or coordinated response towards the revolutions during the reign of Ferdinand VII. Instead there was fierce controversy over the best way to deal with the situation and all governments were bombarded with suggested ways of pacifying the insurgents. The sheer quantity was too great for the government bureaucracy to handle and in December 1816, the Navy Minister, José Vázquez Figueroa, angrily denounced the inefficient administrative system in which decisions were being lost in 'a real morass of conflicting papers'. Five years later, the same confusion prevailed and the ever increasing mountain of paper scattered throughout the administrative offices of government seriously delayed the then liberal administration's attempts to produce a policy.[11] In some respects, this bureaucratic chaos was no more than a reflection of the diversity of interest groups concerned or affected by the fate of the empire. The interests of institutions, public and private, the rivalries of domestic Spanish politics, the secret intrigues and ambitions of individuals, the intervention of foreign powers and many other factors all conspired to prevent the emergence of any systematic or logical policy. Faced with ever-conflicting advice from so many directions at once, governments were uncertain and always hesitant, preferring to try simultaneously inherently contradictory measures. For example, as already stated, there was a strong lobby, during both liberal and absolutist régimes, in favour of using as much military force as could be mustered to suppress the alleged insurgent minority of Americans. At the same time, there was a lobby against the use of force on the grounds, usually, that it was impractical, ineffective and counter-productive. A third group postulated that only direct negotiation with the rebels could produce a long-term solution. A fourth maintained that Spain must demonstrate its military capacity first, in order to persuade the Americans to negotiate. A fifth insisted that foreign mediation was essential but should be supported by at least the threat of military force. Confronted with these and many other pressures, not least the instability at home, all Spanish governments sought to pursue these and other policies simultaneously. Concessions were offered to Americans at the same time as military expeditions were being dispatched.

There is no doubt that the policy-making machinery and administrative structure hindered the decision-making process and contributed to the general confusion. The Spanish bureaucracy of the time was already notoriously inefficient and it was obviously not helped by the frequent changes in the fundamental law and political system of the monarchy. Irrespective of the régime in power, however, arriving at and implementing decisions was slow and cumbersome. During the constitutionalist years, the Cortes debated American affairs on many occasions but every proposal had to be examined and reported on by diverse and often overlapping committees. At times, months elapsed only for the eventual decision to be irrelevant because of changed circumstances in the peninsula or in America, and several deputies bitterly complained at the lack of urgency displayed by their colleagues. Others in both the Cádiz Cortes and those of the 1820s realized that strict observance of parliamentary prerogatives was unsuitable in the crisis facing the nation and they moved that the executive authority be permitted to devise and enact whatever policy it felt was required. The majority would not accept this diminution of their powers and would not permit any major policy decision to be taken without their prior approval. Nor was there much harmony over policy between the legislative and executive branches. At Cádiz, the Regency strongly supported trade concessions, if necessary accompanied by mediation by Britain, as the best hope of ending the revolutions, but both ideas, taken together or separately, were rejected by the Cortes. During the second constitutional era, there was frequent discord between the two branches of government with the cabinet generally preferring a more militant approach than that wanted by the Cortes. Both sides accused each other of acting unconstitutionally and deputies' pleas for up-to-date information on recent developments were often met with unexplained silence or delay by the ministers concerned.[12]

Given the novelty of constitutional government in Spain, especially in the insecure and hostile environment in which it was obliged to operate, it is not surprising that the formulation of policy towards America was difficult. By the same token, it might be expected that under the absolute monarchy, with Ferdinand enjoying unrestricted, supreme power, efficiency or at least speed of decision would be the norm. In 1814, Ferdinand restored the institutional structure which had been in operation before his departure to exile in France in 1808, that is, the consultative pyramid of ministers, councils and committees whose function was to inform and advise the king on all affairs of state. Ferdinand, as an absolute ruler, certainly had the final say in whatever action was taken, but he did not reach his decisions alone. On the contrary, at least in respect of America, he used his consultative machinery to the fullest extent and he created influential new agencies to assist him. But again, disagreement was more prevalent among his advisers than consensus and even on those few occasions when the great weight of opinion was strongly in favour of a particular policy, he at times refused to follow it. Nevertheless, he did spend countless hours presiding over his Councils, listening to infinite expositions and personally interviewing all manner of people with ideas on how to restore his empire. He himself was consistent, never wavering in what he considered his sacred duty to preserve the territorial integrity of his kingdom.

Just as the parliamentary procedure and executive–legislative rivalries prejudiced the formulation of policy under the constitutionalist system, Ferdinand's consultative structure hindered rather than facilitated prompt decision and action. The main problem was the multiplicity and duplication of the administrative system which contained at each level several parallel layers. His ministers were his most immediate official advisers, but their individual responsibilities for American affairs were often ill-defined. This provoked frequent acrimony and rivalry between them which in turn caused some to argue that there should be a separate Ministry with sole jurisdiction over all areas of colonial business. The constitutionalists had reached a similar conclusion and created in 1812 the Despacho de la Gobernación del reino para Ultramar, or Ministry of Ultramar as it became known. This was abolished by Ferdinand in 1814, but he then continued and strengthened the experiment by centralizing all colonial affairs in a new ministry entitled the Ministerio Universal de las Indias. The official propaganda asserted that this would ensure greater efficiency, to the benefit of all Americans whose needs would be better and more quickly cared for. Such hopes and promises were not realized and personal factors as well as continued inter-departmental rivalry soon brought its abolition in September 1815. Ferdinand then ordered that a special colonial office be set up in each of the established ministries. Those concerned most directly with the pacification issue were State, War, Navy and Treasury. In 1816–17, amidst mounting discord between his ministers and more and more evidence that the situation in the colonies was increasingly desperate, Ferdinand again sought a means of improving his advisory and executive machinery by placing a general authority for all matters relating to American pacification in the hands of his Secretary of State, José García de León y Pizarro. He was to devote much of his energy to the American issue during his two years of office but he was to be frustrated by his rivals at court who, according to his own account, were more concerned with scoring political points against him personally than with trying to resolve the colonial crisis.[13] Indeed, it was the Minister of Grace and Justice, whose office was only marginally concerned with the revolutions, who led the campaign against Pizarro's attempt to devise a flexible policy and especially against his insistence that Spain's trading monopoly must be abandoned if there was to be any hope of reconciliation with the Americans.

The various ministers acted independently for the most part but Ferdinand did order regular, sometimes weekly, cabinet sessions in which American developments were discussed and similar meetings were held during the constitutionalist years. At the top of the administrative pyramid and parallel in influence to the Departments of State, especially in the absolutist system, were the royal councils. Again there were several of these which advised on America. The Council of War had a say in military policy, the Council of the Treasury in fiscal matters, the Council of the Admiralty in naval strategy, but by far the most important were the Council of the Indies and the Council of State. The former was closely involved from the beginning of the movements for independence in 1810 until its abolition in April 1812. It was restored by Ferdinand in 1814 and again in 1824 and played an active part in the policy debate. In contrast, the Council of State, or Privy Council, although the superior body in status, was little used by the constitutionalists until 1813, but from then onwards its role was vital and it became the arena for much of the controversy over America throughout the rest of Ferdinand's reign.

In addition to these formal agencies, there were diverse other official sub-committees and working parties specially established to suggest appropriate methods of pacification. The most notable of these was the Junta de Pacificación. This originated from a small working party set up by royal order on 3 December 1815 under the chairmanship of the Duque de Montemar. A parallel group was appointed on 7 September 1816 and the following month the two were ordered to amalgamate, again under the chairmanship of Montemar.[14] This larger, single committee proceeded to meet regularly, issuing substantial reports and programmes of action until 1818. Following Ferdinand's decision in 1814, again taken after widespread consultation, to increase the military effort against the insurgents, working parties of generals and other high-ranking officers were assembled. They were commanded to submit advice on strategy, equipment, the number of men and ships needed for expeditions and the best areas to concentrate Spanish reinforcements. The first of these groups, a Junta de Generales, was appointed in July 1814 under the chairmanship of the Infante Carlos and it was one of several advisory bodies to recommend the dispatch to Venezuela, rather than the River Plate, of the expedition led by General Morillo which, after months of delay, finally embarked in February 1815.[15] When preparations were actively under way in 1818 for a full-scale assault on Buenos Aires, another group of generals was summoned and several papers examining alternative tactics and destinations were presented.[16] The Admiralty still had its own special section concerned with America and, in an attempt to coordinate preparations and strategy, Ferdinand ordered on 17 November 1818 a combined committee with three representatives each from the War Office, Admiralty and Council of the Indies.[17] Each of these committees, as well as the ministers and councils, invited submissions from those supposedly knowledgeable of the situation in the colonies, and unsolicited expositions and suggested means of ending the revolutions were forthcoming from individuals and corporations both in Spain and in America. Hour after hour was devoted to consideration of these often lengthy documents, usually only for them to be rejected for one reason or another. Also the international dimensions of the future fate of the empire produced an endless stream of reports from Spain's ambassadors in Britain, France, Portugal, Russia, United States and elsewhere.

What may be described as the official apparatus of the State during both constitutionalist and absolutist régimes was a labyrinth of intricate and often rival interests in which domestic political considerations inevitably intruded on the search for a considered and agreed reaction to the events in America but, complex as it was, it was by no means the only forum in which policy was discussed. There were many semi-official groups which constituted powerful lobbies and certainly influenced decisions. Among these, there were two of particular significance. One was an *ad hoc* group of representatives of all the merchant guilds, or *consulados*, in Spain. Known as the Junta de diputados de los Consulados, it began with a circular from the Minister of Hacienda on 16 February 1816 in which the guilds were invited to send representatives to Madrid to discuss difficulties that had arisen over the collection of a 30,000,000 *real* loan being raised for the war effort in America. The representatives duly assembled from all parts of Spain and soon were compiling long reports on the causes and consequences of the revolutions, naturally emphasizing the damage being caused to Spanish commerce.[18] They clearly represented the merchant interest and were to have considerable influence on future trading policy. The second semi-official group was also composed of merchants. This was the Comisión de Reemplazos, a small committee set up in September 1811, probably at the initiative of the merchants themselves, for the express purpose of raising the funds needed to pay for military expeditions to the colonies. Its members were drawn from the Cádiz merchant community and throughout the vital years from 1811 to 1820, it was to be at the centre of Spain's attempt at military reconquest.[19] Loosely linked to or supervised by several government departments during this period, to all intents and purposes, it was an independent, private enterprise body, acting on the basis of general directives from above but retaining control of its affairs and its methods of operation within its own hands. In terms of the controversy over the pacification issue and what Spain's policy should be, it was the Comisión which successfully argued the case for a hard-line approach based primarily on the use of military force.

These were the more prominent of the many official and semi-official government agencies confronted with the problem of trying to save the empire. There were many other groups and individuals directly or indirectly concerned; for example, the merchant guilds of those ports which traded with America. The city of Cádiz, through its municipal authorities and guild, independently of the Comisión de Reemplazos and the Junta de Diputados, was always active in seeking to influence policy. The guilds of other ports with less significant trade links with America did not always share the same views as their colleagues at Cádiz and submitted their own evaluations, defending their priorities as best they could. Companies with direct links to America, for example the Philippines Company, were consulted or used on several occasions. Through petitions, treatises, representations, everybody with an idea or an interest made his special plea to king, government and parliament. The paper accumulated constantly and with it, the confusion in government circles. Yet there was another level of influence that was rarely committed to paper but which certainly affected Spain's response. It is known that American agents were operating clandestinely in Spain, seeking to spread confusion and to sabotage military preparations. The masonic movement was also allegedly active at Cádiz and elsewhere from 1810 onwards[20] and there is no doubt that even at the highest levels of government, there were secret dealings, probably corrupt and for personal financial gain, that had a material effect on Spanish actions and policies. In an age when conspiracy and secret societies were commonplace, it is very likely, certain according to contemporary memoirs, that much of Spanish policy was actually decided in private *tertulias* (informal gatherings or meetings) and the proverbial smoke-filled room. We shall never know the full extent to which these clandestine activities and pressures which existed under all governments determined policy and this is particularly the case in the most important of them, namely, the notorious camarilla of Ferdinand. Although some historians have dismissed this as little more than a drinking-club of the king's somewhat bizarre intimates, there remains strong circumstantial evidence and contemporary allegation that it did constitute a real power behind the throne. Certainly Ferdinand permitted some of his friends, who held no official post, to intervene directly in American policy and, it is said, to enrich themselves at the expense of the national war effort.[21]

Hidden from public view, these private deals are difficult to penetrate. Some detailed examples will be provided in later chapters, but it seems appropriate to give a brief illustration at this point. A few of the incidents are fairly well known: for example, the purchase by Ferdinand, in league with a few of his intimates in the camarilla but unknown to ministers, of several Russian ships in 1817.[22] Two years later, Ferdinand gave large areas of Florida to a few personal friends, again secretly, in advance of the cession of the territory to the United

States.[23] The freemasons and American agents, with large funds at their disposal, were particularly active in 1818 and 1819 among the soldiers being assembled at Cádiz for the expedition against Buenos Aires.[24] Accusations of financial corruption, not substantiated, were levelled against the Comisión de Reemplazos and nepotism and personal interest also appear evident in some cases.[25] For example, in 1810 the Regency selected Carlos Montúfar, a colonel in the Spanish army, to go as an envoy to Quito, his native province. He arrived in America in May and soon joined the insurgents, much to the embarrassment of the authorities in the peninsula. Questions were quickly asked in Cádiz as to how he received the appointment and Montúfar provides the answers in a letter to his sister of 10 May 1810. General Castaños, president of the Regency, was, he said, 'my protector and like a father'.[26]

Another of Montúfar's friends was Miguel de Lardizábal y Uribe, a family relative in whose house he had lived for a year and with whom he was on intimate terms. Lardizábal was a representative of his native province of New Spain to the Junta Central in 1808 and, unwilling to accept the doctrine of popular sovereignty, he was soon in dispute with the constitutionalists, eventually leaving for exile in England. With the return of Ferdinand in 1814, he was back in favour and was appointed to head the newly created Ministerio Universal de las Indias. According to one admittedly very biased source, he used his new-found power to benefit his friends,[27] in particular, Francisco Xavier Abadía, a military officer and former Minister of War at Cádiz in 1812. By 1816 he was the Inspector General de las tropas de Indias, concerned with supervising all the preparations for the military expeditions to America. He was given the job, allegedly, by his close friend, Lardizábal. By then, Lardizábal is said to have become disillusioned with Ferdinand's conduct of affairs and he wrote a private letter to Abadía in which he was highly critical of the king. Abadía's brother was in America where the family had substantial investments and Abadía wrote to him to warn him of the worsening situation in Spain. As evidence, he enclosed Lardizábal's letter to him with his remarks about Ferdinand. He advised his brother to leave America and withdraw their capital while he could. He also promised, however, that if his brother wished to remain, he personally would ensure that a strong military force was sent to wherever he chose to invest the family fortunes. This correspondence, including Lardizá-bal's compromising letter, was seized by pirates on the high seas and found its way into the insurgent press. Ferdinand soon learned of it and both Abadía and Lardizábal were arrested and exiled from Madrid.

It was in this situation of a complex and wide-ranging agglomeration of institutions and people that Spanish governments sought in vain to formulate a policy towards the revolutions. The diversity of interests contributed to the paradox of unanimity of objective, that is, reunification of the empire, persisting alongside the disagreement over the means. Yet the most important cause of this continuity of both aspects of Spain's response is perhaps the most surprising. More than anything else, it may be attributed to the fact that the people involved did not change. The reign of Ferdinand attracted exceptionally detailed scrutiny from contemporary observers and participants in the events of the time and in the immediate imperial post-mortem, men naturally sought to justify their actions and defend their decisions. Memoirs, histories, accounts of the time abound, few of which, of course, are in any sense objective. Subsequent generations of historians continued to offer their view of the reign coloured by their own political philosophy and the picture to emerge was black or white. More often than not Ferdinand, in particular, to use the words of Le Brun who in 1826 was one of the first to create the image in print, was depicted as the 'Wicked King . . . Crowned Tiger . . . abhorred by God, abhorred by men'.[28] Liberal historiography created the black legend of Ferdinand's rule, but the other side of the polemical coin is equally to be found in the works of the apologists for the absolutist system. There is no need here to reopen this polemic that has endured for so long, except in one respect. Historians have assumed or asserted that the collapse of the liberal experiment in 1814 and the restoration of absolutism brought with it a complete turnover in the people who governed the nation. The same conclusion is drawn for the years following the collapse of Ferdinand's absolute power in 1820 and that of the second period of constitutional government. In each case, it is assumed that liberals and their supporters disappeared from the public scene to be followed in their turn by the disgraced upholders of absolutism. To some extent, this is accurate. It cannot be denied that some leading liberals were persecuted by Ferdinand from 1814 to 1820 and even more so during the final decade of his life.[29] Similarly, there is no question that supporters of the *ancien régime* who could not accept the 1812 Constitution and who flocked to swear their loyalty to Ferdinand in 1814 and in 1823 were dismissed from their jobs by the liberals when they held the public power. One scholar has recently offered the following details:

personnel shifted frequently; sectors (or virtual political parties) influenced power variously; while councils and ministries came and went. Unavoidably difficult to narrate, the complexity is sensed by realizing that in the period 1808 to 1826 there were no less than 46 ministers of State; an incredible 51 ministers of War (8 in 1823 alone); and 40 ministers of Finance; while the ministry of the Indies was created or abolished at various times in the course of these years. The average tenure of a minister of War was 4.2 months; for a minister of State, technically the premier position, it was 4.6 months. The mere change over in leadership at the imperial center was thus a serious weakness and one that is immediately obvious.[30]

Although the accuracy of these numbers and others so often cited is open to question, the central point of instability, at least at ministerial level, is obviously valid.[31] But the mere statistics are deceptive because they do not go far enough. The key question is what happened to these men when they lost their posts, be they constitutionalists or absolutists. The answer is that in many cases, sufficient to be of significance, the loss of one job for the individual concerned often meant no more than demotion or lateral transfer to one of the powerful advisory bodies in the bureaucratic pyramid. While the changes in government did to some extent bring the exile, and in a few instances, the execution of prominent personalities on the losing side, beneath the leading group of each faction and the main institutions of each régime, many individuals and most administrative offices survived the vicissitudes of the political situation. More remarkable, even than the survival rate of liberals and absolutists who escaped the consequences of defeat to bide their time in obscurity or exile to reemerge when their opportunity arose, was the number of men who were able to retain their careers and their influence in the corridors of power throughout all the years of conflict and change. Politicians, career bureaucrats, diplomats, military officers, clergy, merchants and others managed to serve whatever master controlled their fate, regardless of his political creed.

This continuity of personnel is especially noticeable among those who were active in the years following the Napoleonic invasion of 1808 and the emergence of the liberals at Cádiz. These men did not all disappear from the public scene with the return of Ferdinand but, on the contrary, many were quickly reemployed in public administration, now not to work to the will of a representative government but to the dictates of an absolute monarch. They survived for three main reasons. Some were for the most part not seen to be strongly identified with any particular political philosophy and, while it would be incorrect to assume that they were all indifferent or impartial to the dissensions around them, they appear to have been able to maintain their reputations without offending either their friends or their enemies. They thus avoided becoming victims of persecution when the government for which they worked lost its power. The men referred to in this context were mostly, but not entirely, those who were concerned with or had views about the American issue and, as already indicated, there was little significant difference in the basic attitudes towards this in either constitutionalist or absolutist régimes. Hence an advocate of military force or of peaceful persuasion was just as likely to find support for his views in the halls of the liberal Cortes at Cádiz or Madrid as he was in the ministerial offices in the royal palace. Furthermore, since the diversity of opinion on how to resolve the difficulties in the colonies was so great, almost any proposal which had as its premise the objective of restoring Spanish dominion was likely to find a willing audience. Indeed, there are examples of men who had openly backed the wrong side in the domestic political struggle who were forgiven their sins because it was thought that they had useful suggestions regarding America. Even Ferdinand was sometimes willing to forgive and forget[32] and the evidence of the many people whose careers have been studied in the context of the American revolutions seems to show that the king was not the ruthless butcher of his ministers and advisers as he is traditionally depicted.

As will become evident in subsequent chapters, therefore, the same names recur throughout the years from 1808 to 1824 and, in some cases, well into the so-called 'ominous decade'. The people concerned were able to continue to promote their ideas and special interests as well as to propound their favourite solutions of the imperial crisis. Their presence, either continuously or intermittently, was an important factor in the persistence of the same attitudes and proposed courses of action, especially as there is little evidence, except in a few cases, that they changed their minds regarding America. Their opinions and prejudices were the same in the 1820s, and sometimes much later, as they were in the early years of the war. The hawks remained convinced that a military solution held out the best hope of success and even if some finally recognized the impracticality of such a policy, they persisted in the belief that had it been fully endorsed from the beginning, the empire would not have been lost. The doves kept to their position that only a negotiated settlement could have achieved reconciliation and reunification. In the same way, the institutional obstacles, the division of responsibilities, the duplicity of committees and personal political rivalries continued throughout to inhibit and delay Spain's response. It is futile to speculate how or if the course of history might have been changed had Spaniards been able to agree on what to do, but, certainly for some of the participants, the loss of the empire was at no stage inevitable. For them, it was lost almost by default, by the failure of all central governments to appreciate fully what was happening and to act decisively; in short, a direct consequence of their own generation's hesitant, uncertain and bewildered response. However, seemingly surrounded by public indifference over the fate of the empire, confronted at times by formidable problems of finance, geography, international hostility as well as chronic dangers and instability on the domestic political scene, it is perhaps not surprising that doubt and confusion should reign supreme. Professor Anna has correctly concluded that 'Spain lost America not only because of intransigence but also because of a series of failures of political institutions at home'.[33]

2

Revolution: the view from Spain

The evidence of more than a decade of war, the defeat of the royal armies on the fields of battle, and the creation of independent republics throughout Spanish America were not enough to convince Spaniards that the days of Spain's status as a major imperial nation were over. No Spanish government before the mid 1830s was willing to accept the reality of the loss of the empire, even after international diplomatic recognition had been extended to the new states, because the majority of Spanish politicians, and possibly the people at large in the peninsula, thought that reunification of the empire was a realistic possibility, if not probability, either by means of reconquest or some form of political reconciliation. This conviction was shared by liberals and conservatives alike and it was a conviction based, not on wishful thinking, but on Spaniards' knowledge, assessment and understanding of the revolutions, of what had actually happened in America, why and for what purpose.

Spanish analysis of the movements for emancipation was obviously influenced by a number of factors. For many, their attitudes and opinions regarding the rebels and the insurrections were not, and could not be, derived solely from detached, objective observation of the course of events but rather from an emotional response, strongly tinged with feelings of patriotism and national pride. They could not conceive of any circumstances in which the American territories had either a moral or practical right to seek their freedom from the Mother Country and they looked on American demands not only as unfair but as shameful, unjustified acts towards the nation and people which had given its population and resources to bring to the New World all the benefits of European civilization. There was a feeling expressed in countless reports and memoranda of genuine astonishment and outrage that the Americans should wish to sever all the bonds of union forged over three centuries. This anger at what was considered to be the ingratitude shown by American members of the Hispanic imperial family pervaded Spanish opinion throughout the years of war and into the post-mortem which followed. It was evident almost immediately at Cádiz as the knowledge of what was happening was slowly absorbed and it persisted for years to come in the words and propaganda of men of all political persuasions. 'Do not be ungrateful to your parents; such ingratitude is a scandalous monstrosity', declared Lardizábal y Uribe in a government proclamation to the empire in 1814.[1] For the Spanish merchants, the greatest punishment God could impose on Americans for their acts of infidelity would be to allow them to separate from their Mother Country. Their animosity and ingratitude for the 'infinite benefits' bestowed on them was incredible.[2] For the rebels to reject all the rights and privileges offered them by the 1812 Constitution was, in the words of a newspaper in 1821, 'the height of ingratitude'.[3]

Directly related to the themes of ingratitude and resentment at American behaviour was the defence of Spain's record as a colonial power. The conflict in America stimulated the rebirth of the *leyenda negra*, or black legend of Spanish cruelty at the time of the conquest and in the centuries which followed. It was a polemic which had long irritated Spaniards and, since the gruesome accounts of Las Casas in the sixteenth century, many attempts had been made to defend and justify Spain's actions. With Spanish supremacy and right of dominion challenged by the insurgents, the horror-stories of the past were resurrected and used over and again by supporters of American liberty. Now Spaniards made a determined effort to correct the historical record and to deny all the pretexts for separation being alleged in the rebel propaganda. Almost every writer on American affairs from 1810 onwards displayed the same intention. Far from the corrupt, brutal and avaricious conduct which Americans were claiming Spain had shown towards the colonies, the truth was that the metropolis had always pursued a benevolent and enlightened policy. As one liberal weekly declared in 1811, if Spain had made any mistake in America, it was that of too much consideration for its interests.[4] Spain had civilized the continent, built the cities, roads, churches and rescued the indigenous population from their abysmal state of idolatry, superstition and ignorance, from the 'scene of atrocities' prevailing before the Spaniards' arrival.[5] The laws of the Indies had always been 'gentle, benign and just' and no nation had treated its colonies more magnanimously. America was an integral part of the monarchy, its people were Spaniards with the same language, religion, customs and traditions. Spain had protected it from foreign aggression and Americans had always been spared the oppression of despotic rule imposed in the past on peninsular Spaniards. They were exempt from military service in Europe, they paid fewer and lesser taxes and they had been given every encouragement to develop their industries and agriculture, unrestricted and unhindered despite the damaging effects of such freedom on the economic development of the metropolis. Indeed, there had never been any attempt to inhibit American progress in any field of activity.[6]

Years after the revolutions were over, Spaniards continued to make such assertions, denying that there was any valid reason for Americans to want their emancipation. Well-known sixteenth- and seventeenth-century works on the conquest and early years of colonization, favourable to the Spanish case, were reprinted. In the introduction to Balbuena's *Grandeza Mexicana*, first published in 1603 and reissued in 1829, the editor revealed that his objective was to refute 'the chimerical and dismal ideas of emancipation and independence'.[7] Antonio Cánovas del Castillo, later to be the leading conservative statesman of the century, argued that Spain had made enormous sacrifices for the sake of the empire. We were not usurpers, barbarians or tyrants in America, he declared, nor even a conquering or enemy race. Spain's dominion and government were legitimate and sooner or later, future generations of Americans would appreciate what Spain had done for the continent.[8] In a speech opening the ninth congress of the French Institute of History in 1843, Francisco Martínez de la Rosa, liberal prime minister in 1822, paid tribute to those nations which had contributed to the spread of civilization. 'Forgive me, gentlemen', he said, 'if I state that much of this glory belongs to Spain. This fact indemnifies my country against so many false accusations, so many calumnies propagated against her. Few nations have treated their colonies with such wisdom and kindness; few have ruled them with laws so favourable to the indigenous population.'[9]

Spaniards were also influenced in their response to the revolutions by their attitudes towards the American people. In the early years, especially at Cádiz in 1810 and 1811, when the government was still uncertain as to the nature and aims of the 'troubles', as they were called, official propaganda tended to concentrate on the ethnic links which united the Old World and the New. Perhaps the single word most often used in referring to Americans was 'brothers' and the Mother–child, one-family metaphor was inserted in every context to highlight the bonds of blood and religious faith shared by European and American Spaniards. During the second constitutional period, the same approach was used in an attempt to persuade Americans that their long-term interests would best be served by remaining within the Hispanic family.[10]

Rather different concepts were prominent in the words of individuals. While some politicians were willing to admit that they knew little or nothing about America, other Spaniards displayed prejudice and racist attitudes. The working class in America, one anonymous newspaper correspondent wrote in 1811, did not want manufactured goods. They were accustomed to nudity and content to be frugal with no desire for the commodities which in more advanced countries were now thought to be essentials. The American representatives in the Cortes, rather than demanding political reforms, should be spending their time persuading their compatriots 'to wear clothes and shoes, to sleep in a bed, use household articles and other things'. What a tremendous boost there would be for the shoe industry if they could persuade only three out of five Indians to wear shoes – using two pairs a year would create a demand for six million pairs. If Spain was ever to leave Mexico, the place would be reduced within a couple of years to the abysmal state of decadence it was in at the time of the conquest.[11]

In the Cortes debates at Cádiz on American rights under the new constitution, particularly those concerning citizenship and political representation, there were frequent hostile comments on the castes and non-white population. José Valiente felt that Europeans and creoles should have the same rights as European Spaniards, but the seven to eight million Indians should be offered parliamentary representation 'compatible with their present condition'.[12] The elderly and reactionary Jaime Creus considered the castes to have their origins in a barbaric, immoral and pagan continent and no matter how long they lived in Europe or America, 'we know that they will always retain something of those characteristics absorbed from their mother's milk'.[13] Another writer was even more blatantly racist. He insisted that there was a biological difference between European children and those of American Indians or people of African descent. If, he suggested, you were to educate the children of Indians or Africans in Cádiz, by the age of ten the difference in their level of achievement compared with European children would be obvious.

The non-whites of America needed a long time to develop their physical and intellectual capacity to equal that of the whites.[14] According to Martín Garay, the decadence of American industry and agriculture was because the 'lazy Indians' had not been forced to work and the whole place was 'a country of rampant immorality'. Americans did not like 'to plough or to weave' and there would be no economic development until the Indians and the castes could be forced to labour in the fields and factories. Spanish officials might have been corrupted but how could their conduct be kept pure amidst such endemic immorality?[15] Similar prejudice was evident in a circular from the Ministry of Ultramar in 1812. Colonial officials were asked to provide detailed information on the non-white population in their regions. The minister wanted to know the customs and habits of Indians and castes, how many meals a day they ate, if they were literate, showed any aptitude for music and if they were inclined to be 'liars, bad-tempered and cruel'.[16]

Such attitudes were by no means reserved for the non-white population. The creoles, generally considered to be the instigators and leaders of the revolutions, were also seen with the traditional Spanish contempt for their class. Juan López Cancelada was among the most vitriolic of their critics, repeating again and again in his newspapers that they were imbued with a profound hatred of European Spaniards. They were, however, a weak and cowardly people, men of no education and liars and it was the duty of Spain to protect the innocent castes from their unscrupulous creole masters.[17] The Conde de Puñonrostro advised that Americans were by nature weak and submissive people because of the climate. It was these personality features which had kept them submissive for so long despite their grievances and Pizarro recalled that arrogant prejudice against Americans was prevalent among the king's advisers as well as in the country at large.[18] For Juan Rico, a clergyman representing Valencia in the 1822 Cortes, Americans had the same basic temperament as Spaniards but 'they do not have as many virtues because of the climate and other moral causes'.[19] The creoles, it was said, complained of discrimination but the fact was that they did not compete with Europeans because of their bad upbringing, poor character and natural inclination to prodigality. According to López Cancelada, all trade would collapse if European Spaniards left because 'the creoles abhor the profession of merchant.'[20] Cabrera de Nevares, author of an important set of proposals on the pacification issue, thought the creoles to be 'naturally mistrustful and suspicious' and some to be 'monsters nourished by every kind of crime.'[21] Those who defended the Spanish record, if forced to admit that some injustice did exist in America, usually blamed it on the creoles. Deputy Joaquín Ferrer found it ironic that the creoles, who had benefited most from the conquest, were now denouncing it and it was clear to him that the revolutions were being fought not by the oppressed classes but by the oppressors.[22] For the Conde de Toreno, ardent liberal and life-long defender of Spain's conduct in the New World, Las Casas had been 'a bad Spaniard', son of a foreigner and only Spanish by chance. Spain had nothing to be ashamed of – all the evils that existed in the New World had been caused by the creoles.[23]

The open display of racist prejudice, arrogance and hostility towards the Americans culminated in 1829 with the publication of a three-volume history of the revolutions by Mariano Torrente.[24] Filled with macabre tales of massacres and barbaric behaviour by the insurgents, Torrente claimed that reconquest would be easy because the new rulers were tyrants. They were 'terrorists, monsters of barbarity, corrupt and bloodthirsty' and they had imposed a reign of terror on the innocent majority of loyal subjects. Choosing an impressive variety of terms of abuse, he proceeded to describe the situation in each colony and vilifying all the liberators, he predicted that unless Spain acted quickly, the now disillusioned and misled majority of creoles would themselves be butchered. The coloureds and castes would rise up and take over. In Buenos Aires, the gauchos, or 'fierce men of the pampas' as he called them, would overrun the city. In Colombia, the llaneros or men of the plains would rebel. These men, he said, were 'ferocious, the size of giants, of herculean strength, hardly yet human'. They would pillage, rob and murder and if another Tupac Amaru was to appear in Peru, the whites would be slaughtered and in Chile dominated again by the savage Araucanians. In general, the Indians, he added, were by nature passive, always obedient to Spaniards and retaining their almost idolatrous veneration of the king. As for the mestizos, they were an important social group but easily pliable and willing to support anyone who gave them the opportunity to go on the rampage. They too still recognized the natural superiority of people of pure European blood.

Possibly financed in part, and certainly approved of by Ferdinand, Torrente's colourful history was part of the reconquest propaganda of the time and hence it is not surprising that it was so violently anti-

American.[25] Even so, it was well received by reviewers and seemingly the public, since it was quickly reprinted.[26] This was almost certainly because, despite the extreme statements and poetic licence regarding fact, it corresponded in most respects to the view of Americans already held by many Spaniards. This was particularly the case regarding the rebels. In addition to their preconceived notions, Spaniards since 1811 had been fed a regular diet in their newspapers and in official publications by all governments which offered them a graphic, if sometimes bizarre, idea of their American 'brothers'. Initially, the public image of them presented in the peninsula was that they were ill-informed, misguided men, deceived by foreigners and who would soon realize the error of their ways. This portrayal quickly changed. They became bloodthirsty assassins, barbaric rapists, renegade priests, thieves and jacobins. Francisco Miranda was invariably referred to as 'the traitor'; Miguel Hidalgo was 'the most bloodthirsty man America had ever known'.[27] This portrait was given of José María Morelos: 'Father Morelos gives mass to his soldiers wearing a general's hat, two blunderbusses and a sword in the belt around his vestments.'[28] The Mexican rebels were said in 1811 to be 'as vile as they were infamous, lacking any true or understood religion' and a decade later to have been 'men of the lowest class, unknown, ignorant in military arts and fervid partisans of republican principles'.[29] Agustín de Iturbide was a perfidious ingrate and his supporters defenders of privilege and theocracy.[30] Stories of horrific cruelty and butchery of innocent people abounded. Bolívar was said to have entered Caracas, killed all the Europeans he could find and then wrote letters in their blood to his cohorts asking for replies in similar ink. His orders were that Europeans should have their eyes and hearts torn out while they were alive and that all Spaniards should be lined up to watch until it was their turn.[31] In a published document in 1814, the Comisión de Reemplazos, describing Hidalgo as 'this ignorant, stupid and dishonest imposter', proceeded to offer this description of his successors in the rebel movement:

The whole of humanity shudders when it recalls the atrocities of these monsters; it was not enough for them to ravage, burn and drown in blood the unhappy country in which they were born; they were not content to sacrifice their fathers and their brothers; their implacable rancour was not satisfied with exterminating their victims; those unfortunate people suffered prolonged torture to their dying breath; and just to prove that their hatred extended even beyond the grave, the rebels wrote in the blood of their victims the brutal decree to exterminate the others.[32]

Similar gory illustrations were often to be found in Ferdinand's official gazette. To cite just one example, in 1818 the paper reported the massacre of thirty-four Capuchine missionaries from Catalonia. The settlements they had set up in the province of Guayana had been overwhelmed by hordes of rebels, most of them negroes, sambos, mulattos, with their wicked cohorts Bolívar, Piar, Cedeño. Fourteen of the friars had died from ill-treatment while the other twenty were sacrificed in a barbaric manner with their bodies dismembered and thrown into the river Caraní.[33]

It was in this atmosphere of prejudice and hostility towards Americans displayed openly by some and probably shared by most people in the peninsula, seeming fully justified to them in view of the constant propaganda of the insurgents' uncivilized savagery, that Spaniards were confronted with the need to assess the nature and significance of the revolutions.[34] This problem of evaluating what had happened and was happening in the empire and deciding what to do about it first fell to those politicians, merchants, journalists and others who, by the outbreak of the rebellions in 1810, found themselves in Cádiz.[35] Besieged by the French armies, almost totally dependent for their survival on British support and with their overriding priority the war on the home front for which continued American financial aid was desperately needed, the task facing them was certainly difficult. Not surprisingly, their initial response was indecisive, hesitant and confused, but their reactions, ideas and policies were to form the basis and precedent for many years to come as each succeeding administration struggled to formulate a coherent policy. The bewilderment at Cádiz was partly caused by the difficulty of communications and, more important, the very diverse nature of the sources of information which were available.[36] It is not known exactly when the news of the formation of all the juntas across America was received in Spain. The earliest official discussion of the events at Caracas of April 1810, the first place to depose its peninsular authorities, was held by the Council of the Indies on 9–11 July 1810.[37] With ships and correspondence regularly arriving from America, more details soon became known, but the accounts, often coming from returning private citizens and merchants, were patchy and based to some extent on rumours which the travellers had picked up in their respective regions and ports of embarkation. Throughout 1811, more and more information from envoys and resident colonial officials, private correspondence, foreign diplomats and press was accumulated in government offices but, again, much of this was contradictory and the real significance and extent of the rebel movements remained in doubt.

The Council of the Indies discussed the situation in Caracas in the light of evidence presented to it by former colonial officials and others and concluded that a rebellion against the Crown had taken place with the undeniable objective of independence. The rebel junta had suborned some of the local population with promises of freedom and prosperity and by spreading deceitful, false rumours of the fate of Spain. They had claimed that Spain had been completely defeated by Napoleon's armies and that the French and British governments were going to divide Spanish America between them. There were indications, however, that the people of Caracas now regretted what had happened and that the insurgent leaders were no more than uneducated men, cowards and without weapons. The former intendant, Vicente Basadre, had suggested that a blockade of the main ports in the province would bring about the surrender of the rebels within two or three months. The Council recommended, therefore, that a commissioner with the title of captain-general or governor, accompanied by a military escort of 150 to 200 men, should be sent to Venezuela to inform its people of the true state of affairs in Europe. He should also be empowered to talk to the rebels and pardon or punish them. At the same time, the Regency could announce a blockade and foreign governments, particularly the British, should be requested to see that no aid was given to the rebels. The opening of the Cortes would be welcomed in America and the Regency should ensure a much more efficient circulation of news to prevent the spread of subversive rumours. Finally, it would be as well to instruct the clergy to make certain that the Indians and castes knew where their loyalties should lie.

Hence this first official and confidential assessment of the events in Caracas seems to have been that although something of significance had taken place and independence was the motive regardless of rebel declarations of loyalty to Ferdinand, the situation was not unduly serious. A few days later, the Regency began to act on the Council's recommendations.[38] A blockade was announced and Antonio Ignacio de Cortabarría was appointed as commissioner to Caracas.[39] At the end of August 1810, his instructions were drawn up and probably as a result of further information received since July, the Regency appears to have become rather more concerned. Cortabarría was warned that the Caracas junta already had envoys in London seeking support and that the British government was talking to them in private. Recent unconfirmed reports had said that the British governors at Curazao and Trinidad were secretly helping the rebels. Orders had been sent to the viceroys and governors of New Spain, Puerto Rico, Santa Fe, Havana and other regions to be ready to provide him with money, soldiers and anything he might need. On arrival, he was to inform the people of the creation of the Regency, its recognition by other nations and that their past actions would be overlooked provided that the rebels submitted and recognized the Regency's legitimacy. He was to leave them in no doubt that if they did not comply, force would be used against them.[40]

After some weeks' delay, Cortabarría left Cádiz and arrived at Puerto Rico on 24 October 1810. During the next few months, his first reports back to Spain emphasized that the rebels were few in number, poorly armed and generally distrusted by the population at large. It would be easy to restore order, he claimed, if a small number of soldiers were sent out from Spain, and such a move would also dispel once and for all the rebels' main propaganda weapon that Spain was a defeated and powerless nation. By January 1811, his view had become more pessimistic. The 'famous revolutionary', Miranda, was now leading the revolt which meant that their military tactics might improve. His own efforts at peace talks, the installation of the Cortes and the news of other reforms sanctioned by the Regency had had no effect. The insurgents were describing the Cádiz government as despotic and illegal and they would not recognize the Regency, Cortes or himself. All their talk of allegiance to the Crown was purely to deceive. Even if the king turned up in person, they would reject him. They were seeking independence: 'this has been and is certainly the aim of those revolutionaries'. Nevertheless, the majority of the people were loyal and the pardo population wanted to remain under the paternal protection of their sovereign.[41]

While these reports were being received and digested, developments in other parts of America were also becoming known. Buenos Aires had overthrown its Spanish authorities in May 1810. The first notice of these events was probably that of *The Times* of 7 August and the basic details would be known in Cádiz soon afterwards. The naval commander of Montevideo, José María Salazar, writing on 6 June 1810, sent copies of the proclamations issued by the rebel junta.[42] He also alleged that the loyalist group in the province was strong, even though many people were being intimidated by threats of execution.

The rebels had 350,000 pesos, were recruiting troops, buying weapons and placing their hopes for support largely on the British. A quite different interpretation of what happened was offered on 30 August by José Fernández de Castro in a note to the Regency.[43] He had arrived in Europe from Buenos Aires in 1809 to represent the interests of the city's merchants. He now refused to condemn the insurgents, maintaining that the independence they had declared was not from Spain but from French-occupied Spain. There was no intention of establishing a separate government but it was still essential to be wary of the expansionist ambitions of Brazil which had long coveted the River Plate region. To counter the Portuguese threat, he suggested than an army of 3,000 troops should be sent at once.

Within two weeks, Fernández de Castro had changed his mind. He now accepted, he wrote, the absolute independence aim of the rebels and the army must be sent to suppress the junta as well as to meet the threat from Brazil.[44] In contrast, the judges of the Buenos Aires *audiencia*, who had been expelled by the junta, were more optimistic. Writing from Las Palmas on 7 September, they informed the Regency that the appointment of a new viceroy and the dispatch of only a small military force would be enough to resolve the situation. They were certain that the Europeans there would remain loyal, as would the Spanish garrison. If the junta would not submit peacefully, the authorities of Montevideo could easily isolate it by joining with the interior provinces which continued loyal to the Crown.[45]

Faced with these and other conflicting reports, the Regency appears to have decided that although a rebellion had taken place, the danger arose more from British and Brazilian ambitions than from the strength of the insurgents. This view was reflected in the confidential instructions to the newly appointed viceroy of the River Plate, Francisco Elío.[46] These were dated 20 September and they emphasized the external threat to the area. Elío was told that since the Portuguese royal family had arrived in Brazil in 1808, it had been plotting to get possession of the Banda Oriental. The Brazilians were amassing troops on the borders, protecting Spanish dissidents and encouraging the rebels. All they were waiting for was a pretext to invade. British behaviour was equally suspect. The British government had received the Caracas envoys and there seemed little doubt that it was Britain's intention to promote for its own interest the independence of America. As for the rebels, they were certainly seeking independence and their proclaimed loyalty to the Crown was hypocrisy. They were, moreover, no more than a small group of stupid and ignorant rogues.

On 19 November 1810 the Council of the Indies reassembled to consider Buenos Aires and it also appears to have concluded that, at least as far as the rebels were concerned, there was no cause for alarm.[47] The advice of the Council's fiscal was that once the news of the opening of the Cortes had reached Buenos Aires, it was to be expected that the rebellion would end. If it did not, an experienced viceroy, accompanied by troops, should be sent to Montevideo where he would reestablish the *audiencia* and require the rebels to acknowledge his authority. The Regency could not allow a self-established and arbitrary government to persist in the colony, nor ignore the insults to officials and infringements of the law.

By early 1811 a rather different picture was emerging. In a report dated 30 September 1810, the Spanish ambassador at Rio de Janeiro said that he had recognized at once that the rebels' aim was independence 'despite their prostitution of the name of our sovereign'.[48] Many of them wanted to set up a republic but, as the level of enlightenment required in all social classes for such a political system did not exist in the colony, that would not be achieved. Instead the result would be a barbaric despotism similar to that of the French when the republic was founded. The Buenos Aires junta was already proving the accuracy of his assessment. With its atrocities, murder and confiscation of property, it had terrorized the city into submission. To illustrate the savagery of those jacobins, he described the execution of Santiago Liniers. The firing-squad of eight soldiers had at first wept and refused to fire. Threatened by their officers, four had fired but only one bullet hit Liniers in the arm. An officer then walked across and 'blew his brains out'.

Salazar also warned in regular dispatches from Montevideo that the situation was deteriorating. 'Junta, revolution and independence are synonymous words in these countries', he declared, and his own position was growing desperate.[49] He had no money or resources, rebel spies were everywhere, and the junta was gaining confidence because it knew of Spain's impotence. He had to have urgent military support if the colony was to be saved.[50] The Conde de Maule added to Salazar's warnings with a copy of a letter of 30 October 1810 which he had received from Montevideo.[51] This asserted that the Buenos Aires junta was organizing a large army to liberate the interior provinces and that if at least 2,000 Spanish soldiers were not urgently sent, Peru and the entire southern part of the continent would soon be lost. The rebellion was spreading and the loyal people were becoming more and more disillusioned at Spain's failure to act. In contrast to these assessments, Elío reported from Montevideo on 18 March 1811 that the rebels were weakening, suffering setbacks and unable to pay their soldiers. His own recent naval campaign had been successful and as soon as military reinforcements arrived from Spain, he would be ready and able to end the insurrection: 'I am certain I can put an end to the whole thing once 2,000 troops arrive.'[52]

Similarly divergent accounts of the development of the revolts in New Spain and other areas were also being received by the early months of 1811.[53] However, faced with the imperative need to maintain morale in the peninsula and among the presumed loyalists of America, the Regency had little choice but to play down the importance of the revolts to try to ensure that alarmist rumours did not spread. From the government's own uncertain and hazy impression of events, an appropriate official interpretation was devised and printed in the daily Regency Gazette. The issue of 8 August 1810 saw the first published comment on Caracas. The troubles, it emphasized, were the work of only a few dissidents, already known as troublemakers. The great majority of the people remained loyal and the other Venezuelan provinces had refused to join the insurrection. Fortunately, no blood had been spilt and the consequences were not as grave as they might have been. There was no doubt that the rebels would be defeated once the true state of affairs in the peninsula was known. Caracas did not have the resources to sustain its independence and, most important of all, the British government had expressed its disapproval of the rebel junta's actions.

This first editorial on the American situation became a model for the future, with the Gazette repeating again and again that the rebels in each colony were no more than a negligible minority, in no sense representative of the popular will. As proof of this, constant reports of donations of money and supplies from loyal Americans were printed, as well as myriad declarations of allegiance from all over the empire. Following the opening of the Cortes on 24 September 1810, the Regency missed no opportunity to announce the participation of American delegates and to publish every recognition of the congress that was received. By February 1811, New Spain was being given increasing attention and it was said that there was a universal desire in that viceroyalty for the defeat of the rebels. On 26 February, it was reported that the rebels had lost all hope of victory following a series of crushing military defeats by the royal armies. Every military victory was naturally given extensive coverage, although the capture of Hidalgo and other leading Mexican rebels was reported on 29 June 1811 without comment. By July and August, the Gazette was announcing that opinion in Buenos Aires was changing among the rebels and their supporters who now realized that the blind ambition of the minority was dragging them into a civil war. The rebels' attempt to invade Paraguay had been repulsed, their seditious propaganda in Peru had been unsuccessful and that important viceroyalty was entirely loyal. The honourable people of Buenos Aires were being suppressed by a few malcontents but peace and order would soon be restored. The position in Venezuela was similarly hopeful. In September 1811 it was reported that Miranda had dissolved his illegal congress and executed his opponents. His aim was independence, but the anarchy which had accompanied the rebellion had disillusioned the people. They realized that unity with the Mother Country was the only practical option open to them.[54]

Throughout 1811 and the early months of 1812 the Gazette, followed to some extent by other newspapers,[55] continued to give this impression that what had happened in America was that a small number of men, taking advantage of the French invasion of the peninsula, had seized power, and in one or two areas, notably New Spain and Caracas, they had forced some of the lower classes into acts of rebellion against the Crown. The vast majority of Americans were loyal subjects and would soon reassert themselves against the rebel minority. This optimistic assessment and prediction carefully contrived by official sources was by no means accepted or shared by everybody at Cádiz. 'America is aflame and we must immediately reach the fire that is destroying it, if the metropolis does not want to lose it for ever', proclaimed one newspaper in January 1811.[56] López Cancelada began his own personal campaign to counteract what he thought to be the mistaken interpretation and apathy of the Regency. In a stream of articles throughout 1811, he stressed again and again that the lives of Europeans in America were in grave danger, that the rebellion was spreading and that it was essential to send military reinforcements. He warned that if this was not done, 'we will lose, we will lose, we will lose America forever'.[57] Other papers preached the same message and one correspondent denounced the government for failing to keep the public properly informed and for only reporting victories.[58] Indeed, López Cancelada decided to publish his own newspaper precisely, as he said in the first issue, to correct the inaccurate information that was being divulged about what was really going on in the empire.[59]

For more than a year after the movements for emancipation had spread throughout America, neither the Regency, the Cortes nor the public had any clear picture of what had happened and there was little or no agreement on the significance or gravity of the situation. As Agustín Argüelles recalled in his memoirs, the whole issue was enveloped in confusion and obscurity. Commenting on the attitude of the Cortes, he wrote, 'the prejudices, the struggle of divergent interests, of opposing aims with irreconcilable plans, disfigured the facts and the circumstances, misled opinion and perverted so pitifully the judgement of contemporaries'.[60] Nevertheless, interpretations of the events, attitudes and responses to them were formulated and clarity prevailed at least in as much as the differences of opinion emerged. Despite the vicissitudes of time, the fluctuating political scene and, more important, the changing fortunes of the royal armies in the colonies, these initial, divergent assessments, for the most part and for most of those involved, were to remain unchanged during the next twenty years and more. The main conflict of opinion concerned the numerical strength of the revolutionary movements and the degree of support for the concept of independence among the majority of the population in each part of America. The view propagated by the Regency that only a minority of ambitious and unscrupulous men, mostly creoles, was involved became the accepted assessment and significantly influenced the response of all governments, especially in their belief that military reconquest was a possible option. When Ferdinand returned to power in 1814, he ordered analyses and proposals for dealing with the American problem from various sources. Among those consulted was Antonio Joaquín Pérez, a former conservative deputy at Cádiz, Mexican born and future Mexican bishop. He replied that the rebels in New Spain from the time of Hidalgo onwards included clerics, estate managers, military deserters and lawyers but that they were corrupt and immoral people. The forces of Morelos were similar and no revolution against the established order had taken or was taking place but rather isolated actions by a small number of bandits. Even among the rebels, the name of the king still commanded respect.[61] In October 1814, in a full session, the Council of the Indies discussed America and concluded that there was 'a club of villains' who had plotted independence since 1810.[62] A year later, Juan Antonio Yandiola produced an extensive survey of the revolutions and he again emphasized that the majority did not support the rebel cause. Thousands of innocent people had died because of the perfidious conduct of an ambitious minority. Americans, he argued, had neither the economic capacity nor the necessary skills to be independent and the majority did not want to separate from Spain.[63] In a published pamphlet, possibly sponsored by the Cádiz merchant guild, the same point was made.[64] The solution to the American problem was to utilize the great majority of Americans who were opposed to independence and Spain ought to ensure that those loyalists were provided with the leadership they required. In 1818, several members of a military committee, composed of high-ranking officers, former viceroys and others with direct personal experience of the revolutions, counselled that if Spain could send enough soldiers the whole war would be quickly concluded.[65]

This minority assessment was certainly not the unanimous view of Ferdinand's advisers from 1814 to 1820 but it again became prominent following the restoration of the constitutional system in 1820. The executive, the Cortes, the advisory councils and some of the press used it as one of the many reasons for their refusal to accept independence. Offering a detailed survey of the state of America in his report to the Cortes in July 1820, the Minister of Ultramar, Antonio Porcel, assured the congress that Americans were tired of internal dissension and fanciful promises. The people of Buenos Aires in particular were desperate for peace and he had no doubt that all over the continent, public opinion welcomed the reintroduction of the constitution with the liberties and prosperity it offered through the maintenance of imperial unity.[66] Much of the press carried the same message. According to one paper, the people of Buenos Aires were longing for Spain to rescue them from the anarchy in their city.[67] In March 1821 Ramón Gil de la Cuadra, in his report to the Cortes, declared that New Spain, Guatemala, Venezuela, Panama, Cartagena, Santo Domingo, Puerto Rico and Cuba had all accepted the constitution and that those areas still in rebel hands were rapidly disintegrating into chaos as the minority of rebels fought among themselves for power.[68] In a memorandum to the Council of State in August 1821, the minister said that although it was impossible to be certain of the state of public opinion, he felt that the balance still remained in favour of Spain. The wealthy sectors of society, the businessmen and landowning creole families, the Indians and the castes much preferred to be ruled by Europeans than by the ambitious creole clergy and lawyers who were seeking personal aggrandizement.[69] In 1822, another minister, explaining the basic principles underlying the government's policy, stated that the administration had evidence to prove that the great majority of Americans accepted that only the Spanish constitution could give them any prosperity and that any other step was both premature and put at risk the fate of present and future generations of Americans.[70] After long discussion and debate, the constitutional régime decided to send envoys to the dissident provinces and their private instructions contained the same assessment. Public opinion, they were told, was not unanimously in favour of emancipation. Those who were campaigning for it were largely creoles but the majority of the landed classes, Indians and castes retained their affection for their king and wished to remain united in the imperial family. Many of the rebels were now disillusioned and realized that they had been misled by the promises of the ambitious few.[71]

British diplomats at Madrid in the 1820s seem to have been surprised and frustrated by the persistence of this minority thesis in successive administrations and ministers. Writing to Lord Londonderry in December 1821, Lionel Hervey reported a conversation with the then Secretary of State, Eusebio Bardají.[72] News of the occupation of Mexico City by Iturbide and his army had arrived four days previously and yet, said Hervey, the minister refused to accept that Spain's position in the viceroyalty was as bad as some people claimed. Moreover, 'he persisted in his opinion that there was still a strong Spanish party in the country'. A few months later, in May 1822, Hervey described the views of the liberal prime minister, Martínez de la Rosa.[73] He also was convinced by recent accounts from Peru and Mexico that Spain's position was by no means hopeless and he believed 'there was still great attachment on the part of the inhabitants to the Mother Country'. In January 1825, Cea Bermúdez, Minister of Foreign Affairs in Ferdinand's restored government, told the British ambassador that the information in Madrid 'tended to shew (sic) that the mass of the population in all Provinces was favourably disposed to the king of Spain and that they were only prevented from declaring their real feelings from being kept under by a faction which must one day or other be overthrown'.[74] A few weeks earlier, Ferdinand had sent a circular to his ambassadors throughout

Europe saying that he was consoled by 'the repeated and irrefragable proofs' that an immense number of Americans remained loyal to the Crown.[75] As late as 1830, Henry Addington reported to Lord Aberdeen that the great error of the Spanish cabinet was the obstinate persistence of the idea that 'the Mexicans must be and are anxious' to return to Spanish dominion because of the present state of anarchy in their country.[76]

In was not just ministers in both constitutionalist and absolutist governments who reached such conclusions regarding the extent of popular support for independence. In the liberal Cortes of 1820 onwards, many hours of debate were devoted to the empire and multiple committees concerned themselves with finding an appropriate policy. Again the minority thesis was evident in many of the discussions and reports. For example, in October 1820 deputy Francisco Magariños (Buenos Aires) spoke of the dreadful condition of the provinces he represented but the most recent news he had from Buenos Aires was that the loyalists in the city had welcomed the constitution. Spain must come to their aid because the good people of Montevideo, Buenos Aires and most other provinces were clamouring to return to the benign protection of the metropolis. Those who in the past had been deceived by false promises were disillusioned and tired and Spain could surely not abandon them to 'four egoists who, under the patronage of ambitious foreigners, are only concerned with making their own fortunes out of the ruin of so many families worthy of a better fate'.[77] In a major debate on America in the early months of 1822, deputies José María Moscoso and the Conde de Toreno suggested a compromise position in the light of recent events, especially in Mexico. Spain must sustain and help those areas of America which remained loyal and resist the efforts of rebels to capture them. Spanish policy should vary according to the province; in some, the revolutions might perhaps after all reflect the popular will but there were certainly others where only a minority had terrorized the majority into submission. Envoys should be sent to some areas as peaceful negotiators but to others as liberators of the oppressed people who were suffering tyranny.[78] A few months later, the Overseas Committee of the Cortes accepted that the situation was 'extremely critical and unpleasant', but there was still hope. Spain might well be called upon to settle the feuding factions in New Spain; the rebel governments of Venezuela and New Granada had no 'moral force' and it would not be difficult for the loyalists there to overthrow them, if Spain could provide some assistance.[79]

Few of these advocates of the minority thesis ventured to place any numerical assessment on the number of rebels to justify their case, but López Cancelada showed no such reluctance. In 1821 he took up his pen and resurrected his newspaper, in his words, to save America. He found it incredible that there were now some people in the peninsula willing to abandon the empire. Surveying all the rebel-held provinces and their population, he concluded that there were at most 1,526,000 dissidents and at least 13,474,000 loyal inhabitants. Even among the rebels, there were many who were passive, unaware of what they were fighting for and privately longing for Spain to restore peace and order. To abandon the 9,000,000 loyal castes, the 3,500,000 loyal Indians and the 500,000 loyal creoles would in his opinion be an act of betrayal and injustice by the Mother Country. It would expose them to the 'insane fury of a miserable number of revolutionaries'.[80]

As in every other aspect of the pacification issue, there were those who disagreed with this assessment of the revolutions and their support in America. As already indicated, some had concluded at Cádiz by 1811 that the desire for independence was both profound and widespread. Furthermore, although during Ferdinand's six years of absolutism from 1814 to 1820, the royalist armies, reinforced by thousands of soldiers shipped over from Spain, did achieve significant military success and control seemed to have been regained in several provinces, many of the king's senior advisers knew that the situation was in fact getting worse. Secretary of State Pedro Cevallos warned in May 1815 that the colonies were 'near to breaking completely their bonds of dependency on Spain', and in November of the same year the Council of the Indies advised that hatred of the metropolis was spreading in New Spain and that the Indies in general were in a 'very dangerous state'.[81] José Alvarez de Toledo, in a general appraisal of the Spanish position submitted to the cabinet, contended that the revolution was gaining ground everywhere. New Granada, he predicted, although recently pacified, would rebel again; Venezuela was being destroyed by the war; Lima and the whole of Peru were by no means secure; and Chile, although also recently pacified, was in imminent danger.[82]

From 1816 to 1818, the Junta de Pacificación, the Councils of State and of the Indies and individual advisers all concluded that the revolutionary fervour was increasing throughout the empire. In October

1816, for example, Manuel de la Bodega, in a report for the Junta de Pacificación, painted a vivid picture of the destruction and desolation in America caused by the scale of the war. Whole provinces had been ruined and as many as a million lives lost. The rebellions were spreading daily and the loss of America was inevitable if the causes were not promptly dealt with.[83] A month later the Council of the Indies repeated its view, already expressed on several previous occasions, that the revolts were not just popular disturbances which could be subdued by force and future peace and order thereby guaranteed. What was happening was a full-scale civil war.[84]

The Conde de Casa Flores took a more philosophical view. In a letter to Secretary of State Pizarro, he advanced the premise that in the firm opinion of most great statesmen, the separation of the colonies was inevitable. He did not wish to argue the point but he was convinced that America would reject all its links with Spain unless radical reforms were introduced. We are, he pointed out, in the nineteenth century and nobody can stop the progress of ideas. Spain must find a way of ending its imperialist mentality and the word 'colonies' must be removed from the minds of Spaniards. The administration of the 'overseas provinces', as he felt they should be called, must be changed and modernized.[85] The merchant representatives on the Junta de Diputados rejected the idea that America had reached maturity and that emancipation from the Mother Country was an inevitable or natural stage in its evolution. As far as they were concerned, the fact that Americans wanted independence when their region was still in a 'state of infancy' confirmed their immaturity. Furthermore, it was not the educated people in revolt but the masses of mestizos, Indians and negroes and despite their overwhelming numbers, they had not been able to defeat the minority of loyal Spaniards and creoles.[86]

The Council of State, largely at the insistence of Pizarro, undertook a thorough review of the American situation in 1817 and 1818. Several of the councillors, led by Pizarro, insisted that the situation was critical and that it was essential to find 'a grandiose remedy' before it was too late. Pizarro accepted that the situation was not uniform all over the continent in that some provinces were presently under control, but he was sure that the rebellious 'spirit and disposition were uniform and general'. Buenos Aires and Chile were in a deplorable state, Venezuela was by no means secure, and although he despised the rebel leaders individually, it was clear that judged together and with their allies, they had to be taken most seriously. Britain was giving large amounts of aid to them and that was contributing to the desire for independence 'which, more or less, is the decided objective of all Americans in all areas'.[87]

Following the restoration of the constitutional system in 1820, those who believed that the desire for independence was widespread tried to persuade their colleages that the idea of a minority suppressing a loyal majority was quite mistaken. Cabrera de Nevares declared that 'the insurrection of America is the work of the entire American people', and in the Cortes, José Ibarra who, as he said, had lived for forty-three years in America, emphasized that emancipation was the fervent desire of the great majority of Americans. It was now 'physically and morally impossible' for Spain to prevent independence and the sooner Spaniards recognized it, the better: 'let us recognize our true interests; let us remember finally that we are all of the same blood, language and religion; and let us bring to an end a fratricidal war that can no longer be disguised under any pretext'.[88] Alcalá Galiano supported this view. Clearly, it was a matter of profound and natural regret when an empire disintegrated after so long, but nobody could surely doubt that most Americans wanted to be free. He knew that many considered the revolutions to be the work of only a minority but they were mistaken. Buenos Aires, he noted, had had a dozen or more governments since 1810 but not a single one had sought reunion with the Crown.[89] Joaquín Ferrer, also a former resident in America, insisted that the minority assessment was wrong. Americans had forgotten that before the arrival of Spaniards, they were no more than tribes of savages ruled by bloodthirsty tyrants. They had forgotten all the benefits bestowed on them by Spain, the opulence of their cities, the expansion of their agriculture and industry, their universities and the civilized life provided at great cost by the Spanish people. There was no doubt in his mind that most now wanted independence. They had been indoctrinated in favour of it from the pulpit and the confessional and the extent of support for the rebels had to be accepted.[90] One newspaper was even more emphatic: 'A ministry who believes the renewal of war possible and who counts on arming provinces against provinces, either jokes or speaks in delirium.'[91]

From 1810 onwards, therefore, Spaniards were quite unable to agree on the extent of support for emancipation and their respective minority or majority assessments were to be a significant factor in determining their ideas on what Spanish policy should be. Another area which influenced reactions and policies and on which again there was no consensus was the causes of the revolutions. An infinite variety of explanations was put forward by almost everyone involved and the diversity was almost immediately apparent at Cádiz during the first constitutional period. The first causes to be postulated by official sources attributed the revolts to a lack of information in the colonies about the fate of Spain and to the pernicious influence of French agents who were spreading false rumours that the resistance forces in the peninsula had been completely defeated. The Regency issued several proclamations in an attempt to dispel this erroneous view and, on 1 May 1810, a decree was promulgated to alert the colonial authorities and imposing the death penalty on any spies who were caught.[92] The Council of the Indies, in its report on Caracas of 12 July 1810, asserted that the insurrection had occurred because of the lying propaganda and hence one of the first measures the government should adopt was the improvement of communications with America. In the first public statement about Caracas on 8 August 1810, the Regency accepted this explanation and the envoy Cortabarría was told that he must be sure to inform the people of Caracas of the true condition of Spain, its heroic defence and the valour of its armies. He was to say that the Regency assumed that Americans had been misled because there could be no other reason for their actions. Again, in a proclamation of 6 September 1810, it was claimed that events in Caracas and Buenos Aires were the direct consequence of French intrigue and local ignorance of what was happening in Europe. In November 1810, the fiscal of the Council of the Indies assessed the main causes of the Buenos Aires disturbances as the news of the French invasion of Andalucía and the dissolution of the Junta Central, and in the Cortes in January 1811 the Buenos Aires representatives spoke of 'misunderstood and inaccurate beliefs'.[93] The Regency's commissioner to New Spain likewise blamed the French invasion and the belief that Spain had been defeated. Several months later, the same explanation was offered in a memorandum by American representatives in the Cortes. Among various other reasons, the news of the defeat of Spain, they said, had brought great fear in the overseas provinces and the juntas had been formed for self-defence against the French.[94]

The activities of the British government and especially British merchants were another often-cited cause. Although in public the Regency, and, indeed, most subsequent administrations were obliged to maintain the façade of total confidence in the main ally against the French, numerous informants alleged that Britain had secretly fomented the revolts. Salazar wrote from Montevideo that British merchants were promoting independence in Buenos Aires and Casa Irujo from Rio de Janeiro that the British ambassador there was actively trying to persuade the Portuguese court that the Buenos Aires rebels were honourable men, merely seeking some long-needed reforms.[95] As already indicated, the Regency advised Cortabarría to expect trouble from the British, noting the reception in London of the Caracas junta's envoys. Probably the most anti-British group were the Cádiz merchants. They vehemently and repeatedly attacked British attempts to get trading privileges. In fact, according to them, it was previous trading concessions to foreigners, so harmful to religious faith and economic prosperity in the colonies, that were largely to blame for the present difficulties.[96]

The role of the French or the British, and for some the malign influences and ambitions of the United States and Portugal, were not seen as the sole causes. They were thought to be contributory factors in perhaps the most widely propagated cause, namely what one scholar has aptly called the 'seduction theory'.[97] The advocates of this thesis considered that French, British, United States or Portuguese interests, separately or together, had subverted a few ambitious dissidents in each province who in turn had 'seduced' more of their naive compatriots into the belief that Spain was lost, independence was there to be taken, and that foreign powers would offer protection. The verb 'seducir' appeared in most explanations offered by government ministers and reports from agents. The Regency Gazette constantly denounced the 'seduction' of the innocent. For example, referring to New Spain on 2 April 1811, the editor regretted the loss of life but public order had to be restored: 'the ruin and grief are the sole responsibility before God and man of those wrongdoers who have seduced some of the unwary indigenous people, forcing them to commit excesses and all manner of crimes'. A few weeks later, the Gazette proclaimed that knowledge of the true condition of Spain would be fatal to the rebels 'who have succeeded in deceiving the least educated part of those peoples with their sophistries and false picture of events in Europe'.[98] The *Redactor General* similarly condemned scurrilous priests in New Spain for 'seducing' their docile flocks into senseless rebellion.[99]

Popular though it was to attribute blame to lack of information, foreign intrigues or the seduction theory, or sometimes a combination of all three, there were those who recognized that the actions of previous governments and past Spanish policy as a whole towards the empire were the more likely causes. Several condemned the behaviour of the Junta Central and the Regency. Pizarro criticized the inappropriate proclamations issued by the Seville junta and the poor quality of the envoys sent to the colonies by the Junta Central.[100] The governor of Huancavelica quoted from a government manifesto of 14 February 1810 directed to Americans: 'your destiny no longer depends on ministers, viceroys or governors; it is in your own hands'. It was hardly surprising, he said, that authority had been undermined and there was now continuous conflict between government and people.[101] The potential dangers of the appeals to Americans for loyalty and aid had been foreseen. Once the decision was taken by the Junta Central in 1809 to summon a congress to deliberate on the future form of government for the monarchy, predictions were soon forthcoming that, in the circumstances of the time, any attempt to change the fundamental laws of the nation could well have repercussions in America. The town council of Córdoba had warned that to include colonial affairs on the agenda of the congress was one of the most dangerous steps that could be taken. A desire for independence would soon emerge and if American representatives were allowed to participate in constitutional discussions, it would not be long before they learned how to achieve it.[102] Antonio Capmany had noted that the frequent use of words such as liberty, freedom and independence in official propaganda, while appropriate for the peninsula, might well persuade Americans to seek their own emancipation.[103] Alvaro Flórez Estrada attacked the inept policies of both the Junta Central and the Regency.[104] Gabriel Yermo, on the other hand, blamed the revolt in New Spain on the weak administration of Archbishop Lizana, while Elío thought the ignorant and incompetent members of the *audiencia* were responsible in Buenos Aires.[105]

Others, but few in number, took a rather broader view. In contrast to the more usual defence and even eulogy of the Spanish record in America, there were some who acknowledged the defects of Spanish dominion in the past. The dean of the Council of the Indies, José Salcedo, referred to the despotism, arbitrary rule and notorious venality of the *ancien régime*.[106] Disgraceful appointments, he noted, had been made in the public service, especially in the Treasury departments, and many licentious young men, already discredited by their earlier careers, had been given senior posts in the colonial bureaucracy. Who could be sure, he asked, that the result of such injustice was not now being seen in Caracas, Buenos Aires and Quito? Francisco de Noriega, in a memorandum dated 22 November 1810, recalled that he had lived in New Spain for twenty years and it was his opinion that unjust government by past generations was at the root of the present unrest.[107] Juan Antonio Yandiola listed avarice, bad government, despotism and favouritism as the causes in New Spain and in the Cortes, Argüelles accepted that America had suffered three centuries of misfortune, despotism and systematic oppression.[108] Deputy José Valcarcel y Dato also attacked the cruelty and corruption of Spanish officials in the past and, of course, American deputies frequently expressed similar sentiments.[109] The majority disagreed with this harsh view of their forefathers and denials of past injustice were always prominent. For them, the actions of Spaniards in the New World, the colonial legislation and the general conduct of the metropolis towards the empire could not in any way be blamed as causes of the disturbances. According to Garay, there was nothing for which Spain could be reproached. There was not a single bad law in the whole of the laws of the Indies; America had never been called a colony or colonies by people in Spain but only by foreigners; there were no restrictions on industry or agriculture; great care had always been taken in the choice of officials; and Americans had always had plenty of channels through which to make complaints and have them satisfied.[110]

The argument over the causes propounded initially at Cádiz continued in the debates of the royal councils and in the volumes of advice given to Ferdinand following his return to the throne in 1814. Although, for the most part, the attention of his advisers was concentrated rather more on finding solutions than analysing the causes, the ideas and emphasis on the latter did change to some extent. The most obvious new feature of the analysis was to omit reference to the past misdeeds of the *ancien régime* and at the same time to attribute the revolts to the evils of constitutionalism and the liberal ideology.[111] Indeed, all the resistance governments were blamed and, in particular, the reforms in colonial law enacted by the Cortes which were ridiculed as unjustified, provocative concessions. In the manifesto of the Persas (conservative deputies), the Cortes decree of 15 October 1810 announcing the equality of Spain and America as integral parts of the monarchy was said to have been tantamount to 'awakening the rebellion of the overseas provinces'.[112] Ferdinand was told in May 1814 by the Conde de Vistaflorida that the actions of the Junta Central and Regency had inflamed a situation already made critical by the intrigues of the French and José de Zayas told him that it was the unfulfilled promises and expectations aroused but not satisfied by the previous régime which were the main causes.[113]

The tendency to blame foreign intervention, already well evident at Cádiz since 1810, became even more pronounced among Ferdinand's ministers and officials. His Secretaries of State constantly warned of British ambitions and the Portuguese in Brazil were widely attacked for having encouraged the rebels since the outbreak of the revolts. The attitude towards foreign powers was nevertheless ambivalent because many of the most senior advisers in the court came to the conclusion that the best hope of reunifying the empire was to persuade a foreign government, usually the British, to mediate. They argued from at least 1815 that no other solution held greater prospect of success, but that such mediation could only be attracted by the offer of trading concessions. The merchant lobby, aided by their supporters in the corridors of power, opposed both the idea of mediation and trading concessions, partly on the grounds that it was precisely the relaxation of Spain's commercial monopoly which had caused the spread of seditious ideas which, in turn, had caused the revolts. Everybody agrees, said the Junta de Diputados, that the insurrections started only when foreigners were allowed into the colonies. Envious and avaricious merchants had fomented discord and parricide. Santiago Linier's introduction of free trade at Buenos Aires was one obvious example and the rebellion of the River Plate region might never have happened if he had not been so imprudent. Foreigners were active in New Spain, Sante Fe, Caracas, Cartagena, Chile and all over the continent. They paid people to propagate the idea of independence, they sponsored subversive newspapers, inciting the creoles with promises of aid from their governments.[114] Minister of State Cevallos told the Council of State in the presence of Ferdinand that 'the rebellions had their origin in the spirit of rapacity and ambition of their instigators incited by the suggestions of Bonaparte's envoys and by the diffusion of subversive works which since the middle of the past century have prepared the minds of the people for insubordination against the legitimate powers'.[115] For Juan Lozano de Torres, Minister of Grace and Justice in 1817 and alleged member of Ferdinand's camarilla, the British were the principal instigators of the revolts. He had the utmost contempt for the monarchy's erstwhile allies and urged that they should never be trusted. The British, he remarked, had sacrificed their much-vaunted philanthropic ideas on the altar of their mercantile speculations.[116] Casa Irujo, on succeeding Pizarro as Secretary of State in August 1818, promptly rejected his predecessor's predilection for British mediation via trading reform as a policy option. It was foreign trade, he told the king, that was 'the vehicle of the revolutions'.[117]

By the time the liberal Constitution was reintroduced in March 1820, the constitutionalists naturally added to their list of causes the fact that their reform programme had been suppressed by Ferdinand in 1814. The Conde de Toreno was full of praise for the traditional loyalty of Americans. It had only been their fear of being dominated by the French that had caused the revolts; 'such was the noble principle of the troubles in America'. There had been every chance of reconciliation, he suggested, once the French were defeated, but then the disastrous decree of 4 May 1814 and the 'atrocious system which followed it' had destroyed all hope.[118] Had this not happened, the liberals in general argued, there would have been no question of a resurgence of the revolutionary movements. To some extent, this line of argument rebounded against its many advocates when it became clear that despite all the proclamations and talk that the reintroduction of the Constitution would bring an end to the revolutions, the opposite effect occurred in that they spread and were consolidated. The constitutionalists needed to explain the continuation of the conflict. General Morillo provided a convenient explanation on his return to the peninsula. Reporting to the Minister of Ultramar, he stated that it was the internal rivalries and factional feuding among the rebels 'which has been the cause of the continuation of the war'.[119] Others had a rather different explanation. For some, it had been Ferdinand's policy of military reconquest that had driven Americans to seek their separation from the metropolis and for José Moreno Guerra, representing Córdoba in the Cortes in 1821, it was the same General Morillo who bore the greatest responsibility for the loss of the empire. His illegal acts, his tyranny, and the cruelty of his military campaigns in America, he said, had been the main reason why the revolts had continued.[120] Others in the Cortes believed that the Americans had continued their actions because the promises of equal rights offered by the first congress at Cádiz had not been kept. Flórez Estrada insisted that the concept of one nation, one imperial family, must be made to be seen meaningful by the enactment of genuine reforms and Juan Freire that actions and not words were essential if the disintegration of the empire was to be stopped.[121] On the other hand, there were also those who contended that some of the reforms enacted by the Cortes were to blame, particularly for the Iturbide revolt in New Spain. The Cortes had condemned the sixty-nine signatories of the Persas manifesto and some of the Councillors of State advised that Bishop Pérez of Puebla should be exempted because much of the new unrest in Mexico had been caused by the belief that he was being persecuted. Similarly, they recommended suspension of the anti-clerical legislation which had caused renewed discontent in the colonies.[122] For Esteban Varea, also on the Council of State, the causes of the revolutions were quite clear. They were the distance of 3,000 leagues and more from the centre of government, which inevitably meant that the overseas territories could not be governed efficiently and with the necessary dispatch; the long-standing complaint that almost all worthwhile posts in the civil and ecclesiastical bureaucracy were denied to even the most illustrious Americans; the undeniable fact that there was virtually no Spanish colonial official who did not abuse his authority.[123]

In January 1822, the Minister of Ultramar, Ramón López Pelegrín, presented a report of more than one hundred pages to the Cortes which was intended to be a definitive evaluation of all the evidence accumulated by the government and its committees on the American situation. Everyone, he said, had his own opinion regarding the causes of the movements for independence. Some even believed the conquest to have been a mistake, others blamed the failure to appreciate the effects of the United States' separation from Britain, or the events in Peru in 1781 or the much-discussed problem of bad appointments to posts in the colonial service. The main causes, however, were clear. The French invasion of the peninsula and the false impression that Spain was lost, the more philanthropic than political acts of the Junta Central, the seduction of the people by French and other foreign provocateurs, and the government's own mistakes. Those who blamed defects in the laws of the Indies were wrong. Any impartial examination revealed that they were uniformly protective and helpful and were envied by other nations.[124]

This diversity and range of specific causes of the revolutions, added to the more general belief among liberals that absolutism past and present was to blame, and among royalists that it was all the fault of the reformers, complicated even further Spain's attempts to analyse and understand what was happening.[125] With ever-conflicting opinion, advice and recommendations from all directions, no Spanish government was confident that it had managed to acquire an accurate assessment on which policies could be based. Moreover, despite the mountains of paper and the vast amount of information that poured into Cádiz and then Madrid, each régime always felt that the true picture had not been presented to it. Hence Ferdinand and his ministers and the constitutional authorities repeatedly sought more information, but by the time it was received and absorbed by the cumbersome administrative machinery, it was usually out of date in that the military position in America had changed or new domestic political considerations had to be taken into account. Faced with this fluctuating scene and air of uncertainty, all governments chose the expedient of sending envoys, either officially or in secret, to the colonies with instructions to find out what was happening, assess the support for the rebel cause and, if possible, to negotiate a settlement. The Junta Central sent its agents in 1808, the Regency in 1810, Ferdinand in 1814 and the constitutional government in 1820 and 1822. But again, the reports remitted by these officials were often in direct contradiction with one another or with information coming in from other sources, or had been superseded by the time they were received. The general public, of course, knew even less of what was going on. Just as the Regency had put its own optimistic gloss on its reporting of developments, so Ferdinand, having abolished almost the entire press in 1814, used what little was left to maintain morale and for his own internal political interests. He imposed strict censorship on news leaks concerning events in the colonies and, between 1814 and 1820, there was not a single reference in the official government Gazette to any major American success, while Spanish victories were given extensive coverage. Another Madrid newspaper produced in 1818–19 devoted its first four issues to the empire and managed to discuss its government and economy without once mentioning that there was a war in progress.[126]

For individual politicians, this lack of reliable information became the pretext, or perhaps valid excuse, for their refusal to commit themselves on American issues. Certainly many of the peninsular deputies in the first Cortes knew little or nothing about the empire and often said as much. Part of the problem for the legislators in both constitutional periods was the reluctance of the executive to divulge what information it held and no administration, except perhaps that of Ferdinand from 1816 to 1818, was willing or able to give top priority to the imperial crisis. For example, on 13 November 1810, the Cortes asked the Regency for an up-to-date account of events in Caracas, Buenos Aires and elsewhere. No reply was forthcoming and reminders were sent on 11 and 28 December, again without response. Eventually, the ministers did make statements, but these often contained few or no details beyond those already publicly known from the popular press. A decade later in 1821, the same problem persisted. For much of that year, the Cortes requested the executive to report. The ministers failed to do so and there were accusations against them of deliberate prevarication in an attempt to stop discussion in the congress. In December, deputy Félix Navarrete pointed out that news had arrived of the treaties of Córdoba in New Spain, that Portugal had recognized the independence of Buenos Aires, that there was a Regency in New Spain and that Guatemala and Mérida were now independent. All this, he complained, he and his colleagues had had to learn from press reports and despite the potential magnitude of such events, not a single word on any of them had come from the responsible departments of State and no explanation at all offered to the Cortes.[127]

This executive–legislative rivalry evident in the constitutional régimes was also present in a different form during the years of Ferdinand's absolute rule. Then internal political rivalries in the court clearly had a significant effect on the policy-making process and the atmosphere of personal animosity in the corridors of power was not helped, and nor was Spanish assessment of the revolutions, by a persistent belief that there were secret forces at work in the peninsula conspiring to sabotage any efforts to regain control of the colonies. Much of the information concerning events in America came from American representatives in the Cortes. In the early sessions at Cádiz, few of these had any more recent or firm knowledge than their European counterparts, but as more arrived directly from all over the empire, they produced detailed and extensive accounts of what was happening and what action needed to be taken. This was even more the case in the second Cortes but rather than clarify the minds of Spaniards, the words of the Americans added to the uncertainty. This was because in both congresses, the Americans were viewed with intense suspicion and there were many allegations that, despite all their claims to the contrary, they were in fact using their time and opportunity in Spain to promote their independence. Alcalá Galiano recalled that 'the European deputies regarded the desires and remarks and acts of their colleagues from Ultramar with justifiable – if occasionally excessive – suspicion'.[128] Argüelles said that they manipulated everything towards their ultimate goal of independence and that although they did not openly propose it, 'they threatened it at every stage, if we did not concede all that they asked for'.[129] It was not just the American deputies who were not believed. Vázquez Figueroa referred in 1817 to the 'fallacious and perverse words of those who for a long time have been trying to persuade us that we should willingly emancipate such vast dominions'. Recalling discussions in the Council of State, he wrote that things were debated 'according to the interests of those people who supported them, some of whom and their motives, were not unknown to me. What a misfortune it is for all governments to have these people who prefer their own private interests, even when their nation is dying.'[130]

Whatever the hidden forces, be they secret American agents or freemasons, both of whom were also certainly at work seeking to influence Spanish opinion, there is no doubt that few Spaniards ever achieved a firm and clear picture of what was going on in America throughout the years of war. Biased by their own acquired, if not inherited, prejudices against the American people, misinformed, at times deliberately, or else kept in ignorance of events, they failed to appreciate the full implications of the movements for emancipation as they swept throughout the empire. What Delgado has described as the 'blindness of its politicians and the incomprehension of its rulers' was not brought about by what another scholar has labelled 'apathy' on the part of Spaniards.[131] Rather, such features of the Spanish response were the product of surprise, confusion and a large measure of disbelief as each succeeding régime with its ministers, officials, legislators, advisers and private-interest groups argued the merits of their own appraisal of the situation. Always uncertain of the extent of support for the rebels in the military sense and even more so in the sense of support for the idea of independence among the American population as a whole, the Spanish lexicon had to be scoured to find words appropriate to the assessment of American actions. They were *alborotos, turbulencias, colonias rebeldes, provincias rebeldes, insurrecciones, motines, provincias seducidas, rebeliones, sublevaciones* and *revoluciones*. As for the rebels themselves, it was simply inconceivable for many Spaniards that the majority of their American 'brothers', above all the creoles sharing what was so often said to be a common heritage in every respect, could genuinely wish to destroy the imperial community after so many generations of apparently indissoluble unity. To use the emotive words of a minister in 1822, the overseas provinces were not just a group of people who happened to live in America who, under the pretext of seeking their own welfare, were tearing to pieces the entrails of the mother who gave birth to them. America was part of the Spanish nation; it was part of the world brought to light by the sacrifices of Spaniards; to them it owed its prosperity, whatever knowledge it had, and its very existence.[132] Alcalá Galiano summed it all up nicely. When it came to the question of the events in America, he told his colleagues in the Cortes, Spaniards were like Don Quijote, rational and irrational.[133]

3

The military solution

Origins, 1810–14

Spanish uncertainty as to the causes and degree of support for the revolutions in America was reflected in the fierce controversy and divergence of views over how best to respond to the situation. Myriad ways of restoring Spanish domination were postulated by officials and private advisory groups in Spain and in America, but these were rarely practical, occasionally fanciful and often contradictory. One view, however, which did command considerable support was that the use of, or at least the threat of, military force was essential, regardless of whatever other supplementary measures might be devised. The belief in military reconquest provoked much controversy at times but this largely centred on the extent to which it was necessary and how, when and where it could be most successfully applied. For the advocates of the minority thesis who were convinced that there was never more than a small number of dedicated rebels, the military solution was the most obvious answer to the problem. For those who came to believe that the desire for independence was both profound and widespread throughout the empire, military action seemed wasteful in human and material resources, and even more important, counter-productive in terms of achieving the agreed objective of restoring imperial unity. Ferdinand himself always remained convinced that the use of force was a realistic policy, despite the failure of Spanish arms to defeat the rebels and regardless of the actual defeat of his loyalist forces across the continent by the early 1820s.

The idea of using military force to suppress the insurrections, and the actual embarkation of soldiers, began during the first constitutional régime at Cádiz. In the autumn of 1810 and the early months of 1811, the Cortes and Regency reacted to the events in America with a combination of policies of political, social and economic reform while at the same time ordering redeployment of military units already in

52

the colonies and the blockade of some ports. As it became clear, at least to some, that the rebel movements were not merely temporary aberrations by misguided men and that emancipation was their objective, demands for a much more vigorous and militant reaction were soon forthcoming. It was essential and urgent, it was argued, to suppress the dissidents by force before they could intimidate and oblige their compatriots to join them in their treachery. Among the most ardent advocates of this hard-line approach was López Cancelada. By March 1811 he began to campaign for more soldiers. He strongly advised the immediate dispatch of 7,000–8,000 men and he even offered to find the recruits and the money to pay for them himself, provided the viceroy of New Spain would send the same number of Europeans from New Spain to fight in the peninsular war.[1]

López Cancelada, although the most persistent and vociferous, was by no means alone in his campaign. Force, proclaimed one newspaper, was the only way to defeat the rebels: 'send a few troops from the peninsula and total pacification is certain'.[2] From the colonies, Spanish commanders and officials sent repeated requests for additional forces and supplies. Salazar, naval commander at Montevideo, pleaded almost daily for immediate reinforcements.[3] Elío, within weeks of his arrival at Montevideo, reported that more troops were needed and his replacement, Gaspar Vigodet, demanded as a matter of the utmost priority that 'measures be taken to meet his repeated requests for the embarkation of troops'.[4] Merchants at Lima warned that the garrisons of Peru had to be strengthened and that at least 1,500 men were required.[5] Envoys to the colonies came to the same conclusion. Cortabarría insisted over and again in his letters that the Caracas rebellion could not be stopped unless an expedition of 2,000–3,000 men was quickly sent. Carlota, sister of Ferdinand and wife of the Portuguese monarch João VI, wrote from Rio de Janeiro imploring the Regency to use as much force as it could muster and the Council of the Indies in its reports recommended that reinforcements should be sent, even if only to ensure that the people of America were properly informed of events in Europe and knew that the monarchy had not collapsed.

Not everyone, of course, adopted this hawkish stance. The envoy to New Granada, Antonio de Villavicencio, advocated a policy of tolerance and understanding, warning that military action would antagonize the population and make matters worse.[6] There is also no doubt that many people believed that either the news of the installation of the Cortes, or political and economic reforms with the promise of their incorporation in the new constitution, would be enough to pacify Americans. Once the injustices of the *ancien régime* had been remedied, the American people would have no cause for complaint and would willingly lay down their arms to reenter the imperial family and enjoy the political equality and material benefits offered by the new constitutional system. This attitude, or hope, was most visible in the Cortes where the liberal reformers at first found it difficult to reconcile their beliefs in freedom and popular sovereignty with the idea of using force against their overseas compatriots who, it was thought by some, were seeking no more than to achieve long-needed improvements in their relationship with the Mother Country. The liberals were told day after day by the active and energetic American deputies that force was not the way to settle the problem. It could only be resolved by genuine and meaningful reforms as detailed by the Americans in their several lengthy expositions to the congress. In May 1811, for example, a Cortes committee considered Cortabarría's request for military aid. The Regency, the committee said, appeared to favour the idea but it did not. Using the army would certainly alienate many Americans and there was no guarantee that it would be successful. If the expedition was sent only to Caracas, other rebel areas would become alarmed and improve their defensive preparations. Furthermore, it was unjust to use force until all the avenues of peaceful persuasion had been exhausted. Reforms, the committee concluded, were more likely to achieve peace than military campaigns.[7]

Faced with these pro- and anti-force pressures, and always unsure of what exactly was happening in America, the Regency hesitated. There were several important reasons for its caution. Priority clearly had to be given to the war against the French in the peninsula and the state of the public treasury did not permit the recruitment of additional soldiers who could be properly equipped and nor was there immediately available sufficient ships to transport an army across the Atlantic. The Minister of Hacienda reported in February 1811 that public finances were in a desperate state, with revenues not meeting even a third of expenditure and, with the national public debt rising week by week, there was no source of credit on any large scale.[8] Even the generous American aid was not enough and could not be relied on indefinitely. The government was obviously aware of its desperate need for American financial help and proclamations and appeals for contributions were still being made. To spend such scarce resources on equipping military expeditions to the provinces which had provided them in the first place would jeopardize that essential source of revenue. Furthermore, as the British ambassador was quick to point out, the Regency was even more indebted for its survival to British financial support and that was given in large amounts to be spent on resisting the French rather than on fighting dissident colonials.

Indeed, British concern at the growing clamour in Cádiz for military expeditions to be sent to America may well have been a factor in its offer early in 1811 to mediate with the insurgents in exchange for commercial concessions in the transatlantic trade.[9] Partly in response to American demands, fundamental changes in the trade regulations, involving the formal ending of Spain's exclusive monopoly and the introduction of partial or complete international access to the colonial markets, had been under consideration since at least the beginning of 1811. Prompted by the Regency, the Cortes began its debates on the matter in April and after a few weeks, before the decisive vote was taken, Sir Henry Wellesley intervened with his offer of mediation in America. The possibility of either an independent declaration of free trade by the Cortes which was the policy most strongly pressed by the American deputies, or any infringement of the monopoly system for the benefit of the British, caused great alarm to the Cádiz merchants. Through their *consulado*, or guild, they began an impressive campaign against free trade, publishing representations predicting economic ruin for the nation if it was approved and sending deputations to the Cortes to argue against any change in the existing mercantile code. This pressure was successful and, when the Cortes voted on the key article of the trade reform proposals on 13 August 1811, it was defeated.[10]

Having successfully opposed the free trade lobby, the merchants were equally determined to resist the commercial concessions which the British were seeking in return for their mediation with the rebels. There was considerable support in the Cortes and the Regency for the British proposal as the best means of pacifying the colonies and the merchants realized that they had to offer some practical alternative. They also knew that the government's financial and military resources were already fully committed to the war against the French and that, in the circumstances, it was highly improbable that the Regency would be able or willing to finance any significant military effort in America even if it could be demonstrated that the insurrections were spreading and that prompt military action might be effective. It appears, therefore, that the merchants decided to take the initiative themselves by offering to recruit, equip and finance the first expeditions to the colonies. It is not certain which side made the first approach but the first sign of behind-the-scenes negotiations came in the Cortes in the last week of August. On 23 August, deputy Felipe Aner de Esteve proposed that the Regency be told to take whatever steps it could to pacify New Spain, 'not forgetting the use of force'. A week later, on 30 August, Luis Rodríguez del Monte suggested that Aner and Francisco Gutiérrez de la Huerta be authorized to indicate to the Regency 'the means they have said are immediately available to send to various places in America the reinforcements required to preserve them'.[11] Almost immediately, possibly on 1 September, a small group of wealthy Cádiz merchants met with the Navy Minister to discuss ways and means of raising the finance and equipment required to dispatch reinforcements to several army units in America.[12] The meeting seems to have been preceded by private discussions, presumably known to Aner and others, in which the merchants had let it be known that they were willing to provide the funds. Following these initial talks, the *consulado* summoned an emergency meeting of its governing council, which in turn appointed a working party to report on the matter.[13] This proposed the establishment of a fund of 8,000,000 *reales* which would be used to pay for uniforms and rations and to reimburse the owners of merchant ships which served as troop transports. If this sum could not be raised directly from the merchant community, it was to be borrowed and, to repay creditors their capital and interest within a two-year term, special taxes were to be introduced. These were 1 per cent on agricultural produce and general merchandize entering or leaving Cádiz and other peninsular ports; 1 per cent on gold imports from America; 2 per cent on silver imports; and 3 per cent based on the tariff value of produce from America. These proposals were submitted to the Cortes on 8 September where they were approved and the Regency ordered them implemented.[14]

Thus the Comisión de Reemplazos was established and throughout the rest of the decade to 1820, it was to be the source and stimulus of most of Spain's military campaigns in America.[15] It began its work almost immediately. Recruiting agents were sent to Extremadura, Galicia and the Canaries and a voluntary enlistment centre for men between the ages of sixteen and forty was opened in Cádiz.[16] By 11

October, it was reported in the press that two battalions, to be known as the First and Second American, had already been recruited and were being prepared to leave for New Spain.[17] Warships and transports, uniforms, food and munitions were procured and López Cancelada jubilantly announced in his newspaper on 13 November that the first expedition for Havana and New Spain had embarked.[18] Moreover, he claimed, several thousand recruits had had to be left behind because there was no space for them on the ships. In fact, the convoy had consisted of one warship and three transports, taking 37 officers and 720 men. Within two weeks a second expedition departed for Montevideo with 7 officers and 80 men on one frigate and towards the end of the year, on 30 December, a third set out for Puerto Rico with one warship and one transport carrying 224 officers and men. Within just twelve weeks of its formation, the Comisión de Reemplazos had recruited, equipped and transported 1,068 men at a cost of 3,197,824 *reales*.[19]

As the kings of the sixteenth century had done to found the empire, the constitutionalist régime thus turned in effect to private enterprise to begin the process of reconquering America. Whatever ideological scruples, if any, the liberals felt against the adoption of this bellicose policy, they kept to themselves for no protest seems to have been forthcoming. In fact, there was a protest but this came from Wellesley who warned that military action was futile and that only a negotiated settlement of the dispute could have any hope of success. Also he repeated his objections to the expenditure on such a project when British money was only given for the peninsular war. Standing somewhat on his dignity, Minister of State Bardají replied that British money had not been used, since the expeditions had been financed by the Cádiz merchants and, furthermore, peaceful persuasion had failed and the metropolis was fully entitled and, indeed, obliged to take whatever steps were thought necessary for the security of the nation.[20]

Nevertheless, having given way to the pressure for a more militant and active response, the politicians at Cádiz had clearly compromised their credibility, especially with the American deputies who almost but not entirely unanimously had tried to persuade against the use of force. Discussions on possible British mediation were still going on although by October when the first expedition set sail, the negotiations were running into serious difficulties. Similarly, the liberal propaganda had for months past asserted that the Constitution was sure to bring about the end of the 'troubles'. Now such faith in the new order of things on the near horizon – the Constitution was published in March 1812 – was obviously tempered by reality or at least by the pleas for help pouring in from the colonies. Yet, on the other hand, even given the constraints of the military logistics, the dispatch of only 87 men to Montevideo can hardly have been considered an effective counter-revolutionary force. It seems that it was intended to fulfil several purposes. First and foremost, as a reminder to the Buenos Aires rebels that Spain was not entirely impotent and was prepared and able to use force, an ability which would greatly increase once the peninsular war had been successfully concluded. Secondly, to meet the persistent demands for aid from the hard-pressed colonial officials and commanders and, thirdly, as a morale booster to the supposed loyalist majority who needed to be assured that Spain was not a defeated nation; and finally, to satisfy the Cádiz merchants who more than once had warned that their financial support for the war against the French could not be maintained unless they were allowed and were able to earn money from the transatlantic trade. At the same time, it is possible that the Spanish authorities hoped that a token show of strength, allied to the constitutional reforms in progress and the promise of beneficial changes to come, would be sufficient to persuade the rebels to lay down their arms or the loyal majority to suppress them by their own efforts. In short, to adopt a policy that combined moderation and persuasion backed by the actual use of some, and the threat of greater, military force.

Whether such a policy evolved by accident or design is difficult to perceive but it remained in effect for the rest of the constitutional régime until the return of Ferdinand in 1814. The same arguments over the effectiveness or advisability of seeking to use force continued throughout 1812 and 1813 with López Cancelada and others, including Councillors of State such as Garay, maintaining that there was no alternative while some began to insist that it was a waste of time, men and money. The British mediation proposal continued to be explored even though the early negotiations had failed, and there were those who insisted that the concession of fundamental reforms, including international free trade, was essential for the restoration of peace. The constitution was duly published and quickly seen not to have the assumed or desired effect on the rebels and the demands for further military expeditions increased. The Regency, through the medium of the Comisión de Reemplazos, met the pressure for militancy by dispatching a further twelve expeditions, four of which took 7,231 men to New Spain and three, with 4,127 men, to Montevideo, the rest going to Santa Marta (two), Maracaibo, Costa Firme and Lima. Despite loyalist victories in some regions, notably New Spain and Venezuela where the rebels appeared for a time to have been defeated, there were many reports that the insurrections were spreading in spirit, if not in deed, and that in the River Plate territories, the Spanish position was critical. As the military reinforcements were seen not to be effective in suppressing both the fact and the ideology of emancipation, there were two basic responses. The first wanted larger and larger armies to be sent before the insurgent minority could spread irrevocably their seditious philosophy. The second began to take a longer-term view and questioned whether Spain had the military and, just as important, the naval capacity, not only to end the present disturbances but also to keep the peace in the distant colonies on an indefinite basis. Was it, it was asked, a viable economic proposition even to attempt to do so when it was probable that the cost of maintaining large, permanent garrisons would far exceed the financial benefits accruing to the metropolis from its entire imperial possessions?

The pursuit of reconquest, 1814–20

When Ferdinand returned to Spain in May 1814 to stage his successful coup against the constitutionalist administration and abolish all that it sought to achieve, he was presumably aware of the controversy over how to respond to the situation in his American empire.[21] All the alternatives seemed to have been pursued by the constitutionalists – political, economic and social reforms, possible mediation by Britain, and the use of military force, albeit on what was, in practical terms, a token basis. He also knew that none of the options so far tried had achieved the permanent defeat of the insurgents and it was quickly evident to him that his abolition of the liberal reform programme and his restoration of the *ancien régime* were likewise not going to bring about the desired imperial harmony. Nevertheless, he had his ministers issue the customary proclamations to his overseas subjects with appeals for loyalty and promises of future benefits from the new order of things. He appointed Americans to prominent positions in his government, made changes in the colonial administrative system and promised much better treatment in the future. Although it may have been no more than a propaganda charade, he also began a series of

consultations into the exact causes of American dissension. On 12
May 1814, the day before his triumphal entry into Madrid, a royal
decree was issued in which several Americans resident in the peninsula
were called upon to advise on what needed to be done to restore peace
to their continent. The four men thus consulted replied within three
weeks and all advocated various reforms, but they differed on the use
of force. José Baquícano y Carrillo, Conde de Vistaflorida, a native of
Lima and a Councillor of State, said that Americans were loyal to
their king and that all military action against them should be halted.[22]
The Conde de Puñonrostro (New Granada) did not mention the idea
of reconquest in his reply,[23] but Antonio Pérez (New Spain) recalled
his own earlier efforts at Cádiz to persuade the Regency to send a large
army. He criticized the Regency's tactics, especially for dividing the
few available soldiers by sending only small numbers to several places
with the result that nowhere was completely pacified. Ferdinand, he
said, should now send 10,000–12,000 men to New Spain to ensure that
order was fully restored.[24] General José de Zayas (Costa Firme)
advised that the situation in each province was different and each
required different measures but whatever steps were taken, force was
essential and care should be taken to see that only well-disciplined
men were used.[25]

Ferdinand also ordered the former American deputies to the Cádiz
Cortes to remain in Spain and advise him on his colonial policy. Again
there was no consensus but while this early advice was not notably
jingoistic, there was soon more bellicose pressure from other sources.[26]
The most persistent of these was the Comisión de Reemplazos, still
busily engaged on organizing expeditions planned by the Regency.
The latest, originally intended for Costa Firme, was being prepared in
Galicia, but in April 1814 the orders were changed. It was now to go to
Montevideo and to consist of 3,200 infantry, 200 artillerymen and 600
cavalry. The change of destination was possibly a consequence of a
long representation which the Comisión had produced and, un-
usually, had published in the previous month of March. This painted
a gruesome picture of the situation in America where anarchy,
poverty and destruction were said to prevail everywhere:

Rivers stained with Spanish blood; fields covered with corpses; gallows to
exterminate the good people; rewards offered to the one who immolates the
greatest number of victims; widows, orphans, mourning and grief, in every
family. This is the scene in the rebel towns . . .[27]

The previous policy of moderate response in military terms, allied to
concessions and reforms, had not worked and it was now essential to

launch a full-scale military operation. The first priority had to be the River Plate and the Comisión was certain that the arrival of 3,000 well-disciplined troops at Montevideo would end the revolt in that region. In other regions – Costa Firme, Guayana and Coro – the situation was the same and at least 3,000 men should be sent urgently. Also in New Spain, an additional 2,000 men were needed to enable the viceroy to secure peace and, finally, a reserve army of 3,000 should be assembled in the peninsula ready to go wherever required. Its existence alone would be a useful deterrent to potential rebels. All of this, the Comisión added, would cost a large amount of money and private capital could only afford to finance the priority Montevideo expedition. It was now up to the nation to find the funds for the others.

The Comisión's emphasis on the River Plate clearly reflected the merchant interest and the fact that their profitable trade in hides and other Argentine products had been almost entirely cut off since the outbreak of the revolt in Buenos Aires in 1810. It is reasonable to assume that Ferdinand was quickly aware of these views expressed in the published document because the Comisión, based at Cádiz, promptly appointed two individuals to represent it in the capital once the king was in residence. In Madrid, they continued to press their case for a major expedition to the River Plate. In August they submitted a report to Ferdinand indicating the best places to land in the region, the tactics that would have to be employed and urging that a blockade of Buenos Aires should be imposed as soon as the expedition had landed. Clearly, they pointed out, the attitude of the Portuguese in Brazil was crucial and they should be persuaded to cooperate and possibly permit the ships to use Brazilian territory. An envoy should be sent to Rio de Janeiro to get an agreement and his costs would be borne by the Comisión.[28]

The Comisión de Reemplazos and its Madrid agents were not alone in pressing Ferdinand to take a hard line with the rebel movements. In July his sister Carlota wrote from Rio de Janeiro with unequivocal advice: 'This can only be done by force. You must send soldiers and in large numbers, both land based and naval; and cavalry units, without horses because there are plenty here; but they should bring everything else they need'.[29] Also in July, Ferdinand established his first military advisory committee, the Junta de Generales, chaired by his brother Carlos, and it promptly recommended the shipment of a strong army.[30] Similar pressure came from various parts of America. From New Spain, for example, viceroy Félix Calleja insisted that he had to have more soldiers. He could contain the rebels but not defeat them and he wanted to declare martial law. To make this effective, he had to have an additional 6,000–8,000 men from the peninsula, together with large quantities of weapons. The town council of Caracas reported that although Bolívar and the rebels had been defeated and expelled, there was still widespread discontent among the castes, banditry was rife and the economy paralysed. A garrison of 4,000 was required to maintain public order and to ensure peace.[31]

Similar advice from other sources was given to Ferdinand in the summer of 1814 and the majority view was certainly that he should relegate, if not abandon, the idea of concessions or negotiations in favour of a substantially increased military effort. It seems probable that this advice from so many quarters confirmed his own inclination to attempt the military reconquest of his empire and it offered a partial solution to one of his principal problems on the domestic political scene. In contrast to the position of the Regency which, while fighting the French, never had enough soldiers available to contemplate large-scale military action in the colonies, Ferdinand found with the end of the war on the home front that he had too many. According to one estimate, there were no fewer than 148,643 men on active service.[32] The problem was what to do with this 'improvised army'.[33] It was impolitic to disband the hundreds of different units and oblige all the successful guerillas with their recent but in many cases valiantly earned officer status to return to their humble civilian life. On the other hand, the Treasury could not afford to maintain them and there was growing hostility between the older generation of trained regular army soldiers and the new irregulars.[34] Ferdinand's solution was to compromise by absorbing some into the regular army while, despite protests and resentment, to disband others. Although it can only be supposed, since there appears to be no reference to it in the documentation of the period, it seems not unreasonable to assume that Ferdinand's decision to send thousands of men to the colonies was affected by his need to resolve the problem of too large an army in Spain.

Whatever his reasons, by the middle of August Ferdinand had resolved to make military action his principal response to the rebellions. He decreed that an expedition of 10,000 men was to be prepared with Field Marshal Pablo Morillo as the army commander and Field Marshal Pascual Enrile as the admiral in charge of the navy. During the next few weeks preparations began and further consultations were undertaken, particularly concerning the destination of the expedition. This consultation process culminated on 3 October when two opposing views were expressed. Perhaps because they knew that the Council of the Indies was to meet on that day, the Comisión de Reemplazos representatives, Gómez de Liaño and Torres, submitted another memorandum in which they again pleaded for urgent action.[35] The situation in the River Plate was deteriorating rapidly, they said, and the rebels now had 15,000 men, with skilled officers. Because of past neglect, an expeditionary force of 12,000 including 3,000 cavalry was vital. Once again the two men detailed possible landing sites on the coast of Brazil and suggested ways of recapturing Paraguay and other inland areas.

The Comisión de Reemplazos' preference for the River Plate as the primary target was not shared by the Council of the Indies. Having surveyed the development of the revolutions since 1810 and the inadequacy of previous measures, the Council concluded that a military expedition should be promptly dispatched to Caracas.[36] It should be commanded by an experienced general able to keep rigid discipline among his men. Both these reports were presumably made known to Ferdinand almost at once, but two days later, 5 October, he decided to send an expedition to New Spain under the command of Pascual de Liñán.[37] On 7 October a meeting was held to review the overall position and among those summoned to give evidence in person was José María Salazar, now back in Madrid after his service as naval commander of Montevideo. Two decisions appear to have been taken. Gómez de Liaño and Torres were told on the same day that it had been agreed to send an expedition to the River Plate as soon as possible.[38] Secondly, it was decided to send Salazar as a special envoy to Rio de Janeiro.[39] He was to ascertain the best means of employing the expedition, the number of land and naval forces needed and what the probable Portuguese reaction would be. Finally, on 16 October, Ferdinand approved a plan drawn up by the military committee for recruiting the 8,000 men to be commanded by Liñán in the expedition to New Spain and on 7 November lists of the military units from which the recruitment was to be made were published.[40]

The published lists issued on 7 November referred to two expeditions – the first was called the División Expedicionaria a Montevideo under the command of Morillo, and the second, in order of priority, was that of Liñán to New Spain. The position, therefore, appeared to be that Ferdinand had chosen to take the advice of the Comisión de Reemplazos and make the River Plate his first priority, and certainly this was the impression that was allowed to circulate both in Spain and abroad, and it was reinforced when Salazar set sail from Cádiz on his mission to Rio de Janeiro on 31 December. Nevertheless, the whole process of consultation and public reference to the River Plate as the first target seems to have been designed to mislead the many American observers both inside and outside Spain.[41] The Council of the Indies had made almost no reference to the River Plate in its meeting of 3 October and it had advised concentration of the military effort on Caracas. Other officials had reached similar conclusions and, when Morillo's instructions were drawn up and approved on 18 November, it was clear that Venezuela was to be his destination. He was appointed captain-general of Venezuela, governor of Caracas and president of the *audiencia* and his programme, in brief, was to be as follows. He was to establish peace in Caracas, occupy Cartagena and assist the authorities in New Granada. With those primary objectives achieved, units of the expeditionary army could be sent to Peru and, if possible, to New Spain. A minimum of force was to be used and bloodshed avoided where possible. Morillo was to maintain good relations with the existing Spanish authorities but he was also given broad political and judicial powers. He was authorized to alter any part of the instructions if circumstances so required.[42]

All these meetings and decisions were, of course, conducted in the greatest secrecy, especially Morillo's instructions and his destination. The Comisión de Reemplazos, believing that it had won the argument over the destination, was only too willing to begin preparations, acquiring equipment, ships and collecting the large sums of money involved. Despite the diligence of the Comisión, however, it was not easy to find all the necessary resources and there were inevitably delays. Recruitment was slow, even with the offer of extra promotions, and according to Rafael Sevilla, an infantry officer, the men had to be guarded to prevent desertions. Sevilla was a family friend of Morillo and nephew of the naval commander, Enrile, and he has provided a graphic account of the mobilization and eventual sailing of the expedition. The men were told daily from December 1814 onwards that departure was imminent and all believed that they were going to the River Plate. Finally, on the morning of 17 February 1815, 18 warships and 42 transports raised anchors in the bay of Cádiz with thousands of friends and relatives waving from the shore. After a week at sea, Morillo announced their true destination, much to the consternation of his almost 10,000-strong force. We all knew, Sevilla recalled, that the rebels of Buenos Aires and Montevideo were divided among themselves and that a strong loyalist party was merely awaiting the arrival of reinforcements from Spain before rising up to overthrow the rebels. On the other hand, the men also knew that the fighting in Venezuela had been especially savage, with no mercy shown. The shock news that they were going there caused great discontent, but Morillo's oratorical powers were apparently enough to calm the situation and the expedition proceeded according to plan.[43]

The Morillo expedition confirmed Ferdinand's commitment to a hard-line approach to the revolutions and there were high hopes in Madrid that it would be quickly effective, not only in the immediate area of its operations but in the consequential effect of its presumed success on other rebel forces who would now realize that Spain fully intended to regain control of all parts of its empire. Morillo did indeed enjoy some success in his early campaigns and Ferdinand announced in May 1815 that a further 2,500 men had recently left Cádiz for Panama and other places and that he had decided that an army of 20,000 was to be raised to 'crush the revolutionary seed'.[44] The Comisión de Reemplazos was instructed to find 25,000 tonnage of ships and to have the expedition ready to depart by the autumn. Although this target date was not achieved, two other smaller expeditions were sent in 1815, to Montevideo with 308 men and to Lima with 1,479. In total, 17,139 men were sent in the single year of 1815, a greater number than the total of all previous years since 1810.[45]

Despite this impressive logistic achievement, it was soon realized that military action alone would not be sufficient. At the end of March 1815, Ferdinand had ordered the Council of State to advise on measures to bring peace to the empire. The Council met a few days later and Minister of State Pedro Cevallos summarized the policy that had so far been followed, namely as much force as could be mustered, but also continued negotiations with European powers which might be willing to cooperate and offer assistance. He warned, however, that Britain was openly trading with the rebels, Portugal was seeking to expand its borders and the rebels were well aware of Spain's poverty. The colonies were, he said, 'already near to breaking all their links of dependency' and it was becoming manifestly clear that Spain would have to make concessions in order to get help. Commercial privileges should be offered to Britain to persuade it to help with the pacification.

Most of the councillors present supported the opening of talks with Britain with the offer of trading concessions and several noted that Spain did not have the military capacity to suppress the revolts. General Xavier Castaños emphasized the shortage of ships and Juan Pérez Villamil considered that the idea of a major expedition to Buenos Aires should be abandoned. 'At present and in our circumstances', he said, 'it is wishful thinking.'[46]

This mood of pragmatism became even more pronounced later in the year. Cevallos had approached the British representative in Madrid 'to offer a participation in the trade with America', and he had expressed his anxiety 'to engage the British government to assist Spain directly or indirectly in her expeditions to America, either by furnishing transports, or by rendering Spanish ships of war serviceable for the conveyance of troops, or by a loan of money to be applied to this service'. The British diplomat, Charles Vaughan, refused even to forward such proposals to London and they were dropped by Cevallos.[47]

There were at least two other facts bringing this disillusion with the military policy. First, the Comisión de Reemplazos was experiencing more and more problems in its attempts to find the ships, uniforms, supplies, munitions and money to pay for them. The Morillo expedition and the three smaller ones of 1815 had cost 105,722,136 *reales* and, despite several new taxes and forced loans introduced to raise this money, the Comisión found it increasingly difficult to raise the additional large sums it needed for any new expeditions. The initial enthusiasm of the merchant community, itself badly hit by the declining colonial trade, disappeared to be replaced by resistance to new demands for funds and the taxpayers displayed their traditional reluctance to pay whatever the designated purpose of the levy. Secondly, the news filtering back from Venezuela was not encouraging. Early in 1816, Morillo made the first of what were to be several requests to be relieved of his command and rumours of desertions to the enemy, poor morale, inadequate equipment and supplies soon circulated in the peninsula.[48] Victory was going to be neither quick nor easy.

Ferdinand does not appear to have been unduly perturbed by these problems of finance, *matériel* and lack of lasting success on the battlefields. His response to the situation was to set up new committees and to appoint new ministers. In particular, Vázquez Figueroa was named as Minister of the Navy and in his first memorandum to the king, dated 21 February 1816, he began what was to be a long campaign to have the military strategy changed to more emphasis on the navy and less on the army. He was careful to stress the importance of a strong navy in maintaining imperial control. If, he said, Spain had had a proper naval force, the American provinces would not have sought to separate from the Mother Country and the anarchy and horrors of civil war would have been avoided. 'Without a strong navy', he warned Ferdinand, 'there can be no doubt that you are authorizing the decree of permanent emancipation for a great number of your subjects.'[49]

During the next few months, Vázquez Figueroa lobbied vigorously on behalf of his department and, at least to some extent, his case seems to have been accepted by his colleagues.[50] Ferdinand, however, continued to be unconcerned by the lack of ships or money to buy them and towards the end of May he confirmed that a large expedition for the River Plate should be organized.[51] A week later, the Council of State met again and on this occasion there was an air of renewed militancy.[52] The Minister of State reported on talks which had recently been held in Madrid with the Buenos Aires representative, Bernardo Rivadavia. Secret discussions had been in progress for some time with representatives of the rebel government and Rivadavia had come from London to Madrid to continue the dialogue. Nothing was achieved and the talks ended with mutual hostility and recrimination. Cevallos told the Council that Rivadavia should be ordered to leave Spain at once and that decisive military action should be taken to suppress the insurgents in the River Plate. In the comments which followed, some councillors supported the use of force, but others advised caution, pointing to the weakness of the navy and shortage of money.

Similar doubts about the wisdom of relying on military action were also expressed at this time by the Council of the Indies. Ferdinand had asked the Council to recommend specific measures he could take to end the rebellions. The councillors were pessimistic in their reply. The revolts, they said, were far more terrible and disastrous than had been previously thought and only major changes, notably in the trading monopoly, held out any hope of success. The rebels would fight to the death and military action alone would not work. It would indeed be counter-productive, as Morillo's experience in Venezuela demonstrated. By using only military methods and being unnecessarily repressive, he had alienated large sections of the population. Moreover, the military expeditions were draining the peninsula of its people and resources and the country could not afford to keep on sending them. But, as it was politically important to be seen not to be entirely weak, some reinforcements would have to be sent, but the numbers should be reduced to what the American provinces where they were to go could support. It was vital to find better, more disciplined soldiers and more skilled officers, led by a general who could attract support and respect in America. Morillo was no doubt brave and honourable but he lacked the political acumen essential in so dangerous a situation.[53]

Despite these voices of caution, the majority of the Council of State favoured the expedition to the River Plate and this clearly coincided with Ferdinand's own wishes. Hence the decision was taken and preparations begun. Francisco Xavier Abadía was named Inspector General de las Tropas de Indias with responsibility for supervising the organization in conjunction with the Comisión de Reemplazos which set about finding the equipment, supplies and money.[54] The Navy Ministry began a desperate search for ships of all types but, within only a few days, problems began to be encountered and Vázquez Figueroa complained bitterly that he could achieve nothing unless money was provided by the Treasury. By the end of August 1816, it was becoming clear that the expedition would be delayed. The original intention had been that it would be ready to depart in 1816, but Vázquez Figueroa now enquired of the Minister of War if this was still the target date. If not, he wanted to suspend the recruitment of sailors because the absence of so many men was harming, among other things, the fishing industry.[55]

These difficulties encountered in the preparations for the new expedition added to the doubts which influential members of the royal administration already felt about the whole policy of military reconquest. More such doubts were forcefully expressed in a report of 8 October by the military committee presided over by General Joaquín Blake,[56] and by November the Council of the Indies was even more convinced that the military policy was a mistake. Meeting in full session to consider a series of pacification measures proposed by a French army officer living in London, the councillors took the opportunity to restate their opposition to relying on reconquest.[57] The revolts in America, they said, were not popular disturbances which could be permanently suppressed by force. They were civil wars and the insurgents were determined to separate from Spain. There was no base which could serve as a starting-point for reconquest and even if there were, an army of 10,000–12,000 men would be needed together with corresponding naval support and all would cost a vast amount of money. There was no more money available and no navy and even if peace could be restored by military means, it could not be enforced on an indefinite basis. Reform of the trading monopoly and British mediation were essential if the 300-year-old empire was to be saved.[58]

It is possible, although unlikely, that Ferdinand did not know of this rising opposition among his advisers to the military policy, or, if he did know of it, he gave it little attention. On 8 November, the day preceding the Council of the Indies' report mentioned above, the Minister of War, Campo Sagrado, wrote to Vázquez Figueroa on the king's instructions to inform him of several decisions that Ferdinand had taken.[59] First, given the problems of getting everything ready quickly, the expedition to the River Plate was to be postponed until 1817, although preparations were to continue so that it could leave in August of that year. Secondly, with the utmost urgency transport ships were to be prepared to take to Veracruz the Zaragoza infantry regiment, which was to be equipped with 2,000 rifles, 1,000 swords and 1,000 pairs of pistols. That expedition would be commanded by Field Marshal Pascual Liñán and it should be escorted by the frigate *Sabina*. Thirdly, as soon as possible, an expedition was to be organized for Upper Peru, consisting of the Burgos infantry regiment and other units. It was to travel via Cape Horn and land at Arica. Finally, the Navy must take energetic steps to stop pirate activity as recommended by the military committee.

In the Council of State on 20 November, Vázquez Figueroa set out in plain terms his reaction to these orders. The frigate *Sabina*, he said, could be used as an escort but only if money was made available to bring it to a seaworthy condition. As for the River Plate expedition, forward planning was seriously hindered by one major unknown factor, which was the attitude of the Portuguese in Brazil. If they were cooperative, then three or four frigates, some brigantines and lesser vessels would be adequate. If, on the other hand, the Portuguese were hostile, then a much stronger force was essential. Three or four warships at least would be needed and these could not be provided by the planned departure date of August 1817 for several reasons: the dry docks were not ready and there was no money to hand to purchase timber and other indispensable materials; time was needed to train personnel; and such expeditions could not be organized without considerable advance notice. Finally, he added, he could do nothing without resources.[60]

Vázquez Figueroa's reference to the attitude of the Portuguese in Brazil reflected a development which had recently added to the already grave doubts about the viability of any attempt to reconquer the River Plate provinces. In the preceding months, a complex web of political and diplomatic intrigue had resulted in what for Spain was a wholly unexpected event – Portuguese armies from Brazil had invaded the Banda Oriental. The Spanish government had well appreciated for some time that any expedition to the River Plate would have to be able to establish bases on the coastline of Brazil or the Banda Oriental and that to secure this strategic requirement, Portuguese cooperation was desirable, if not essential. Spanish diplomacy had been in part directed towards obtaining such cooperation but had not made much progress. Then an opportunity to achieve this objective, among many others, arose when it was suggested that Ferdinand and his brother Carlos should marry Portuguese princesses. There is no need to relate all the political dimensions of this proposed marital alliance.[61] It is sufficient to note that one major consideration was the assumption that closer family ties with João VI would pave the way for Portuguese assistance in America. Negotiations were conducted in the greatest secrecy by members of Ferdinand's inner clique, with even Minister of State Cevallos not being informed, but as the arrangements were being finalized, João VI ordered his armies to cross into the Banda Oriental. Ferdinand had been warned of troop mobilization in the border areas but, in view of the impending marriages, nobody in the peninsula expected an invasion. Hence when the news of it arrived in Madrid in August 1816, the initial Spanish reaction was muted and hesitant because it was not known whether the Portuguese were acting as a hostile invading force or to defeat the rebels on behalf of Ferdinand. A note was sent to Andrés Villalba, the chargé d'affaires at Rio de Janeiro, instructing him to ascertain the real motives of the invasion. He in fact had already concluded that the action was a hostile move but, lacking senior diplomatic status and suspecting some secret deal between Ferdinand and João, he could do little except make timid protests. When Cevallos explained these developments to the Council of State in late August, he voiced his suspicions and urged Ferdinand to demand the return of the occupied territory. The situation, however, had become even more delicate because the Portuguese princesses had already left Brazil for Spain, and arrived a few days later. After much deliberation and confusion, it was decided to proceed with the marriage ceremonies and these took place on 5 September. More discussions took place in the Council of State and elsewhere in an attempt to find a response to the invasion and eventually, in October, it was decided to seek international mediation to what was finally recognized as an act of hostile aggression.

Thus Vázquez Figueroa stated with obvious reason that he had to know the probable attitude of the Portuguese before he could say what strength the naval forces should be. He did not get a definite answer. Cevallos replied that he could not predict what the Portuguese attitude would be in the following August when the River Plate expedition was due to embark, but, in his opinion, the larger and stronger force should be prepared. The Minister of Hacienda in turn asked to be supplied with a breakdown of the costs and an estimate of the total.[62] Ferdinand, who presided over the meeting, then made what was a rare recorded personal intervention. He had, he said, listened to the persistent complaints about the lack of resources but he urged the councillors not to lose heart. He himself was confident that every problem had its remedy and, whatever the condition of the Treasury, they should bear in mind the maxim of great merchants 'who to sustain their credit, hide their real situation and never appear less in financial difficulty than when they are on the point of bankruptcy'.

More correspondence circulated between the ministerial offices, and considerable pressure to get things moving was put on Vázquez Figueroa by his cabinet colleagues. Nothing, however, seems to have been done and an atmosphere of bitter recrimination developed. The Minister of War demanded the ships he needed from Vázquez Figueroa and he in turn demanded the money for them from the Minister of Hacienda. Vázquez Figueroa finally lost his temper with the general prevarication and reluctance or inability of the Treasury to provide the funds. In the Council of State on 11 December, he angrily denounced the bureaucratic red tape and inefficient administration. His own incessant appeals for urgent aid for the navy were being ignored and yet the whole of Spanish commerce and the very preservation of the empire were at stake. Other councillors supported him and José de Ibarra, chairman of the Treasury committee, tried in vain to defend himself against the angry criticism being levelled at him.

It may be that the growing antagonism among the senior members of the royal administration over the military policy was no more than a reflection of the pressure put on them by Ferdinand to produce results. It is also likely, however, that despite all the ambitious schemes and announcements by Ferdinand, most of them suspected, to use Heredia's phrase, that all their plans for a full-scale expedition to the River Plate amounted to no more than building castles in the air, given the acute lack of finance and ships, and the unexpected Portuguese dimension. Although the pressure from the more bellicose individuals and lobbies such as the Comisión de Reemplazos continued, it was undeniable that Ferdinand's grandiose objective of total military reconquest was grinding to a halt. Three expeditions were dispatched in 1816 – one each to Portobelo, Havana/Puerto Rico and Veracruz – but the total number of officers and men was only 4,344, less than the liberal constitutional régime beset by the problems of the peninsular war had managed to send in 1813. Moreover, there were clearly other factors which encouraged a general reappraisal of the military policy. It was evident that the quick military success expected in those regions to which large armies had been sent was not being achieved, and Morillo in particular remained in difficulty, still making frequent demands for more help which could not be entirely met. Then there were the many reports that the rebellions in other provinces were far from under control and that the military policy so far pursued had been counter-productive. Again, Ferdinand's own private assessment of the situation is unknown, but it seems likely that he did realize that he was no nearer achieving his objective than he had been on his return to the throne. Someone had to take the blame and hence, as he so often did, Ferdinand decided to change his ministers, presumably in the hope that the new incumbents could better implement his policy or produce a more effective one. At the end of October, Cevallos was removed from the Ministry of State to be replaced by Pizarro, who recalled in his memoirs that on taking office, he found the whole question of the pacification of America in a deplorable state which had reached 'a state of incredible exaspera-tion'.[63] A few weeks later, in the hope of being able to improve the fiscal situation and almost certainly with the American crisis in mind, Ferdinand dismissed López Araujo from the Treasury – he went to the Council of State – and appointed Garay in his place.

It was against the background of new ministerial appointments, the growing body of opinion in the advisory councils that the military policy was futile, the knowledge that the rebellions were getting worse and the fact that Spain did not have the resources to prevent them, that the Council of State reassembled in the presence of the king on 22 January 1817.[64] Campo Sagrado, who had retained his post as Minister of War in the cabinet changes, introduced the American issue and stated plainly that he had concluded that the policy of sending military expeditions was a waste of men and money.[65] He had compiled an account of the number of men dispatched to the colonies since 1811 and the cost. According to his calculations, excluding officers, 33,127 men had embarked from the peninsula at a cost of 214,102,746 reales. Yet peace had not been restored and there seemed no sign that it would be. In other words, he said, the policy was wrong and manifestly not the right way to achieve the objective. Therefore, he proposed, all such expeditions should be suspended and future policy based on negotiation. Ferdinand listened to this for once quite unequivocal statement and then asked each of the councillors to comment. Most agreed with Campo Sagrado's analysis and the Minister of War then asked for a formal resolution, because a decision had to be taken on whether the next planned expedition should proceed. A decision was then formulated and agreed as follows:

That in view of the information provided by the Ministry of War concerning the serious damage caused by the expeditions against the American insurgents, the said expeditions shall be suspended, but secretly and without public knowledge; that aid be given to the Navy which is the force most needed to preserve the Americas; that negotiations with England shall be activated without delay; and that the Duque de Montemar be reminded to forward the report pending.

Thus the Council of State voted to shelve, but not abandon, the idea of military reconquest and instead to renew efforts to persuade Britain to mediate. Support for this decision came two weeks later when the Junta de Pacificación produced its long-awaited appraisal of the situation.[66] It advocated a series of reforms and it was quite emphatic concerning the military policy. Spain, it said, had no money, no navy, no useful treaties with influential powers, no credit and no concerted plan for defeating the rebels. Alone, it was incapable of restoring peace. Even if the military means were immediately available to end what were now civil wars, that would not resolve the problem, because it would be imperative to continue to send military expeditions for a long time in the future. Such a prospect was neither possible nor politic because a large standing army not subject to discipline in regions already devastated could easily be converted into a hostile threat and bring about 'our own ruin'. The only solution was a prudent political policy of substantial reforms backed by a carefully chosen and controlled military presence sufficient to ensure that the changes were observed but without spilling blood.

The report of the Junta de Pacificación together with its comments on various plans and proposals it had been asked to evaluate were presented to the Council of State by Pizarro on 19 February 1817.[67] Pizarro informed the Council that the file was so large and of such critical importance that he felt the councillors needed time to consider it and to formulate their own responses. He advised that discussion should be postponed and this was agreed. It was not in fact until September that the report was examined. In the meantime, despite the decision to postpone further expeditions, four were dispatched to Lima, Havana, Portobelo and La Guayra respectively, the total number of officers and men amounting to 4,321. Also the preparations for the River Plate expedition continued with men being recruited, ships acquired, including several secretly purchased by Ferdinand from the tsar, and Vázquez Figueroa constantly complaining of the lack of resources for the navy. On 9 May, the Minister of War, on instructions from Ferdinand, circulated army inspectors, reminding them that the target recruitment figure was for the time being 6,000. The Inspector de Infantería suggested various methods of recruitment; for example, using 12 or 13 per 100 men from each unit of infantry, cavalry, artillery and engineers.[68] Ferdinand also ordered that the navy budget should be substantially increased and Vázquez Figueroa decided to conduct a thorough review of the naval forces although, as he recalled, little practical benefit came from it. He still faced the problem of not knowing exactly what he was supposed to be preparing and whether the expedition would have to fight the Portuguese at Montevideo as well as the rebels at Buenos Aires.

The return of Pascual Enrile to Madrid on 1 June did little to help the situation. He had sailed with Morillo in 1815 as the naval commander of that expedition and he travelled back to Spain to make representations on behalf of Morillo and especially to defend the actions the general had taken. As already indicated, it was widely thought in government circles that Morillo had pursued an unnecessarily harsh policy against both the rebels and the loyalist population which had been alienated from the Spanish cause. Enrile was received by Ferdinand on 12 June and later interviewed by the cabinet and twice by the Junta de Pacificación.[69] He presented a long and diffuse account, incorporating thirty-nine proposals ranging over commercial and economic policy and other areas, but his main emphasis was on strengthening the military effort. In his opinion, force was the only way to keep America under control.[70] Given the disillusion with the military policy, it is not surprising that Enrile's ideas were not well received in Madrid and he was told that his commission was terminated, although he did continue to press his case in several other memoranda.

Enrile's was not the only voice to be heard while the Councillors of State were preparing their positions for the crucial September debate. Many other reports, some requested by ministers from people supposedly knowledgeable about colonial affairs, and some unsolicited, circulated in the corridors of the royal palace.[71] Most advocated a wide variety of reforms as the best hope of bringing peace and the ever-present lobby on behalf of foreign mediation continued to press its case. By 10 September when the Council of State met to begin its examination of all the options, there was no consensus in favour of any one policy. Indeed, the number and diversity of proposals seemed infinite and it fell to Pizarro as Minister of State to try to coordinate them into a coherent and practical policy.[72] He began by offering his own plan of action. Following an introductory analysis mainly on foreign affairs and the international dimensions of the American problem, he listed twenty-two points in which he incorporated a mixture of priorities, options and firm proposals. It was easy, he admitted, to criticize any single article in his plan but it was designed to be viewed as a whole. In brief, he advocated a coordinated policy based on political and mercantile reforms including, if necessary, British mediation. He made it clear that one of the premises on which his scheme was based was that Spain did not have the military power to suppress the revolts by force. On the other hand, the British guarantee of successful mediation that he wanted required that Britain would provide military assistance to end the rebellions if the insurgents would not accept or respect the mediation.[73]

Pizarro's presentation occupied most of the 10 September session and only five councillors made brief comments giving qualified approval for some of his ideas. The next session was held on 17 September and, unable to be present, the Minister of Justice, Juan Lozano de Torres, had asked for his prepared statement to be read.[74] In this he began his offensive against Pizarro's plan in general and against free trade in particular. He denounced the idea of British mediation and strongly urged that the expedition to the River Plate should be sent as soon as possible. He wanted various other changes in military strategy and administration and he openly favoured giving priority to a policy based on military action. In subsequent sessions, a clear split in the Council emerged on the question of free trade and the two factions, led respectively by Pizarro and Lozano de Torres, bitterly and angrily argued their case. Eventually, such was the conflict of opinion on this issue and the diversity of alternative measures put forward, it was decided to appoint a sub-committee to try to collate all the ideas expressed. José Ibarra, Guillermo Hualde and the Duque del Parque formed this committee and in due course presented their findings. These were given in the form of three categories of measures: direct, indirect and military. The first two concerned political, social and economic reforms and foreign mediation. The third, or military section, proposed the following: a military expedition should be organized against Buenos Aires and other places in a similar state of rebellion; soldiers should be sent to those provinces partly in rebellion to stop the disorder spreading; without delay, ships should be armed to protect the merchant marine and to defend the coasts against pirates. Each councillor was then asked to comment on all the measures in each category and, while the division of opinion persisted on the free trade and mediation proposals, those concerning military action provoked no discussion and were agreed unanimously. Eventually the other matters were brought to a vote and Pizarro was authorized to open negotiations with foreign powers to ascertain if some form of mediation in exchange for commercial concessions could be arranged.

To some degree, Pizarro and his supporters had won their case, having gained approval for at least the main plank of their pacification programme. But at the same time they had compromised in the sense that the militarists, led by Lozano de Torres and the recently appointed Minister of War, Francisco Eguía, had persuaded the Council to sanction the River Plate expedition as well as other secondary military measures. Nevertheless, Pizarro, who had little or no faith in the idea of military reconquest, had gained what he wanted, which was the time and an opportunity to see if he could find a solution to the American problem by way of international mediation allied to reforms. However, the diplomatic initiatives he made to persuade other nations to assist either directly or by mediation brought no quick results. By April 1818, he knew that his policy was in danger of being submerged within the prevarication and general confusion that characterized the administrative system or, more probably, of being sabotaged by the militarists who were in closest contact with the king. He decided to try yet again to convince his colleagues of the gravity of the situation. In the Council of State session of 28 April he submitted another, shorter set of proposals.[75] In his preface to these, he warned that action independent of mediation must be taken at once if America was to be saved. He had three proposals: the expedition to Buenos Aires should be reconsidered by a committee of generals; Spaniards in exile should be offered an amnesty; and spontaneously and immediately, the king must authorize foreign participation in the American trade. Ferdinand quickly suppressed the amnesty idea and once again no agreement could be reached on the free trade issue. The military expedition also provoked some disagreement. Guillermo Hualde reminded his colleagues of the lack of finance and ships. The Duque del Parque noted that the whole thing was very risky and expensive and the Duque del Infantado expressed his doubts because of the unknown attitude of the Portuguese in Brazil. There were other councillors, of course, who were more bellicose. Manuel López Araujo wanted at least 10,000 men sent as soon as possible and Pedro Mendinueta thought that the expedition should be dispatched at any price. Some, for example Vázquez Figueroa, reserved their position until the whole plan for the expedition had been examined by the military officers and after more argument, including a suggestion from the Duque del Infantado that it should go to Mexico or Caracas but not to Buenos Aires, the matter was referred to the military advisers.

The military committee, which included former viceroys and military officers with considerable recent experience of conditions in the colonies, met two days later on 8 May.[76] Following the presentation of five prepared papers, protracted discussion ensued but there was little agreement reached. As several speakers had qualified their statements on such grounds as the attitude of the Portuguese or the availability of resources, the voting record is not entirely clear, but there was certainly a sharp division of opinion with apparently seven opting for Buenos Aires as the priority destination and seven for Peru, including the chairman, Joaquín Blake.

If Pizarro had hoped for firm guidance from the military committee, he was disappointed. He recorded in his memoirs that after three hours of often rambling and irrelevant discussion, nothing positive was achieved.[77] Nevertheless, when the Council of State reassembled on 22 May he duly reported the committee's deliberations. His interpretation of the meeting was that although there was a division of opinion, it was more apparent than real. Those who had argued that the expedition should go to Peru had done so, he said, largely on the supposition that resources for a larger force for Buenos Aires could not be found. Assuming they were, almost all the committee favoured Buenos Aires as the target. The councillors then proceeded to make the same points as they had previously, but it soon became apparent that a large majority now wanted Buenos Aires to be the destination and this was in due course agreed.[78]

Further talks in cabinet meetings and between government departments were held and, although the decision to proceed with the expedition seemed to have finally been taken, there were more delays and renewed misgivings.[79] These were brought to a head at the end of June by an alarming report from the Duque de San Carlos, ambassador in London. He sent his secretary, Joaquín Francisco Campuzano, to Madrid to present personally to Ferdinand his assessment of the situation. Speaking both as ambassador and an old personal friend, San Carlos told of the victory of San Martín at Maipú (April 1818) which marked the final defeat of the Spanish forces in Chile and he warned the king that the position was very critical. The policy of repression had failed and Spain could not achieve reconquest without foreign aid. The only solution was to make great sacrifices, including offering territorial concessions. The conference of European powers at Aix-la-Chapelle was soon to open and that offered perhaps a final opportunity to see if something could be salvaged from the empire.[80]

San Carlos' note seems to have been greeted with a mixture of despair and anger in Madrid. Ferdinand ordered a small group to consider it and Gómez de Liaño submitted his reaction a few weeks later. He did not dispute San Carlos' picture of the situation in America. Peru, he said, could not hold out much longer now that Chile had fallen and it could not resist the armies of Belgrano and San Martín. The only thing that Spain could do was to embark an expedition of at least 16,000 men to the River Plate from where the revolutions were spreading across the continent. As for San Carlos' hopes of attracting foreign aid at Aix-la-Chapelle, there were only two things which could be offered: trade concessions or territory as San

Carlos had indicated, but the cession of territory would be an infamy on the honour of Spain and could never be countenanced. Hence the trade proposal, regrettable though it was, was indispensable.[81]

While the news from San Carlos was being digested, more ominous information was received. Vázquez Figueroa summarized it in a message to the colonial authorities.[82] A plan of operations, he told them, was being formulated in London in aid of the rebel cause. Several heavily armed ships from Britain and the United States were to travel to the coast of Chile and Lord Thomas Cochrane would soon leave London to assume their command. An army of about 3,000–4,000 men was being mustered in Chile and General Robert Wilson would also leave London in about three or four weeks to command it. Together with the forces of San Martín and Bernardo O'Higgins, they would attack Lima and another group would head for Acapulco. A renegade Spanish army officer, Mariano Renovales, was also due to leave London within a couple of weeks with two ships and about 2,000 men to attack Venezuela. Other ships and considerable numbers of men would be leaving Britain to join the rebels in the near future.[83]

This information was learned in Madrid in late June and early July and it immediately distracted attention from the River Plate expedition. In a top secret note to Pizarro, Minister of War, Eguía said that Ferdinand had decided that the following action must be taken at once. A warship was to set out for Lima; an armed frigate was to go to Havana/Veracruz within the current month; another was to go in August with 400 men; and an armed frigate was to escort 2,000 men to Venezuela to help Morillo. Thus, within the three or four months the rebels needed to put their plan into operation, Spain would have, Eguía claimed, 1 warship, 3 frigates, 2 armed corvettes, 2 brigantines and several armed merchant vessels. Those would be sufficient to defend Peru, reinforce Morillo and help defend New Spain and Havana. It would allow time to get the River Plate expedition ready and that would bring about 'the total pacification of America'.[84]

This plan seems to have been concocted by Ferdinand and Eguía alone and Vázquez Figueroa was not impressed. He commented that the ships were simply not available and there was no money to acquire them. A few minor vessels might be fitted out but nothing near to what was envisaged. The royal navy, he added, was less than that of Portugal or Holland and morale was desperately low because of the indifference with which the service had been treated for so many years past. Hence the whole plan was quite unrealistic.[85]

Nevertheless, despite these all-too-evident truths, ministers and councils continued to meet and talk about plans for reconquering the River Plate. On 31 July, the Junta de Pacificación again concluded that trade reform was the best solution but, at the same time, a show of strength must be organized with a supreme effort made to get 16,000–20,000 men ready to be embarked in case all else failed.[86] The next day, 1 August, four ministers – Pizarro, Vázquez Figueroa, Eguía and Garay – met to review the situation. Much of what they said comprised recrimination and frustration at the mistakes of the past. Pizarro lamented that for a few thousand *reales* and a few honours, Artigas could have been won over to the Spanish cause; New Spain could have been completely pacified if action had been taken early enough; Morillo should have gone to Buenos Aires. They all expressed misgivings about the River Plate project. Garay did not believe that it would restore peace. It simply would not work and there was no money, he said: 'there are no resources, there are no taxes, the ecclesiastical estate cannot do any more, and nor can the civil'. Vázquez Figueroa repeated his fears of Portuguese opposition but he did agree to prepare an up-to-date budget for the expedition and, two days later, he sent this to Garay.[87]

After so many months of meetings, reports, analysis and inaction, Ferdinand was finally obliged to conclude in the middle of August that there was no possibility, however urgent it might be, of sending the River Plate expedition in 1818. On 29 August, Vázquez Figueroa wrote to Eguía informing him that the king had decided to postpone the expedition because the optimum time of year for its departure would soon have passed. Also, given the threat of the foreign mercenaries, it was important to aid those territories likely to be attacked. Hence a warship should be sent to Callao and a frigate or brigantine to Veracruz. Another frigate was to escort troops to Cuba and a brigantine with 2,000 men was being sent to help Morillo. Other ships had to be found to protect the merchant marine. All of these plans, Vázquez Figueroa added laconically, depended on funds being available, without which nothing was possible.[88] His cynicism was justified because, despite all the royal commands for immediate dispatch of so many expeditions, in fact throughout 1817 and 1818 little had been achieved. Four expeditions carrying reinforcements had set sail in 1817, to Lima, Havana, Portobelo and La Guaira respectively, carrying a total of 4,321 officers and men. Even fewer left in 1818. One expedition sailed from Cádiz for Lima with 1,950 men on one warship and ten transports but this was intercepted and captured by rebel pirates before it could arrive at its destination.

The River Plate expedition was thus postponed yet again but it was by no means abandoned. In August 1818 Ferdinand confirmed a series of appointments of those who were to command it. Enrique O'Donnell, Conde de la Bisbal, was to be the army commander with Brigadier Francisco Maurell in charge of the navy. Also the ever-present problem of finding the resources was handed to the Comisión de Reemplazos and several new taxes and forced loans were decreed. Ferdinand had obviously not given up hope that the expedition would eventually set sail, but, having sat through and listened to the endless discussions about its viability, there is no doubt that he finally tired of the prevarication, hesitancy and doubts of so many of his advisers. As far as he was concerned, the objective was clear, namely the reconquest of the empire, and it was the job of his ministers and councillors to see that the objective was achieved. He does not seem to have been impressed or even believed the argument that Spain did not have the resources to implement the military policy and, in the atmosphere of intense personal rivalry and hostility at the court, there were always those who were willing to encourage him in this belief. For example, Vázquez Figueroa claimed that his political enemies told Ferdinand that the estimates he had prepared for the River Plate expedition were deliberately inflated in order to force the delay, if not abandonment, of the entire project. According to Pizarro, Eguía, Lozano de Torres and their militarist cohorts were not concerned with Spain or America. Their aim was solely to achieve the dismissal of himself, Vázquez Figueroa and Garay. Certainly, there was little, if any, unity in the government and Vázquez Figueroa was not alone in complaining of his colleagues' refusal to cooperate. Pizarro and Vázquez Figueroa were constantly wrangling with Eguía and Lozano de Torres and Ferdinand seems to have followed his usual practice of favouring first one and then the other, informing them of some decisions but not of others. Pizarro and Vázquez Figueroa also both allege in their memoirs that favoured members of the administration, or the camarilla, corruptly used the few resources of the war effort for their own personal benefit. Vázquez Figueroa described Eguía as 'brusque and also ignorant' and, referring to the inner clique, lamented, 'Oh, if only there had been a formal enquiry into all their transactions, ideas and deals.'[89]

From Ferdinand's viewpoint, whatever the reasons for the personal or political animosities in his administration, his ministers had failed to resolve the imperial crisis. Pizarro had had almost two years to produce a diplomatic solution or to find some kind of effective policy combining diplomacy with the limited use of force. He had failed to achieve either of these alternatives. Vázquez Figueroa had not revitalized the navy and the reconquest was failing because of the shortage of ships. Garay had not produced the revenues to pay for any policy, especially not for one involving expensive military expeditions. The reasons for their failure did not interest Ferdinand. He would not accept the defeatist attitude of some of his advisers; he would not believe that the money could not be found; he was convinced, as he said in the Council of State, that every problem had a solution.

For him, the immediate problem was simple to resolve. If his present ministers were ineffective, he could dispense with their services. Early in September, Pizarro and Garay were dismissed and they were followed a few weeks later by Vázquez Figueroa. The survivors in the cabinet for the time being were the militarists, Eguía and Lozano de Torres, and this indicated that Ferdinand had decided to revert to his original policy of 1814–15, that is, to place all his faith on a military solution. His new Minister of State was quick to tell Ferdinand what he wanted to hear. The new minister was Carlos Martínez de Irujo y Tacón, the Marqués de Casa Irujo. He had served in diplomatic posts in the United States where he had married the daughter of Pennsylvania's chief justice, and then in Rio de Janeiro where he had been ambassador in 1810 when the Buenos Aires rebellion started. In his reports at that time, he had revealed his intense disdain for the insurgents and he now proceeded to make it clear to Ferdinand that he had not changed his views. In a note to the king a week after his appointment, he placed on record what he had already told Ferdinand in person.[90] He dismissed Pizarro's ideas, especially his emphasis on trade reform and foreign mediation. Anyone familiar with the British, he declared, should have known that such a policy would fail. San Carlos should be instructed to stop all talks on mediation with the British and preparations for military reconquest should proceed at once.

Casa Irujo's hard-line, militant approach was approved by Ferdinand and San Carlos and the ambassadors in Paris and Vienna were told not to discuss mediation. Henceforth, all attention and effort was to be devoted to the River Plate expedition, but Ferdinand had clearly decided that he would no longer rely on his ministers to get it under way.[91] Garay's replacement at the Treasury was José Imaz who was given only an interim appointment. According to Pizarro, he was far from being a dynamic personality – all he did was 'see, listen and say nothing'.[92] Vázquez Figueroa's post went to Baltasar Hidalgo de Cisneros who had been viceroy in the River Plate in 1810. He had had a distinguished naval career, including fighting at the battle of Trafalgar and more recently, he was the captain-general of Cádiz. But rather than place authority for the expedition in the hands of any of his ministers, Ferdinand chose to appoint Antonio de Ugarte y Larrazabal. Popularly known as Antonio I, Ugarte was from Vizcaya. A man of humble origins, he came to Madrid at the age of fifteen and earning his living as a servant, dancing-teacher and divers other occupations, he gradually used his lively wit and personality to ingratiate himself into court circles. With the Russian ambassador Tattischef as his patron, he found his way into Ferdinand's inner circle of unofficial advisers and, a clever operator behind the scenes, he soon amassed power and wealth, the latter corruptly according to liberal historiography. It is said that Ferdinand never took a decision without first privately consulting him and that he made no appointments without his approval.[93] Ugarte had been one of the few people involved in the purchase of the Russian fleet in 1817 and he was now on 1 July 1819 given full authority for the organization of the expedition. As Ferdinand left Madrid to take the waters at his favourite resort of Sacedón, he wrote to Ugarte as follows:

With the laudable aim that the fitting out and departure of the great expedition does not suffer any delay, I authorize you during my absence at Sacedón to dispatch without delay correspondence relating to the said expedition, and all matters pertaining to it, whatever they may be, keeping me informed of all you do and working in accord with Alós [Minister of War] who should sign the correspondence.[94]

The subsequent events of 1819 have probably received more attention from historians than those of any single year in the nineteenth century and there is no need to repeat them here. Contrary to the pessimistic assertions of so many of Ferdinand's previous advisers, the expedition was organized, 14,000 men together with ships and supplies were assembled in the Cádiz area, and it seemed that the reconquest of the River Plate was about to begin.[95] As Wellesley reported to London, 'both the King and his Minister appear(ing) to entertain the most confident hopes of the successful issue of the expedition preparing at Cádiz . . .'[96] However, a bewildering range of conspiratorial groups, including freemasons, agents of the insurgent American governments, especially that of Buenos Aires, liberals, constitutionalists and all manner of secret societies, were energetically promoting subversion in the army. With an existing strong fear and reluctance among the men to make the hazardous journey across the Atlantic to fight what was rumoured to be a barbaric enemy, it was not difficult to raise the level of discontent to that of rebellion. On 1 January 1820, Rafael del Riego raised the banner of revolt and, as an afterthought, made his objective the restoration of the constitutional system of government enacted in 1812. Support was soon forthcoming and by March, Ferdinand was forced into another volte-face and into acceptance of the representative system he so abhorred. For the time being, the River Plate and indeed America were forgotten as the nation went through the upheaval of restoring the 1812 Charter and laying the foundations for the so-called liberal triennium. The problem of what to do with the men, ships and supplies, for the most part ready and waiting at Cádiz, was now in the jurisdiction of the new constitutional cabinet and Cortes.

Ferdinand's dream of the military reconquest of his American empire had not only failed but had cost him his powers as an absolute monarch. It was not a policy that he had initiated. It was inherited from his liberal predecessors and while he increased the number of troops sent to the colonies and placed more reliance on it, he was sufficiently flexible to permit the search for an alternative, also started by his predecessors, to continue. Whether Spain could have reconquered America must remain in the realm of speculation, but as far as Ferdinand and the militarists around him were concerned, especially the Cádiz merchants, there was no doubt. Always convinced, despite the mounting evidence of defeat on the battlefields, that the insurgents were supported by only a small minority of the American people, military victory was a matter of will and determination, of organization and efficiency. There was no moral or political dilemma, as there was to be for some liberals later. Rebellion against the divinely appointed ruler challenging the essential foundations and unity of the kingdom could not be tolerated. Given the supreme nature of the mission and what Castlereagh called 'their proud and vindictive character',[97] the reality of Spain's impotence could not be accepted and the pragmatists at court who, from 1816 onwards, persistently warned of the lack of resources came to be seen as defeatists. Their arguments against over-reliance on military means and their point that even if successful in the short term, a formidable military presence would have to be maintained indefinitely, were anathema to Ferdinand. He simply could not believe such an analysis and instead his own assessment of the situation was strengthened by those who, like Lozano de Torres and Eguía, told him what he wanted to hear, that is, that the Spanish cause was not as bad as the defeatists made out and could easily be rescued if enough force was used.[98] An air of unreality thus pervaded at Madrid as all the planning of expeditions continued to preoccupy the royal administration. The French ambassador in 1818 commented on this with undisguised disdain:

I never cease to be surprised at the calm with which they view the future here and the confidence they have in their armies. On the basis of these, they isolate themselves, scorn the advice of friends and clash with those whose friendship they ought to be seeking to preserve. And what resources do they count on to sustain such arrogant language and confront events? They have a cabinet lacking in unity where each minister is daily exposed to the risk of being sacked; an army callous and extremely discontented; a navy that cannot put to sea, despite the acquisition of the new fleet, because their stores are empty, their arsenals without work, their sailors without rations and their ports unprotected. Added to this, the Treasury is completely empty.[99]

The liberal triennium, 1820–3

In the two weeks from 9 March 1820 when Ferdinand took the oath to the 1812 Constitution and 22 March when a new Cortes was summoned, the victorious liberals wasted no time in setting up their new régime. A Provisional Junta was chosen, ministers were appointed, the inquisition was abolished, press freedom restored, the Supreme Court and the Madrid town council reconvened. It was also at once apparent that the imperial crisis was to be high on the agenda of priorities. On 10 March, the Ministry of Ultramar was reestablished and Antonio Porcel, a former deputy at the Cádiz Cortes, was named as the first minister. It was decided that the overseas provinces must be informed as quickly as possible of the new order of things and the Provisional Junta suggested five measures that could be taken immediately. These were that Americans should be sent instructions to prepare for elections to the new Cortes; the king should issue a manifesto emphasizing the benefits for Americans from the new system; a cease-fire should be ordered; if the insurgents refused to send deputies, they should be urged to send commissioners to tell the new government what they wanted and how reconciliation could best be achieved; political and military commands should remain unified in some of the provinces for the time being.[100]

These proposals, accompanied by a note from Antonio González Salmón, interim Minister of Hacienda since November 1819, were referred to the Council of State. González Salmón told the councillors that the king had made it clear that any cease-fire which might be recommended must not leave Spanish forces at a strategic disadvantage to allow for the possible renewal of hostilities at a subsequent time. Furthermore, any agreement with the rebels would have to include a clause to the effect that neither side would increase the number of its soldiers during the cessation of hostilities. The king also wanted to send two or more commissioners to each rebel province, except New Spain which was almost entirely pacified, and in due course their instructions would be referred to the Council for comment. He also enclosed a draft of the manifesto that Ferdinand proposed to issue to Americans.[101]

None of the five measures provoked much disagreement and all were approved with minor amendments. The cease-fire was to be held until such time that it was certain that the insurgents had rejected the constitution and refused to send commissioners. An amnesty, it was thought, should be published simultaneously with the cease-fire declaration.

A week after this session of the Council, the new Minister of War, Pedro Agustín Girón, Marqués de las Amarillas, a close personal friend of Ferdinand, drew up a report on the military policy so far followed since 1810.[102] He outlined the early years of the revolutions, the creation of the Comisión de Reemplazos and provided various figures of the expeditions and number of men involved. He now asked the Council to advise if the military expeditions should be suspended while at the same time keeping the Comisión de Reemplazos in operation. The king felt that, in view of the recent events in the expeditionary army at Cádiz and the readoption of the constitution, further expeditions should be halted for the time being but officers who had asked to be allowed to go to America should be permitted to do so. Also, replacements already ordered to go to New Spain should be authorized to leave and if Morillo needed more men, they should be sent. To meet these several needs, it was important to keep the Comisión de Reemplazos, which would have to find the money for them.

This report was passed to the Council's war sub-committee which concluded that all available resources should be concentrated on preparing warships 'to assist the most important and needy places especially at Costa Firme and the Pacific'. On 18 April, the Council met and it was agreed that for the time being no new expeditions should leave and that the replacements Ferdinand had indicated could be sent. The most important thing, the Council felt, was to have naval forces in America which would watch the progress of talks with the insurgents, protect commerce against pirates and give encouragement to the loyalists. The Comisión de Reemplazos should continue until the Cortes decided what to do with it and the funds which it currently had should be spent on getting the ships to Costa Firme and the Pacific. The governor of Cádiz, Cayetano Valdés, should be given the job of liaising with the Comisión and organizing the ships. Finally, the recruitment of volunteers for America should not be stopped or neglected. A reception centre should be set up in a town in Extremadura which was convenient for travel to and embarkation from Cádiz or Galicia.[103]

It is clear from these early meetings and decisions that neither Ferdinand nor the new constitutional authorities were willing to renounce the use of force and rely on what was supposedly to be the voluntary return of the insurgents to the imperial family now that the constitution had been restored. In essence, their view was that military action might be suspended for a time to allow the results of negotiation and the political changes in the peninsula to be known, but they obviously still considered military reconquest a practical option open to them. This is not particularly surprising because, despite the radical shift from absolutism to constitutionalism, many of the men at the centre of power remained the same. The Provisional Junta contained long-standing militarists such as Lardizábal, Manuel Abad y Queipo, bishop-elect of Michoacán, Colonel Vicente Sancho, and former Minister of State at Cádiz, Ignacio Pezuela. The Council of State had been purged but the faces were not new. Eight councillors attended the sessions in March–April 1820. With one exception, all had served on the Council during Ferdinand's previous administration and some had been active on committees during the Cádiz Regency. General Blake, Francisco Requena, José Aycinena and Esteban Varea had been members of the Council of the Indies or other royal committees. Antonio Ranz Romanillos, soon to become director of the Royal Academy of History, had served on many committees since the 1790s. Bernardo Roa, Marqués de Piedrablanca, had been

on the Caracas *audiencia* and Francisco Castaños, the victorious
commander at Bailén in 1808, had worked for both the Regency and
for Ferdinand. Gabriel de Ciscar was a naval officer and former
Regent at Cádiz. These men were familiar with Spain's policy
towards America of the previous decade and, to a considerable extent,
they had taken part in its formulation. They were now faced with a
new situation on the domestic political front but the colonial crisis
remained the same and so did their attitudes towards it. Hence they
produced no radical new initiative and retained their faith in at least
the possibility of victory by force of arms. Ferdinand's first proclamation to his overseas subjects, dated 14 April, well summarized the
liberal position. He urged unity, deplored the horrors of war, made
promises of benefits to come and ended with an implied threat that if
Americans did not accept his paternal offerings, they would be forced
into submission.[104]

The persistence of the idea of military reconquest did not find
favour among some sections of the press, freed once again to comment
on national affairs. On 29 April, the *Aurora de España* carried an article
from a Cádiz newspaper protesting against the preparation for an
expedition to Venezuela still going on in the bay of Cádiz. It was
incredible, commented the editor, that the government was still
contemplating such action which was so contrary to the peaceful
reconciliation that was the only and obvious answer to the dissensions
in America. If the news from Cádiz was true, America would certainly
separate and, unless the opposite policy was adopted, 'we should from
this moment consider as null and void all our relations with that
hemisphere'. In the provinces, the press seemed to take a similar
position. The *Diario de Barcelona* while printing accounts of loyalist
victories and rebel chaos, especially in Chile, was quite unequivocal
about the military policy; 'We will not hide the fact that in our
opinion, the idea of subduing America by force is absurd.'[105]

While Ferdinand and his advisers were deciding that the military
policy should not be abandoned, elections were being held for the new
Cortes and on 9 July the representatives, including a number of
Americans, assembled for the opening session. In his inaugural
address, Ferdinand again offered a mixture of promises and threats if
the insurgents rejected, or would not cooperate in, a negotiated
settlement. The next few days were spent largely on receiving reports
of the activities of the various branches of the executive since March.
The Junta de Gobierno referred to the urgent need to dissolve the

Buenos Aires invasion force still billeted on the outskirts of Cádiz. The force of reason, it said, should now replace that of bayonets but if the disturbances continued, congress should give the executive 'more appropriate methods of pacification'. The Junta also reported the decision to suspend further expeditions, but added that supplies were being sent to Morillo because, even when agreement with the rebels was reached, it would still be necessary to defend the provinces against foreign aggression.[106] In his report, the Minister of State, Evaristo Pérez de Castro, former deputy at Cádiz and recently ambassador at Hamburg, surveyed the lack of progress on the diplomatic front. The attempt to use international mediation to resolve the Portuguese occupation of Montevideo had failed, possibly, he said, because the River Plate expedition, that 'necessary auxiliary of mediation', had not sailed. The Minister of War, Marqués de las Amarillas, provided the representatives with a detailed picture of the military situation in America. Men numbering 15,625 had left for North and South America between 1811 and 1813 and another 27,342 had gone since 1814, a total of 42,967. At the present time, there were 41,036 regulars in New Spain, 12,016 in Venezuela, 6,199 in Peru and smaller numbers elsewhere. But, he emphasized, the military position was not promising. While New Spain was largely but not entirely at peace, the rebels dominated to the south and Morillo was in a critical state, without hope unless he received more support. Army morale was low, discipline lax and supplies inadequate. Peru, although still under control, was at risk from insurgent-dominated Chile and Buenos Aires. Spain, he noted, had had in 1814 an army of 190,000 men and 17,000 horses. That had been reduced, partly by the expeditions to America, to the present strength of 53,705 men and 7,083 horses.

The Navy Minister, Juan Jabat, who had been one of the first envoys sent to America in 1808 by the Junta Central and who, according to Pizarro, was an idiot, also offered a statistical survey of the navy. Not long ago, he said, we had 287 warships on active service. Now there were only 4 and 10 useable frigates. It was vital to repair others, especially two warships to be kept in reserve for Lima in case the one en route there met with some mishap. Echoing his predecessors, he warned that the navy, so important for maintaining the empire, must be developed. Finally, the Minister of Ultramar, Porcel, summarized the actions so far taken by the new government. If, he said, peace did not result from the concessions, benefits and constitutional freedoms open to Americans, the continuation of the war would not be the fault of Spain. He noted that the government had been criticized for sending armaments to Venezuela. But it was important for the monarchy to be seen to have military power at the very time when it was prepared to talk peace: 'the government knows that it is better to achieve things by reason rather than by force; but it also knows that force is the best support of reason'.[107]

In all of these ministerial reports, there was no attempt to disguise the fact that the use of force was not being ruled out, and while this may have been mere sabre-rattling in the hope of impressing the insurgent régimes at a time when it was intended to start talks, it all sounded familiar and no more than a repetition of what the royal councils and others had been saying for years. The liberal press was again not enthusiastic. As one paper asked, what philosophical or rational justification was there for Spain's use of force to retain a colony? To threaten military action if Americans failed to conform with Spanish ideas was a tactical error because threats offended the pride of people and nations. Moreover, even to talk of using force after the experience of the past six years was just silly. If the overseas provinces could not be kept by peaceful persuasion, it was better to accept their separation.[108]

For its part, the Cortes does not seem to have placed America very high on its agenda of priorities. Amidst the fervour of their perhaps unexpected return to power, the liberal reformers hastened to enact their programme of change in the political, economic and social structure of the monarchy. Soon beset by internal rivalries, split into factions and in the certain knowledge that, despite his public loyalty to the constitution, Ferdinand was conspiring against them, they found that America was among the least of their immediate problems. Throughout the remaining months of 1820 and the early part of 1821, the deputies were content to await the effects on the insurgents of the new liberal order and the results of negotiations. The ministerial reports were passed to committees for evaluation and it was agreed in September 1820 that an amnesty for the rebels should be proclaimed. Also it was generally felt that a conciliatory approach was the best, if not the only, policy to adopt. By and large the Cortes was, therefore, willing to leave America to the executive and although there were occasionally demands by individual representatives for action, sometimes military, the majority of the assembly favoured a negotiated solution.[109]

This peaceful approach was still not shared by all the ministers and councillors. The ministers made their second annual reports to congress in March 1821.[110] The Minister of State made almost no reference to America but the Minister of War gave a fairly detailed survey. Cuba, Puerto Rico, Guatemala and most of central and northern America were quiet. In South America, Morillo's army was very weak, but four transports carrying supplies for his men had left the peninsula on 11 November 1820. Furthermore, an armistice had been signed with Bolívar on 26 November. The Navy Minister reported that the four transports had definitely arrived safely and that warships were being urgently prepared for service in the South Pacific.

The picture which the executive chose to present in public was reasonably confident, but the same was not to be found in private meetings. The Council of State in particular now had a stream of matters referred to it and its attitude began to harden.[111] In April 1821 the Minister of War referred alarming reports from Peru, emphasizing that more troops and naval support was essential, and the Council agreed that at least three warships and two frigates should be sent. Even graver news was received soon afterwards. The armistice with Bolívar had collapsed and fighting was again taking place. Morillo had himself returned from Venezuela to defend his personal record and to plead for aid for the 2,000 men he had left behind, which was all that was left of the 10,000-strong army which had set sail in 1815. He painted a depressing picture. The region was devastated and could not maintain the army. Desertions were rife, there was hunger, fever and shortages of all the essentials of war among the Spanish veterans. His successor, Field Marshal Miguel de la Torre, and his men had no hope of survival unless they received help directly from the peninsula. It was a matter of national honour and pride that they should not be abandoned to their fate. Guayaquil, Maracaibo, Santa Marta were already independent and Cartagena and other areas again in revolt. The Council of State greeted Morillo's account with alarm and urged the government to send a strong naval force to Venezuela as soon as possible.

Then, to the surprise and astonishment of all, the Minister of Ultramar told the Cortes that Agustín de Iturbide had abandoned the loyalist cause in New Spain and joined the insurgents.[112] The new rebellion there was spreading rapidly and Iturbide was, the minister warned, an experienced officer and 'fearful enemy'. Orders had been given to Pascual de Liñán, who had 2,000 infantry and 640 cavalry, to keep a watch on rebel movements and contain them. The Cortes immediately debated these developments in New Spain but, apart from deploring the mistakes of the past, most speakers insisted that if Americans only appreciated the benefits to be derived from the constitution, their discontent would end. Nothing concrete was agreed except to refer the matter to a committee which in turn produced an inconclusive report. It was presented by the Conde de Toreno who said that after long discussions with ministers and others, the committee felt that specific proposals for dealing with the crisis should come from the executive. All the Cortes could do was to urge the goverment to act.[113]

While the news of the Iturbide revolt was being absorbed in the Cortes, the Council of State was in turn considering the situation. It met on 6 June to discuss Venezuela and, in subsequent sessions, New Spain was on its agenda. A clear split now developed between those who still wanted an increased military effort and those who believed that reconquest was impossible. Several councillors argued that to send more land forces was counter-productive, ineffective and impossible because of lack of resources. The only hope was to rely on naval strength. In contrast, Esteban Varea and Ignacio de la Pezuela both demanded that military aid, including land and naval forces, must be sent to Venezuela, and Ranz Romanillos, Miguel Gayoso and Antonio Porcel wanted the military suppression of anyone in America who did not obey the Constitution. Warships should be sent at once to the Pacific because that was the most effective means of pacification and vital for the preservation of the River Plate, Chile and, indeed, the whole empire.

Early in August, following a request by the Cortes of 27 June, the Minister of Ultramar asked the Council to conduct a thorough investigation into the whole American problem and to suggest measures of pacification that could be adopted in the light of recent events. During the next three months, the Council began to assemble all the evidence and factual data that it could find and ministers were asked to submit up-to-date assessments. In his submission, the Minister of Ultramar stressed that the military situation was changing constantly with first one side and then the other in the ascendance and there was no way of predicting what success a new expedition would have. Orders had gone to Cuba to send soldiers to Veracruz and men would have to be sent to Cuba as replacements; an infantry regiment was being formed at Cádiz for that purpose. It was up to the Council to advise if even more men should be dispatched from the peninsula.

Eventually, after many sessions, on 7 November the final report of the Council was completed.[114] It covered a wide range of options, including reforms of various kinds. As far as military action was concerned, the Council's majority view was that the most effective action that could be taken was to build a strong naval presence to protect loyalists and demonstrate naval supremacy. Warships should be sent to Lima and at least four armed vessels to Veracruz. As for land-based forces, while acknowledging their usefulness, the problems involved were such that available resources would be better employed on the navy. Nevertheless, in those places where reinforcements were absolutely necessary, the minimum number required should be sent and ships should in any case carry munitions and military supplies. The Council recognized that the funds for the military and naval forces might not be readily forthcoming and, if this was the case, the government should approach foreign powers, notably Britain, to ask for aid, offering in return commercial concessions. Finally, the promises, so far often unfulfilled, of extra pay and promotions for those soldiers who had gone to America must be implemented.

The Council's formal report was a summary document of its proceedings, but the range of ideas put forward in discussion and the disagreements were such that it was thought appropriate to attach as appendices the individual opinions of several of the councillors. Pezuela, Varea and the Marqués de Piedras Blancas all pressed for stronger military action. Pezuela repeated his view that nothing would have any effect unless it was backed by force. Varea wanted naval and land forces used and Piedras Blancas suggested a forced loan of 8,000,000 pesos be levied to be spent on buying warships in the peninsula and abroad. All the ports and coastlines of the rebel-held provinces should be blockaded. Porcel, La Serna and Vázquez Figueroa wanted more money spent on the navy. Four councillors – Aycinena, Luyando, Flores and the Prince of Anglona – ridiculed the idea of using the army. They began their joint opinion by referring to advice once offered to Spain: the conservation of America did not rest on bayonets but on a bridge constructed of battleships of 74 cannon. Over the past twelve years, they pointed out, more than 40,000 men had been sent to America at a cost of 25,000,000 pesos and all had been wasted. That policy had been 'impolitic, destructive and ineffective', and even if the soldiers, transports and money were available, there was no way the war could be sustained indefinitely. The military policy had been adopted because of the 'blind petitions' from the merchants of Cádiz and Mexico. The only hope left now was to attract British support by abolishing the trading monopoly and granting the British special commercial privileges. In the meantime, whatever money could be raised should be spent on getting two or three warships to Peru which had been pleading for them in vain for the past two years. For Gabriel Ciscar, there was no hope. The whole idea of physically defeating the insurgents or holding onto America was quite impractical. It just could not be done, he said, and it was a waste of money and effort even to try. The time had arrived in his opinion for Spain to accept the independence of the American territories within a federal political system.

The Council's report and the individual opinions were passed to the government and in turn the cabinet prepared its own assessment. In January 1822, Ramón López Pelegrín, Minister of Ultramar, submitted his final appraisal to the Cortes of all the accumulated evidence and opinion.[115] He summarized the events of the previous decade, praising the successes, albeit temporary, of Spain's military effort. Unfortunately, he thought, it had been misdirected and if the money had been spent on the navy, things would have turned out differently. The government still believed it essential to prepare for war by strengthening the navy, if only to prove that offers of negotiation were not being made from a position of weakness. A two-year cease-fire should be declared in all the overseas provinces and this would allow time for talks on the list of reforms that he proposed.

López Pelegrín's report and that of the Council of State were discussed in the Cortes, which began its second major debate on America on 24 January 1822. Most of the American provinces had by then achieved their *de facto* independence. Brazil had annexed the Banda Oriental, Mexico had declared its emancipation, Lima had been occupied by the insurgents, Cartagena had surrendered and Spanish armies were in disarray and retreat. The deputies knew of these events and that international recognition of the new nations was soon likely to be granted, and yet there were still a number who clung to the belief that reconquest was a viable proposition. The Conde de Toreno refused to rule out the idea. We must choose, he said, between force and reconciliation. He did not know if Spain had the military capacity to reconquer America, but even if it did, it was better to start with conciliatory steps. If Americans refused to talk, then they must be treated as savages and Spain was not entirely devoid of moral or physical power. Dolares introduced another concept, stating that he would never agree to independence because that would remove the possibility of reconquering the empire at some time in the future when circumstances might have changed. Palarea wanted military preparations continued and Marcial López objected to any talks with the rebels. We should, he proclaimed, be getting ready to suppress them by force and by no other means.[116]

These militarist voices were in a minority in the Cortes where the majority recognized the reality of Spain's military impotence. Such was not the case with the Council of State and some ministers. In March 1822, the Navy Minister pleaded once again for more funds to get warships ready. Six months later, he was still making the same plea and still planning to send ships to America. He wanted for active service, he said, three or four warships, six frigates, three or four corvettes, seven brigantines and other smaller vessels and these were to be deployed off Mexico, Havana, Venezuela and in the Pacific.[117]

Throughout the final year of the constitutional triennium, ministers, councillors, advisers and some members of the Cortes continued to hope and believe that military reconquest was possible and reinforcements were sent to Havana and from there to San Juan de Ulúa, the island fortress off Veracruz which was the last remaining Spanish-controlled point in the old viceroyalty of New Spain. Even the return of bitter and disillusioned officers and men from America did not dispel the faith that at least Peru could be saved if only the loyalist army still resisting the rebel advance could be supported from the peninsula. International recognition of the new republics, initially by the United States in 1822, and the declaration of the Monroe Doctrine did not change the attitude of the Spanish militarists. They would not accept that the situation was irreversible and they could not accept the ignominy of defeat. Their attitudes were the same as those that had prevailed since 1810 and this is, as already noted, at least partly because many of those in power in the triennium had been involved or in positions of influence throughout the evolution of the American-policy. For them, the problem was mainly one of resources. If money could be found, they were convinced that reconquest was always possible and this was because they believed, and were often told, that there were large numbers, perhaps a large majority, of the American population merely awaiting assistance from the Mother Country before rising up to overthrow the insurgents. By 1820, it was generally acknowledged that the policy of the previous decade of relying on mostly land-based forces had been wrong in as much as it had not worked. Changing the strategy to naval power would, it was believed, be more effective and bring victory. Then, there was another new argument used by the militarists. Thousands of Spanish soldiers had been taken to the colonies and it was a matter of national pride and morality that they should not be abandoned. As so few Spaniards were willing publicly to accept American independence, those remnants of the Spanish armies had to continue to be supported and there could be no question of their withdrawal from the battlefields. Moreover, no Spanish government, including the radical liberal administrations of the triennium, gave up hope that a foreign power would be willing to offer military aid for the reconquest of the empire. Many Spaniards also remained persuaded that the new republics would soon collapse and indeed were already collapsing into anarchy which made it all the more incumbent on Spain to fulfil its moral obligation of protecting the loyalists and all the easier to defeat the divided insurgent régimes. As the Minister of Ultramar told the Council of State, Chile had had three or four leaders and Buenos Aires a hundred or more. There was no central authority in control of New Spain and factions were terrorizing the whole continent. The military situation was fluid, changing from day to day, and 'perhaps tomorrow will offer another perspective and fresh hopes of peace and security'.[118]

Epilogue

The defeat of the constitutional régime by the invading French armies and the restoration of Ferdinand as an absolute monarch in October 1823 did not bring any change in Spanish policy as far as military action in America was concerned. Even the defeat of the loyalist army at Ayacucho on 9 December 1824 was greeted with disbelief in the now controlled press. On 19 April 1825, a Cádiz newspaper carried reports from Havana which, it was said, told of the surrender of the Spanish army. But, it added, a recently arrived traveller from Lima had said that the whole thing was made up by the Colombians and this had been corroborated by others. There was no doubt, concluded the Cádiz paper, that the so-called surrender was yet another American invention.[119] In Barcelona, the city's long-running El Diario published the news of the battle and then later said the reports of defeat were false. When the truth was finally known, the word Peru was not mentioned in El Diario for the next six months.[120]

Ferdinand remained as determined as ever. In January 1825, Spain's foreign minister told the British chargé d'affaires that the king 'will never cease to employ the force of arms against his rebellious subjects' and a year later the British diplomat reported that as long as there was any possibility of a military expedition to America 'no Spaniard who approaches the king will ever venture to think seriously of anything else'.[121] Thus the sycophants, office-seekers, wheeler-dealers and anyone who could come up with a scheme for reestablishing Spanish dominion received a hearing at court. Constantly told by official and unofficial advisers that the new republics were in chaos and that the majority of Americans were desperate for the return of Spanish rule, Ferdinand never gave up hope. Meeting in June 1824, the Council of the Indies proposed a solution to the long-standing problem of resources. It was no longer possible, the councillors advised, to contemplate the reconquest of all the overseas provinces at the same time in view of the shortage of money, men and ships. The programme of reconquest, therefore, should start with the nearest and richest province which, once recaptured, would provide the resources for expeditions to other areas. New Spain was the obvious candidate. It was politically unstable and most of the population wanted to return to the benevolent rule of their Spanish monarch. The Indians, mestizos, sambos, negroes and mulattos had gained nothing from independence and many of the white population had lost so much that they were now against emancipation. The circumstances could not be more favourable for Spain and an expedition of 6,000–8,000 men, supported by a naval force, would be enough to achieve the objective. The expedition should be dispatched at once in the sure knowledge that the many loyalists would immediately join the liberation army.[122]

Other solutions to the resources problem were also forthcoming. Among the more bizarre of these were several schemes involving the creation of a mercantile company along the lines of the East India Company. Antonio Carrasco, a former Treasury official at Buenos Aires, advanced one such idea. He proposed a company open to shareholders from any nation. It would arrange two expeditions, the first of 10,000 volunteers to recapture the Banda Oriental and other River Plate territories, and the second, a strong naval force to fight the rebels in the Pacific. His estimated cost of one million pesos would, he reckoned, be recouped by the merchant investors within two years of their trading monopoly being enforced, and the entire Banda

Oriental could be offered as security against the funds expended. A similar project was vigorously canvassed by the rather more significant and influential French financier of the time, Gabriel Ouvrard. He had been contracted to supply the Duke of Angoulême's army as it invaded Spain in 1823 and once it had successfully placed Ferdinand back in control, Ouvrard emerged to propose a new Spanish company with a capital base of 400 million *reales* which was to be given a thirty-year monopoly of the American trade. Its first task would be to raise an army of 30,000 adventurers to be used to enforce its commercial privilege. It would also demand a four billion *real* indemnity payment to Spain by the insurgent provinces, the company taking 10 per cent.[123] Attempts were made to get other distinguished European banking families interested, for example, the Rothschilds, and according to a British diplomatic report, it was confidently expected that shares would be eagerly sought by all the rich men of Europe.[124] Neither of these plans made much progress but the idea was not abandoned, being resurrected in 1827 by Goyeneche, Conde de Guaquí.

There were dozens of other imaginative, if odd, ideas put forward whereby the military reconquest of the empire might be achieved.[125] Miguel de Lastarría, Peruvian by birth and a former colonial official in Chile and Buenos Aires, had been active in government circles since his arrival in the peninsula in 1803. He had written several memoranda on the American revolutions and he had managed to get them evaluated by bodies as senior as the Junta de Pacificación, for which he had acted as secretary for a time. By 1826, he was living in Seville and, at the age of sixty-seven, still urging Ferdinand to regain his empire by force. He wanted priority to be given to the Banda Oriental, suggesting among other things that alliances should be made with the Araucanian Indians to provide the necessary manpower. Francisco de Paula del Villar, a minor bureaucrat, was even more ambitious. He wanted 20,000 men sent to New Spain and another 20,000 to Buenos Aires and the cost of 500 million *reales*, he believed, could be raised from the six groups most interested in reconquest: aristocracy, clergy, commerce, farmers, manufacturers and military.[126]

The schemes and projects kept coming forward throughout the 1820s and when serious divisions did develop in America, for example, the Argentine–Brazil war of 1825–8, hopes were always raised in Madrid that an opportunity for military action was at hand. Loyalists and Spanish agents in the new republics continued to send back reports emphasizing how little effort would be required to regain control and for years there were rumours of imminent loyalist reactions in America and the curious belief that Dr Francia, dictator of Paraguay, was somehow secretly preserving the territory for the king of Spain and that he would hasten to aid any invasion force. All the rumours and reports that favoured the Spanish cause were believed by the king and his advisers who convinced themselves that nothing had changed. For them, it was always only a small minority of rebels who were violently oppressing the loyal majority. In 1828, the Council of State composed another long assessment of the situation, recommending that the diplomatic efforts to get international support, which Ferdinand had continued to explore since 1823, should be stopped. It was now time, the councillors said, for Spain to settle the issue itself and to do so by force. Lack of funds was still a problem but in their view, the revenues coming from Havana were sufficient to raise the credit needed for the expedition to New Spain. The former viceroyalty should be the first target because once recaptured, its rich revenues could be utilized to reconquer the rest of the empire, and it was well known that there were still many loyalists there, especially in the Mexican army. Hence an invasion force should be built up in Cuba, secretly in order not to alarm the British or French, and the reconquest should begin.[127]

The decision was taken and reinforcements shipped to Havana in the greatest secrecy. Apparently only Ferdinand and his inner circle were involved in the preparations and the British chargé d'affaires defended his failure to forewarn his government by claiming that he had no way of finding out what was going on because not even the king's ministers were informed.[128] By July 1829, all was ready and a force of some 4,000 Spanish soldiers led by Brigadier Isidro Barradas left Cuba and landed in Mexico on 26 July. Carrying additional weapons for the loyalists they had been assured would flock to join them, they quickly captured the town of Pueblo Viejo and having stripped it of its food supplies and munitions, they moved on to Tampico, the main port in the state of Tamaulipas. There Barradas issued a proclamation in which he declared that in the name of the king of Spain, he had recovered a part of the viceroyalty of New Spain. Then, taking about half of his men with him, he left for Altamira which lay about twenty miles to the north.

Antonio López de Santa Anna, leading part of the Mexican army, arrived at Pueblo Viejo and set up his camp about a mile from the

Spaniards in Tampico. The two towns were separated by the Panuco river and on the night of 20 August, with about 500 men, Santa Anna crossed the river and attacked the Spanish positions. After a night of bitter and bloody street-fighting, a truce was arranged. Barradas returned and during the next two weeks, there were minor, sporadic engagements. Little or no local support was forthcoming for the Spaniards and their plight grew daily worse with more and more men succumbing to disease and food increasingly difficult to obtain. The Mexicans prepared their final assault with an army of 5,000 men. The attack began on the night of 9 September with the fighting lasting for about twelve hours, at which point Barradas requested a cease-fire. The next day, having lost 900 of his men, he agreed to surrender and leave Mexico. The Spaniards handed over their weapons and supplies and the Mexicans undertook to care for the sick and wounded until they were fit to travel. All the defeated Spanish soldiers promised never to return to, nor attack, the republic of Mexico. The men sailed back to Havana and Barradas, fearing the reception awaiting him in Madrid, went to the United States.

Ferdinand's reaction to the news of this humiliating defeat has not been recorded but there was nothing which could convince him of the futility of his pursuit of military reconquest. Not long after the information from Mexico would have been known in Madrid, it was reported to London that another expedition was being planned and 'that the necessary preparations are in considerable forwardness'.[129] Planning was in fact under way for an expedition of 25,000 men. Seeking to explain the Spanish intransigence and profound conviction that reconquest was possible, the British Minister to Spain, Henry Addington, reported to the Earl of Aberdeen as follows:

The great error which, as it appears to me, pervades the calculations of the Spanish Cabinet in respect of Spanish America, and especially Mexico, is that they obstinately persist in the conviction that because Mexico is at the present moment in a state of anarchy, therefore the Mexicans must be and are anxious to terminate such a state of things by returning to the Spanish dominion.[130]

In fact, no further expeditions were to set sail from Cádiz, but it was only the death of Ferdinand in September 1833 which brought them to an end. His belief in the necessity, the feasibility and his own regal responsibility to reconquer his American empire never wavered. He was always convinced, in the words of his publicist, Mariano Torrente, that 'America has been lost against the will of America.'[131]

4

The logistics of reconquest

For most of the Spaniards who participated in the forlorn attempt to save the empire by military means, the failure to do so was at no stage inevitable. For liberals and conservatives, constitutionalists and absolutists, whatever their opinion of the military policy, it was above all the lack of resources in men and ships, and the money to acquire them, which ultimately prevented Spain from reestablishing its imperial dominion across the American continent. Yet, despite a severe economic depression exacerbated by the critical loss of revenues from the colonies both from direct taxation and the collapse of trade, some 47,000 soldiers were recruited, equipped and transported to fight in America, a number not far short of the total regular army in the early 1820s. In the circumstances of the time, with all governments, if not bankrupt, always chronically short of money, this fact provokes a number of questions. How and where was the money found, where were the hundreds of ships and vast quantities of military *matériel* acquired, how and where were the soldiers recruited and what was their attitude towards the prospect of crossing the Atlantic to fight their American 'brothers' for the sake of imperial unity? It is with these and analogous matters that this chapter is concerned.

According to the royal committee which investigated the activities of the Comisión de Reemplazos, thirty military expeditions had sailed to the colonies in the years from 1811 to 1820 and two others, including the large River Plate expedition, had been prepared but did not leave.[1] Their destinations were as follows: seven to Veracruz with 9,685 men; two to Santa Marta with 522; one to Maracaibo with 214; one to La Guaira with 118; three to Portobelo with 4,960; two to Costa Firme with 13,703; five to Montevideo with 4,524; five to Lima with 6,122; one to Puerto Rico with 224; and three to Havana with 7,009. In all, forty-seven warships with 1,004 cannon and 177 transports, a

General summary of net revenues

Years	Peninsula	America	General	Total
1811–20	321.094.481.21	67.091.720.16$\frac{1}{2}$	3.301.553.281$\frac{1}{6}$	391.487.755.31$\frac{2}{3}$
1821–26	15.234.961.15$\frac{7}{8}$	21.169.694.7	41.298.51$\frac{1}{2}$	36.445.953.28$\frac{3}{8}$
1827–30	17.145.200.9$\frac{3}{4}$	5.196.396.23	–	22.341.596.32$\frac{3}{4}$
	353.474.643.12$\frac{5}{8}$	93.457.811.12$\frac{1}{2}$	3.342.851.33$\frac{2}{3}$	450.275.306.24$\frac{19}{24}$

Expenditure

Years	Personnel	Matériel	General	Total
1811–20	137.856.241.24$\frac{5}{46}$	186.405.283.17$\frac{7}{8}$	26.233.455.22$\frac{4}{6}$	350.494.970.30$\frac{4}{6}$

Credits in favour of the Comisión de Reemplazos

1811–23	91.007.867.25$\frac{1}{6}$
1823–26	13.551.381.31
Total	104.559.249.22$\frac{1}{6}$

Debts owed by the Comisión de Reemplazos

	Capital	Annual interest
Interest-bearing debts	111.818.669.12$\frac{1}{3}$	8.267.997.26
Interest-free debts	2.991.523.30$\frac{5}{12}$	–
Unpaid interest to end of 1830	100.885.414.12$\frac{1}{4}$	–
	215.695.607.20$\frac{11}{22}$	8.267.997.26

combined tonnage of 47,086, left the peninsula, carrying 2,390 officers and 44,689 men.

Matilla Tascón has analysed in detail the income and expenditure of the Comisión incurred in arranging these expeditions. (See above tables.) In sum, the attempted reconquest of America had cost in the region of 500,000,000 *reales* and the average per capita cost of each soldier sent to America was between 5,000 and 8,000 *reales*.[2] These figures certainly represent only the minimum direct expenditure because allegations abounded of corruption, misuse of funds and money spent on purposes other than the military campaigns for which it was intended.

The organization and financing of the expeditions was placed in the hands of the Comisión de Reemplazos. For the first three years, 1811–13, with French armies occupying most of the peninsula, the recruitment of men and supplies was almost entirely from Cádiz, Extremadura and the Canaries, areas which the French did not control.[3] When voluntary enlistment proved inadequate, the Comisión requested the allocation of men from regular army units, and the area of recruitment thus spread over much of the country, with reception centres being set up in several places. Perhaps the most acute problem of supply was obtaining enough ships, particularly transports. Compensating the merchant owners was very expensive, but even more difficult was the scarcity of vessels of all types. The Comisión had to resort to embargoes and also to buying ships on its own account when it could, both within Spain and abroad. Shipowners in Cádiz, Catalonia, Vizcaya and other regions were obliged to hand their ships over to the Comisión. Some were also forced to repair them, get them to Cádiz and maintain them there until they were needed, all at their own expense.[4] Similarly, general provisions had to be found. In the words of the 1831 report, 'all kinds of armaments, equipment, food, medicines, crockery and other utensils' were all needed in large quantities.[5] Some of the items were not always readily available and it was often almost impossible to have them manufactured. The Comisión's agents travelled all over the country, buying wherever they could. Uniforms were acquired in San Sebastián, gun carriages in Galicia, casks in Cartagena, and special contracts were agreed with manufacturers for rifles, biscuits, clothing and other supplies, with the Comisión also establishing or financing workshops to produce whatever was needed.

All these multiple operations required extensive and often complex financial support. The initial enthusiasm of 1811 meant that loans were at first readily forthcoming from the Cádiz merchant community, but, with the overseas trade declining year by year as the American revolts spread and the danger from pirates increased, raising money from private sources became difficult, if not impossible. Hence a series of taxes had to be introduced by the central government which assigned the revenue from them to the Comisión, although some of the money was often diverted to other commitments. There were complaints in 1816, for example, that the city treasurers of Cádiz and Barcelona were appropriating funds and, as a result, work on some ships had had to be stopped.[6] The taxes imposed in 1811 were extended indefinitely and in 1813 the Comisión was given control of the sale of mercury.[7] This was used in various ways, one of which was to meet charter costs, calculating the value of the metal at the government fixed rate of 38 pesos per *quintal*. Sometimes, shipowners would not accept payment in mercury and the available supplies were sold in auction. On other occasions, it was sold on credit and the practice in America was cash payment within three months. These dealings in mercury had yielded more than 30,000,00 *reales* by 1820.[8]

By 1815 the Comisión reported increasing problems in finding more funds. The Morillo expedition had absorbed 92,150,309 *reales* and costs were rising. Interest rates on borrowed money rose and food costs alone for Morillo's men were 11,000,000 *reales*. Added to increases in *matériel* costs and army pay, the per capita cost of the Morillo army was 7,520 *reales* compared with an average of 3,000 *reales* for the first three expeditions of 1811 when interest rates, food, charter costs and general expenses were lower. Ferdinand responded to these difficulties by ordering the Cádiz *consulado* to help with revenue from the war subsidy tax. This was a 1.05 per cent levy on imports and exports first introduced in 1805, and in 1818, when preparations for the River Plate fleet were under way, the revenue was assigned exclusively to the new expedition. It had produced 23,464,454 *reales* between 1814 and 1818 and some of this was used to pay off existing debts to creditors.[9] Also in 1815, the Inspector General de Indias, who had been given responsibility for the war subsidy tax, proposed that the tax on retail shops originally introduced in 1799 should be used for the rehabilitation of the navy and for ships for the American campaigns. A royal decree was duly issued on 13 July, requiring payment of 100 *reales* a year minimum by all manner of retail businesses, including bookshops, chemists, glass and leather goods, cafés, inns and taverns. Payment was to be made in two instalments, each in advance, to the local municipal authority which was to forward the money to the Comisión.[10] In fact, it seems that there was considerable payee resistance and resentment that a small retail shop was expected to pay the same amount as a large store. The Inspector de Indias reported that the tax was only being collected in Cádiz and two more royal decrees were promulgated in 1816, ordering officials throughout Spain to promote payment and collection, although it appears that these had little effect.

It was not only shopkeepers who were exhorted to contribute to the war effort in America. The bullfight *aficionados* in Madrid were charged 1 *real* on their tickets and theatre-goers in the capital had to pay an extra half a *real*. In Cádiz and other provincial towns, the rate was fixed at half a *real* for both entertainments. The municipal authorities were again ordered to collect these taxes on behalf of the Comisión. Other taxes were imposed on imported wheat and flour, the revenue to be collected by the *consulados* throughout the country, and similar levies were charged in various parts of America.[11]

Direct taxation was accompanied by other means of raising funds. There were individual donations, but much more common were forced loans, especially from the merchant community.[12] The largest was for 30,000,000 *reales* payable by the *consulados* in three instalments over a period of ten months. This loan was administered directly by the Comisión which was to circulate bills at the designated intervals which had to be accepted by the regional *consulados*. Interest at 8 per cent was payable eighteen months from the date of the loan and the so-called Reemplazos taxes, that is those of September 1811, were mortgaged to guarantee repayment. The total sum was divided among the *consulados* who promptly protested at the amount and the distribution. For example, the governing council of the Málaga guild, which had been assigned 3,000,000 *reales*, discussed the matter on 28 February 1815 and decided that it should be put to a full meeting of the members.[13] A week later, the general meeting took place and, after many complaints of poverty, it was resolved to request a reduction in the amount to 1,000,000 *reales*. This request was turned down by Madrid and the government emphasized that the expeditions to America were urgent and in the interest of all merchants. In the light of this rejection, the committee decided to investigate ways and means of raising the money from throughout the region and eventually devised a scheme whereby each class of member, for example, landowners, businessmen, merchants, manufacturers, would be allotted a certain proportion. General meetings of representatives from all areas in the province were then held to discuss the proposed scheme and bitter argument ensued, with the landowners in particular insisting that they had no money because their properties had been destroyed during the war against the French. On the other hand, they maintained the merchants were still earning money from trade and could much more easily get credit. Furthermore, as the main beneficiaries of transatlantic commerce, they should pay the larger part of the loan. After long and always irate exchanges, an allocation was agreed and the 3,000,000 *reales* divided among the various areas of the region, with Málaga contributing more than a third of the total.

The opposition to the 30,000,000 loan evident in the Málaga reaction seems to have been typical of the attitude taken by other *consulados* and provincial associations. Years later, the Valencia Junta de Comercio y Agricultura asked for repayment of the 803,000 *reales* demanded of it in 1815 and of the 53,533 *reales* taken from it by force.[14] Barcelona's share of the loan was almost 5,000,000 *reales*, half of which was assigned to the city's merchants and manufacturers, but, despite threats and repeated demands, little was actually paid. The local committee pleaded as its excuse that the collection process was unavoidably slow.[15]

Early in 1816 Ferdinand decided to summon representatives from each of the guilds to discuss the general problem of financing the campaigns in America.[16] These merchants assembled in Madrid and as a result of their deliberations, the 30,000,000 loan was cancelled and replaced by one of 10,000,000 to include the 2,000,000 already collected. No interest was payable and the capital was to be repaid from 5 per cent of the customs revenues.[17] The Cádiz customs had already been used. In three royal decrees of 1815, 6,000,000 *reales* from the customs dues were assigned to the Comisión, payable at the rate of 500,000 per month. The existing demands on the customs were so great, however, that this was not paid and a decree of November 1816 reduced the amount to 300,000 per month which was to be remitted to the Comisión to enable it to meet the debts incurred in organizing the Morillo expedition.[18]

Taxation and loans provided most of the Comisión's finances, but many other sources were also used. It speculated profitably in government bonds and also benefited from the sale of surplus food stocks and other supplies not used in the expeditions. Income also came in from America. Substantial sums were sent by loyalists initially for the war against the French, but some of this was diverted to the Comisión. Copper stocks in the Mexico City warehouse were given to it and these were shipped to Spain where they were sold and yielded more than 200,000 *reales*. One of the ways used to meet the charter charges of ships used as troop transports was to pay the owners only a small proportion in advance and to give them a note for the balance against the respective American treasury department which was obliged to redeem it on arrival of the ship. More than 25,000,000 *reales*-worth of such notes were issued between 1811 and 1820.[19] Attempts to tax American-based merchants in similar fashion to those in the peninsula seem to have been made in vain. In December 1814, the Comisión suggested that a loan be imposed on the American *consulados* and, shortly afterwards, the sum of 12,000,000 *reales* at 8 per cent interest was decreed, but apparently no revenue was forthcoming. The Mexico City guild replied that it had no funds, that of Veracruz began to deliberate on the matter and Guadalajara did not reply. Faced with this failure to cooperate, it was decided to levy the taxes already in operation in Spain on behalf of the Comisión throughout the colonies. The Comisión then began to issue notes payable from the revenue to be collected by the American *consulados* and this technique was much more productive, yielding over 26,000,000 *reales* between 1811 and 1820.[20]

Following the final decision in 1818 to proceed with the River Plate expedition, a number of new taxes and schemes were devised to enable the Comisión to find the very large amounts of money needed.[21] A further 18,000,000 *real* loan was forced on the *consulados* and the Department of Public Credit was told to provide 48,000,000 *reales*, which was quickly reduced to 36,000,000, provided 3,000,000 a month for a year was delivered to the Comisión. The Guadalquivir Navigation Company was ordered to pay 2,000,000 *reales* which was to be without interest but, in exchange, the Company was permitted to import a quantity of cotton textiles and to offset the import taxes due on these against the loan. Several other companies and institutions were required to make large contributions. For example, the Philippines Company and the National Bank of San Carlos were each instructed to pay 6,000,000 *reales* and this was later altered to 8,000,000 and 4,000,000 respectively. The Company did pay about 5,000,000 in cash and effects but the bank managed to escape with only 230,000 in cash and an additional several hundred thousand in bonds, valued at current rates, which were subsequently returned to it when the expedition was abandoned.

Even Ferdinand himself made a substantial contribution from the Privy Purse, amounting to 15,483,980 *reales*, some of which was taken from the money set aside for the maintenance of his parents. The different regions throughout the monarchy were ordered to find specified sums and at least one, Navarre, sent more than 4,000,000 *reales* instead of the 1,794 soldiers it had been told to provide. Payments due from the French government to meet war damage and compensation claims were made over to the Comisión and there was a variety of emergency loans raised by way of promissory notes and advances from the Comisión's own members. Finally, on 14 January 1819, Ferdinand authorized the Comisión to raise a loan of 60,000,000 *reales*, two-thirds in cash and one-third in bonds, 10 per cent of the principal being redeemed each year and 8 per cent interest to be paid. Security for this loan was to be the revenues from the war subsidy, wheat and flour, and public entertainments taxes. These conditions were revised in November 1819 to allow payment of two-thirds in bonds and one-third in cash and the interest rate was increased to 10 per cent. In due course, 17,531,337 *reales* in cash and effects was received.

Not surprisingly, considerable opposition from the already hard-pressed potential lenders affected by these new measures was soon aroused. At Bilbao, for example, the 18,000,000 forced loan on the *consulados* seems to have caused a serious division in the town's merchants.[22] The amount assigned to Bilbao was 500,000 *reales* and most members of the guild, no doubt reluctantly, paid their share, but twenty-three refused. The *consulado* and government authorities brought pressure to bear on them but one, Agustín Antonio Lequerica, persistently rejected all appeals to comply. As a result, his house was forcibly entered and his personal possessions confiscated to the value of the amount he had been allotted. He was the most recalcitrant, but there is no doubt that other objectors were similarly incensed. The Comisión used promissory notes to purchase supplies and then these had to be redeemed by the merchants. Having been told that it was to guarantee 500,000 *reales* in this way, the *consulado* had held a general meeting on 5 August 1819 which appointed a sub-committee to decide on the details of how much each member should pay. It was to the allegedly unfair distribution which this sub-committee recommended that the objections were made, even though the amounts in some cases were negligible, one being for only 96 *reales*. The Málaga *consulado* was asked to find 868,000 *reales* as its share of the 18,000,000 loan, which it was told would be spent on weapons for the River Plate expedition. The latter had been ordered 'as the only way of pacifying the Americas'. The governing body of the guild met in February 1819 to discuss the matter and set up a committee to look at it in detail.[23] There is no further reference to the loan in the *consulado*'s records.

Even confronted with such difficulties, the Comisión was able to find 123,735,871 *reales* for the River Plate expedition. This was spent as follows: 50,059,035 *reales* on provisions, medicines, uniforms, munitions, artillery and pay; 71,234,201 *reales* on the ships, charter costs and demurrage charges at Cádiz. Other expenses absorbed a further 2,000,000 *reales*. Only a small part of these costs was recovered after the expedition was abandoned.[24] Supplies and equipment fetched over 6,000,000 *reales* and some of them were given to the regular army. Approximately 9,000,000 *reales* was used to purchase ships which were incorporated into the navy and the cost added to the national debt. A further 935,046 *reales* from the sale of the supplies was spent on the small expedition of four ships to Venezuela in 1820.

The report on the Comisión's activities unfortunately does not indicate where these various supplies, and particularly the 43 warships and 94 transports, were to be obtained for the River Plate expedition. Some ships were certainly commandeered within the peninsula, some were chartered and others were bought or hired by the Comisión's diligent agents. A Catalán deputy in the 1820 Cortes, Guillermo Oliver y Salvá, a merchant by profession and former member of the committee of *consulado* representatives, referred to ships lying idle at Cádiz and at other ports which had been embargoed from their owners for the River Plate fleet.[25] Three years later, a goverment official at Cádiz asked the Madrid authorities for a prompt decision on bids made in a public auction for two frigates, formerly the property of the Comisión. They were costing money to maintain, he said, and they were rotting.[26] At least some of the ships were also acquired from abroad. In 1819, the Spanish consul at Bordeaux signed two contracts with the French firm of Balguerie, Sarget et Cie under which the company undertook to supply and equip ships totalling up to 12,000 tons. The contracts, according to an official Spanish enquiry in 1828, were unduly harsh, with severe penalty clauses if the expedition was delayed in Spain or at the port of arrival beyond a specified time. The company contracted the ships in England, although it is not clear how many did eventually reach the peninsula. It was not paid at least some of the agreed price and duly sued the Spanish government in a French court for 6,154,270 *reales*. The court ordered Ferdinand to pay within ten days and, if he failed to do so, his assets, held by the Paris banker Alejandro Aguado, were to be seized. In their report on this judgement, Ferdinand's advisers urged him to make a strong protest to the French government and to ignore the court's ruling. If the company had a claim, they stated, it should be made directly to the Spanish Treasury.[27] In addition to using such foreign companies, Spanish agents also chartered ships in England which were reported to be delayed at Liverpool by industrial action by dockers, and *The Times* (11 February 1819) warned shipowners that they would have to accept all risks themselves, regardless of whether the ships were flying a British or Spanish flag.[28]

In 1817, Ferdinand and some of his intimates had arranged the purchase of warships from the Russian tsar. Apart from the king, only the Russian ambassador Tatischeff, Eguía and Ugarte were involved in the negotiation and such was the secrecy in which the deal was made that it subsequently provoked much controversy and resentment. Apparently, Ferdinand, encouraged by Tatischeff, first asked the tsar to allow warships to be built for Spain in Russian shipyards, and the tsar responded to this request by offering the immediate sale of several ships.[29] On 11 August 1817, Eguía and Tatischeff signed an agreement in Madrid whereby the tsar was to sell five warships with 74 cannon each and three frigates with 44 cannon each. The price was 13,600,000 roubles or 18,000,000 *reales* and Ferdinand offered as a downpayment the £400,000 compensation the British government was to pay Spain for agreeing to abolish the slave trade.[30] Ferdinand promised to pay the balance by 1 March 1819 but did not do so and the debt was refunded in another contract negotiated by Ugarte with Tatischeff on 27 September 1819. In the meantime, the Russian ships sailed into Cádiz in February 1818 and the government Gazette in Madrid promptly announced their arrival, emphasizing their value for the American campaign and the fact that Ferdinand personally had been instrumental in acquiring them. The ships were, it said, 'completely armed and ready to make long voyages'.[31]

It is over this last point, the condition of the ships, that argument now began. Vázquez Figueroa, Navy Minister at the time, was not formally told of the purchase until the ships reached the peninsula.[32] In his memoirs, he recorded that Baltasar Cisneros, Captain-General of Cádiz, told him on the basis of detailed surveys by engineers that the ships were 'totally useless' with the exception of one warship and one frigate. Ugarte, Vázquez Figueroa added, tried to bribe him not to tell Ferdinand the truth about them but he did so. Other contemporary accounts also state that the ships were not seaworthy. One newspaper in 1820, for example, declared that they were in a deplorable condition, with rotting timbers and fit for nothing but scrap.[33] This dispute over their condition is still not resolved. In 1908, Saralegui devoted a monograph to the affair, asserting that the ships were indeed rotten. In 1971 Professor Fontana claimed that Vázquez

Figueroa lied when he said that Cisneros had reported the ships to be useless. The truth, according to Fontana, was that Cisneros had said that, with only one exception, they were all fit for service.[34] Whatever the truth of the matter, and there is perhaps no better illustration of the way in which personal and factional rivalries intruded on Spain's American policy, it seems that little use was made of the Russian fleet. Again according to Vázquez Figueroa, the frigate *María Isabel* was used on the Lima expedition in 1818 and subsequently captured by the Chilean rebels. The warship *Alejandro I* also eventually went to Lima and was later scrapped. Somewhat ironically, the Comisión de Reemplazos had to find 11,000,000 *reales* to repatriate the Russian crews who had brought the ships to Spain.[35]

Vázquez Figueroa's anger at not being told about the Russian fleet was partly because, at the same time, he was secretly trying to buy ships in France. He had commissioned Brigadier Honorato Bouyon, the best marine engineer in the country in his estimation, together with two other engineers to go to Bordeaux and other French ports to find out what was available. They found two corvettes and one schooner and, with the approval of Ferdinand, these were purchased and later sent to Havana. The construction of two other ships was contracted at Bordeaux and they were also completed, again with the consent of the king.[36]

By 1820, when the constitutional government decided to suspend new military expeditions, the activities of the Comisión de Reemplazos over the previous decade had resulted, in the words of a Cortes deputy, in 'a multitude of creditors with an array of contracts, conditions and origins'.[37] Certainly, there were many creditors who began to press for payment. Felipe de los Eros, for example, was a broker at Cádiz who had supplied foodstuffs from 1811 to 1820 and he claimed that he was owed 1,465,180 *reales* by the Comisión. He wanted payment for the produce, his own services and for money he had advanced to pay wages and other costs.[38] Leandro José Viniegra and Federico Rudol owned merchant ships which were contracted to carry foodstuffs and munitions to Venezuela and they were also not paid.[39] The transfer of the French compensation and indemnity payments to the Comisión inevitably left many people with unpaid claims from the war in the peninsula. These included individuals and companies in many parts of the kingdom and some, including the Cinco Gremios Mayores of Madrid and wool merchants from Burgos and elsewhere, petitioned the Cortes for the debts to be recognized.[40]

The *consulados*, of course, had made substantial contributions to the war effort and although specific taxes were usually assigned to them to repay their loans, they rarely received the full amount. They too began to petition the Cortes, and those at Málaga and Santander particularly asked if the customs levies designated for repayment of the money spent on the expeditions could continue to be collected.[41] In 1821, the committee of guild representatives made a similar request, asking that the sums owed to the *consulados* from the 10,000,000 loan of 1816 and that of 18,000,000 of 1818 should not be incorporated into the general national debt, but rather should continue to be repaid from the customs revenues. The Cortes committee which examined the claim reported that the first loan had been repaid and that the *consulados* had in fact only paid about half of the second. Nevertheless, it was felt that the customs dues should still be used to repay them what they were owed.[42]

Directly and indirectly, the financing of reconquest and the provisioning of the expeditionary armies had clearly affected a wide range of the propertied classes across the country, and there can have been few people who were not affected, however slightly, by being forced to contribute to loans or by way of the many taxes on imported and exported goods, as well as on their entertainments. Nevertheless, despite the presumably highly patriotic endeavours of the Comisión and the presumably praiseworthy pecuniary sacrifices of the merchants and businessmen, neither was noticeably looked on with much favour by the Cortes after 1820. The many creditors of the Comisión formed themselves into groups to present their case, but they found strong antipathy and resentment towards them. Juan Antonio Yandiola acknowledged the existence of such feelings, but he declined to go into the reasons for them. Instead, he told the Cortes, the attacks being made on such patriotic people were unjust. Their claims were fair and their contracts had to be honoured if the credit-worthiness of the government was to be maintained.[43]

Another influential figure who spoke up on behalf of the creditors was José Manuel Vadillo, a lawyer, merchant and former mayor of Cádiz who represented the town in the Cortes in 1820 and who was soon to become Minister of Ultramar. He presented the Cortes with a statement from a group of creditors asking for repayment. In contrast, deputy Moreno Guerra denounced the members of the Comisión 'about whom he would speak to congress one day, so that their bad conduct was known publicly to the whole nation'.[44] Unfortunately,

Moreno Guerra did not keep his promise to provide his contemporaries, and posterity, with such information. The Cortes continued to deliberate on the problem of the creditors, but without reaching any decision on their claims and, with the Comisión in effect dissolved, the responsibility for collecting the various taxes and loans passed to the Junta Nacional de Crédito Público. It set about the slow and complex procedure of liquidating the Comisión's accounts, but nothing was finalized in the first congress. Eventually, a committee was set up to examine the several pleas from the creditors and in October 1821 it recommended that the debts should be recognized and settled where possible, using to start with the funds the Comisión had had in hand when it was dissolved. In the debate on the committee report, there were objections on technical grounds and alleged inadequate information, but the Minister of Hacienda did say that, however imprecise the figures, it was clear that the shipowners, those people who had provided the money for the return of the Russian crews, the suppliers of food and all the other materials had not been paid in full since 1814. Vadillo added that many ships had been chartered abroad for the River Plate expedition and their foreign owners paid promptly, whereas their Spanish counterparts were being denied their money.[45] Again, no action seems to have been taken and in April and December 1822 the creditors submitted further representations. Finally, in January 1823 the Cortes agreed to recognize as part of the national debt those amounts owed to legitimate creditors of the Comisión. A full liquidation was to be carried out and creditors were told to elect five of their members to participate in the review of the accounts which the former Comisión members were ordered to produce.[46]

Probably because of the collapse of the constitutional régime later that year, the liquidation was not completed and it was one of the problems inherited by Ferdinand when he reassumed control. In December 1826 he appointed a new committee whose brief was to collect and collate all the relevant information and present a detailed report on the activities, income and expenditure of the Comisión. After five years, in 1831 the committee's report was finally delivered to the king and in August 1833 the Comisión's debts were formally accepted into the national debt. Terms were offered to creditors and the Treasury took over responsibility for the Comisión's finances. To assist with the payment of interest charges on the debt, various taxes were applied in Cuba and Puerto Rico, including the war subsidy tax and that on flour and wheat. Following several public announcements requiring creditors to present their claims, the list was finally closed on 31 December 1836.[47]

It was, of course, not just ships, *matériel* and money that Spain had to find for the reconquest. More than 47,000 soldiers made the long and hazardous voyage across the Atlantic in the bid to save the empire. For the most part, we can never know the identity of those men, their thoughts, their motives, their hopes. In the early years at Cádiz, it appears that recruitment was largely voluntary and, according to López Cancelada, there was no shortage of volunteers. Soon, however, there were signs that enthusiasm for the venture became muted to say the least and the government had to resort to conscription and make offers of special payments and promotions to persuade men to join the expeditions. In 1814, Ferdinand offered extra benefits to the officers and men who volunteered for the Morillo army and the offer was repeated in 1815.[48] Rafael Sevilla, who sailed with Morillo, recalled that while the officers had had to be bribed, the men still had to be guarded to prevent desertions. The selection of regular army soldiers was supposed to be by lot, but everyone knew that the results could be arranged. In 1818 and 1819, while recruitment was being carried out for the River Plate expedition, Ferdinand again offered promotions. He told the commander-in-chief, however, that these were not to be distributed until the actual day of embarkation, again presumably to discourage desertion. In fact, La Bisbal did announce them beforehand, and, when the expedition was cancelled, the recipients demanded that they be allowed to keep their new status.[49]

These promises of promotions, pay and crediting men with additional years of service if they went to America were rarely kept and they added to the widespread aversion of Spaniards to fight in the colonies. Both the constitutionalists at Cádiz and Ferdinand tried to censor the news from America, but rumours of the savage character of the fighting and the dangers of disease, climate and lack of support were soon rampant in the peninsula. Governments tried to counter this with proclamations, appeals to patriotism and by emphasizing the grandiose national objective of saving the empire. Ferdinand's controlled press was careful to praise the valour and heroism of the army as well as to pour scorn on the fighting abilities of the rebels. Odes in honour of the River Plate expedition were published regularly in 1819 and it was repeatedly stressed that victory was close at hand.[50]

These attempts to persuade the military of their patriotic duty failed to counterbalance the rumours from America. One contemporary described the attitude of the men on the Morillo expedition as follows:

The troops were exceedingly dissatisfied; several of the regiments were meanly deceived and conducted under false pretences to the place of embarcation. Others could not be got on board without first being disarmed; and their hatred against the colonial war, joined to their fear of the dangers of a long voyage and of an unwholesome climate, took such possession of their minds, that they would all to a man have consented and have given themselves up to any enterprise, however arduous it was, provided that they might thus escape the expedition.[51]

Five years later, there was no change, and very few of the thousands assembled at Cádiz awaiting their embarkation to the River Plate wanted to leave or felt any sense of patriotic mission. The activities of American agents liberally distributing bribes, of masonic factions and of political conspirators, and the dangers of a yellow-fever epidemic raging in the Cádiz region merely added to the atmosphere of dissent and subversion. Officers preferred to make their careers in the peninsula and the men were dissatisfied with their conditions, their pay and, above all, they were afraid of what lay ahead of them.[52] The conspirators successfully contrived to depict Ferdinand as their enemy, rather than their American 'brothers', and, when the Riego rebellion began, American prisoners held at the Carraca arsenal were released. Colonel Antonio Quiroga, a leading officer in the Riego revolt, told his men that it was no longer possible to subdue America by force and when ships appeared off Cádiz, he declared, 'our brothers from southern America join us for the defense of our cause; we are receiving powerful aid from them'.[53] Reluctant to be there at all, it is no surprise that many of those who were transported so unwillingly to the colonies promptly deserted or proved impossible to discipline. At moments of defeat, they were suspected of treachery and some politicians in Madrid tended in private to blame the loss of the empire on the incompetence and cowardice of the military commanders and their men. Antonio Pérez told the Council of State in 1816 that the commanders had a vested interest in the continuation of the insurrection because they were growing rich through theft and corruption.[54] Almost ten years later, the Council considered a proposal to court martial the officers defeated at Ayacucho.[55]

Ferdinand and his ministers were well aware of the unpopularity of military service in America and they knew that their dreams of reconquest could not be achieved unless the colonial war could be turned into a national crusade. The Council of State had reported in 1821 that it was almost impossible to persuade soldiers that to make the journey to the colonies was to defend 'su patria'.[56] In 1824, one Pasqual Churruca suggested ways in which this might be done and told Ferdinand of the mistakes of the past.[57] The most important cause of the soldiers' reluctance to go to America, he said, was their fear that they would never return. A fixed term of service with each man receiving a signed document stipulating its maximum length was essential. All back pay due to those who had returned should be paid. It was a scandal to tell mutilated men that their pay arrears could only be paid by provincial treasuries in colonies which had declared their independence and might never again be part of the monarchy. Better rewards had to be offered publicly to those who agreed to go and places in the royal guard might be reserved for men who distinguished themselves, as well as special battalions established for veterans. Public opinion in the army had to be convinced of the justice of the cause and the press should be used to highlight the wealth of the colonies, to blame Spanish poverty on their separation and to eulogize the deeds of the *conquistadores*. Parish priests should remind all soldiers that it was their duty to defend the empire and the nation's undoubted rights to it.

Ferdinand did adopt such a propaganda exercise and the new editions of works favourable to the conquest published in the 1820s and, particularly, Torrente's three-volume history of the revolutions were parts of it. But it was too late, and the Spanish army, consisting largely of men who had risen spontaneously to fight the French invaders in 1808, was unwilling to fight to preserve the empire. No doubt there were exceptions but they were few and far between. One was Luis Fernández de Córdova. He was the son of a Spanish naval officer who had gone with his family to Montevideo in 1803 to serve in the coastguard; he had tried to resist the insurrection in the River Plate but he was caught and executed by the rebels at Potosí in December 1810. His wife and his seven sons were left destitute and only through public subscription and the help of friends were they able to return to Spain. Several years later, in 1819, one of the sons, Luis, volunteered for the River Plate expedition because he was determined to avenge the death of his father.[58] Personal motives of this kind perhaps inspired others, but for the majority of young soldiers in Spain, the loss of the empire was a matter of little or no concern.

5

Economic and commercial reform

There were few people in Spain who believed that peace could be restored in America solely by the use of force, or that the military suppression of the independence movements would afford anything more than an ephemeral restoration of imperial harmony. For most of the politicians, merchants and others familiar with the course of events, it quickly became clear that while force may be to a greater or lesser extent necessary, it would have to be accompanied by concessions. Even if only a small minority of the American population was actively in rebellion against the Crown, there was no doubt that discontent and dissatisfaction were widespread among all social classes and that public opinion needed to be persuaded of the benefits of being part of the Hispanic empire. There were many subjects of complaint, long voiced by Americans against colonial policy and practice, and perhaps none were more persistent than those in the area of economic affairs. Although some substantial, positive changes had been introduced by the Bourbon kings in the eighteenth century, the economic relationship between Spain and America remained based on the monopolistic and highly restrictive system created by the Hapsburg dynasty. While the practice certainly differed from the theory in important respects, the empire continued to be a dependency of the metropolis, prohibited by law from seeking to promote any independent economic activity which was not closely regulated by nor in the interests of the Mother Country. As far as most Spaniards were concerned, no apologies or excuses were required to justify this situation. For Garay, Toreno, Argüelles and many of their contemporaries, America had been created by the sacrifices of their forebears and it rightly existed for the benefit of Spain. As Argüelles put it in the Cortes in 1822, in reply to those who advocated even a limited recognition of independence, why should Spain abandon its 300-year-investment without recompense?[1]

It was only when revolution spread across the continent and the danger of losing control of the empire completely became a real possibility that Spaniards were reluctantly persuaded to reassess their traditional imperialist attitudes. But reform, concessions to Americans, acceptance that the status quo could not be restored, such changes were inevitably problematical and difficult to achieve. The idea of concessions brought about by the treacherous acts of colonial subjects taking advantage of the crisis in the peninsula was not easy for Spaniards to swallow, and giving in to American demands in such circumstances was offensive to national pride and dignity. Moreover, to grant reforms in response to threats of separation was tantamount to a confession of impotence and might well accelerate rather than retard the disintegration of the empire. For the more pragmatic, the age-old prejudice and imperialist arrogance towards the colonies could no longer be sustained and they realized that change was essential, but there were many factors to be taken into account. In the first place, the fundamental purpose of all Spanish decision and action was to prevent the emancipation of America. Hence, every reform suggested was given weighty consideration, but its approval or rejection rested entirely on the assessment of its impact on the overall objective of ending the insurrections. This was no easy matter because, however desirable a change in past practice might be for economic or other reasons, it was only to be judged in the context of pacification and there were few, if any, changes that could be made for the benefit of some without offending others either in Spain or in America. Of course, colonial legislation had been designed for the benefit of Spaniards and it followed that changes in it could only be to the detriment of the personal interests of those individuals and corporations that had long profited from it. Domestic political considerations had, therefore, to be taken into account when deciding on American reforms, because to settle American discontent by concessions would be futile if the effects of the same concessions were to provoke discontent at home.

There is no better illustration of the political problems involved in seeking to end the revolutions by reforms than the position of the merchant community. Those merchants, shipowners, insurance brokers and the whole range of ancillary professions directly engaged in transatlantic commerce were heavily concentrated at Cádiz, but their dependents and influence extended across the peninsula and into most American territories. As men of commerce, they were rarely manufacturers or producers and it did not concern them that a substantial proportion of the goods they traded were of foreign origin. For them, what mattered was that whatever was sent to the American markets must be managed by them, carried in Spanish ships, sailed by Spanish crews from Spanish ports. Their very survival, they loudly maintained, and that of all Spanish commerce, rested on the monopoly system whereby foreign ships were forbidden to sail directly to colonial ports. They would certainly tinker with the mercantile code, with customs and tariffs, but always on the premise that all cargoes going to America went from the peninsula where they could collect their commission and keep control.

The political clout of the Cádiz merchants far outweighed their numerical strength. As the purveyors of the resistance régimes from 1808 onwards, and with the national authorities of Regency and Cortes in and wholly dependent on the city of Cádiz throughout the war against the French, the political pressure exercised by the city's merchants was irresistible.[2] There was simply no answer to the threats posed by their *consulado*. If you do not allow us to make money from the American trade, they warned, 'who will supply the armies? Who will pay for them?'[3] The constitutional authorities at Cádiz found it politically impossible to enact major reforms for the benefit of Americans against the wishes of the merchants. Ferdinand, while less dependent on them, still needed their services and the customs revenue they earned, as well as their money to finance the attempted military reconquest, and he too found that the political disadvantages at home of radical change exceeded the potential benefits in America.

The Cádiz merchants, however, were not the only powerful group affected by economic reforms. Despite gaping cracks in the monopoly system in the years before 1810, a substantial proportion of the cargoes dispatched across the Atlantic were still of Spanish origin and, were Americans allowed to buy direct on the international markets or to develop their own industries, many Spanish manufacturers and producers would be adversely affected because they could not, and they often said so, compete with cheaper, better quality foreign merchandize. Their protected American markets would disappear and there was little chance of their finding alternative outlets elsewhere. Less well organized or vociferous than the Cádiz lobby, these Spanish entrepreneurs were nevertheless not without their spokesmen in the corridors of power. Opposing the idea of permitting the British to trade directly with America, Garay reminded his colleagues on the Council of State in 1813 that it would not be just the Cádiz merchants who would suffer, but also 'our manufacturers of cotton products, or hardware goods and a thousand other things; those in ruined Catalonia, of silks in Valencia, linen in Galicia, hats and drapery all over the kingdom'.[4]

When it came to trying to solve the American problem by way of reforms, therefore, no Spanish government could ignore the interests of the nation's merchants, shipowners, manufacturers, landowners, entrepreneurs and indeed all the propertied classes who profited directly or indirectly from the existing economic relationship with the empire. A delicate political judgement had to be made in assessing the benefits towards the pacification objective against the harm thereby caused on the home front. Consequently, surveying the reforms that were actually enacted alongside those proposed, it is immediately apparent that the majority of those suggested were rejected either because of their presumed minimal impact on the American rebels or their major impact on interested groups in the peninsula. Hence support for change was at best lukewarm and the initiative for it almost always originated with the Americans themselves. During the first constitutional period, the American deputies in the Cortes produced two programmes of reforms, as well as myriad individual projects, which, they assured their sceptical European counterparts, if granted, would bring about a rapid end to the disturbances in the empire. Embracing a variety of political and administrative changes as well as international free trade, they demanded changes in the following areas of economic activity: taxation, especially the question of the Indian tribute and the *mita*; monopolies; industrial and agricultural production; land distribution.

The question of the Indian tribute illustrates the complexities of reform. Those who advocated its abolition contended that, apart from its innate injustice, its suppression would assist in regaining or retaining the loyalty to the Crown of the Indian population of America. There was little opposition to this viewpoint and the payment of tribute by Indians was formally abolished on 13 March 1811, and exemption was later extended to the castes.[5] Uncontroversial though its abolition was, the effects of the change were more complex. The money raised from tribute payments was substantial and significant in viceregal revenues. In Peru, for example, three-quarters of the population were tributaries and the viceregal government found that one-third of its revenues had disappeared. In Mexico, the estimated loss of income was as high as 1,000,000 pesos and at least some of these losses had to be borne by parish priests, encomenderos and other beneficiaries in the colonies.[6] Alternative sources of income had to be found and in Peru the viceroy decided that the Indians should pay the same taxes as any other inhabitants, since they had been declared to be Spaniards in the 1812 Constitution which had provided for no special exemptions for any group. In Mexico, the viceroy contemplated restoring the *repartimiento de las justicias* whereby the judiciary had once enjoyed a profitable monopoly on the sale of 'bulls, mules and horses'. This privilege had been ended in the eighteenth century, but it was now suggested that it should be restored to make up some of the deficit caused by the loss of the tribute revenue.[7] But, to reimpose taxation in this way on the Indians was to defeat the original purpose of removing the tribute, that is, to keep their loyalty. On the other hand, it was dangerous to antagonize those who benefited from the tribute and hence they had to be compensated in some way. As usual, following many complaints and requests for advice from colonial authorities, the problem of how to resolve this dilemna ended up in the Council of State. In August 1813, its Treasury committee wrote a report on the matter concluding that there should not be 'diversity in taxes between Spaniards and Spaniards'. In other words, all subjects in the monarchy must pay according to their means. It was up to the Cortes to decide the level of taxation but it should be noted that variations in taxes were always dangerous and could be provocative in America where there was such diversity of 'classes, customs and interests'.[8]

The Cortes did not resolve the problem and it was one of the matters to which Ferdinand's administration turned its attention in 1814. In his decree of 4 May 1814, Ferdinand had declared void all the legislation of the preceding régime, but in the case of the tribute, and *mitas* and personal service which had been abolished on 9 November 1812, it was decided to proceed more cautiously. Ramón de Posada was asked to prepare a report, keeping in mind the following: the likely effects of restoring the levies in America; the need to increase revenues; the wish not to overtax American subjects; methods of compensating those affected in the event that it was decided not to restore them. Posada accepted that the loss of revenue was substantial and serious for the colonial treasuries, but to reintroduce the taxes would, he said, 'give new weapons to the insurgents'. Also, although it seemed to him fair that Indians and castes should be treated equally with the white population in respect of taxation, it would be dangerous to apply that principle in the present circumstances of discontent. Hence, in short, Posada advised a prudent silence for the time being with no new or renewed taxes which might exacerbate the situation.[9] Nevertheless, the difficulties for both the Treasury and individuals associated with the end of the tribute persisted and on 1 March 1815, following more consultation, the tax was in part reintroduced on the grounds that discrimination or exemption from tax in favour of any one class was unjust. Henceforth, the tribute, or 'contribution', as it was renamed, was to be imposed in those regions that requested it and, where there was opposition, it was to be pointed out that paying it was better for the Indians than being liable to all the same taxes as Spaniards.[10]

There were similar difficulties with the other economic reforms sponsored by the Americans. In their proposals of December 1810, the American deputies had asked for the abolition of all royal monopolies, but in the Cortes debate in February 1811, the Spanish deputies were reluctant to be pushed into what they thought was a radical step, regardless of its possible welcome effects in the colonies. Jaime Creus warned that there was no way of anticipating the effect of the proposed measure and Ramón Lázaro Dou thought that while some monopolies might be harmful, others were not and yielded large revenues. Juan Climaco Quintana reminded his audience that the tobacco monopoly had produced 116,000,000 reales in 1807 and Manuel García Herreros wanted the Americans to indicate how the loss of income was to be made up.[11] This and other opposition was sufficient to persuade the Cortes to vote to postpone the decision on the general proposal. Argüelles had suggested in the debate that, although he was against wholesale abolition, there might be a case for suppressing some monopolies in some regions and this suggestion was adopted. The government monopoly of mercury mining was ended, at least in part because the main source in Spain, the mines at Almadén, had been seized by the French and it was essential to find alternative sources to keep the Mexican silver mines in operation. Monopolies on leather, alum, lead and tin in Mexico were abolished in February 1812 and, a few weeks before the collapse of the constitutional régime in 1814, it was decided to end the tobacco monopoly, although that decision was not implemented.[12] Again, the main criterion for evaluating these measures was the balance of benefits in respect of stopping the insurrections, and affected interest groups were always quick to protest. For example, on 27 May 1812 the viceroy of Santa

Fe, following the example of the Cortes, decided to end the monopoly on the manufacture and sale of *aguardiente* in Panama. He did this, he said, because it was one way of counteracting the propaganda of the 'disloyal and depraved' of Cartagena and Santa Fe who were claiming that the much-heralded Cortes reforms were not worth the paper they were written on. He wanted to give 'a public testimony to the contrary' and to reward the people of Panama for their continued loyalty to the Crown. Moreover, both the viceroy of Lima and the captain-general of Guatemala had abolished the monopoly.[13]

The day after this decree, the dean of the *audiencia* of New Granada, who was also a member of the local treasury committee, sent a confidential letter of complaint against the viceroy's actions and the dispute was referred to the Council of State. Adopting on the one hand a typically conservative position, the Council declared that however loyal the people of Panama were, they could not be rewarded with the scant resources of the public treasury in such difficult times. The example of what other viceroys had done was irrelevant, because their powers differed and because nothing justified an official exceeding his authority. The viceroy should be reprimanded. At the same time, it would now be unwise to reimpose the monopoly 'after the people have tasted the liberty'.[14]

The supporters of the viceregal action in Panama had cited another recent Cortes reform as part of their case. This was the law of 9 February 1811 which gave Americans the freedom to grow and cultivate whatever they wanted and to develop manufacturing industry and crafts. It seemed to the Panama merchants that, given this freedom, it followed that they should be allowed to produce brandies and that the royal monopoly was no longer tenable. The Council of State disagreed. The Cortes decree 'favours the manufacture of those articles which are not the source of one of the public revenues'. In other words, the freedom of industry and agriculture was not quite the reform requested by the Americans. It had been approved without dissent in the Cortes, because the Spanish deputies assumed that there was little or nothing produced in the colonies which would be in direct competition with Spanish products, and there were those who believed that Americans were in any case mentally incapable of industrial or entrepreneurial skills. The reform was thus qualified in as much as Americans were free to produce anything as long as the product was not a royal monopoly, and it had already been decided not to abolish the monopolies.

Another area in the economic sphere, much debated and often

promoted as a sure way of helping the Spanish cause in America, was land distribution. For López Cancelada, it was possibly the most important single reform that the Cortes could enact and he argued at length that giving land to the castes was a certain means of ensuring their loyalty. He condemned, as he always did, the rich creole landowners of America and, blaming them for popular discontent, he advised repeatedly that the theoretical paper rights being granted would have no effect unless they were accompanied by more tangible changes. Writing in January 1812, he declared:

Spaniards. Is there any reason why one individual should own fifty leagues of land and 200,000 people who live on it should be without a few inches where they can call a lettuce their own? What does being made an integral part of the kingdom mean to them? What use is a wise constitution except to show them the way to liberate themselves from hunger and poverty?[15]

A year later, he was still on the same theme, insisting that it was the monopoly of land by the creole class which was at the root of the insurrections.[16] Some of the American deputies also pleaded for land to be distributed. Pedro Bautista Pino (New Mexico) told the Cortes in November 1812 that neither the constitution nor the specific reforms so far introduced were enough to stop the revolts. What was needed was help for the millions of landless castes and while force might command their respect, it would never stop their despair. Every inhabitant should be given land and, at a stroke, that one measure would eliminate support for the rebels.[17]

To some extent, the constitutional authorities took note of these and many similar pleas and a limited distribution of land was decreed as well as the sale of uncultivated or unclaimed land. There was also a variety of more specific reforms in the mining industry, taxation and commerce. More American ports were allowed to trade, the tax on *pulperías* (taverns) was lifted and the production of mezcal brandy was freed from all restrictions. Yet the sum total of the reforms in the economic activities of the colonies approved at Cádiz amounted to very little and did nothing to stop the progress of the revolts or to diminish support for them. The Spanish deputies in the Cortes always moved cautiously and, although radical in political terms in the context of peninsular affairs, they were conservative when it came to changes in America. Their successors in the liberal triennium were no more adventurous and, although the previous concessions were confirmed and the new American deputies again advocated a host of reforms, little new legislation was achieved. López Cancelada still maintained that the way to stop independence was to give land to the castes, and Ministers of Ultramar talked of the need for major changes in agriculture, mining, fiscal policy and industry. Enquiries were ordered, plans drawn up and promises made but most were left unfulfilled. In June 1821, the Overseas Committee recognized that there had been much talk but little action in the past, which they attributed to the problems of distance and bureaucracy. They suggested an immigration scheme designed to attract new population by offering land and tax concessions, but, after several debates, it was referred back to the committee for further consideration.[18] Of course, by the 1820s, it was obvious that particular reforms would not in themselves halt the revolts. Most of the ministers and deputies were aware that some kind of political solution was demanded and that there was always the danger that even more talk and promises could be counter-productive. They continued to hope, and in part to assume, that a negotiated settlement was possible and, despite a decade of enquiry and detailed programmes of reform put forward by Americans, it was still believed necessary to ask what it was the rebels wanted in the way of new legislation. The envoys dispatched during the triennium were instructed to offer changes, to make promises and, above all, to find out what was required to pacify the rebels. In his intended seminal survey of the situation of January 1822, López Pelegrín still included the distribution of royal and vacant lands to the Indians and castes as a vital step. The earlier decrees of 4 January 1813 and 8 November 1820 had shown, he claimed, the useful benefits of such a measure among which was the creation of groups whose interests would thus be tied to the Crown. Everyone knew, he wrote, that revolutions are supported by the have-nots in society and opposed by the haves.[19] Lucas Alamán (New Spain) tried to disillusion his Spanish colleagues. The idea of creating a new group of landowners who owed their good fortune to the Cortes was wishful thinking, because the vast areas of vacant, usable land which everyone seemed to assume were available simply did not exist.[20]

In view of the paucity of significant measures of reform in the economic field introduced by the liberals, despite their often-stated belief that reform equalled reconciliation, it is not surprising that Ferdinand and his absolutist advisers were even less persuaded of the value of a policy based on concessions. For them, as we have seen, military action appeared to offer the best hope of success and little in the form of concessions was permitted. This was not for want of advice to the contrary, for many of Ferdinand's advisers believed, like the constitutionalists before them, that changes were needed, if only to reduce rebel support and thereby make military victory easier. Of the various areas of economic activity discussed, excluding commerce for the time being, that which attracted most attention was the development of American industry and agriculture. General Zayas told Ferdinand in June 1814 that some of the American complaints were justified and that it was important to regain popular support. We are both farming and industrial nations, he said, and we should concentrate on that fact by stimulating agricultural production in America and industry in the peninsula. There should also be tax and tariff reductions and a general improvement in the standard of living of Americans.[21] Manuel de la Bodega, strongly critical of the military policy, also urged measures to promote industry and agriculture and a much more conciliatory approach as being the only way to reduce support for the rebels and to ensure a solution that had any hope of permanency.[22]

The Conde de Casa Flores tended to support Bodega's rejection of a military solution. Voicing the hitherto unspoken fear that emancipation might be inevitable and unstoppable, he pleaded that the whole system of colonial government should be overhauled because, as he declared, we are in the nineteenth century and the progress of ideas cannot be halted. Among his proposals was that Americans should be allowed to grow whatever crops they chose and to develop any related industries.[23] Alvarez de Toledo made the same plea for restrictions on production to be lifted and the Conde de Ofalia, hoping to negotiate international support at the congress of Aix-la-Chapelle in 1818, made the abolition of restrictive laws on industry and agriculture a priority reform.[24] Even Lozano de Torres, strong supporter of military action and mostly reactionary towards any idea of concessions, agreed that changes were needed to benefit American industry, although he qualified this by saying that there should first be an enquiry into what was appropriate.[25] In 1817, the Council of State voted without dissent to confirm the freedom of agricultural, industrial and manufacturing production in America and to make improvements where needed.[26]

These and other influential men at the court, for example, José Ibarra, acknowledged that the revolutions could only be suppressed permanently by offering substantial concessions. The distribution of land also had its advocates. Miguel de Lastarría, author of several memoranda on the revolutions and secretary of the Junta de

Pacificación in 1816, wanted the suspension of the law by which vacant Crown lands were to be sold; instead, the lands would be adjudicated without cost to anyone willing to work them. Royalty owned *estancias*, or large livestock estates, should be divided and distributed and there should be tax concessions to encourage people to settle in frontier regions, especially near Brazil.[27] López Lisperguer, responding to Ferdinand's invitation to advise him on what changes were appropriate, wanted land to be given to the Indians, although it should not be taken from either Spaniards or castes.[28]

Other changes were advocated and not adopted. Enrile, for example, proposed the abolition of the monopolies on tobacco and brandy, improvements in the monetary system, reduction in tariffs on American products and the establishment of a School of Mining.[29] All of these changes were put forward always on the grounds that it was vital to win the support of popular opinion in the colonies, to cut away the propaganda advantage of insurgents who alleged, with justice it was agreed by some, that the so-often promised reforms, promised by both the constitutionalists and by Ferdinand, had not materialized. There were, in fact, several reasons for the failure of any Spanish government to do as Casa Flores suggested, and devise a wholly new legislation more in keeping with the circumstances of the time. First, none was ever convinced, despite all the advice and the loud demands of Americans, that changes would have any effect on the rebel movements. There was always the fear that concessions would be seen by the rebels, and, perhaps more important, by foreign powers, as a sign of weakness, an indication that Spanish resolve and determination over the empire were bending under the pressure of opinion and events. Futhermore, after the initial set of changes approved between 1810 and 1812 which included far more than economic affairs, it was apparent that there was little or no reduction in insurgent activity. Most important of all, however, was the fact that almost every change suggested was opposed on political or economic grounds by individuals or groups. Some wanted no change at all. Yandiola, for example, reporting on the situation in New Spain in 1811, advised repressive measures. Universities and colleges where Americans learned subversive doctrines should be closed and, while there should be new legislation, it should be more rigid and less liberal. American factories which competed with Spanish industry should be closed.[30] The liberal *Semanario Patriótico* strongly denied that the economic development of America had been in any way restricted.

Agriculture, it said, was flourishing in New Spain, as evidenced by rising tithes, land prices and demand for land and, although industry had not progressed at the same rate, that was not the fault of Spain but rather of the natural indolence of the creoles. Also, compared with the working class of Spain, 'the Indian is a privileged subject'.[31]

Others took a similar view. The Persas manifesto of 1814 attacked the earlier concessions which had encouraged rather than discouraged the rebels.[32] Yandiola repeated his ideas in 1815 and the Council of the Indies in 1816 came out firmly against any more concessions.[33] It pointed out that none had had any effect in the past and all that had happened was that Spain had been manoeuvred into admitting an 'imaginary oppression' in the colonies. There was not a single province or village which had voluntarily returned to allegiance and there were simply no further positive offers that could be made. Furthermore, granting reforms to those 'monsters of the human race' implied that their complaints were justified and that the Crown was to blame for the situation. This was manifestly untrue and there was no basis for the charges being levelled against the metropolis. One of the most reactionary and the most influential in terms of economic change was Garay. Commenting on the memorandum of Casa Flores in 1816, he vigorously defended the laws of the Indies as a model of legislation which could not be improved. Since the conquest, he insisted, the American territories had always been considered as provinces of the kingdom and never as colonies. Americans had been encouraged to cultivate whatever their climate allowed and the decadence of industry and agriculture was entirely attributable to the failure to oblige the 'indolent Indians' to work.[34] The committee of *consulado* representatives was equally hostile to a policy of concessions in its several memoranda of 1816 and 1817.

These were powerful voices defending their interests and opposing any change. Allying their protests to the ever-popular defence of the Spanish record in America, they argued consistently that reforms were unnecessary, or were undesirable because of their impact on peninsular industry and agriculture, or were politically dangerous because they would be interpreted as weakness or, finally, because they would have no effect on the rebels.

By far the single most controversial reform considered as a means of bringing the revolutions to an end concerned the Spanish trading monopoly with the empire.[35] It had long been a subject of heated debate, especially during the final decades of the eighteenth century.

Cádiz, Barcelona, Málaga, Santander and other city-ports in the peninsula and in America had opposed any attempt to permit direct international trade with the colonies. Nevertheless, in times of war, for example in 1797, the impossiblity of meeting the demands of American markets solely from Spain had obliged the Crown to permit neutral nations to ship their merchandize directly to America. Once peace in Europe had been restored, the monopoly was reimposed, much to the annoyance of free trade partisans in Spain and in America. The free trade issue, therefore, was not new as a measure of economic reform, but the nature of the debate changed from 1810 onwards in that it was now conducted in the context of the search for a pacification policy. Although the economic arguments of the monopolists and the free traders remained much as they had been in the past, a new political dimension was now added with the case for change or the status quo argued in terms of the likely effect on the American situation. The respective merits of the economic debate, while not becoming irrelevant, assumed secondary importance compared with the political dimension. In essence, the problem became one of the lesser of two evils. To grant international free trade would, said the monopolists, destroy Spanish industry and commerce and alienate the powerful merchant classes, while not to grant it, replied its advocates, would hasten, if not cause, the loss of the empire.

It is not clear when trade reform was first specifically considered as a way of reconciling the dissident Americans. Certainly it was being debated in public by May 1810 when a Regency decree, subsequently withdrawn as spurious, changed the existing mercantile code.[36] It was also referred to in the reports of agents and others on the causes and nature of the revolts, but it was not until the Cortes opened its sessions in September 1810 that serious attention and lobbying began. American deputies included reform of the commercial code as one of their priorities and in January 1811 the Regency told the Cortes that it had concluded that the laws on trading relations with America needed to be modified. There were sound practical reasons for such a reform, the Regency declared, but the most important factor was the political considerations of Spain's relationship with its main ally, Britain. The British were short of bullion and Spanish resistance to the French invaders was dependent on British financial and military support. Hence, the Regency suggested, there was a coalescence of interests. By giving British merchants access to American markets, mutually beneficial effects would result; Britain could sell its goods,

Americans would be able to export their produce, Spain would derive fiscal benefits from the increased trade and, most importantly, Britain would be in a better position to support the war effort against the French. Finally, the Regency stipulated that this relaxation of the monopoly was not to apply to all foreign nations, only to Britain and for a specific number of years under strict regulations.[37]

The Regency clearly viewed even a limited infringement of the monopoly as a political expedient to meet the peninsula's urgent problems rather than as an economic reform for the benefit of the American provinces. Nevertheless, the American deputies continued to press for direct international trade for their regions and, when the Cortes debated the issue in the early months of 1811, it appeared that there was considerable support for the idea. The Cortes Trade Committee introduced a set of proposals which, taken as a whole, amounted to the ending of the monopoly and some of the changes were agreed.[38] The key clause, however, which would have permitted foreign ships into American ports, was rejected on 13 August 1811 by 87 votes to 43. There were two principal reasons for this defeat of the free trade lobby. During the weeks of debate, the British ambassador and dominant figure at Cádiz, Sir Henry Wellesley, offered British mediation between Spain and the colonies in exchange for sanction of British trade with America for at least as long as the mediation lasted. A Cortes committee advised acceptance of the British offer, including the trade concession, but it reserved the right of the Cortes to continue to deliberate on a general reform of the commercial system.[39] Despite this qualification, the idea of trade concessions, which had hitherto seemed to enjoy good support on economic grounds, was now directly associated with the mediation proposal and British mercantile ambitions. As the more conservative politicians no doubt noted, there now existed the possibility of achieving the pacification of America through British mediation at the cost of only a limited and temporary concession rather than the complete abolition of the monopoly.

Throughout these discussions on trade reform and the newly introduced factor of British mediation, one other vitally interested party had watched developments with particular concern. This was the Cádiz merchant community. The city's merchants and their supporters, for example, López Cancelada, when they saw the mounting pressures for change, either to reconcile Americans directly or through British mediation, or to meet British demands for help in return for their support against the French, decided to initiate a private and public propaganda campaign against any relaxation of the monopoly. On the same day that the Secretary of State informed the Cortes of the British mediation offer, 1 June 1811, the deputies' attention was also drawn to a pamphlet circulating in Cádiz which predicted the ruin of New Spain if free trade was introduced.[40] A week later, the Cádiz *consulado* asked the Cortes to suspend discussion of trade reform until it had had a chance to explain its views to the deputies. This request was granted and a lengthy exposition from the *consulado* was presented on 25 July.[41] It stated the traditional monopolist case that the opening of American markets to other nations would cause the collapse of the Spanish and American economies and that it would worsen the situation, giving the rebels even more grounds to campaign for independence.

More pamphlets and press articles making similar points quickly appeared and this pressure, together with the complication of the British mediation proposal, was sufficient to persuade the Cortes not to sanction direct foreign trade. But the free traders did not give up. On 28 August Alvaro Flórez Estrada presented the congress with copies of his essay on the virtues of free trade, forcefully reasoning that the monopoly system had to be ended if peace and prosperity were to return to both hemispheres.[42] Private discussions were also allegedly in progress with a view to promoting another free trade initiative in the Cortes,[43] and the Cádiz merchants knew that they had to forestall this renewed pressure and at the same time offer some practical assistance to the government to dissuade it from giving in to continued British demands in either the mediation or trade negotiations which were currently under discussion. Hence the *consulado* organized the Comisión de Reemplazos and paid for the dispatch of the first Spanish soldiers to be sent to fight the rebels. The merchants proclaimed that military reconquest was the best policy, but they also realized that their hawkish views were not shared by everybody at Cádiz. It remained essential for them to press the economic case against free trade and early in October they submitted to the Cortes a second defence of the monopoly.[44] They asked the congress to receive another deputation and 'after a long discussion', the deputies agreed to hear again the *consulado*'s case. What effect this had is not known, but the prospect of complete free trade as a measure of purely economic reform seems to have been finally shelved, if not abandoned.

Although the Cortes committee on trade reform remained in existence and the mediation talks with Britain continued for a few more months, there was no further significant attempt to breach the monopoly system during the first constitutional period, despite the repeated warnings of Americans and others that the measure was the only one to offer any hope of persuading the rebels to lay down their arms. There can be no doubt that the merchant lobby, especially with the practical demonstration of aid in the form of the Comisión de Reemplazos, had skilfully protected its interests, waging an organized and effective campaign both in its formal representations and in the press.[45] The intervention of the British aid and mediation questions had complicated the issue and raised doubts in the minds of at least some of those who might have been persuaded by the economic case for free trade or of its possibly beneficial effects on the American rebels. Few Spaniards trusted the British and they had little faith in their ally's frequent protestations that it genuinely wished to see peace in all the American provinces. Most suspected that the British desire to get even a limited foothold in the American markets was merely the first step in their attempt at complete domination. Wellesley was never able to allay these suspicions and he often remarked in his messages to London that as long as the Cádiz merchants were opposed to British ambitions, there was little hope that they could be realized.[46] The Council of State was divided on the matter with some councillors, for example, Andrés García, Pedro Cevallos and Ibar Navarro, strongly critical of the monopoly which was only 'advantageous to a few bold entrepreneurs who in the shade of so vicious a system impoverish both Spain and America'.[47] Nevertheless, it was the views of Garay which prevailed. He bitterly denounced British hypocrisy; its actions had been 'injust and unseemly' and it was privately encouraging the insurgents while publicly offering to mediate with them. As far as he was concerned, free trade could well destroy Spain and America and it should not be admitted as one of the bases of the mediation.[48] Hence the mediation proposal also foundered principally on the free trade issue. For Garay and others like him, whatever the benefits in America, the price was too high to pay or too risky to contemplate.

The restoration of Ferdinand to the throne in 1814 led to a reappraisal of policy and, as we have seen, the several reports of 1814 leave no doubt that the militants in his administration were in the ascendancy, with the result that it was decided to concentrate attention and effort on the military solution. When the Council of State met in May 1815, however, just a few weeks after the departure of the Morillo expedition to Venezuela, Minister of State Pedro

Cevallos told his colleagues that the only solution to the American situation was to seek the assistance of any foreign power which, in exchange for commercial privileges, would help to bring the revolutions to an end. There was much support for this assessment and even though several councillors found the idea of trade concessions repugnant, they recognized that, in the circumstances, there was no alternative.[49] A few weeks later, the Council of the Indies reached the same conclusion, and also found that British mediation still offered most hope, 'although it might be in exchange for rewards in the form of commercial concessions'.[50]

In a letter to Castlereagh dated 16 November 1815, the British envoy, Charles Vaughan, confirmed what appeared to be the new attitude of compromise prevalent in Madrid. Cevallos, he said, had told him that the king now agreed that Britain could be given exclusive trading rights in the colonies in return for assisting with their pacification. The Spanish attitude, he continued, had undergone 'a material change . . . The opening of the trade is no longer so repugnant to the Spaniards and they begin to feel the impossibility of subduing their colonies to allegiance by force.'[51] Vaughan's interpretation, an accurate assessment of the mood towards the end of 1815, failed to take into account the vicissitudes in Spanish policy and bureaucracy or the competing interests at play in the corridors of power. During the next three years, 1816–18, an intense struggle developed between those who, disillusioned by the failure of military reconquest, favoured a more moderate policy by which most meant the use of limited force tempered with reforms and those who wanted an increased military effort with few, if any, concessions. The conflict between these rival groups came to centre on the issue of free trade and particularly its use as a bargaining counter in persuading other nations to help in restoring Spanish control of the empire.

In the early months of 1816, the pro-military lobby retained its predominance, but by the autumn of that year, those who favoured free trade as a direct means of reconciling Americans or as a way of attracting foreign support began to make their voices heard. On 22 October, the Duque de Montemar submitted a preliminary report of the deliberations of the recently established Junta de Pacificación.[52] The committee had paid special attention to the trade issue, Montemar said, because it offered the best hope of success. It rejected the monopolists' arguments which were the product of self-interest and much the same as those used against the 1778 reforms, although it acknowledged that the merchants had helped the government and that their voice was still influential. The present commercial system, however, hindered the prosperity of both Spain and America and its reform was urgently needed. It was quite clear that it was now a good moment to seek British mediation once again in exchange for trading privileges. Spanish merchants must accept that there was no other means of pacifying America.

Other members of the Junta de Pacificación produced their own memoranda. Manuel de la Bodega, for example, insisted that any reforms, and any British mediation, would fail unless freedom of commerce was granted. He dismissed the monopolists' predictions of economic collapse and added that it was manifest to all that 'The present state of knowledge and general opinion imperiously demand the system be changed.' He could not understand how there could be any controversy over the subject when it was so clear that the colonies would be lost if it was not granted.[53]

During the next year or so, those who favoured trade reform found themselves backed by many of the highest-ranking officials in the royal administration. On 9 November, the Council of the Indies reminded Ferdinand that in July 1815, September 1815 and May 1816, it had advised that British mediation obtained through trade concessions offered the best hope of success in America. Action had to be taken at once if Spain's 300-year-old empire was not to be irrevocably lost. Even a limited trade treaty with Britain would suffice. It would aid political moves, end contraband, bring increased revenues to the Treasury and great benefits to the colonies. Peace would surely follow. Without that single measure, there was no hope of saving the empire.[54] In December 1816, the Conde de Casa Flores joined this mounting chorus of free trade advocates. The monopoly was not politic, he said, whatever its intrinsic merits. Britain was vitally interested in American commerce, already trading to the value of 42,000,000 *duros* and it was advantageous to use this fact.[55] Finally, in the Council of State in January 1817 the militarists were defeated, further military expeditions suspended and the decision taken to reopen talks with the British government.[56]

Whether this pressure against the monopoly was coordinated behind the scenes is not known, but it did coincide with the ministerial reshuffle which brought Pizarro to the cabinet as Minister of State with overall responsibility for American policy. It was Pizarro who now took advantage of the changing opinions in an attempt to devise a more flexible approach. He presented the Council of State with the file that had been compiled on methods of dealing with the American situation.[57] Among all the reports and memoranda that it contained, the most recent, dated 8 February 1817, was from the Junta de Pacificación which repeated its view that only trade reform had any hope of providing a long-term solution. The right to trade must be offered to foreigners immediately, even if only on a provisional basis, in preparation for the complete reform. Talks with Britain should start at the earliest moment and the British should be given favoured nation status, though not exclusive privileges.[58]

With this unequivocal opinion by the Junta de Pacificación, the pressure in favour of free trade was so strong that it seemed irresistible and, when the Council of State finally began to consider America in September 1817, Pizarro quickly added his voice in support.[59] Direct pacification by Spain was preferable to mediation, he felt, but, if the latter was essential, then it should only be by Britain and restricted to Buenos Aires and Caracas. If Britain guaranteed success, commercial privileges should be given in return. Furthermore, free trade should be authorized in those regions already pacified. During the next two months the Council devoted all of its weekly and sometimes twice-weekly sessions to American policy, and Pizarro's plan provoked bitter controversy. By 1 October he realized that his free trade proposal was the sticking-point and he decided to concentrate on it. It was essential, he maintained, to see the issue not in the light of economic theory or its possible effects on the peninsular or American economies. It had to be judged only in the wider context of restoring peace to America and it should be evaluated as the most effective measure yet devised for achieving that fundamental objective. Free trade was not just convenient, it was necessary. As was obvious to everyone, the Americans in effect already had it and nothing could be more impolitic than to try to ban it. More heated and angry debate followed and on 20 October the Council finally arrived by a majority vote at a resolution which authorized Pizarro to open talks about mediation with foreign powers, offering them, in exchange for their help, reforms in the commercial system and, gradually, direct trade with American ports.

Pizarro's attempts to implement this resolution and the diplomatic initiatives he made to foreign governments brought no quick results. Hence, in April 1818, he proposed to the Council of State that spontaneously and immediately, the king should authorize foreign

participation in the American trade; a participation, he said, that
Spain could neither refuse nor stop and that having already been
agreed in principle, awaited no more than a public announcement.[60]
Again, more discussion and dissent ensued and a few weeks later
Pizarro made what turned out to be his last attempt at getting a policy
based on free trade.[61] In a nineteen-point memorandum to Ferdinand, he repeated that it was vital to sanction direct trade by
foreigners with designated ports and under specific tariffs. The whole
of Europe, he declared, was in varying degrees supporting the
movements for emancipation because it believed that Spain would
never abandon its exclusivist mercantile code. That belief had to be
disproved.

Pizarro's case again received strong backing from the Junta de
Pacificación and various other senior advisers, including the Conde de
Ofalia and the internationally renowned Wilhelm von Humboldt,
but all to no avail.[62] More diplomatic notes to European courts and
clear signals that Spain seemed at last prepared to abandon the
monopoly system in return for international help brought no positive,
or even encouraging, response. In September, Pizarro, who to a
significant degree had staked his reputation on the free trade proposal,
was dismissed to be replaced as Minister of State by the Marqués de
Casa Irujo. He promptly rejected the policy of his predecessor,
especially any concession on free trade to the British, and he advised
Ferdinand to proceed with preparations for military reconquest as
quickly as possible.[63]

Thus the idea of using the concession of international free trade as a
means to quell the revolutions was finally rejected. It had originated
at Cádiz, promoted by American deputies as a reform which would
benefit their continent and which they posited as an essential step
towards the restoration of imperial unity. Considerable political and
intellectual support for this assessment of the potential impact in
America was achieved, but the Spanish government at Cádiz and
those of later years had always viewed the proposal mainly as a
bargaining counter to be used in obtaining British or international
cooperation in ending the revolts. The economic consequences of
ending the monopoly and, according to the free trade lobby, the
beneficial impact this would have in the colonies, were relegated to
low priority, and free trade was seen as a political lever to be used only
if unavoidable. Yet, despite all the pressure from the Council of the
Indies, the Duque de Montemar and his Junta de Pacificación, the

many expositions from official and unofficial advisers, the majority support on the Council of State and the determined campaign led by Pizarro, Ferdinand was not convinced that his only choice was to declare the end of the monopoly, even when it was evident to nearly everyone that international commerce was in operation throughout the overseas provinces.

There are several possible reasons why Ferdinand refused to act. It may be stated that, as in other areas of national policy, he was unwilling to depart from the traditional orientation of the *ancien régime* and its concentration upon the immediate fiscal needs of the State and reliance on revenues from commercial activity, especially the colonial trade. In the words of Vicens Vives, Ferdinand upheld 'a stagnant policy, or closed monetarist traditionalism.'[64] Pizarro failed in his attempt to persuade the king to view the ending of the monopoly not as a measure of economic reform but only in the context, and as the best means, in his opinion, of saving the empire. It may also be deduced that even though the evidence of the collapse of the colonial trade and the *de facto* breakdown of the monopoly system was overwhelming, Ferdinand did not accept that the Spanish cause in America was lost and that events, particularly in the sphere of trade, could not be reversed. He allowed, and sat through, the prolonged debates in the Council of State on all manner of alternative policies, but he always kept open the possibility of the military option. He appears to have decided in September 1818 that the major expedition to the River Plate offered more hope of success than any policy of reform or foreign mediation based on trade concessions.

In addition to the king's own conviction, the supporters of the free trade reform faced other difficulties. The advice to Ferdinand was never unanimously in favour of ending the monopoly. Juan Antonio Yandiola had argued in favour of retaining it and Rafael Morant, a respected official of the Treasury, in a report specifically on the trade issue, had also supported the existing system. Spain had every right to the monopoly, he claimed, and should resist the pressure to abolish or even reduce it.[65] In the Council of State, while the majority supported the idea as a last resort if America was to be saved, most did so with reluctance. Garay, who had long defended the monopoly, Mendinueta, Vázquez Figueroa and others only gave it qualified support and several wanted it conceded only within the context of foreign mediation. Some rejected the idea outright as unnecessary, ineffective, counter-productive and an insult to national pride. At the

head of this group was Juan Lozano de Torres, who vehemently
maintained that allowing foreigners directly into the colonial trade
was certain to lead to emancipation.[66] He was backed in his inflexible
attitude by Eguía, Araujo, the Duque de San Fernando and the
Duque del Infantado. They and their allies constituted a powerful
lobby in favour of the monopoly and, according to Pizarro and
Vázquez Figueroa, they used the free trade issue for their own
personal and political motives. Pizarro wrote that they were not
concerned with Spain or America. Their aim was solely to achieve the
dismissal of himself, Vázquez Figueroa and Garay, and they seized on
the free trade controversy as one means of doing so.[67]

Furthermore, despite the repeated attempts to persuade Britain or
other European powers to mediate in exchange for commercial
privileges, and the strong body of opinion in the court that favoured
this as the best, if not the only, hope of restoring control over the
colonies, the various negotiations from 1811 onwards were frustrated
largely because the British always refused to meet Spanish demands
for military aid in the event that the insurgents refused to negotiate.
Casa Irujo's analysis of September 1818 reflected the widespread
suspicion of British motives and ambitions in America. He was by no
means alone in his anti-British attitudes, and even among those who
favoured the mediation–free trade policy either out of conviction or
expediency, there was always an element of doubt over the safety of
placing the future of the empire in such untrustworthy hands. Pizarro,
Garay and others in the Council of State clearly indicated that for
them, British involvement was a last resort without which the empire
would be lost. This opinion of the British was neatly summarized in a
foreign policy survey of June 1820: 'as much lack of good faith as excess
of mercantile ambition'.[68]

Ferdinand and some of his closest intimates may also have had
rather more private and mercenary reasons for their attitude. While
the official ban on direct foreign trade was maintained, privileges or
concessions were given to individuals with money or influence. When
the liberals returned to power in 1820, they cancelled such privileges
retrospectively and many prominent people who had negotiated a
private deal suddenly found themselves in difficulty. They naturally
protested, pleading that they embarked on their contracts in good
faith with the government headed by Ferdinand. Most of these
concessions were designed to overcome the principal obstacle to
Spanish commerce with America during the period of the revolutions.

The voyage across the Atlantic, never free from risk, rapidly became extremely hazardous for Spanish merchant vessels because of the activities of pirates, some licensed by the rebel régimes and others, independent operators. Spanish shipping suffered mounting losses year by year and many merchants were not prepared to risk their ships and cargoes, nor to pay the inflated insurance charges imposed by the brokers at Cádiz. The solution for the Spanish trader was to seek to keep his business afloat by sending his merchandize under the comparative safety of a foreign-owned flag, but as foreign ships were not permitted under the monopoly code to sail directly to American ports, such a procedure, widely adopted though it was, was nevertheless technically illegal except in a few places, for example, Cuba and Panama, which had been given special exemptions. Goods imported or exported on foreign ships to those few places where they were allowed were subject to a substantially higher tariff than those transported in Spanish bottoms.

Some examples, uncovered by the liberal investigators, will illustrate the sort of deals that were made.[69] Field Marshal Juan Downie was personally authorized by Ferdinand to import cargoes of cacao and sugar, paying only Spanish dues. In return for the favour, Downie alleged, he made Ferdinand three 'gifts' of 100,000, 25,000 and 10,000 *duros*, 'which sums served as encouragement for the concession of the privilege'. The liberals did not find any evidence that the money was actually handed over even though the king repeatedly requested it. The Marqués de Casa Irujo, convinced opponent of free trade, received a similar favour from Ferdinand to import cacao directly from foreign ports paying only Spanish dues as if the merchandize came straight from Venezuela. He insisted that it was in no sense a favour but only to repay him for the 500,000 *reales*-worth of bread with which he had supplied the royal armies from a mill he owned in Cádiz.[70] The Conde de Puñonrostro, another of Ferdinand's intimates, was allowed to import 100 tons of cotton goods free of all taxes,[71] and the United States consul at Málaga, George Barrell, received a permit to dispatch a cargo to America and return with American produce in foreign ships, but paying only Spanish taxes. The London merchant house of Gordon and Murphy was allowed to export to Veracruz 1,000,000 *duros*-worth of merchandize in foreign ships on ten separate expeditions. As soon as each expedition reached the peninsula with the return cargoes, a payment of 200,000 *reales* had to be made in Madrid. Export and other taxes were reduced. Luis

Clouet, a native of Louisiana, was authorized to send 25,000 pesos-worth of goods from the United States to Havana, paying only one-eighth of the taxes due. The Marqués de Echandia was allowed to send six expeditions to America with foreign and national-produced goods in foreign ships which were to return with American produce. He also was to pay only the excise due on the Spanish flag. The Prussian chargé d'affaires, Bertold Shepeler, was granted a licence to import grain, cacao and sugar using foreign ships.

There were many other similar cases uncovered by the liberals, with Ferdinand's friends and also foreign diplomats being notably prominent among the beneficiaries; for example, the Duque de Alagón, Pedro Vargas and the Baron de Kolly. The merchant community was not excluded; among those to benefit were Manuel Agustín de Heredia, a prominent merchant in Málaga; Francisco Bringas, owner of a porcelain factory in Madrid; Benito Patrón, of Cádiz. As far as the constitutionalist deputies in 1820 were concerned, these multiple deals were illegal and corrupt. Flórez Estrada demanded a full investigation of the corrupt officials who must have been involved. Moreno Guerra said that everybody had long known what was going on: 'arrangements were made with the Minister or accountant, and the privilege thus obtained'. Victorica repeated the demand for an enquiry because he did not see why corrupt ministers should escape, but Toreno, speaking for the committee, advised caution: 'We should not enter into an enquiry which would bring us up against, I repeat, political inconveniences of the greatest importance.'[72]

It is quite clear that, despite the official public insistence that all Spanish trade with America should be conducted in Spanish ships sailing from the peninsula, those in power, including Ferdinand personally and some of his ministers, were quite willing to break the commercial monopoly to reward their friends or in return for financial contributions. In effect, the maintenance of the fiction of the monopoly enabled them to profit by selling the right to break it, and it followed that were free trade to be formally sanctioned, a lucrative source of income would disappear. Of course, we cannot know if these secret intrigues significantly influenced Ferdinand's attitude to the free trade lobby or if it was a factor in the hostility to the proposals demonstrated by ministers such as Lozano de Torres and Eguía, or such intimates of Ferdinand as Ugarte, all three of whom were accused by Vázquez Figueroa of corruption.[73]

Whatever the impact of such underlying factors, there is no doubt that the most obvious cause of the failure to use free trade as a means of reconciling Americans was the opposition of the Cádiz merchant community which, although it led the pro-monopoly group, was supported in its attitude by representatives from all the *consulados* in the peninsula through the committee of guild representatives. Together they mounted a most adept and formidable defence of their own interests, always challenging any attempt to change the commercial system or their own privileged status in it. A minority group in numerical terms, as Bodega and others often pointed out in their reports, the merchants were highly successful in their use of oral and written representations, first to the Cortes and later to Ferdinand.[74] Above all, their financial aid and promotion of a policy of military force were instrumental in the failure of the free trade campaign. They offered an alternative to a policy of negotiation or reform and this certainly corresponded to Ferdinand's own preferences and to those of senior advisers in all administrations.

In terms of the academic debate over the detrimental effects on the peninsula's economy of opening up the colonial trade against the possible benefits of persuading Americans to lay down their arms, the merchants won their case. It was argued in many detailed expositions by the Cádiz *consulado*, but the most influential synthesis was probably that from the committee of *consulado* representatives of 26 August 1817.[75] They asserted with considerable force that the rapid decline in Spanish commerce and general prosperity could be halted only if the traditional trading monopoly was rigorously enforced. In their view, it was precisely the infringements of the monopoly, permitted by previous governments, which had caused the disturbances in America and the economic collapse of Spain. Concessions to foreign traders, privileges to receive foreign ships and goods directly into Cuba and Panama, fishing permits granted to British and United States' citizens to fish off Patagonia and the Pacific, had all facilitated the contraband trade, rampant all over the empire to the detriment of peninsular and colonial interests.[76] One by one, they answered the free traders' arguments, providing detailed statistical evidence of former trading patterns, balances of trade and predictions of future developments. For example, to the free traders' point that Spain could no longer supply American markets, they calculated that a capital of 15,000,000 *duros* was needed to finance the colonial trade, a sum which, they said, could easily be raised in only three or four of the country's main commercial centres. Also, the goods needed were available, either from home production or imports, and there was no reason why Spain should not import goods and retain the monopoly as France, Britain, Holland and other imperial nations had always sought to do. Merchant ships were certainly in short supply but that could easily be remedied. There were still 150 Spanish ships trading with Havana and elsewhere, another 100 were American-owned, many more were under construction in American ports. If others were required, they could be acquired abroad in less than four months. It was not, they insisted, for lack of men, money or ships that the monopoly was in danger, but because the Spanish merchant community had lost confidence that it would be sustained. If that confidence was restored, and the monopoly rigidly enforced, all the needs of Spanish and American commerce would be met. It was true that Spanish merchants could not compete with foreigners, but this was simply because of the enormous burden of taxation placed on goods exported from the peninsula. Imports into Spain attracted at least 28.2 per cent tax: when the same goods were sent to America, a further 9.2 per cent was paid; on arrival, another 18 per cent. Adding other levies, the taxation on Spanish trade with the empire totalled 61 per cent, to which internal taxes in the American territories had to be added. No wonder, declared the merchants, that we cannot compete and that foreign contraband is so flourishing. The solution was obvious: taxation on trade must be reduced and taxes on Spanish-produced goods exported to America eliminated in order to stimulate home production; all imports of foreign goods directly into America must be banned; and all trade should be carried only in Spanish ships.

With these and many other points, the merchants set out to show that not only Spanish economic prosperity but also control of the empire rested almost entirely on the monopoly system. Carefully playing on the ever-present fear of British and other foreign ambitions and long-standing rivalry with Spain, they offered Ferdinand the best of all worlds, subtly appealing to his national pride and conservative instincts. To grant free trade, they told him, was to give away the empire and thus betray generations of their forebears. To maintain the monopoly was to ensure future prosperity and imperial unity.

The reformers, including these who believed in free trade for its intrinsic merits or in the mediation context, were faced with the apparently insoluble problem of persuading their compatriots to reject this traditional conservative Spanish view that the monopoly had been and would be in the future of great benefit to the monarchy.

This was not wholly an area where reasoned opinion or economic theory prevailed. Those, especially the more pragmatic, who accepted that the exclusivist practices of the past could never be fully restored, had to overcome what the Conde de Fernán Núñez aptly described as a 'prejuicio'. In a letter to Castlereagh in October 1816, he succinctly stated the complexities of the free trade controversy:

With regard to the exclusive commerce, independently of its resting in the fundamental laws of the Colonies, it is advocated by those who enrich themselves through it. These, though few in number, make themselves heard throughout the monarchy; and notwithstanding the respectable judgement of some economists who weigh the true results of things, the multitude suffers itself to be misled by the idea of advantages which exclusive commerce holds out at first sight. England, who has in herself abundant proofs of the power of prejudices, will not be surprised at the force which the exercise of that commerce must have acquired, and at the precaution necessary to be employed in reforming it.[77]

It was this prejudice that was never overcome, and the restored liberals after 1820 found themselves subjected to similar pressures of fact and feeling. They were to display the same resistance to basic change in the mercantile code. The pro- and anti-monopoly arguments of the previous decade soon reverberated once again around the halls of the Cortes and the same predicted effects of national ruin or imperial harmony were paraded. There were also still those who believed that the trading monopoly could be used as a negotiating ploy either directly with the Americans or in attracting foreign mediation. In some respects, however, the approach of the liberals in the constitutional triennium did change in as much as the idea of trade reform was now discussed more as a means of rescuing Spanish commerce than in the context of the American wars and many, perhaps accepting that imperial dominion could never be recovered, were anxious that favourable trade treaties should be negotiated with the dissident provinces before it was too late. Hence much time and attention were devoted to stimulating trade, without permitting direct foreign access to American markets, and to reforming the customs tariff.[78] In July 1820, the Minister of Hacienda, José Canga Argüelles, proposed the extension of a system of entrepôts at the ports which, while not being free ports, did envisage significant reductions in import–export taxes, although Spanish merchants were still to be required to use only Spanish ships in their transatlantic trade.[79] A few days later, the Cortes heard the report of its Treasury committee which suggested the suspension of the 1778 mercantile code to permit temporarily the import–export trade with America to be conducted in foreign ships which would be treated for tax purposes as if they were Spanish. The advantages of doing this, it was claimed, would be that 'the mercantile code for trade with America will thus correspond to the present state of the seas and the national navy'.[80]

This proposal provoked the first major debate on Spanish commerce, and both monopolists and reformers soon made their voices heard.[81] Deputy José Vargas Ponce, for example, contended that Spain had the ships and sailors to sustain the monopoly. The problem as he saw it was the use of large ships of 1,200 tons which, if lost to pirates, bankrupted the merchants. What we should do, he proclaimed, was to return to the size of ships used at the time of the conquest and the convoy system should be reintroduced.[82] Perhaps surprisingly, there was considerable support for this reactionary view, but others denounced the ideas as impractical, impolitic or out of date. José de Sacasa, representing Guatemala, said that the restrictive commercial laws were barbaric, tyrannical and despotic, but he then made the odd observation that if the trading system was liberalized, pirates might well offer their services as ordinary merchants and thus the independent governments in America would be weakened. The Minister of Hacienda tried to introduce some realism into the debate. We are not discussing the merits or otherwise of the monopoly system, he said, but rather how to revive Spanish trade with the colonies. As far as he could judge, there was no way of doing so except by using foreign ships. His cabinet colleague, the Minister of Ultramar, disagreed. Pirates would still attack any ship regardless of its flag if it was known to be carrying Spanish goods. Spanish sailors would have to leave to get work with foreign shipping companies and the nation's naval strength would be irrevocably depleted. The Conde de Toreno agreed that it was shameful to have to use foreign ships for the nation's trade but he saw no alternative. For Moreno Guerra, however, to approve the proposal was to hand America to foreigners and that was worse than granting independence.

After much more debate and a referral back to the committee, this idea of allowing Spaniards to use foreign ships even on a temporary basis was rejected, and it seemed clear that the Cortes was no more willing to infringe the monopoly than Ferdinand had been. In August it was decided that goods could be shipped to Cuba in foreign vessels for a period of three months, paying a tariff surcharge of 4 per cent, but even this provoked protests from the *consulado* and merchants of La

Coruña, and when American deputies tried to get the same privilege for other American ports, their initiative was refused. Another opportunity to end the monopoly came in the debate on tariff reform, but, introducing the committee report, Guillermo Oliver made it clear that while a general and equal tariff for the entire monarchy was appropriate, it was still felt that direct international trade would do more harm than good.[83] American deputies again pleaded for access to foreign markets and Juan Freire reminded his Spanish colleagues that the monopoly system had been one of the causes of the revolutions. Any attempt, he warned, to use tariffs to give even more preferential treatment to Spanish products would finally cut the bonds of union between the metropolis and empire. In contrast, Juan de Valle defended the monopoly, quoting at length from representations in its favour from the merchant guilds of Mexico City and Veracruz.

The debate on tariff reform soon attracted the ever-vigilant Cádiz merchants and, indeed, merchant interest from all over the peninsula. The Cádiz *consulado*, now campaigning to have their city declared a free port, supported the idea of a general reduction in tariffs to stimulate trade, as long as it was conducted exclusively in Spanish ships.[84] Much of the case put forward by the committee of guild representatives in 1817 was resurrected and it was now emphasized that what concerned Americans was not the end of the monopoly which protected their industry and trade but, rather, cheaper goods of both Spanish and foreign origin. The solution, therefore, lay in wholesale tariff reductions in all stages of the trade cycle with the removal of many of the restrictions or bans on imported products and special privileges for Spanish shipbuilders and shipowners. In short, according to the Cádiz *consulado*, the traditional protectionist policy had become counter-productive, harming industry, agriculture and trade throughout the empire. Tariff reductions would stimulate all areas of economic activity and remove a main cause of discontent in America. No new mercantile code was needed or should be devised for the American trade until the effects of these tariff changes were known and Spanish prosperity restored.

The Cádiz *consulado* received some support for its ideas from, for example, San Sebastián and Santander, which also petitioned to be designated as free ports, but there was also significant opposition. Málaga, Burgos, Seville and especially Barcelona expressed strong dissent. The Barcelona Junta de Comercio argued in favour of protectionism, predicting the total collapse of industry and agriculture in the peninsula and in America if it was abandoned, because there was no way that Spanish manufacturers or farmers could compete with foreigners. Tariff reductions and free ports might make goods cheaper for Americans but the cost to the Spanish economy was too great to bear. Attacking the unproductive economic base of Cádiz, they told its merchants to give up their commission trade and invest their capital in productive enterprise, as the Catalans were doing.[85]

It was not only the merchant guilds that were deeply divided over tariff reform. In the debates in the Cortes, several speakers emphasized the likely beneficial effects on Americans but petitions soon began to pour in from all over Spain against any reduction or liberalization of the tariff on foreign products. Iron producers from Navarre wanted a total ban on foreign imports of their type of products into Spain and America; manufacturers of silk and porcelain from Valencia and of nails from Mataró, Vich, Cardona and Ripoll wanted a similar ban; and from Cádiz itself, carpenters, cabinet-makers and noodle producers pleaded for protection against foreign competition. The point made repeatedly by these and numerous other petitions to the Cortes, always implied and sometimes explicit, was that if the revival of Spanish trade and the reconciliation of Americans depended on cheaper foreign imports, these could only be achieved at the expense of domestic industry and the price was just too high to pay.

In several other respects, the liberals continued the attitudes and position of Ferdinand and his predecessors towards the imperial problem. At least part of their reluctance to end the monopoly was the continuation of the belief that it could still be used as a bargaining counter to reconcile Americans directly or as a means of attracting foreign military support or mediation. In its major report of November 1821, the Council of State clung to the idea that the 'destructive monopoly' had been the most supreme cause of dissension in the colonies. It was now absurd and iniquitous to try to sustain it: 'Of necessity, this monstrous system has had to come to an end and has become completely incompatible with the ideas of the age'. Hence, free trade should be granted and preferential treatment offered to those foreigners who would assist with bringing the revolts to an end. In their individual report, councillors Aycinena, Luyando, Flores and Anglona recommended renewed efforts to persuade Britain to help in return for trade privileges. Certainly, they acknowledged, the end of the monopoly would mean a sacrifice by merchants who, since 1810, had fought to retain it even at the expense of losing America, but now free trade was essential and justifiably demanded by Americans. Moreover, it was evident that 'nobody is indifferent to buying expensive rather than cheap goods, nor to buying inferior products when superior ones are available; and, as in all exclusive commerce, there are many opportunities for this to happen, the desire bursts into a clamour, the clamour is raised to a complaint, and the complaint becomes a pretext for some to make independence not only commendable, but necessary'.[86]

The Council of State's recommendation to try again for foreign mediation or direct aid was adopted by Minister of Ultramar, López Pelegrín, in his set of proposals put to the Cortes in January 1822.[87] He regretted, he said, having to suggest it, but Spain could not alone pacify America. He also advised a temporary suspension of the monopoly for a period of six years during which direct foreign trade would be permitted, a step which would convince Americans, he thought, of the benefits of the constitutional system and stop the subversive activities of foreigners. Also, it happened to suit Spanish interests for the moment but in the future, when the merchant marine had recovered, the concession could be revoked. Hence he was advocating only a temporary suspension. López Pelegrín's modest reform did not make any progress and both the government and Cortes chose to instruct the envoys to the rebel provinces to try to negotiate as a matter of priority trade agreements which would be beneficial to Spain.

By the end of 1822, with the *de facto* separation of much of the empire established and with traders from all over the world flocking to American ports, it seems that an air of reality, or at least acceptance of it, began to permeate the metropolis. According to Canning, the Minister of State, Evaristo de San Miguel, admitted 'that it is utterly hopeless for the Mother Country to look to the practical establishment of that exclusive system, which still exists in her law with respect to her late possessions in America. He has the candour to admit that the time is come when Spain, instead of dreaming of bringing back the practice to the law, must, so far as relates to her maritime jurisdiction on the American coast, conform her law to the necessity which defeats her practice.'[88] A few days later, on 7 January 1823, the Cortes agreed to extend the privilege of international trade granted to Cuba to other ports of the empire, but only for a period of ten months. The government was instructed to propose whatever changes in the mercantile code and tariff levels were needed to 'secure the most advantageous means of conserving and increasing the political and commercial relations of Spain with America'.[89] Finally, with the French armies once again rapidly taking over the country and with the last remnants of the constitutional authorities struggling to survive in Cádiz, the few remaining members of the Cortes agreed to permit foreign ships to carry cargoes from Spain to America. Even this concession, however, was to last only for the duration of the war against the French.[90]

The liberals, therefore, could never bring themselves to the point of abolishing Spain's traditional commercial monopoly and, ironically, it was left to Ferdinand to try finally to use the promise of free trade as an incentive to reconcile the Americans. On 9 February 1824, following advice from the reconstituted Council of the Indies, once more headed by the Duque de Montemar, he issued this decree:

A direct commerce shall be maintained in my American dominions with Foreigners, Subjects of the Powers, the Allies and Friends of Spain: their ships are to be admitted to American ports as to those in Spain.[91]

A regulatory law deciding import–export dues, the location of customs houses and other matters was to be issued and until these details were settled, the present trading pattern was to be maintained. It was to be expected, said Ferdinand, that American Spaniards would see in this resolution 'a fresh proof of my strong desire for their advancement and prosperity'. On the day before this decree was signed, Ferdinand's ministers had discussed it. José García de la Torre and Juan de Erro both wanted to delay publication because they hoped that foreign powers then talking in Paris would accept the offer of commercial concessions that had been made to them, and give in return 'the most solemn guarantees of an effective cooperation towards the pacification of the Americas and their total incorporation to the peninsula; of never recognizing the independence of any of the Spanish possessions in that hemisphere, nor its several revolutionary governments, nor any sovereignty in them other than that of his Majesty and his successors as Kings, together with the other benefits which should be furnished to our flag and products'.[92]

Such words could well have been spoken fourteen years before and certainly the sentiments they express had been enunciated repeatedly by governments and politicians of all political persuasions. They illustrate the fact that the attitudes of Spaniards towards the policy of using economic reform as a means of persuading Americans to lay down their arms did not change throughout the years of revolution. Liberals and conservatives, constitutionalists and absolutists, shared a common belief in the right of Spain to the empire and to whatever economic benefits that might be derived from it. They would not, perhaps they could not, change and, despite all the advice from Americans and from their more pragmatic compatriots that change was vital, above all in the commercial monopoly, no fundamental reform was enacted. The pressures of tradition, patriotic pride and domestic politics were too strong. There had to be another way of saving the empire.

6

The aftermath of imperial decline

The impact of the loss of America on Spain's international trade has been exceptionally well documented in recent years. A substantial scholarly literature has charted the trading pattern year by year and an enormous amount of statistical information is now available. It demonstrates the obvious, namely, that with the empire reduced to Cuba, Puerto Rico and the Philippines, Spanish trade with the American continent collapsed and, as a direct consequence, its trade with the rest of the world suffered a sharp decline. Nowhere in all the books and articles is this more succinctly demonstrated than in the brief analysis by Josep Fontana of the balance of trade in two years, 1792 and 1827.[1] A comparison of these two relatively normal years reveals that Spain's total foreign trade fell by approximately 75 per cent. As far as America was concerned, the loss was even greater. Imports from the former colonies fell from 740,000,000 *reales* in 1792 to 100,000,000 in 1827, with money receipts of only 15,000,000 compared to 421,000,000 and the value of goods at 84,000,000 as against 318,000,000. The colonial products which had for so long supplied the markets of the peninsula were reduced in some cases to almost nothing. Dye woods and Tabasco pepper, for example, virtually disappeared. Raw cotton, cacao, indigo and myriad other raw materials which Spain's manufacturers had traditionally refined for reexport to America or to their European customers showed a drastic decline. Similarly, Spain's exports to America were reduced to comparatively negligible proportions. With the commercial monopoly safeguarding their interests and with Spanish industry never able to produce the type, quantity and quality of goods demanded by American consumers, Spain's merchants had grown rich and prosperous importing foreign manufactures for reexport to the empire. Now that foreigners could ship their wares directly to their markets, there was no need for them to travel to Cádiz or any of the other peninsular

150

ports licensed for the transatlantic trade. Textiles had been the largest single imported item and by 1827 had declined by 85–90 per cent. Nevertheless, despite the backwardness of Spanish industry, another economic historian has shown that while never sufficient, Spanish-produced merchandize shipped from Cádiz still provided approximately half of the exports to America,[2] but the once-secure market for olive oil, wheat and wine had gone and by 1827, the fall in the export of Spanish products was of the order of 90 per cent. The figures for brandy alone demonstrate the seemingly catastrophic impact of the loss of the closed colonial markets: in 1792, the value of brandy exports had equalled 607,400,000 *reales* and the corresponding amount for 1827 was 37,000,000.

There is no need here to relate the broader aspects of the industrial, agricultural and commercial paralysis which afflicted Spain during the first decades of the nineteenth century and which have been so ably analysed by many scholars. The significance of the statistics is absolute. The revolutions in America compounded the already disastrous effects of the six-year-long war against the French and Spain's economy sank into a severe and prolonged recession. Merchants, financiers, entrepreneurs, manufacturers and agricultural producers were confronted with a critical situation. The city-ports that derived their prosperity directly from the American trade were clearly the most badly affected, and none more so than Cádiz. Its affluence and activities had suffered major blows since the 1790s with Spain's futile involvement in European conflict and the increasing volume of illicit direct foreign trade with America that accompanied and followed the temporary suspension of the monopoly system in 1797 and in later years. Paradoxically, the French invasion of 1808, however, had brought a revival, with the city becoming both the mercantile and political capital of the kingdom. With its large resident foreign community of businessmen of English, French, American, Dutch, Irish, German and many other nationalities, it offered a cosmopolitan and invigorating atmosphere perhaps unique in Europe. Its lively *tertulias* and masonic lodges, theatres, active cultural and artistic life, not to mention the occasional French cannon bombardment during the two-year siege of the city and the ever-present danger of yellow fever, all made it, according to the memoirs of those who experienced it at first hand, an exciting and lively place to live.[3] It was above all a city of commerce, a middle-man's town, with little or no productive industry other than furniture; a place for merchants, shipowners, insurance brokers and all the ancillary professions drawn by the American trade. The warehouses were filled with sugar and tobacco from Cuba, gold, silver, cochineal and indigo from Mexico, cacao from Caracas, exotic timbers from Guatemala, leather and tallow from the River Plate. Ships from all parts of Europe brought their goods for storage and shipment to the colonies and there were textiles from Catalonia, rice and silks from Valencia, wines from Alicante and dozens of other products from all over the peninsula. In the single year of 1810, 3,890 ships entered the bay of Cádiz.[4]

By 1824, it was all over. The politicians, bureaucrats, journalists and hangers-on attracted to the centre of power had returned once and for all to Madrid. The foreign nationals closed the doors of their offices and left. Of the 623 merchant companies existing in the good times, 227 had gone bankrupt: of the 300 shipowners, only 20 were left; the population declined from 70,000 to 40,000.[5] The once-great emporium of Western Europe was reduced to a minor provincial town with its trade only a fraction of what it had formerly been: in 1826, 639 foreign ships visited Mexican ports and, of these, one was from Spain.[6] The Cádiz merchants had fought a long battle to retain their businesses and their affluence but the loss of their trading monopoly with America was a mortal blow from which the city would never recover. Its *consulado* had cajoled, pleaded and threatened all national authorities but to no avail. Frustration followed the arrival of poverty and in 1821, refusing to recognize the officials appointed by the Madrid government, the city tried to make itself into an independent republic. Two years later, again host to an unwilling Ferdinand and the liberals he detested, and besieged by the French armies, the *consulado* well summarized its plight in these words:

Cádiz, now persecuted by sea by its most implacable enemies; invaded by land by the usurper, disturbed in its very midst by domestic strife born of opinions; blockaded by children of its colonies; by everybody robbed, obstructed in its business and abandoned by its most powerful capitalists.[7]

Although Cádiz was the most severely and directly affected, it was not the only city to experience the consequences of the loss of America. Barcelona, prior to 1810 the thriving capital of Catalonia and second only to Cádiz in the volume of its trade with the empire, suffered major setbacks to its expanding mercantile and manufacturing activities. Unlike Cádiz, Barcelona was not dependent for its prosperity on the American markets because its merchants conducted a substantial part of their business with European and North American clients. Also, again in contrast to Cádiz, Barcelona and its hinterland were developing an industrial base with textile production fuelling a much more general growth. The Catalan industries, however, were clearly susceptible to international economic factors and especially to foreign competition. Furthermore, as much of the city's trade with the colonies was in locally produced merchandize, general economic depression which reduced domestic production had an immediate impact on the merchants who did not enjoy any significant share in the reexport trade in foreign goods. The widespread economic destruction throughout the region during and after the war against the French thus brought the collapse of industrial and agricultural production and when this was followed by the loss of the American markets for Catalan textiles (America took two-thirds of the output), paper, brandy, almonds, cork and other goods, bankruptcies and unemployment were soon evident.[8] Exports to America from Catalan ports in 1815–19 were a seventh of what they had been in 1803 or 1804.[9] The Barcelona Junta de Comercio appealed for help. Thousands of families all over the province, it said, were destitute because there was no work. Factories were closed, workers dismissed and there was poverty and misery everywhere. There was no way Catalan industry could compete with foreign competition and there was no home market for their goods because consumers throughout the country were impoverished. A protectionist tariff was essential and Cádiz was mistaken in its belief that trade with America could ever be revived.[10]

It is clear that for the merchants of Cádiz and the merchants, manufacturers and farmers of Catalonia, the separation of America caused profound difficulties. We know little in detail about the specific effects on other regions but a similar situation seems to have prevailed. In Andalucía, for example, the textile industry of Córdoba and Puerto de Santa María, already reeling from the pressure of foreign competition, could not withstand the added blow of the loss of the American markets. Much of the industry, especially in cotton, disappeared altogether. Seville, once the flourishing capital of the colonial trade, was also badly hit. Its silk industry fell from 16,000 looms to 2,500 and production of other articles declined by two-thirds.[11] Unlike their colleagues in Cádiz or Barcelona, the Seville merchants were producers and exporters of their own merchandize to the colonies, 'authentic direct exporters of the products of artisan industry', as Professor Bernal has described them.[12] With their markets in America gone, they tried to find alternative outlets in

Europe but to no avail. Forty-eight bankruptcies occurred in the city between 1807 and 1821 and the established merchant community was virtually destroyed.

It must be emphasized, of course, that in those areas like Seville in which the empire was of relatively marginal interest compared with Cádiz, the independence of America was not the sole cause of their economic difficulties; rather it was the final straw which exposed the fundamental weakness and inefficiency of Spain's economy. The position is well illustrated in the case of Antonio Ximeno. One of the founders of Seville's new *consulado* in 1784, he had developed a successful business through international trade with North and Central Europe, America and within the peninsula. He was a large-scale property owner, particularly of farming land which provided much of the wool, wine and oil he used in his commercial activities and he traded in a variety of other goods. His success brought him many material comforts, for example, three *coches birloches* and one *berlina*, and he was a well respected, established figure in Seville's bourgeoisie. By 1815, he began to tell his multiple creditors that he was in difficulty. Among the reasons, he said, was the losses he had sustained with his business in America. His merchandize, exported mainly to Lima, could not be disposed of because of the revolutions and hence he had no funds coming back from his investments in the colonies. There were other contributory factors, for example, the fall in wool prices in England, and Ximeno was forced into bankruptcy in 1816, after which it took almost twenty years to sort out his affairs.[13]

The Ximeno case may well have been typical of the experiences of producers of products for the colonial markets across the peninsula, but, although the statistics of decline are available, we lack information on what happened to the farmers, landowners, manufacturers and others who found that they no longer had American customers to buy their products. It has already been indicated that the exports of brandy collapsed. It is not known, however, what became of the individual producers, their equipment or their workforce. Chile alone imported some forty different types of Spanish goods – textiles from Valencia, Murcia and Granada; textiles, paper, hats and hardware from Catalonia; books from Madrid; linen from Galicia; crockery from Alcora, Seville, Málaga and Talavera.[14] In every province of the realm, small workshops and crafts of every description found that the demand for their wares had disappeared, at least in America, and, presumably, they had to find alternative markets or go out of business.

Certainly, it may be stated in general terms that many ceased production. In July 1820, Canga Argüelles gave the Cortes some details, approximate only he admitted, of a few products. In 1799, 49,000,000 *arrobas* of wines had been produced and in 1818, 37,000,000; production of olive oil had decreased from 6,000,000 *arrobas* to 3,000,000; and *sogas y barrillas* from 214,161 *quintales* to 6,983 in 1815.[15]

While little information is available of the fate of those people who provided the merchandize for the colonial trade, it is possible to trace the fortunes of some of the import–export merchants who earned their living from organizing its sale and distribution. As indicated, bankruptcies occurred in Cádiz, Seville and elsewhere. In Barcelona also, there was much insolvency and, fortunately, the records of many of the city's merchants have been preserved.[16] They reveal the experiences of largely Catalan companies throughout the years of revolution in America, the problems they faced, their attitudes towards the rebels and the sometimes desperate devices to which they resorted in an attempt to preserve their fortunes and their businesses.

Cristóbal Roig y Vidal headed a company with a large network of agents and associates, often family relatives, in the Americas and in important European commercial centres. The company dealt in the usual colonial products of sugar, cotton and other agricultural goods and exported diverse cargoes from Spain. Increasingly, however, the business was affected by the danger of pirates, operating not only in the American hemisphere but also in the Mediterranean.[17] By July 1816, Roig was writing to an associate at Genoa that the situation with the pirates was so bad that it was no longer safe to send ships flying the Spanish flag to America. His solution was one to which other Spanish merchants had resorted to stay in business. He had, he said, control of an excellent ship in port at Barcelona which he wished to send to Havana or Montevideo but it would have to sail under a British flag. He asked if this could be arranged and added that it would also be necessary to find British sailors for at least half the crew. To make absolutely certain that the Spanish ownership of the vessel would not be discovered, he suggested that its owner would make a simulated sale of it to the Genoa-based company. This would then provide the crew, decide what cargo should be carried, and share in the profits.[18] On the same day, Roig also wrote to Bland and Co. at Gibraltar offering the same deal. They would 'buy' the ship and provide a British flag and crew.[19]

The result of Roig's attempt to get round the pirate problem by
using a British flag is not known, but certainly this was one solution
which seems to have been fairly widespread among Spanish merchants, both on the outward and the return journeys. Not all the
merchants resorted to simulated sales. As indicated in the previous
chapter, some obtained special permits from government officials and
during the early 1820s, when there was a scramble to retrieve
investments in America, many petitioned the Cortes. For example,
the Barcelona company of Vilardaga, Juliá y Reinals, asked to be
allowed to receive a cargo of cotton brought in on the United States
ship *Manufactor*, being the property of Mariano Serra y Soler and
Bernardo Estrada who had fled from Chile. At Santander, Joaquín
Villalva and partners imported cacao from Guayaquil on an English-
owned ship and they also were excused the premium imposed on
foreign flags.[20]

Cristóbal Roig was also not lacking in other ideas in his efforts to
make profits. In September 1816, he instructed his agent at Mahon to
buy and send him all the small arms, cannon and munitions that he
could acquire. Very few ships were leaving for America at that time,
he said, but soon the new wine crop would be arriving and shipping
would then pick up. Arms would be needed for protection and he
would sell them.[21] Whether he was able to make money from this arms
dealing is not known, but within a month or so he was becoming
increasingly disillusioned with the difficulties of trying to trade with
America. He wrote to a nephew in Havana that the risks involved
were now too great and he strongly advised him to put his money into
land. Even so, he went on, there was still one trading activity which
did justify the risks. This was the slave trade with Africa which yielded
at least 25 per cent more profit than ordinary cargoes. He had, he
admitted, an interest in several slaver expeditions and intended to
invest in more.[22]

Although in 1817 Spain was in the final stages of negotiations with
Britain to end the slave trade in return for some £400,000 compensation which Ferdinand used as a deposit on the notorious Russian fleet,
there is no doubt that Barcelona merchants continued to participate
in it as their problems with the colonies became more and more acute.
It is clear from the Roig correspondence of May–June 1817 that the
firm was preparing an expedition to Africa to obtain a cargo of slaves
destined for Lima. A branch of a Cuba-based company had an
interest in it, as did the ship's captain and pilot.[23] On 2 August 1817,

Roig wrote to Marseilles to enquire the insurance rates for an armed brigantine going to Guinea and then Havana with a cargo of slaves. In another letter a few days later, he again emphasized that under no circumstances could the ship sail under the Spanish flag, nor was there to be any evidence available of the Spanish interest in it, because of the danger from pirates.[24] Once more the result of this project is not known but Roig was still involved in probable slave trading expeditions in 1822. In July of that year, he corresponded with a firm in Genoa concerning possible insurance rates for two ships going to Zanzibar and then on to Havana. The company replied that nobody would now insure Spanish ships going to America and Roig eventually had to settle for the high insurance available at Cádiz.[25] Obtaining insurance cover became increasingly difficult for all Spanish merchants as the war in America and especially the piracy danger spread. Rates obviously increased at Cádiz which was the main centre for insurance on the transatlantic route, and also in the various other European cities where the Barcelona merchants tried to get cover. It was in 1822 that Roig finally decided to withdraw from the American trade. He instructed his diverse agents and relatives in America to wind up his affairs and remit his capital to Europe.[26]

The retrieval of capital from the colonies during these years of war was no easy matter. Roig, and most other Barcelona merchants, seem to have been able to overcome the problem in one of two ways. The most secure was to ship bullion or specie in a British vessel, and several of the companies had banking agents in London. The alternative, and this was used by Roig from 1816, was to invest the cash in produce on the grounds that the pirates were rarely interested in commodities which involved evident difficulties of disposal. In November 1816, Roig told his brother, Juan, who was based in Havana, never to remit the firm's profits in coinage. Instead, he was to invest any funds in cargoes of sugar or coffee and, for even greater security, to try to ship this produce in either an American, British or French vessel going to Trieste, Marseilles or Genoa. The cargo was to be registered in the names of three separate individuals. As Roig pointed out, apart from reducing the risks from pirates, additional profit could always be made from its sale in Europe.[27]

Another family firm which used this same method of investing its funds in colonial produce to get its capital back from America was that of Domingo Parés y Cía. The Barcelona branch, headed by the son, Ramón, wrote to the father at Cádiz in May 1814 that it was indeed a good idea to order their agents at Veracruz to invest their funds in grain and sugar from Havana, remitting the cargoes on several ships so as to reduce the risk of total loss.[28] Similarly, in 1816 Alfonso Arenas shipped barrels of red wine, sacks of hazelnuts and almonds and a quantity of olive oil valued at over 7,000 pesos. 'I decided not to expose this sum', he wrote, 'to the great risk from the pirates.' He also told his agent to spend the money on sugar, to be dispatched in several different vessels.[29]

The correspondence of the Valentín Riera company reveals other problems the merchants faced. His firm conducted a substantial trade with the United States as well as with the colonies. Its letter-books start in 1805 and continue to May 1810, after which there is a gap of four years to June 1814. Like many other merchants, the company was forced to cease almost all its activities when the invading French armies occupied Barcelona. Writing to Jos Bell and Jos Watson at Philadelphia on 24 August 1814, a few weeks after reopening for business, Riera reported that 'trade in this side is not yet systemized on account of the extraordinary prejudices occasioned by the arbitrary and despotical government of the French who swallowed the fortunes of the inhabitants where their forces predominated, for which reason there is much trouble in recovery of the debts contracted in the beginning of the revolution'.[30] Clearly, the French invasion posed a major problem for the merchants, many of whom quickly moved to Tarragona where their guild was temporarily established. When Tarragona fell to the French, the more determined established themselves in Mallorca and the Cádiz Regency government authorized Palma as a port for the American trade for the duration of the war in Catalonia. At least one company did not recover from the disruption which these enforced moves entailed. This traded under the name of Caruana, Ciappino y Cía and in 1811 it was operating from Valencia and Palma. By 1815, because of the losses sustained as a result of the French invasion, the company was insolvent and attempts were begun to sort out the accounts. Writing from Barcelona on 3 January 1818, the owner stated that he was now virtually destitute and had a wife and seven children to feed. Moreover, his eldest son, a ship's captain, just as he had been making some progress in restoring the family fortunes, had been captured by pirates and had lost everything.[31]

Despite such losses caused by the French, the Riera firm survived and appears to have been one of the few remaining which continued to be interested in the Buenos Aires market. Writing to John Hodge at Marseilles in 1816, Riera said that he had been reliably informed that ships of all nations were being admitted there 'without having the least hindrance for going in and coming out thence'. Many articles were in short supply in Buenos Aires and therefore highly profitable; for example, brandy, black silk handkerchiefs, satin ribbons 'from half to two inches wide, the narrowest are more saleable, black and white are not so preferred', French silk stockings, paper fans, 'Straps of three branches to keep up the breeches, strings of guitar 4th, 5th and 6th', candlesticks, white writing paper and 'silk girdles, crimson and other colours'.[32]

The merchants who were heavily involved in the Argentine trade probably suffered the greatest losses of all those in the colonial markets, partly as a result of the policies and actions of the rebel administrations which controlled Buenos Aires continuously after 1810. Many no doubt tried to save their investments but it is likely that few were successful. One exception may have been the Gaspar Soler company which was able to write to an agent in Madrid in October 1815, with obvious relief, that information just received from two gentlemen recently arrived from Buenos Aires had confirmed that its assets there had not been lost, although they had not been able to get them out of the province because its authorities had threatened the death penalty against anyone caught exporting funds belonging to Spaniards. Nevertheless, one of the recent arrivals was returning shortly and would be able to realize the capital and return it.[33] Not everyone in this family was so fortunate. Writing in the following year, 1816, he excused the delay in the firm's correspondence which was the result of a family tragedy. An aunt, whose eldest son had recently died and all of whose assets were in America and had now been lost, had committed suicide by throwing herself from the third floor of her house.[34]

Another family firm which suffered from its involvement with Buenos Aires in particular and America in general was owned by the Catalá family. The father, Juan, was one of the few Barcelona merchants who was also a textile manufacturer, specializing in silk products which he shipped mainly to Buenos Aires before 1810.[35] By 1812, he had reached the conclusion that it was prudent to end his connection with America and he wrote to several firms in Buenos Aires asking them to realize all his assets there, invest the money in hides and send these to Cádiz in batches of one thousand per ship between May and November, preferably registering the cargoes in names other than his own. He wrote in the same vein to Cartagena, asking for his capital to be put into a cargo of cotton and also to Puerto Rico where he wanted cacao but not coffee. Again, whether he was successful in getting his capital back in this way is not known, although several years later in 1819, he was warned that he could expect little of what he was owed from the estate of a deceased business partner at Veracruz.[36]

As was perhaps to be expected, few of these merchants expressed in their business correspondence much comment on political events in the peninsula or Europe at large, but there is no doubt, and in this respect they often did express a view, that they shared the commonly held opinion that the revolutions in America were the traitorous work of an ambitious and unprincipled minority. The records of one company, however, prove the exception to this absence of political comment. Manuel and Ramón Llano y Chávarri were from the Basque province of Alava from where they emigrated to Mexico, probably in the year 1800.[37] The two brothers formed a partnership in 1804 and during the next decade or so built up a substantial commercial enterprise, trading within the viceroyalty of New Spain and in the import–export cycle with the peninsula. Presumably because of the political situation in the colony, some time in 1816 they decided to return to Spain and after spending some time in France, partly to assess the opportunities there, they settled in Barcelona which henceforth became the base of their operations. By 1819 they had established an international network of agents, employees and associates. In Mexico City, their brother remained the principal representative. At Veracruz there were formal and informal partnerships with several merchants, most important of which were Cayetano Canaleta and Buenaventura Mandri. At Havana, their close friend and partner was Domingo Martorell, himself a member of a large trading house. In London, there was Joaquín Ruíz de Alzedo who until 1825 was the main banker of the firm's profits from the American trade. Naturally, within Spain the associates were many and varied. Among the most prominent was a cousin, Francisco Antonio, in Madrid, and in the key port of Cádiz, Juan Bautista Dotres who was the father-in-law of Ramón.

The company's American interests were normally within the Cádiz–Havana–Veracruz triangle and the brothers seem to have been willing to deal in more or less any product on which there was profit to be made. The Catalonian hinterland provided much of the produce and purchasing agents were employed throughout the region. At Reus, the agent was responsible for buying mainly almonds, hazelnuts and some wine. In Valencia, Juan Sagristá provided access to local products as and when they were required and articles such as paper items were obtained from La Riba, Tarragona and elsewhere. One factory owner at Calella, Salvador Guitart, sold his entire production of stockings exclusively to the Llano y Chávarri firm and other textile manufacturers at Mataró, Olot and elsewhere supplied various merchandize.[38] Goods were also obtained from Madrid and other areas of the peninsula as well as from France. Although occasionally the cargoes were shipped directly to Havana from Barcelona, it was more usual to send them first to Cádiz where Dotres arranged the transport and insurance. Once in Havana or Veracruz, they were sold and the funds used to purchase return cargoes of sugar, grain, tobacco, cacao and any other colonial produce for which there was a profitable market in Europe.

During 1819 and 1820 the two brothers prospered with regular and profitable shipments of a variety of goods.[39] By early 1821, however, their correspondence reveals growing concern with the political events in Europe and in America and the increasing difficulties of trade. In a letter to Martorell at Havana in January 1821, Ramón reported that the market at Veracruz was stagnant and that Canaleta had not been able to dispose of any of the stock from the warehouse. Until the situation was clearer, they had decided to proceed cautiously and to make no further shipments for the time being. To Rafael de Villalobos, an associate at San Luis Potosí, Ramón said he did not think it prudent for the moment to meet his order for one hundred bales of paper because the situation in Europe was verging on general war. He also authorized Canaleta at Veracruz to sell the textiles he had on credit because of the difficulty he was having in disposing of them. As for the Mexican rebels, they would never, he insisted, get their independence but even so, prudence and tact were advisable.[40]

By June 1821 this mood of caution had become rather more pessimistic. Writing to Francisco in Mexico City, Ramón expressed his reluctance to make further shipments to Mexico because of news they had recently received from Canaleta. In a letter of his from Veracruz, dated 20 February 1821, he had written as follows: 'This country is now destroyed and is daily getting worse with the emigration of so many honourable men because of the deplorable state of all America which in my opinion is lost.' Furthermore, their nephew, Francisco Gámez, who had just returned from Mexico, had told them 'that those dominions are taking giant steps towards separation and as the first action is always the sacrifice of Europeans and their fortunes, it is a sensible precaution for them to safeguard their capital in places offering more security than New Spain'. Everyone was so concerned about what might happen in America that they dared not send various goods which they had had in store in Cádiz for the past three months.[41] From Havana, Martorell had written in April warning that the situation in New Spain was deteriorating rapidly. The viceroy had taken 'very energetic measures' which permitted some optimism but if they failed, the fate of the kingdom was sealed.[42]

These warnings and predictions of imminent disaster seem to have brought the two brothers to a crucial decision. They began writing in June 1821 to associates at Veracruz instructing them to sell off all their assets and arrange for the transfer of the proceeds to Europe. They were now convinced, Ramón said, 'that all our overseas possessions are lost and we will have great difficulty even in retaining the islands'. They urged Mandri to sell everything, even at a loss if necessary, and return to Spain before it was too late. Trade with America was no longer worth the risks involved.[43] The confirmation of Iturbide's rebellion reached Barcelona in June and more letters were dispatched with instructions to wind up the company's affairs. Canaleta was told to try to exchange the textiles for indigo, grain or anything else if he could not sell them and their brother Francisco was advised that independence was inevitable and that he should sell up and return home.[44]

During the remainder of 1821, the firm's correspondence contains more and more references to the situation in New Spain and, among other things, reveals the intense contempt and mistrust the brothers had for the Mexican rebels and their leaders. Writing to Martorell in September 1821, Ramón predicted that an armistice would soon be signed with Iturbide but that his policy of conciliation towards Spaniards was no more than an expedient to gain full independence. Nevertheless, any period of peace, however brief, was just what Spaniards in America needed because it would give them an opportunity to rescue their capital and leave. The firm would not send any more goods because the Mexicans just could not be trusted. By 28

November, news of the treaties of Córdoba, signed in August by
Iturbide and the recently arrived Spanish *jefe político*, Juan O'Donojú,
had been received but Ramón had little faith in its promises. If
Americans were aware of morality, he wrote to Martorell, and of their
own interests, the treaties would guarantee their welfare and ours, but
their real intentions were only too well known. It was still their view
that America was lost. Cuba might well be the next to revolt and
Martorell should begin to wind up their affairs on the island. A few
weeks later, writing to Veracruz, Ramón spoke of the 'fearful anarchy'
which was to be anticipated in New Spain in view of the Mexican
character and inability to accept any form of government or live in
peace over a long period.[45]

By January 1822, the brothers were convinced that there was no
future for Spaniards in America. The Mexicans were imbued with a
deep hatred for Spaniards and they should all get out while they
could. They themselves had definitely decided to terminate all trade
with the country and they were sending their nephew, Francisco
Gámez, to the colony to settle their affairs. Ten days later, Ramón
seemed even more alarmed at developments and again urged his
brother Francisco to leave before it was too late. He reminded him of
the fate of Spaniards in Buenos Aires when that province separated
from Spain. He should settle everything at once, even at a loss, for his
life was worth more than any profit. Also, he added, he would not
write in future so frankly about Mexico because he had no doubt that
the new authorities there would be opening private correspondence
and his views might well endanger his brother's safety.[46]

The experience of the Llano y Chávarri company and those
previously described afford some insight into the effects of the
American revolutions on individuals and the difficulties they faced as
they struggled to survive. To some extent, the merchants in Barcelona
were more fortunate than their colleagues at Cádiz because they were
not wholly or even largely dependent on America. They were
international merchants active in markets wherever profits were to be
made, including the slave trade, and as such they had the essential
contacts in Europe and the United States which enabled at least some
of them to transfer their activities to other areas once the colonial
sphere became too dangerous or closed to them. Nevertheless, by the
same token they were more susceptible to national and international
economic pressures and in common with their colleagues across the
peninsula their most vociferous complaint was always about the level

of taxation imposed on them. The committee of *consulado* representatives had calculated that the various levies on exports to America amounted to 61 per cent and there were all manner of other taxes, forced loans and contributions to be met, not least those imposed on behalf of the Comisión de Reemplazos to meet the costs of the military effort in the colonies. The little evidence available seems to confirm that outside of Cádiz, the merchants and indeed all other property owners greatly resented the demands made on them by the central government and they saw little reason why they should continue to contribute large amounts of their scarce profits to a futile attempt to reconquer the empire. Scholars have recently suggested that it was the realization by the bourgeois class that the régime was incapable of recovering America or restructuring the national economy that persuaded them to support uprisings against Ferdinand and the *ancien régime* in particular, and the known presence of merchants in anti-Ferdinand conspiracies seems to confirm this interpretation.[47]

The burden of taxation which increased substantially during Ferdinand's reign despite Garay's effort to reform it was a direct reflection of the crisis in the colonies, because Spain had traditionally relied on the taxation of commerce and trade for a major proportion of national revenues. With the paralysis of commercial activity in the domestic economy and the collapse in overseas trade, as well as the virtual destruction of the once-rich American mining industry, national income fell accordingly. In 1796 the customs had yielded 233,680,954 *reales*; in 1821, the amount was down to 80,993,329 *reales*.[48] The Minister of Hacienda told the Cortes that national revenue in the financial year from June 1821 to June 1822 had been estimated to be 765,000,000 *reales* but only 352,939,064 had been collected. From America, it had been expected to receive 60,000,000 *reales* but a mere 60,000 had been forthcoming.[49] Needless to say, the national debt, already a heavy burden on the exchequer, increased and the government found more and more difficulty in meeting the demands on it. Among these were claims for salaries and pensions from the military and bureaucratic personnel returning from the overseas provinces. In a mood of generosity and perhaps wounded pride, the Cortes had decreed that the salaries of displaced colonial officials should be continued on their return to the metropolis and the Treasury set aside the sum of 10,000,000 *reales* to meet that commitment. It was not enough, the Minister told the Cortes in June 1822, because 'battalions of employees, both military and Treasury, were arriving', and there was not a ship returning from America that did not bring 150 or 200 emigrants from Lima, Venezuela and all the rebel provinces. Again what happened to the mass of these individuals is unknown, although as deputy Vicente Salvá suggested, it is likely that they joined the ranks of the nation's growing number of *cesantes*, or unemployed civil servants.[50]

Some of the returning military, however, especially veterans of the Peruvian campaigns, despite early hostility towards them and accusations of cowardice or treachery at Ayacucho, were able to resume their careers. Among many who attained senior positions in the army and in national political life in later years were Rafael Maroto, appointed in 1838 commander-in-chief of the Carlist armies of the north during the first Carlist war (1833–9); Generals I. Alaix and Ramón Rodil, both ministers in the 1830s and 1840s; and the nation's first military dictator (1840–3), Baldomero Espartero. According to the contemporary press, some of these *ayacuchos*, as they became known, were, as Carr puts it, 'a particularly cohesive group' and it is possible that they formed a kind of informal military clique for mutual support based on their shared experiences in America. Certainly, *ayacuchismo* in the late 1830s and during Espartero's Regency became an important phenomenon in the political turmoil of the time and was deemed worthy of a novel by Galdós, *Los Ayacuchos*.

The disintegration of the empire was, therefore, visible for all to see in both material and personal terms. The collapse of manufacturing and agricultural production, commerce and shipping, the poverty and unemployment, the widespread individual bankruptcy as well as the chronic fiscal situation at the national level; indeed, all the indicators seemed to confirm that the revolutions in America had contributed towards, if not directly produced, a major crisis in the nation's history. Yet, although few Spaniards ever lost or gave up hope that in some way the empire could be reconstructed, either by force or by negotiation, there were those who believed that the final end of Spain's role as a major imperial power was a blessing in disguise. They advanced the thesis, debated in fact since the seventeenth century, that America had always been a burden, depriving the peninsula of its population, its skills and its capital to such an extent that it had had a negative rather than positive effect on the country's development. In 1822, the newspaper *El Independiente* contained the following:

the Americas were always onerous to Spain; far from producing clear benefits, only courtiers took advantage of them, who obtained its vice-regencies and intendancies. National commerce drew no other profit from them than the sale of a few favoured products. If the necessary passage of a few foreign goods through our customs left a niggardly commission, most times [it fell into] foreign hands.[51]

Another paper, *El Espectador*, thought the burden of the colonies was responsible for the crisis in the Treasury which in turn was the main danger to the constitutional system. Hernán Cortés, the paper declared, had brought more glory than real benefit to Spain.[52] A decade later, George Flinter, a high-ranking army officer and author of several works on the revolutions, wrote that the American continent had been the 'graveyard of Spanish industry for three centuries' and that were it not for independence, the metropolis would have become a colony of the colonies.[53] His pamphlet circulated widely and was influential in forming opinion in the years of the imperial post-mortem and his views were well supported by other politicians and commentators. In 1835, for example, one newspaper declared that the possession of America 'never caused more than our ruin and our impoverishment'.[54] José Canga Argüelles, former Treasury Minister and active political figure throughout the years of war, wrote in an article published in 1842 that the colonization of America had brought ruin to the towns and cities of Spain. The once-great trade fairs at Burgos and Medina del Campo had been destroyed and the wealth that had come from the colonies had been dissipated in what he called 'a regrettable ostentation of opulence' whereby Spaniards had spent their money on useless, imported luxury goods rather than investing it in productive enterprise. For centuries Spain had been no more than a channel through which foreign manufactures from France, England, Holland and elsewhere were transported to America and while the import–export merchants grew rich on this trade and foreign industry flourished, Spain had sunk into industrial stagnation.[55]

The controversy regarding the beneficial or harmful effects of the once-massive imports of silver was also resurrected. As one writer put it, 'the gold of America was everything and Spanish industry and labour almost nothing'. 'The treasures of Mexico and Peru extinguished the torch of our genius', proclaimed a newspaper in 1835.[56] The dependence on silver was said to have brought inflation, decimated industry, prevented investment and suppressed the entrepreneurial spirit of the Spanish people. Moreover, it was not just in the economic sphere that America had damaged the Mother Country. Illusions of imperial grandeur had made Spaniards lazy and torpid and had been a significant factor in the rising despotism of the kingdom's rulers. With American wealth at their disposal, kings had become less dependent on the Cortes and the traditional rights of the people had been oppressed. Since the reign of Charles V (1517–56), 'despotism was victorious and American treasure, if not the only, was at least the main reason'.[57] The Inquisition was one institution which had increased its power because of the extension of its functions to America and, as for the merchants who had gained so much profit, 'after routine trips, after putting into uncultured ports, after wrenching gold from nascent societies in exchange for trinkets, [he] returned to his country more despotic, more wealthy, more cruel but not more independent and enlightened'.[58] After all was said and done, another writer maintained, what we received from America was venereal disease, yellow fever and the vomit. Also it was the destruction of industry, agriculture and commerce which caused the enormous increase in the number of unproductive clergy, military, lawyers and celibates which had been so harmful to economic progress.[59]

These people welcomed the end of imperial responsibilities and foresaw the dawn of a new era of economic emancipation for Spain. Spaniards would now have to invest their capital in industry rather than trade. Commodities imported for so long would be produced at home or given even greater stimulus in the remaining loyal island colonies. Private initiative and enterprise would once again flourish as it had done before the discovery of America. 'We must', advised a newspaper article of 1821, 'work as if there were no longer America and count on our inexhaustible earthly fountain of riches and transport ourselves in our imagination back to the fifteenth century.'[60] In 1853, the Royal Academy of History held a competition for the best essay on the influence of America on Spain's economic development. The winning entry by José Arías, published as a book the following year, strongly supported this view that America had been a constant and oppressive burden on the peninsula. Since its separation, there had been a revival in the long-lost natural skills, industry and inventiveness of the Spanish people who were now producing the goods on which future prosperity depended.[61]

Not everybody, of course, adopted this view that America had brought so much ruin in so many ways. There were those who were in no doubt that the loss of the empire was a catastrophe for the monarchy. P. Martínez said it was absurd to argue that American silver had harmed industry and Javier de Burgos ridiculed the idea that the colonies had been of no benefit. It would take centuries, he thought, for the country to recover from the blow and stand on its own.[62] José Presas, in another influential book published in 1828, argued that since Spain had lost control of America, its factories had been ruined, its crafts and industry crippled, its agriculture depressed, the working classes unemployed and the entire country 'in the utmost poverty'.[63] Many other writers blamed the decline in industrial and agricultural production on the virtual disappearance of the American markets and, in the 1830s, following the death of Ferdinand, the pressure to recognize the independence of the new republics was almost always associated with predictions of substantial economic benefits to be gained from a renewal of commercial relations. As Jacinto Salas y Quiroga put it in 1838, Americans were used to Spanish products and after a decade or so of sampling foreign alternatives, they wanted their old supplies restored. Peruvians, he said, liked Catalan wines, not those of Oporto; they wanted their silks from Valencia, not from Lyons; their iron from the Basque country, not from Cornwall. Spain must, he continued, take advantage of these inherited tastes and preferences, recognize independence and resume trading with the Americans.[64] The same opinion was commonly expressed in the press; the 'rebirth of our navigation and commerce,' declared one paper, would follow a renewal of relations and the Council of Government reached the same conclusion:

Let us not lose time in taking advantage of the principal recourse which remains for reviving our commerce, agriculture and industry. The Council does not find a more effective and expeditious measure than that of re-establishing the commercial relations between Spain and the dissident provinces of America.[65]

For one group of people, the value or otherwise of possessing an empire was a particularly sensitive topic. Having loudly insisted for years, and indeed for generations, that Spain would be destroyed if it lost its dominion in America, the merchants, including those at Cádiz, were prepared to allow, in what they called the 'famous question' of the day, that the ultimate balance of benefit might be against the Mother Country. We have bought many things from the colonies, they said, that we could have acquired more cheaply from other places and while we have sold foreign-made textiles to Americans, there was scarcely one of the 12,000,000 Spaniards who did not buy American chocolate, sugar or leather.[66] The Comisión de Reemplazos, desperate for reconquest, also accepted that the conquest and colonization of the New World had been prejudicial to the peninsula, depriving it of its population, industry and skills. Also, the ambitions of other powers to get possessions on the American continent had involved Spain in numerous, costly wars which had drained it of its resources. With the consequent decline of domestic industry, Spaniards had been forced to become commission agents for foreigners but this meant that the colonial markets were now essential for the few goods that were produced.[67] The Catalans had their own viewpoint on the subject. Nothing is more certain, declared the Barcelona entrepreneurs, than that Spain neglected the wealth of its own soil for the riches of the transatlantic trade but all the benefits went to Cádiz and the rest of the kingdom was treated as a foreigner. It was only when the Cádiz monopoly was broken and other provinces allowed to participate in the trade that some benefits for the nation as a whole were felt.[68]

The *consulado* representatives disagreed.[69] There were many causes for the ills of Spain, they said, but possession of America was not one of them. Rather they were the result of wars in Europe, the increase in privileged, unproductive classes, the excessive wealth of the Church, the expulsion of the Moriscos, neglect of education and bad tax policies. Spain had ignored America to its cost. It was only with American treasure that the European empire in the Netherlands and Italy had been kept for so long and as for the allegation that population loss had occurred because of the colonization, that was illogical. Populations, they argued, expand or decline according to the wealth of the environment and only when poverty prevails do people emigrate. The loss of population, therefore, was the effect, not the cause, of national decline and nine-tenths of those who had gone to the colonies had been from Galicia, Asturias, Vizcaya and Catalonia which were now the most populous provinces in the land.

Such arguments concerning the economic significance of the empire and the consequences of its loss intrude and persist in most of the analyses which were made from the early 1820s onwards. The structural changes and adjustments that may have occurred as the country adapted to its non-imperial role are areas which remain to the investigated. In recent years, economic historians have begun to analyse some aspects, particularly regarding Catalonia, and it seems clear that in Barcelona the reinvestment of capital retrieved from the colonies during and immediately after the revolutions played a

significant part in the revitalization of Catalan industry and agriculture. The Llano y Chávarri brothers, for example, were successful in
rescuing at least some of their assets and bringing them back to
Europe, where part was invested in urban and rural properties and
the rest used to finance continued trading within Spain, buying grains
from the Santander and Seville regions and selling largely Catalan
wines and other products. Similarly, it appears to be accepted that the
recovery in the Catalan textile industry which expanded rapidly in
the 1830s was partly financed by reinvested capital brought from
America.

Professor Fontana, among others, has suggested some broader
effects.[70] With the loss of colonial imports to sell to the rest of the world,
Spain's balance of trade, rarely if ever in surplus, went into serious
deficit. In the past this had been compensated for by the import of
American bullion, but the loss of this once lucrative source of revenue
served to exacerbate the increased deficit in the trade in goods. The
country's imports thus had to be paid for in money and this brought a
severe shortage of currency – by 1842 almost half the coinage in
circulation was French – which in turn contributed to the deflationary
spiral reflecting and causing the general economic crisis. The large
variety of Spanish products which could no longer be shipped to the
American continent could not be absorbed in the depressed domestic
market. This led to a basic shift in the structure of the economy with
the agricultural-based central provinces becoming consumers of the
manufactured commodities of the peripheral regions. In short, Spain
was obliged to seek ways of adapting to a peninsular-centred,
integrated trade cycle and this had innumerable implications concerning land distribution, transport, communications and the other
aspects of the infrastructure, which were to be the business of future
generations of politicians, landowners and industrialists.

Whatever the underlying changes that did take place, there is no
doubt that the loss of the empire caused a painful, perhaps ultimately
beneficial, process of adaptation for many of Spain's emerging
bourgeoisie. It has been suggested that the popularity of the view,
expressed so often in the 1820s and 1830s, that the end of imperial
responsibility was to be welcomed, was because it served as a
convenient palliative to lessen the sense of loss which Spaniards might
otherwise have felt when they realized that their empire was gone
for ever.[71] Certainly, while other European nations were busy seeking
to establish overseas dominions, Spaniards read in their newspapers
and in their books that imperial power did more harm than good.

7

A new relationship

The revolutions in America could not be suppressed by military means and Spaniards were unwilling to countenance any significant measure of economic reform. It was, however, a time of ideological ferment and radical political change, with bourgeois reformers challenging the powers and privileges of the established institutions and the very constitutional basis of the *ancien régime*. They wanted to dismantle much of the institutional structure of the past and to create in its place their version of the modern, secular state resting on the twin foundations of civil equality and popular sovereignty. They were political revolutionaries and it is not surprising, therefore, that some believed that a form of political accommodation with the insurgents was always possible and that a new relationship with the overseas territories could be forged. They did not think in terms of independence for the empire because in their new order of things, the emancipation of their American brothers was neither necessary nor desirable. Nor, indeed, would Americans want to be independent when they fully appreciated and understood the benefits they were to receive once the mistakes of the past were rectified, abuses corrected and honest government restored.

The utopia on the horizon would take time to achieve and the reformers understood that it was important to allow Americans to participate in the evolutionary process. But what should that participation be, what form should it take and who exactly in America should be invited to contribute to the building of the new society? As heirs to the strong centralizing tendency of the eighteenth century, the politicians at Cádiz could only conceive a continuation of that tradition whereby their new-found freedoms and egalitarian privileges emanated from and were protected by the centre of the empire. But that brought other dilemmas. If something was good for the peninsula, was it necessarily good for the diverse and different overseas provinces? Moreover, was it needed, wanted or safe to give such liberties? Should all reforms be applied uniformly across the empire? Popular sovereignty was the cardinal principle of the new era, but did that mean that non-Spanish-speaking Indians, illiterate castes, negroes and the wild men of the pampas had the same rights as white, God-fearing Spaniards living in Valencia or Santander?

Political change was clearly no easy matter and whatever reforms were proposed in American rights or in the government of the empire, there was ever present one paramount consideration: the unity of the kingdom had to be preserved. If the seditious events of 1810 had not taken place at Caracas, Buenos Aires and elsewhere before the doors of the Cortes were opened on 24 September, then perhaps the liberals might have been willing to extend some of their sacred principles to the American people. But by the time the ideological revolution began at Cádiz, a state of war in effect existed between metropolis and empire and informed Spaniards were well aware that this was no ordinary protest to correct a wrong, but a serious attempt at independence. Hence, just as reforms in the economic field were evaluated, any change in the status or rights of Americans could only be assessed in the context of its probable effect on the insurgents and the support they were attracting. Ideological or even constitutional principles were important but, however much so, they could not be allowed to contribute to the disintegration of the empire. Pragmatism, in short, was to prevail over principle and the reformers in both periods of constitutional government found themselves obliged to seek some way of reconciling their sincerely held beliefs with the reality of revolution in America.

For some of the constitutionalists and certainly for Ferdinand and his supporters, there was no need for any radical and separate political reappraisal of the relationship between metropolis and empire. Each side felt that its respective political system offered the solution to the American problem. It did not perhaps offer a complete solution but certainly provided the basic framework within which American needs and complaints could be readily satisfied. While in 1814, Ferdinand may have wanted to turn the clock back to 1808 as far as Spain was concerned, he and his ministers came fully to recognize that changes were required if the alleged causes of colonial discontent were to be removed, and the liberal governments quickly reached the same conclusion. They knew soon after 1810 that there was little or no hope of persuading the diehard, and astute, rebel leaders to lay down their arms, but they did believe it possible and practical to destroy the basis of their popular support by offering reforms in several areas of colonial life.

As always, there was no agreement on exactly what reforms should be offered to Americans and each that was proposed was immediately controversial. The most direct source of information as to what was needed came from the Americans themselves, both from the colonies and, more important, from the American deputies to the Cortes and American-born advisers resident in the peninsula. Their case for change rested on the promise made to them by the Spanish authorities in the months following the French invasion. Well aware that Napoleon was trying to subvert Spanish dominion in America and that the collapse of the legitimate monarchy in the metropolis was stretching the constitutional bonds of imperial unity to breaking-point, the Junta Central and its successor, the Regency, had made what seemed like substantial concessions. Both declared that hence-forth the American territories were no longer colonies, 'but an essential and integral part of the Spanish monarchy', and that Americans would be entitled to have their own representatives in the governing bodies of the kingdom.[1] Although for practical reasons, not least the difficulty of travel, American representation in the Junta Central was in fact minimal, the principle had been enunciated and, when the Cortes was summoned in January 1810, Americans were duly invited to elect their deputies. Then the problems began because the decree of convocation envisaged American representation as comprising one member per 100,000 white inhabitants, whereas the peninsular deputies were to represent the towns, the provincial juntas and the population by one per 50,000 inhabitants. In other words, while American representation was a bold and in the eyes of some Spaniards a very dangerous concession, it was to be numerically far less than the Spanish. Also there was the immediate practical problem of the time needed to organize elections in America and of travel to Cádiz. To meet these difficulties, it was decided that up to 30 substitutes, chosen from Americans resident in Cádiz, would be permitted in the Cortes until such time as the properly elected deputies arrived.[2]

The same practical problems affected the choice of Spanish deputies and when the Cortes opened on 24 September, there were 104 members present, including 47 substitutes of whom 30 represented America. The Americans at once began to make their presence felt. Over the first three weeks of the sessions, they pressed almost daily for a formal declaration confirming the earlier statement that their continent was an integral part of the kingdom, that American Spaniards had equal rights to European Spaniards, and for a general amnesty or pardon to be promulgated regarding recent events in America. The peninsular deputies prevaricated for a time by raising various objections, especially over whether the *gente de color* or people of at least partial African descent should be given the same rights as Americans of Spanish origin. Eventually, a composite motion, excluding the black population, was agreed on 14 October and issued the next day. The following is the relevant section:

The general and extraordinary Cortes confirm and sanction the incontrovertible concept that the Spanish dominions in both hemispheres form one and the same family and that therefore, the natives originating in the said European and American dominions are equal in rights to those of this peninsula. It remains the responsibility of the Cortes to deal opportunely and with special attention with all that may contribute to the welfare of those of America and also with the number and form which the national representation in both hemispheres should have in the future.[3]

This somewhat grandiloquent decree was undoubtedly a victory for the Americans in the Cortes even though some, but not all, had wanted their compatriots regardless of racial origin to be included but it was also, as the Spanish deputies well understood, a statement of principle or perhaps declaration of intent without any specific commitment to actual change. The Americans, of course, also knew this and proceeded to draw up a programme of reforms which they felt flowed naturally from the fact that they were now equal to their European-born compatriots. At the top of their list, presented on 16 December 1810, was the demand for equality of representation in the Cortes. When the debates began on 9 January 1811, it was immediately clear that this was to be a contentious and bitterly disputed issue. In brief, the American case was that if, as declared in the 15 October decree, the American creoles, mestizos and Indians had the same and equal rights as those people born in the peninsula, then they should be represented in the Cortes according to the same rules as the Spaniards. Therefore, elections should be held in all the overseas territories as soon as possible in order that deputies could be chosen and promptly participate in the business of the Cortes and, above all, in its forthcoming deliberations on the new Constitution. Speaker after speaker from the American side assured his audience that the unfortunate disturbances in America would certainly come to an immediate end if equality of representation was approved and the American people could see that their interests were to be fully represented in the centre of power.

It all seemed very reasonable and the logic of the American case appeared irrefutable. Here, according to the Americans, was a ready means of restoring imperial harmony, a reform that would demonstrate the genuine nature of Spanish concern to improve the lot of their American brothers. Yet the Spanish deputies would not agree. Throughout many irate and acrimonious debates, they blocked the proposal, raising all manner of technical objections and difficulties: the electoral basis of the present assembly could not be changed in retrospect, especially not for one interest group alone; there was inadequate statistical data for the American population, its social composition and distribution; the problem of travel time meant that it was impossible for American deputies to be elected and reach Spain in time for the present Cortes. In the light of these and many other such obstacles, the obvious thing to do, suggested the Spaniards, was to postpone the matter until the new Constitution was debated. The Americans became more and more angry, they cajoled and threatened, they promised peace and more financial aid, they warned of dire consequences and they staged melodramatic walkouts from the debating chamber.[4]

Eventually, the issue was resolved on 7 February 1811 with another compromise which reaffirmed the principle of equality of representation, approved by 123 votes to 4 against, but which rejected, by 69 votes to 61, the proposal that it should apply to the present Cortes. Two days later, an appropriate decree was published to the effect that American representation in future Cortes should be 'entirely equal in the manner and form to that to be established in the peninsula' and that the detailed arrangements should be fixed in the constitution on the basis of 'perfect equality'.[5] All that had happened was that the issue had been deferred and when the constitutional debates began soon afterwards, the same bitter controversy ensued. Americans made the same points and Spaniards hedged and prevaricated. All inhabitants of America were to be Spaniards but the right of citizenship, and with it the right to vote, was denied those of African descent. Future American representation was to be based on 'the population composed of those native born who from both lines are derived from the Spanish domains'. In other words, the black population was not to be enfranchised. Equality did not extend that far.[6]

The representation issue undoubtedly soured relations in the closed and at times highly charged atmosphere at Cádiz where the defeated American lobby was not slow to express its disillusion with what they saw as the duplicity of their Spanish colleagues. As far as they were concerned, the first test of their newly proclaimed equality had revealed that it was no more than a worthless paper privilege. To a large extent, the remaining ten of their eleven proposed reforms received similar treatment, with those involving significant economic or trade changes being rejected or shelved. They had argued very strongly that only by adopting their programme of reform and actually proving in a tangible, practical way that equality did exist could the movements for independence be brought to an end. The Spaniards took a different view. For them, the declaration of equality had been proclaimed in order to ensure continued American loyalty and financial aid in the struggle against the French and, secondly, in the hope that it would in itself persuade the insurgents to lay down their arms. The implementation of the principle was another matter and each and every change that might logically flow from it required careful analysis and assessment of its potential impact in the peninsula, in America and in the relationship between the two.[7] In other words, a balance had to be struck: change was not automatic but depended on its beneficial or prejudicial impact on the central objective of retaining imperial unity. Equality of representation had indeed been granted in the decree of 15 October, but there was never any intention that it should at once be taken literally simply because in terms of population there were more Americans than Spaniards and, if parallel electoral systems were adopted, the Americans would have a majority in the Cortes. Having so recently, and with such courage, assumed the right of popular sovereignty in the face of a centuries-old tradition of absolute monarchy of divine origin, the Spaniards were obviously in no mood to hand over even the possibility of power to their former American subjects. Moreover, the issue failed the ultimate test. The Spanish deputies were deeply suspicious of their American counterparts and many were inclined to doubt all the talk that equal representation was such a vital matter in the overseas provinces or that it would have either the positive or negative effects on the rebels that were being claimed. In short, the American demands were neither necessary nor justified as a means of ending the revolutions.

The implications of equality were also far more than the Americans cared to admit. The Cádiz *consulado* argued that if the declaration of equality meant that Americans should enjoy all the same advantages as Spaniards, then it followed that they should also make the same sacrifices. Yet, the merchants pointedly asked, how many Americans were in the peninsula fighting for freedom, how much American blood had been spilt in defence of the Mother Country? Nobody blamed them for not coming to fight and all they had been asked to provide was money. Equality could clearly not be absolute. It had to be regulated in accordance with the situation and the needs of each party. To grant unrestricted international trade would be like being assassinated by a brother.[8]

The Cádiz merchants had a direct interest in opposing equality in all things but they were by no means alone in their opposition. Garay, opposing the concession of free trade, maintained that to apply equality in everything, especially economic affairs, was nonsensical because it was not in the interests of Americans. The function of law was to do the most good for most people and to apply it universally was often mistaken because it was against the common good. Equality of treatment in commerce would lead to the destruction of the American economies and Americans did not want free trade, they did not want to be 'equal' in that respect because they knew the harm it would cause.[9] According to Councillors of State Andrés García, Pedro Cevallos and Ibar Navarro, who favoured free trade, the declaration of equality was an act of unprecedented magnanimity in a noble attempt to stop a 'social war' in America, but it obviously did not mean absolute equality in everything.[10] Alcalá Galiano recalled that the constitutionalists were 'generous in the abstract and judiciously frugal in the practical application of the rights it was recognized that Americans had'.[11] Finally, the Council of State well summarized the Spanish position on the equality issue:

But it must not be understood that by that declaration [of equality], suddenly, at a stroke, all the laws which have ruled those provinces for three hundred years were to be overturned; nor can anyone believe that such a thing is practical or appropriate because the self-interest of those who are to benefit demands that in such a vast and delicate matter, progress should be without that haste which might ruin or retard the commendable aims of the reform.[12]

For Ferdinand, of course, there was no dilemma. He was told in the Persas manifesto of April 1814 that the equality law had been like a clarion call to revolution in the colonies and Garay, becoming increasingly reactionary, advised two years later that the laws of the Indies could not be bettered. There was, he wrote, not a single bad law and the worst thing that could be done to Americans was to force on them the same taxation system as applied in the peninsula, because all they had had to pay hitherto were a few indirect taxes. The idea of equality between Spain and America was 'a political monstrosity', never seen in any empire. The situation, condition and needs of the Indies were such that they must for their own sake continue in their colonial status.[13] The Council of the Indies in its advice to the king was rather more pragmatic. Concessions, changes, reforms had all been made but there was no evidence that any had had the slightest effect on the rebels. Equality, which the Council insisted Americans had in fact enjoyed since the conquest, had been offered but again without effect. There was no point in making any more changes in colonial law, except in the commercial monopoly.[14]

Spaniards, therefore, were never willing nor did they ever intend, despite all the protests and threats from Americans, to apply the concept of equality in every sphere and they do not appear to have considered themselves to be in what Professor Anna has called 'a hopeless dialectical trap', nor did they see any 'inherent ideological contradiction' in proclaiming the principle of equality without implementing it in all respects.[15] Their attitude, regardless of their ideological convictions about the future of the peninsula, was always conditioned by their assessment of the likely effect of any reform on the support for the insurgents and its effect on the domestic scene. Hence they were selective, distinguishing between what they thought good for the Mother Country and what they considered appropriate, in the circumstances of revolution, for America.

Some changes could certainly be sanctioned. One of the Americans' most persistent demands was for equality of opportunity and achievement in jobs in the civil, military and ecclesiastical bureaucracies. American creoles had long protested against their exclusion from high-ranking office in colonial administration and there was profound resentment at what they considered unfair discrimination against them. Three of the eleven points in their 1810 reform programme thus concerned jobs. They asked for equal opportunity for Americans, both Spanish and Indian, in all appointments; the allocation of half the posts in each American province to those born there; establishment of advisory committees in America to choose those to be appointed to public office.[16] The Spanish response to these three demands illustrates the compromise that was always adopted. The second and third were deferred and in effect shelved permanently because to grant them would reduce the power and influence of the central authorities in the metropolis. On the other hand, the first involved another declaration of principle and implementation would rest in the hands of ministers and others in Spain. Hence it was approved without dissent and on 9 February 1811 a suitable decree was published.

As always, not everybody agreed with the decision. López Cancelada, for example, strongly refuted any suggestion of discrimination against Americans and he published various statistics to prove his point[17] but, for the most part, it is clear that successive Spanish governments did feel that here was one concession, sufficiently important to Americans and which did not involve any loss of Spanish control, that it was worth granting. Pizarro favoured more jobs being given to Americans and Lozano de Torres added that it was important not just to ensure that they obtained jobs in their own provinces but also in Spain. Other Councillors of State, for example José Ibarra, included equality of job opportunity in their pacification programme and in the list of measures which the Council proposed to Ferdinand in 1817, the idea was approved without dissent although Garay felt it was better to give Americans jobs in Spain, 'because it is never politic for Americans to have the government of their country in their own hands'.[18]

The same belief that the jobs issue would have an effect on the support for the insurgents continued to prevail into the 1820s. José Aycinena, José Luyando, Luis Antonio Flores and the Príncipe de Anglona all thought some offer of more posts would have a useful effect and the Marqués de Piedra Blanca went even further and some way towards accepting the original American proposal of 1810. He advised the appointment in each overseas province of a three-man committee, not excluding, he added, a royal person, with authority to fill all vacant posts subject to the approval of the Madrid government. Esteban Varea supported this idea with a similar scheme which would ensure that all minor posts would be filled by Americans with only the most senior civil and ecclesiastical officials being selected in Spain. He felt that the job issue was one of the three basic causes of the revolutions and one which had alienated the most illustrious families of America.[19]

Almost all of these councillors and most of the other advisory bodies

who advocated the appointment of more Americans were agreed that
it was not just the exclusion of Americans from administrative
positions which had contributed to the support for the rebels but,
perhaps even more significant, it was the poor quality of the officials
sent from Spain. As early as its first report on the events in Caracas in
1810, the Council of the Indies warned that better people would have
to be found to staff the colonial bureaucracy because the arbitrary and
despotic behaviour of so many officials was a constant source of
complaint by Americans. Many speakers in the Cádiz Cortes both
from America and the peninsula stressed the vital importance of
eliminating financial corruption, nepotism and other nefarious
practices and Ferdinand in turn was told by his advisers that a
guarantee of honest and efficient personnel would do much to calm
the situation and restore American respect for Spanish rule. The
Duque de San Carlos recommended that all senior officials should be
retired as soon as possible to be replaced by people against whom there
could be no possible complaint. The Conde de Casa Flores and José
Alvarez de Toledo also included the better choice of officials as
essential in any pacification programme and the Councils of State and
Indies both endorsed that view in several of their reports to Ferdinand
and to the constitutional authorities.

The traditional image of the Spanish bureaucrat as a man 'without
roots, poor and with no education' who looked on his time in America
as an opportunity to satisfy his 'lust for gold' was widely acknowledged
to be accurate.[20] Whether the men sent to staff the colonial
administration after 1810 were any better than those who went before
is impossible to judge but, certainly, both Ferdinand and the
constitutional régimes often proclaimed their good intentions in this
respect. They also took great pains to assure Americans that, while
equality of representation and control of appointments would not be
conceded, there would nevertheless be much improved representation
of their interests in the imperial government. Hence the liberals
sanctioned in the 1812 Constitution continued American representation in the Cortes and their new Council of State was to have at least
twelve Americans among its forty members. The Regency executives
contained at least one American and there were others at ministerial
and senior levels. Ferdinand promised that they would be represented
in the Cortes he intended to, but never did summon, and he repeatedly
emphasized that more Americans would be given posts in his
administration. In a proclamation of July 1814, Lardizábal, newly

appointed Minister for Overseas Affairs and himself Mexican-born, high-lighted the number of Americans the king had appointed to influential posts. The Council of the Indies had been reconstituted and five Americans put on it, 'something for which there is no precedent'. There was an American at the head of the Council of Castile and the Duque de San Carlos, born in Lima, was the Minister of State. Such appointments were visible proof, declared Lardizábal, that Ferdinand intended that the interests of Americans would henceforth be looked after more sympathetically and more justly.[21]

In addition to giving Americans a more prominent role in the government of the empire and generally improving the quality of the colonial bureaucracy, all Spanish régimes believed that administrative changes were necessary and a useful way of removing discontent. A great variety of minor reforms was introduced and governments continued to deliberate at length on the creation of new *audiencias* or bishoprics as if the situation in America was normal. Many changes flowed from the adoption of the constitution, for example, reform of provincial and municipal government, the press and the Church, but in some places in America reactionary colonial officials refused to implement them. The brevity of each of the constitutional periods was such that the reforms brought few practical benefits. Instead, the rapidity of events in Spain and the number and diversity of the changes planned or decreed provided not the much-heralded improved efficiency and speed in dealing with the problems but even greater administrative paralysis.

Almost all departments of State, councils, *ad hoc* committees, official and unofficial advisory bodies were always eager to suggest reforms or to stop them and the government bureaucracy could not cope with the constant stream of advice and opinion. The constitutionalist response to the problem was to establish a separate department or Ministry for Overseas Affairs which, as the Council of Indies was by then abolished, would in future coordinate the direction of policy and handle the day-to-day government of the empire. The Regency promised in a proclamation in August 1812 that the new department would be solely concerned with the welfare of Americans and that it would encourage a range of economic and social improvements.[22] Although it did issue various circulars and seek to begin a system of acquiring correct and current statistical information on American needs and problems, the new ministry did not survive for long, disappearing with the rest of the constitutional administrative apparatus when Ferdinand returned in 1814. Nevertheless, Ferdinand also recognized the need for centralizing American affairs and he created the Ministerio Universal de las Indias, with Lardizábal as its first minister. Again, the motive and proclaimed intention were to centralize and thereby improve colonial administration and thus remove sources of complaint by Americans. With his undoubted penchant and perhaps conscious wish to divide and rule, Ferdinand soon began to set up other bodies, for example, the military and merchant committees, and by the time the Ministerio Universal was abolished in 1815, the administrative system was again in chaos with inter-departmental and personal rivalries inhibiting effective administration. By November 1816, the Council of the Indies was again arguing for a single, coordinating authority and when Pizarro as Minister of State was given this responsibility, he found the conduct of colonial affairs to be chaotic. The following year, Vázquez Figueroa strongly advocated the recreation of the Ministerio Universal, saying that the division of responsibilities between ministers did not work and that it was essential to provide Americans with a focal point for their complaints. He also felt that there should be a separate royal council and Supreme Court for America.[23]

No notice was taken of Vázquez Figueroa's suggestions but years later, the same idea persisted that reform of the administrative system would help to reconcile the insurgents. In the Council of State in 1821, Vázquez Figueroa, supported by La Serna and Porcel, repeated his arguments in favour of a single ministry. There might perhaps even be two, he thought, one for North and the other for South America but, whatever was decided, it was vital to give higher priority to colonial affairs than had been the case in the past. Some way must be found of avoiding contradictory measures from different departments, administrative anarchy and the delays in decision-making so inevitable when ministers were fully occupied with peninsular affairs.[24]

While the restructuring of the colonial administration both in Spain and in America was seen by some as an important ancillary measure, there were other more direct methods of pacification which found favour with all régimes. The idea of granting amnesties or pardons to those who had taken up arms against the king first arose at Cádiz and a general pardon was offered in the decree of 15 October 1810. According to the press in the next few months, it had a significant impact in America and henceforth military commanders and other colonial officials were encouraged to use amnesties as a means of undermining the rebels' strength. In 1813, Garay was in favour of announcing an unrestricted pardon to all those who recognized the Constitution, Cortes and Regency and the Council of State accepted the idea as one of the conditions on which British mediation could be based.[25] Even Ferdinand was willing to forgive and forget and, in July 1814, he offered to overlook all past offences of those who gave themselves up to the authorities. Failure to do so, he added, would oblige him to use force.[26] The Council of the Indies advised a few months later that the king should publish a general pardon for all rebels who surrendered within twenty-four hours and similar suggestions were made by individuals and advisory committees.[27] Thus Ferdinand repeated his offer of a royal pardon in January 1817 when he was able to use the occasion of his recent marriage as a pretext.[28] Pizarro also included a general amnesty as an essential measure in his major package of pacification proposals presented to the Council of State in the autumn of 1817. Garay, Ibarra and even the reactionary Eguía supported the idea, although Rivas felt such a concession to be degrading and the Duque de Veragua pointed out that the several amnesties offered by Morillo in Venezuela had not done much good. Nevertheless, Pizarro's proposal was one of the so-called 'direct measures' which was approved by the full Council.[29] No action was taken, however, partly because a few months later Pizarro attempted to widen the scope of the amnesty to include exiled opponents of the régime in Europe. To his mind, such dissidents were deliberately fomenting subversion and aiding the rebels in America both materially and with propaganda: 'I believe, therefore', he said, 'that to recover America, an almost unrestricted amnesty is very urgent.'[30] There was some support in the Council of State for this opinion, but Ferdinand promptly refused to have anything to do with such a gesture towards his sworn enemies. On 5 May 1818 he sent a curt but clear instruction to the Council: 'I order you not to speak in any way in the Council of State of giving an amnesty to those exiled from Spain, under any pretext.'[31] The idea of an amnesty for America only was nevertheless not abandoned entirely and it was used in the diplomatic notes which Pizarro circulated in an attempt to get international support at the congress of Aix-la-Chapelle. At about the same time, the summer of 1818, the Conde de Ofalia, in a long and detailed memorandum to Ferdinand, also recommended a full amnesty for dissident Spaniards and Americans.[32]

With the reintroduction of the Constitution in 1820, accompanied by the usual plethora of promises of better treatment for Americans, it was quickly realized that however persuaded the rebels might be of the advantages to them offered by the new situation in the peninsula, it was still necessary to assure them that they would not be called to account for their previous actions. Hence another amnesty was soon proposed and a Cortes committee advised that it would be a noble act to forget the opinions and conduct of the insurgents. The committee was sure, it said, that an amnesty would bring about reconciliation.[33] The Minister of Ultramar was also convinced that it would restore peace and almost all of the deputies who spoke in the debate agreed. Thus, on 27 September 1820, a general pardon was decreed for all Americans who accepted the constitution.[34]

This widely held belief that amnesties of one form or another would make a significant contribution to peace reflected Spanish assessment of the support for the rebel movements. Both liberals and absolutists agreed that a policy of limited military force was essential, but it was also thought that popular support for independence was at most tenuous, with many of those fighting against the royal armies unwilling victims of press gangs and other forms of involuntary conscription. All Spanish governments also, of course, appreciated the propaganda value of being seen to be magnanimous and they were aware of the need to attract and keep the support of public opinion in America. For three hundred years one of the main agents for ensuring popular loyalty to the Crown had been the Church and, in particular, the rural parish priests whose influence over the minds of their parishioners was unchallenged. It was to be expected, therefore, that the Spanish authorities would immediately seek to use the influence of the clergy to undermine popular support for the rebels, but in the early years of the revolutions there was some hesitation because of the known presence, not least in the persons of Hidalgo and Morelos in New Spain, of many clergy in the insurgent armies. For the most part, the senior ecclesiastical hierarchy, however, did condemn the rebellions and in June 1813, the Minister of Ultramar called on the episcopacy of America to persuade their priests and flocks to remain loyal to the Crown.[35] With the return of Ferdinand and the subsequent release of the Pope from his confinement by Napoleon at Fontainebleau, the possibility of using the Church arose again and Ferdinand published a decree in October 1814 urging the clergy to use all their influence through the pulpit and their teaching to arrest 'the almost general corruption of customs'.

Talks with the Papacy were soon started and on 30 January 1816, Pius VII published an encyclical addressed to the clergy of America in which he called on them to help to stop the revolutions. He also sanctioned the establishment of a new order of nobility for loyal Americans to be known as the Order of Isabel la Católica. Then, following more pressure from Spain's formidable ambassador at Rome, Antonio Vargas Laguna, Ferdinand was granted the use of part of some episcopal revenues and those of the cathedral chapters and monasteries, funds which were to be spent in the planned River Plate expedition. Several of Ferdinand's advisers continued to press for more use to be made of the Church and in 1817 the Council of State made the same point in its revision of policy. After 1820 the liberals, despite their anti-clericalism, were also recommended to take note of the significant influence of the clergy. In June 1821, the Council of State suggested that the bishops and priests of Mexico should be asked to persuade the people not to join Iturbide's rebellion and some of the councillors felt that the recent anti-clerical legislation, particularly that affecting the religious orders, should be suspended because it was counter-productive in that it was antagonizing a group whose support was essential. Francisco Requena wanted half the ecclesiastical posts to go to Americans and he suggested that they should also be appointed as diocesan bishops in the peninsula.[36] During the next few years, Spanish diplomats persisted in their efforts to get stronger papal support and on 10 February 1825, the Madrid Gazette included what purported to be a papal encyclical addressed to the archbishops and bishops of America. This was dated 24 September 1824 and the Pope again called on the clergy to persuade their flocks to abandon their rebellious actions and return to the fold of 'our beloved son, Ferdinand'.

The authenticity of both the papal encyclicals has been challenged by several scholars,[37] but their appearance, authentic or not, does illustrate the fact that the Spanish government considered that the clergy were a useful tool to be used whenever possible in the propaganda war which it was accepted had to be won if any kind of permanent reunion and harmony was ever to be reestablished in the empire. It has already been noted that the press was also employed by all governments to persuade public opinion against the idea of American independence and to convince Spaniards that the war was going well. Ferdinand, who imposed strict censorship on news of events, went even further. Pizarro wrote in his memorandum of June

1818 that 'this is the age of charlatans and a gazette can often save [the expense of] an army'.[38] He urged Ferdinand to mount a propaganda campaign to present Spain's case using secret agents, diplomats and planted articles in the press of Europe. Ferdinand then apparently conceived the idea of secretly funding a periodical in London to be known as *El Observador Español de Londres*. A cleric, Miguel Cabral de Noruña, was appointed to direct it and Minister of State Casa Irujo told the Duque de San Carlos, then ambassador in London, that the purpose of the venture was to sway public opinion to the Spanish cause. Seven numbers were in due course produced but by March 1820, the paper collapsed with only four subscriptions received all from the same subscriber, although most of the run was dispatched for circulation to America.[39]

All of these various areas of reform and attempts to win over public opinion, both in Europe and in America, were always accompanied by a willingness to negotiate directly with the rebel leaders. Both constitutional administrations sent envoys to try to reach a negotiated settlement of the conflict but their missions invariably made little or no progress because their instructions included the proviso that independence could not be accepted.[40] The Cortes at Cádiz decided in 1811 at an early stage in the revolutions that talks could be held with the rebel juntas, but only with those which had recognized the government in Spain and not made any claim to sovereignty. As for those which did not accept the legitimacy of the Regency and Cortes, Spain would not initiate any conciliatory steps although it was always willing to listen to any reconciliation proposals from the dissidents. Even Ferdinand was willing to allow direct talks with those who had challenged his divine right to dominion in America. In 1816 the rebel government of Buenos Aires ordered Bernardino Rivadavia and Manuel Belgrano to seek talks with Ferdinand and, following preliminary discussions in London and Paris, Rivadavia was invited to Madrid. There he met with senior government officials including Minister of State Cevallos, but no progress was made and the meetings ended in acrimony and mutual hostility with Rivadavia being ordered out of the country.[41] With the failure of all attempts at direct talks with the rebels, the final method of negotiation was to seek third-party mediation or intervention and, as will be demonstrated in the next chapter, this was to involve the most sustained of all Spanish efforts and hopes of resolving the crisis.

This brief survey of some of the multiple avenues explored by all

Spanish governments regardless of their political creed confirms that no stone was left unturned in the attempt to prevent the disintegration of the empire. Measures of political and administrative reform, concessions on jobs, propaganda and negotiations were all hailed by their respective advocates as providing a sure road to peace. Pizarro, Bodega and many others seem to have been convinced that a negotiated settlement based on concessions in one or more areas was always feasible and, indeed, offered the only hope of an enduring peace. It is clear, however, that the various suggestions, excluding free trade which of course was rejected, amounted to relatively minor adjustments, to tinkering with the imperial machine. The radicalism of the liberals in peninsular affairs did not extend to America and, while they sought to implement a political and social revolution at home, they would not accept major surgery in the colonial status of America. Nevertheless, there was one proposal backed by a few Spaniards which indicated that they were prepared to countenance fundamental change in the relationship between metropolis and empire, either as a genuine, far-sighted realization that the clock could not be put back or perhaps as a last forlorn attempt to salvage something from what they came to believe was a struggle that could not be won.

The idea of establishing some form of Spanish commonwealth or federation, or dividing the empire into separate kingdoms each headed by a member of the royal household, did not originate in the revolutionary era. The Conde de Aranda had outlined such a scheme in 1783 and Manuel Godoy, among others, promoted similar projects in the early 1800s. At Cádiz after 1810, there was talk of resurrecting the idea but now mainly in connection with Carlota Joaquina, sister of Ferdinand and wife of the Portuguese monarch resident in Brazil since 1808. With the collapse and exile in France of almost the entire royal family, Carlota herself had canvassed the possibility of claiming the Regency of Spain but, unsure of her attitude towards them, the constitutionalists had refused to give her claim any serious examination. She had also advanced the idea of herself becoming Regent in Buenos Aires during the enforced absence of Ferdinand but again, this fell on deaf ears in Cádiz where the constitutionalists were well aware of Portuguese pretensions to that region. Then in September 1812, as the fifth member of the Regency was about to be chosen, deputy Ramón Feliú (Peru) caused an uproar in the Cortes by suggesting that as all other measures to restore peace had failed, Carlota should be appointed a Regent and should proceed to New Spain to reestablish control. As far as he was concerned, the idea was essential if America was to be saved. The reaction of his colleagues was hostile and so noisy that when he offered to withdraw the suggestion, nobody heard him.[42]

A more detailed and radical strategy came in 1815 from Luis de Onís, ambassador in the United States. He outlined a number of extreme options including the cession of territory to the United States or to France, bribing United States congressmen and sending a royal prince to lead a large army. He also reintroduced the idea of using the infantes. If separation became inevitable, he wrote, America could be divided into separate kingdoms with a prince of the royal household on the throne of each region.[43] Once again the proposal made no progress in Madrid but it still seems to have been current in 1819. On 24 September of that year, Castlereagh informed Wellesley that the French government had advised Ferdinand to send a prince to the River Plate and efforts were being made to persuade Russia to concur. Castlereagh added that, in his opinion, 'it is the wisest policy they could adopt'.[44]

It seems that, although raised from time to time, this idea of allowing autonomous kingdoms to be set up in America in some form of federal system was not given any serious consideration during the decade from 1810 to 1820. During the second constitutional régime, however, circumstances had changed and with Spain's hold on the empire almost entirely destroyed by 1821, some Spaniards were more willing to entertain any option, as long as it was short of outright independence. Now the suggestions for a radical restructuring of the empire came from several directions. In May 1821, a cabinet meeting attended by former viceroys and other colonial officials concluded that America should be divided into three kingdoms, one in the north and two in the south, to be ruled by Ferdinand through resident royal princes or, if there were too few of the latter available, through a three-man regency in each one.[45] Ferdinand was quickly appraised of the cabinet discussion and just as quickly he let it be known that he would never give his consent. On 24 May a series of questions was put to him for his comments. Had his ministers, he was asked, said anything to him about sending infantes to America? 'They have insinuated it, but not officially', Ferdinand wrote in reply. Was it his intention to oppose the departure of the infantes as unconstitutional and to gain time? 'Yes', answered Ferdinand.[46] According to the French ambassador, Ferdinand refused even to consider the idea because he suspected it was a conspiracy by his enemies to persuade him to act unconstitutionally and then have a pretext 'to take him to the guillotine'.[47] The king's hostility might well have put a stop to all further talk but just two weeks later, on 4 June, news of Iturbide's rebellion in Mexico was released to the Cortes. In the Plan of Iguala, Iturbide envisaged the creation of a monarchy led by Ferdinand or a member of his family or indeed, of any other ruling dynasty. The immediate reaction of the Cortes and the executive was hostile, but in the debate the Mexican deputy Gómez de Navarrete announced that he and his colleagues intended shortly to present a plan of some relevance.

On 25 June, José Miguel Ramírez, deputy for Guadalajara in Mexico, on behalf of all the American representatives, read a fifteen-point project for restructuring the empire which, he said, provided the only means of restoring peace.[48] It proposed three separate Cortes, one for New Spain and Central America, one for New Granada and Tierra Firme, and one for Peru, Buenos Aires and Chile. These new assemblies would have full legislative powers for their respective territories and executive power in each would reside in a delegation headed by a person nominated by the Spanish king, not excluding members of the royal family. There would be the various ministries, a supreme court and council of state. In other words, the Americans now advocated a kind of imperial federation with almost total autonomy for the American part of the empire. Although Minister of State Bardají had apparently said just a few days earlier that he intended to recommend a federal union, the opposition to the American-sponsored project was immediate and widespread.[49] Ferdinand, it was already known, would never give his support and the cabinet concluded that it was unconstitutional. The Spanish deputies in the Cortes found the whole thing too much to swallow and pleaded lack of authority to make such a major innovation. Public opinion also, it was said, was not ready for a change of that magnitude and finally, nothing could be done without the agreement of Spain's allies and there had been no time to consult them.

The regular Cortes sessions ended a few days later and for the next few months, formulation of a policy towards America rested with the executive. The federal concept was still not forgotten. In the Council of State, the Marqués de Piedra Blanca advanced his idea of a three-man committee, which might include a royal prince, to govern each territory and enjoy some limited autonomy. Esteban Varea was also in favour of a similar committee to consist of a governor and two advisers, at least one being American, with the power to decide all government affairs within the law, although legislative power should remain in the Spanish Cortes. Gabriel Ciscar was significantly more adventurous. There was no way, he insisted, that Spain could force or maintain America in its former dependent state and it was a waste of money to try. America could simply not be ruled from Madrid because of the distance and the inevitable delay in decisions. Furthermore, he stated, 'the propagation of these truths and the enlightenment of the century have spread throughout the world knowledge of the principles of natural law; they have produced a general repugnance or open opposition to the recognition of authorities established in another hemisphere'. The moment had thus arrived for America to be divided into four or more independent states joined together and with Spain by way of a federal system constructed according to the needs of each party.[50]

Ciscar's proposal was too radical for the Council of State, but he was not alone in his conclusions. At about the same time, Miguel Cabrera de Nevares finished his own assessment of the situation. He had left Spain in 1815 and after spending five years in Europe, he had gone on a business trip to America, living for two years in Buenos Aires. On his return, he had a two-hour meeting with the Minister of Ultramar who asked him to prepare a report on the state of America. This was done and with 200 copies presented to the Cortes on 14 November 1821, word of its contents soon spread.[51] On the next day, López Cancelada denounced it as 'the result of all the mistakes made up to now', and a few weeks later, another newspaper published lengthy extracts from it.[52] The editor strongly supported Cabrera de Nevares' ideas and emphasized their importance in view of the most recent news, received on 12 December, of the declaration of Mexican independence. Then in January 1822, deputy Fernández Golfín introduced in the Cortes Cabrera de Nevares' views and his proposed treaty with the American provinces. He rejected the idea of sending yet more envoys to find out what Americans wanted. Everybody knew it was complete independence and neither national pride nor grief could disguise the fact that Spain had lost the struggle to prevent it. Thus, Spain should recognize independence and seek to obtain the best settlement available, negotiating with each new nation a trade treaty and a subsidy for the metropolis. There should also be established an Hispanic–American confederation consisting of the American states and Spain, to be headed by Ferdinand and his successors with the title of 'Protector de la Gran Confederación Hispano–Americana'. Within two years, or earlier if possible, a federal congress would be assembled in Madrid with representatives of each of the member states in the confederation and it should deal every year with matters of general interest, without prejudice to the national constitutions.

Deputy Felipe Paul immediately objected to this scheme as no more than the thoughts of a private individual. He preferred the recommendations of the Overseas Committee that another group of envoys be sent to listen to proposals. For the next two weeks, the Cortes debated what to do. The Cabrera de Nevares plan received little support and it was eventually resolved to send commissioners and to reject the Mexican Treaties of Córdoba to which Spain's own representative, Juan O'Donojú, had put his signature.[53]

The Cabrera de Nevares project received possibly the greatest attention and generated the most discussion of all the schemes for federal arrangements with either independent states or with autonomous provinces governed by a member of the reigning dynasty. As it was now clear that neither Ferdinand nor the constitutionalists were willing to accept any form of American emancipation, that particular solution to the imperial problem was shelved, only to be taken out now and again in future years by mostly foreign governments. In 1826, for example, it was reported that the Austrian ambassador and the papal nuncio in Madrid were again pressing the idea of sending an infante and in 1830, the French favoured the creation of an independent monarchy, ruled by a Spanish prince, in Mexico. But while everything around him was changing, Ferdinand remained resolute. The British ambassador reported: 'I doubt whether his Catholic Majesty would have much less objection to recognize Mexico as independent under one ruler, even though his own brother, than under another entirely foreign to his family. In fact I am persuaded that no consideration would induce his Majesty at this moment to relinquish his title to any part of his former American dominions.'[54]

All attempts to preserve the empire through some form of political accommodation, concession of more but not total equality for Americans, pardons, amnesties, gaining popular support, through propaganda, using the Pope and the clergy to show Americans the error of their actions, reform of colonial government in myriad ways and even the introduction of a revolutionary liberal constitution; all had been in vain. The military solution had also failed and the combination of

military force allied to reform had had no better success. There was
only one option left open to any Spanish government and that was to
seek outside support, to persuade another, more powerful nation to
help to keep the empire intact. It is to the diplomatic solution that we
must now turn.

8

The diplomatic initiative

Throughout all the years of revolution and long after the battle of Ayacucho, Spaniards believed that one or more foreign countries could or should be persuaded to stop the wars and restore their dominion in America. Some favoured external intervention as the best of all solutions, especially after it became clear that there was no likelihood of military success nor any real possibility of convincing the insurgents by peaceful means to return to the imperial family. After three centuries of trying to keep foreigners out of the overseas provinces, Spaniards were now willing to plead for their assistance in retaining them even though to do so was thought by some to be a humiliating confession of the monarchy's impotence. It was once again, however, a question of the lesser of two evils. If there was no other way to save America except to go cap in hand around the courts of Europe, then that was what must be done and whatever concessions were required to attract support would have to be granted. There was also a feeling that the nation's allies owed Spain a debt and a duty to come to its aid because of its heroic efforts in resisting the French invasion, which was widely blamed as the prime cause of the outbreak of revolution in the colonies. Spain had stood almost alone in the defence of legitimacy and when the European Powers decided to restore the dynasties of the pre-Napoleonic era, Spanish diplomats were not slow to remind them of the legitimacy of Spanish dominion in America and of the implications of that regal dominion being overturned by force anywhere in the empire. At the international congresses held to reconstruct the map of Europe, Spain tried to put its case for assistance and, apart from this usually public diplomacy, private contacts and negotiations were diligently pursued with Spanish representatives emphasizing not only their political case but also appealing to dynastic and family loyalties. Many ideas and suggestions were floated of ways to persuade sympathetic régimes to provide military aid or to intervene directly in the fighting, but the most persistent and best-supported initiative was to seek mediation by one or more of the European Powers.

The country most associated with the mediation policy was Britain. From 1810 onwards, it was realized that the British attitude to the revolutions could determine their success or failure for, with the world's most powerful navy, British ships controlled the seas and its neutrality or acquiescence was essential for any military campaign based on forces dispatched from the peninsula. Just as important was the alliance between Spain and Britain in the struggle against Napoleon and, while Spain needed British support in the peninsular war, Britain knew that American bullion was vital for its own economic and military progress. It did not seem to Spanish eyes, therefore, that Britain would see any immediate advantage in helping the insurgents, at least not until the French challenge had been defeated and the European scene settled. Hence it was no surprise when in August 1810, following talks in London with representatives of the Caracas rebels, the British government indicated its willingness to act as a mediator between them and the Regency authorities.[1] With the first news of the creation of the rebel juntas then being digested in Cádiz, nothing more was heard of the proposal during the next few months, but there were two parallel developments which would in due course influence the mediation talks.

The first involved the Regency's chronic shortage of money with which to fund resistance to the French and even to meet the daily expenses of government. In December 1810, there was talk in the Cortes of negotiating in a formal treaty a cash subsidy from Britain and, although doubts were voiced about the likely demands the British would make in exchange, it was eventually agreed that the Regency should investigate the matter.[2] A few weeks later, the Regency responded with a secret memorandum to the Cortes which recommended that Britain should be given special commercial privileges in order to ensure its continued financial and military support.[3] The Cortes formally received the Regency memorandum on 15 January 1811 and set up a committee to consider its ideas. During the next weeks, the committee began collecting data, including previous commercial treaties and details of particular concessions made to various British mercantile interests. In the meantime, the American lobby had begun to press for the complete abolition of the trading monopoly, seeking to have transatlantic commerce opened to all nations and not solely to Britain, and when the Cortes committee presented its report on 29 March, it was clear that the British subsidy idea had now been subsumed in the more general controversy over free trade. The debates on the committee's report and on the free trade issue began in April and were still in progress when, on 27 May, Wellesley sent a note to the Minister of State, Bardají. In this, following instructions he had received earlier that month from London, he formally offered the British government's mediation between Spain and the colonies in exchange for Spanish sanction of continued British trade with America for at least as long as the mediation lasted. Bardají duly informed the Cortes of the proposal on 1 June, adding that, in the opinion of the Regency, it was the only way open to Spain of bringing the disturbances to an end. He suggested that the mediation talks could be based on the following points: rebel recognition of the Cortes and Regency; the election of American deputies; obedience to the laws issued by the Cortes. As for the trade concession to Britain the Regency repeated its earlier view in favour, pointing out that if Britain did not see commercial advantages in a united Spanish empire, then it would work to destroy it. Granting trading privileges would on the other hand remove any need for the British government to continue its dealings with the rebel juntas.

The Cortes listened to Bardají's exposition and then referred the matter to a committee which reported its findings some two weeks later.[4] It approved of the British mediation proposal but added several important conditions. The indispensable basis of any talks was to be that the rebel provinces agreed to recognize the constitutional government and to send deputies to the Cortes. There was to be a reciprocal suspension of hostilities and arrested royalists in America were to be set free and have their property restored. Grievances and complaints by the insurgents would be heard and remedied where appropriate. The talks should last a maximum of eight months during which Britain could continue to trade with the rebel provinces. If the talks failed, Britain should suspend all contact with the rebels and help Spain to suppress them by force. Finally, in the official answer to the British note, the reasons for accepting it should be explained, 'safeguarding the decorum of the government'. The Cortes quickly approved these terms, making only one significant change in extending the duration of the negotiation to a maximum of fifteen months.[5]

Almost as soon as Wellesley learned of the Cortes decision, and before any official notification, he went to see Bardají.[6] He told the

Minister of State that his government would certainly not accept article 7 of the Cortes plan, namely that Britain would use force against the rebels if the talks failed, and he pointed out that if the overseas provinces found out that Britain had adopted such a belligerent attitude, it would make the task impossible for the mediators. Bardají replied that the condition was quite reasonable but that it could be kept separate and secret.

Following these private meetings, Bardají sent Wellesley a formal note on 29 June. He defended Spanish actions in America, praised recent reforms and repeated complaints against Britain for having entertained representatives of the rebels in London and for other indications which had seemed to favour the rebel cause. Nevertheless, he continued, Spain accepted the proposed mediation under the terms stipulated by the Cortes, of which article 7 was to be kept secret, and he invited Britain to nominate individuals to proceed to Buenos Aires, Santa Fe, Venezuela and Cartagena. Two days later, Wellesley responded. The secret article would certainly be rejected and if the colonies lost confidence in Britain, the French would at once seek to take advantage. His government had no ulterior motive in its offer to help and all it wanted was the reunification of the empire to ensure that no part of it fell into French hands. Mexico was of great importance for strategic and economic reasons and must be included as the revolts there were no less formidable than anywhere else. He concluded that he had sent all the details to London and awaited instructions.

Nothing further happened on the diplomatic front for the next few months and this gave opponents of the mediation idea their opportunity. The Cádiz merchants were determined to block any attempt to infringe or abolish the trading monopoly. They lobbied vigorously in public and private against the concession of free trade as a measure of economic reform and, as we have seen, the proposal to introduce that change was defeated in the Cortes. By the same token, the merchants were vehemently opposed to any trading privileges being granted to Britain which, they argued, would have just as devastating an effect on them as the more general reform. Britain, they said, is supposed to be our closest ally and yet it is promoting the one reform which will destroy us. There was no doubt in their minds that British aid would still be forthcoming even without any trading privileges and, if the British had to be rewarded, there were other less dangerous ways of doing so. They could, for example, be allowed free access with their goods to specified ports in the peninsula and as long as their merchandize was shipped to America only in Spanish vessels, there would be no danger of economic collapse.[7] Also, of course, the Cádiz merchants at this time organized the Comisión de Reemplazos and the first dispatch of soldiers to America as a practical demonstration that in their opinion Spain did not need foreign mediation.

The mediation proposal and the free trade reform were thus now inextricably linked and, once the Cádiz lobby began to exert its formidable pressure against both ideas, there was little chance of them being approved. But, in addition to the American problem, the Regency remained desperately short of funds for its immediate needs and in December 1811, the idea of getting a subsidy from Britain was again raised. On 17 December, deputy Morales Gallego introduced a proposal in the Cortes to authorize the executive to negotiate a war subsidy in return for which Britain would be granted the right to trade directly with the colonies under a strictly controlled system regulating the ports, the number of ships each year and only in designated goods. This initiative was approved and Bardají informed Wellesley of what was required. First, Spain wanted the British government to guarantee a loan of £10,000,000 to be raised in London; secondly, there was to be a formal subsidy treaty with Britain maintaining 100,000 Spaniards 'completely armed, clothed and equipped'; thirdly, Britain was to provide a number of transport ships to be placed under the control of Spain. Wellesley protested at the size of these demands, pointing out that Britain had already provided large amounts of money and supplies for the armies in the peninsula, but he did agree to forward them to London.[8] Spain's ambassador, the Duque de Infantado, soon found that no agreement would be reached.

In fact, the subsidy talks were superseded when on 30 January 1812 Wellesley finally gave his government's official reply to the Cortes' terms for the proposed mediation. Britain rejected the so-called secret article, demanding that it be suppressed before any further talks could take place. Several notes were then exchanged in which the Regency tried to argue the case for keeping the article, but Wellesley refused to give way. With an impasse reached, the Regency reported the situation to the Cortes in April, emphasizing that Spain remained dependent on British support and how important it was not to offend so powerful an ally. The Cortes' mediation committee recommended that the offending article could be removed as a condition of the mediation, provided it was understood that Spain retained the right to use force without being hindered by Britain. Wellesley's response to this change was to press for the complete suppression of the article and he also refused to accept the Regency's demand that Britain should cease all communication with the rebels if the mediation failed. Again the Regency gave way and Wellesley apparently decided to extract even further concessions. He again raised the question of the inclusion of Mexico and urged that more reforms, especially the abolition of the trading monopoly, must be enacted if Americans were to be persuaded to remain in the empire. The Minister of State rejected these latest British demands. The vast majority of the people of Mexico were loyal, he said, and the rebels consisted of no more than a few scattered bands of brigands which the legal authorities could and would defeat. Moreover, it would be improper to send a British envoy to talk to the insurgents when properly elected deputies from Mexico were already attending the Cortes. As for the trading monopoly, that was not germane to the mediation, which merely concerned special privileges for Britain in exchange for its assistance.

Wellesley replied on 12 June and listed ten points which he considered essential as the basis for any talks with the rebels. These included a cease-fire, an amnesty, confirmation of reforms already enacted, free trade, equal job opportunity, increased powers for municipal authorities in America, recognition of the government and Cortes by Americans and a commitment by Americans to provide financial aid. More letters were exchanged and again an impasse was reached. The Regency refused to agree to the inclusion of Mexico or to the abolition of the trading monopoly, and Wellesley continued to insist that both were essential. Eventually, the Regency had no choice but to refer the matter again to the Cortes which, after some debate, voted on 16 July by 101 votes to 46 to shelve the whole mediation proposal.[9]

Nevertheless, the idea was not abandoned and in September 1812, following talks with Spain's ambassador, Castlereagh put forward an amended version of the British position. The formal talks would be restricted as Spain had always insisted to those provinces where a *de facto* independence had been established and a Spanish commission, accompanied by a secret British agent who would act as an adviser, would go to Mexico. That province must be included because without the supplies of bullion it provided, Britain might well not be able to afford to keep its armies in Spain and would have to order Wellington to withdraw to Portugal. Finally, the abolition of the trading monopoly remained an absolute prerequisite for the success of any mediation. Notes were again exchanged with both sides seeking clarification, but the Regency would still not accept the inclusion of Mexico nor the trading reform and Wellesley would not withdraw them. He reverted to a large extent to the ten-point programme he had tabled the previous July and which had already been rejected.

By November 1812 it was clear that no progress was being made and the Regency decided to seek the advice of the Council of State which, having been reformed under the new constitution, was in regular weekly and even at times daily session. The Minister of State referred the whole file of the negotiation with nineteen separate sets of documents, starting with Bardají's statement to the Cortes of 1 June 1811, and the councillors began to compile their separate opinions. García, Cevallos and Ibar Navarro produced a joint memorandum in which, although critical of British behaviour and support for the rebels, they still concluded that the mediation should be accepted. They saw no reason why Mexico and the other allegedly peaceful provinces should not be included and be offered the same concessions as the more recalcitrant areas such as Buenos Aires and Caracas. The main sticking-point in their view seemed to be the question of trade. As far as they were concerned, the monopoly was extremely damaging and should be abolished. The interests of the merchants, a minority group, should not be allowed to prejudice the greater public good any longer because there was no doubt that 'exclusive commerce is incompatible with the public prosperity'. They then launched into a bitter attack on the monopoly as 'unjust, pernicious and unconstitutional' and they warned that the British threat to side with the rebels if Spain refused to be flexible must be taken seriously.[10]

Garay was also preparing his position at the same time. He disagreed fundamentally with the whole idea of mediation. The rebels wanted independence and thus it followed that no mediation could work. Only military action could stop them and Britain was unwilling to use force. The question of trade was difficult and complicated and it required exhaustive examination before any decision could be taken. The British could only be allowed to trade directly with America on a very strictly controlled basis and only in return for help with arms, money and equipment which should be arranged in a subsidy treaty. The British were hypocrites; they openly permitted Miranda to use London for his conspiracies and they were encouraging the rebels while simultaneously offering to mediate with them. They were betraying their treaties of friendship with Spain and their argument that France might move in to take America was nonsense. It was Britain to which the rebels had turned for support and which was providing it. British behaviour had been 'unjust, indelicate and harmful to the countries united against the common tyrannical enemy'. In short, to give in to British demands would be dishonourable and an insult to national dignity.

Garay concluded this stinging attack on the British by saying that he would agree to a joint British–Spanish peace initiative but only on the basis that Spain's commitments would be to implement the Constitution and offer an amnesty, but to do nothing for the time being about the trading monopoly. The Regency and British ambassador could publish, he suggested, a joint manifesto for which he offered a draft, and then send joint commissioners to Buenos Aires, Santa Fe and Chile. All that was needed in Mexico was to circulate the manifesto.[11] When the full Council of State met to consider these and other individual opinions, it is clear that Garay's views prevailed. Although the final report moderated the anti-British tone, his suggestions were by and large adopted. The Council advised that the mediation could be accepted because all other measures to achieve peace had failed. The conditions of the talks should be as Garay had advocated, with the free trade issue being the subject of a special enquiry. Meanwhile, a separate commercial treaty in which Britain would be given privileges in exchange for aid could be negotiated.[12]

No action was taken on this report, perhaps because the Regency appreciated that in the absence of any move to abolish the trading monopoly and to include Mexico, it was obvious that Britain would not agree to proceed. The early optimism that mediation would provide a solution to the colonial crisis had been quickly dissipated and the sole result of almost two years of negotiations was an atmosphere of mutual recrimination and anger.[13] Ferdinand's return and his decision to rely largely on military methods seemed to preclude any further efforts in the international arena. The restored régime did, however, successfully conclude related treaties with Britain signed on 5 July and 28 August 1814, in which Spain promised that if the transatlantic trade regulations were amended, Britain would be given favoured nation status, and the British government in turn gave an assurance that it would stop the continued flow of arms and supplies to the rebels. The much-hoped-for success of the Morillo expedition did not, of course, materialize, and even within weeks of its embarkation in February 1815, it had become clear to some of Ferdinand's ministers that a renewed diplomatic initiative was necessary and justified. In the Council of State sessions of April and May 1815, Minister of State Cevallos reintroduced the diplomatic option.[14] On 3 April, he began by surveying the current situation. Nothing, he said, had been omitted in the search for a solution to the American problem. Military action had been taken and talks held with those powers whose cooperation was to be expected. Brazil had been asked to observe the reciprocal guarantee signed with Portugal in 1777 and the chargé d'affaires at Rio de Janeiro had been authorized to try to bribe the rebel leader, José Artigas, into submission. Protests against British favours towards the insurgents had been sent to London, but the most that could be realistically expected was that the British government would do as it had agreed and stop the supply of munitions to the insurgent armies. Britain was being approached for a loan to help the war effort in America but there was little or no chance of it being granted.

On 23 May, Cevallos turned to his more specific proposals. Portugal had broken the 1777 pact and was seeking to expand its borders. Britain had failed to fulfil its commitment to preserve the territorial integrity of the kingdom and it was trading directly with the colonies. No altruistic help could be expected from either country. On the other hand, if commercial privileges were offered, it might be possible to persuade another nation to help and, in his view, preliminary talks should be reopened with Britain. Most of the councillors agreed with Cevallos' analysis and it was formally resolved 'to seek the interposition of Britain for the pacification of the provinces of the River Plate and South America, by means of commercial advantages to be offered'.

The following day, Cevallos wrote to the British ambassador asking to reopen talks, but Wellesley's reply was not immediately encouraging. He noted the failure of the previous negotiation and he warned that Britain would not get involved again before Spain made clear the specific details of what it intended as the basis of mediation talks. In the ensuing correspondence both sides revealed their preconditions. The British wanted Spain to agree to abolish the slave trade and to discuss a new commercial treaty. Ferdinand wanted evidence of Britain's good faith, and, in particular, Cevallos asked for a public condemnation by London of Lord Strangford's support of the Buenos Aires rebels.[15] Then the Council of the Indies advised in favour of

British mediation in exchange for commercial concessions and Ferdinand ordered further enquiries into the implications of ending the monopoly. Again the Council recommended reform, suggesting that the British should be allowed a progressive entry into American markets, starting with Cuba and Puerto Rico and gradually extending to Guatemalan, Peruvian, Venezuelan and other ports.[16] Although the slave issue was now complicating the talks, by November 1815 Vaughan was able to report to Castlereagh that Spain was more willing to be flexible.[17] Cevallos had asked him for troop transports or a cash loan and, when these were refused, he confirmed that Ferdinand had agreed to Britain being given exclusive trading privileges 'provided the British government can succeed by any means in its power in reuniting the Spanish American colonies with the Mother Country'. To the surprise of Cevallos and his colleagues, Castlereagh's response was to reject any idea of exclusive trade for Britain. To give such an advantage to any mediating power, he wrote, 'would render her interposition odious and destroy all her just influence'. Spain must, he continued, provide proof of its willingness to adopt 'liberal principles' if it hoped to induce the Prince Regent to engage in any mediation.[18]

Once again little or no progress was made in arranging any mediation and during the early months of 1816 attention turned more to the slave trade problem, which Spain seemed to see as offering an opportunity to extract both monetary compensation from Britain and its support in America. The negotiations continued intermittently throughout the year with Britain refusing to give in to Spanish demands and relations becoming increasingly strained. They were not helped by the Portuguese invasion of the Banda Oriental which, it was believed in Madrid, would not have occurred without British acquiescence. There were other incidents of friction and more protests from Madrid against the supplies being sent to the rebels from British ports. In fact, the year 1816 was not notable for Anglo-Spanish accord and yet among the several royal councils and individual advisers, there was a renewed consensus for the need to approach Britain again for its help against the rebels. In October the Duque de Montemar told Ferdinand that British mediation remained essential and that it could only be obtained by reforming the commercial system. The merchants who were so opposed to such a change, he said, must be persuaded that it was the only way left of preserving the empire.[19] Other members of the Junta de Pacificación, for example, Bodega, reached the same conclusion and the Council of the Indies reaffirmed its support, warning quite bluntly that without British help, America would certainly be lost.[20]

As these various reports were being prepared in the royal palace in Madrid, Spain's ambassador to London, the Conde de Fernán Núñez, wrote to Castlereagh, but the new spirit and desire for cooperation among his advisers does not seem to have extended to Ferdinand. Fernán Núñez reported that his king expected British assistance in resisting the Portuguese invasion of the River Plate territories and with regard to mediation, Ferdinand did not agree that the British suggestions of more pardons and commercial reform would be of much use. On the contrary, 'His Majesty thinks that the proposed measures and the unarmed Mediation of Great Britain will be of no avail towards quelling the insurrections of America.' If Americans knew that Britain would never use force, they would simply ridicule any negotiation and any reforms by Spain. Furthermore, Fernán Núñez argued, it was the duty of Britain 'in the scale of justice' to cooperate against the rebels; it was in its commercial interest to do so because the prolongation of the conflict was destroying the American economy; and it was in Britain's strategic interest to have Spain strengthened rather than weakened by the loss of its empire. For all these reasons, therefore, Ferdinand called upon Britain 'to modify her system of neutrality and to support her Mediation with force'.[21]

The aggressive tone of these demands and Ferdinand's insistence that Britain should agree to resort to force if necessary certainly surprised Castlereagh. He told Wellesley that the note 'seems most studiously framed in contradiction of every principle upon which this Government has hitherto professed to regulate its conduct'.[22] It was possible, he surmised, that Ferdinand was deliberately trying to provoke Britain into dropping the whole idea so that Spain could turn to other Powers for help or revise its entire policy towards the insurrections. Castlereagh's suspicions were perceptive because, by the end of 1816, the Spanish government had decided to broaden its appeal for support to include whatever nations were willing to help. Henceforth, while British dominance on the international scene meant that it could never be entirely excluded and negotiations continued with London, Spain turned increasingly to other nations, seeking their individual or joint support. Ferdinand had not achieved much from his various manoeuvres at the Congress of Vienna or at the Peace of Paris but when the Holy Alliance was formulated in

September 1815, it seems that he began to see an opportunity to appeal to the principles the Powers had pledged to uphold, particularly the rights of legitimate dynasties. Thus, in July 1816 Francisco Cea Bermúdez, ambassador at St Petersburg, was instructed to impress on the tsar the economic and political importance of defeating the revolutionaries in America and stopping them becoming dependent on Britain. In December, he was told to seek Alexander's agreement that France rather than Britain should lead any mediation.[23]

While these largely exploratory soundings were being made, other avenues were explored. Among the more curious was an offer of help from the ever-adventurous Sir Home Popham. The Spanish government was obviously well aware of the British admiral's exploits in the River Plate in 1806 and when he claimed in June 1816 that he had ideas on how Spain could reconquer the colonies, Spanish attention was alerted. Popham offered to travel to Madrid to explain his thoughts in person to Ferdinand and he had several interviews on the subject with Fernán Núñez in London. Ferdinand was naturally suspicious and nothing came of the contact, although it is possible that more discussion took place in secret afterwards.[24] Despite this and other international contacts that were being made, attention was still officially focussed on Britain. When the Council of State met in January 1817, in the presence of the king, there was little dissent to the Minister of War's submission that the policy of using force had been an expensive failure and should be replaced by one of negotiation. Some councillors, for example Garay, Pizarro and López Araujo, felt it tactically unwise to give up at least the pretence of military action but it was generally accepted that the time for talks had arrived. Hence it was resolved to suspend, secretly, planned military expeditions, to give more resources to the navy and 'to activate at all cost negotiations with England'.[25] Soon after this meeting, the Junta de Pacificación presented its appraisal of the situation and Pizarro handed the file to the Council, suggesting that discussion of it be postponed until councillors had had time to examine its contents. The Junta had argued very strongly in favour of abolishing the trading monopoly and thereby attracting British mediation by peaceful means with the insurgents. Such an alliance with Britain, it advised, was politic and just, in no way offensive to national decorum or dignity, and it offered the only way open to stop the spread and ultimate success of the revolutions.

Pizarro, anticipating the Council's attitude, had already approached Wellesley, and Fernán Núñez informed Castlereagh that Spain was now prepared to grant the rebels an amnesty, a more liberal mercantile code and better opportunities for jobs.[26] Hence, British conditions for acting as mediator appeared to have been met. But there remained other outstanding issues to be settled between the two countries and Pizarro surveyed them in a communiqué of 6 April 1817.[27] There were four matters pending: abolition of the slave trade; British mediation with Portugal; the pacification of America; Spanish relations with the United States. In Pizarro's analysis, the British reluctance to mediate in America was a petty retaliation for Spain's refusal to agree to the terms offered for abolishing the slave trade. He pointed out that the £600,000 sought as compensation was less than Cuban merchants alone would pay to prevent abolition. In America as a whole, there were manifest signs of chaos and anarchy and every chance that new governments formed there would be hostile to British interests. Only by restoring Spain's imperial unity, he contended, could Britain's long-term commercial interests be safeguarded. Similarly, it was in British interests that Portugal should restore the Banda Oriental to Spanish dominion and that Britain should continue to be seen to be impartial and just, principles which 'England sustains with so much honour'. Britain could surely not allow the European balance to be upset nor the creation of an 'immense power' in the New World more friendly to the United States than to Europe, and everybody was concerned to see that the North American republic did not take advantage of the revolutions to expand its own borders. In short, according to Pizarro, there were now mutually beneficial circumstances prevailing for both Britain and Spain and he was surprised at the dilatory, indifferent attitudes displayed in London.

Pizarro seems to have been trying in this note to keep all his options open to ensure that even if British support in America was not forthcoming, it might still be available in other areas. Shortly afterwards, Cea Bermúdez replied to the instructions of the previous December, advising that the tsar thought that relying on British involvement was dangerous and that it would be better for other Allied Powers to participate in any talks with the rebels.[28] Dimitri Tatischeff, Russian ambassador in Madrid and alleged member of Ferdinand's camarilla, confirmed that his government now favoured foreign intervention, but also that Spain must make substantial concessions.²⁹ Also, although unknown to Pizarro, Ferdinand and his more intimate advisers had already begun, or were soon to do so, the talks with Tatischeff which led to the contract for the purchase of the Russian ships. Then, coincidentally, there were several other developments which seemed to indicate that the moment was propitious to raise the American problem at a European level. Ferdinand, after long hesitation, agreed to sign the Act of the Congress of Vienna and that of the Second Peace of Paris; a treaty to abolish the slave trade was in its final stages and was signed in September; finally, news arrived in Madrid of the March 1817 revolt at Pernambuco in Brazil. What was needed was an opportunity and this was anticipated at the forthcoming ambassadorial conference to be held in Paris. Pizarro circulated a communiqué to the ambassadors in which he set out to demonstrate that there was a significant link between the Portuguese invasion of the Banda Oriental, the Pernambuco revolt and the revolutions in America.³⁰ European governments, he said, were fully aware of the revolutionary spirit which had caused so much ruin in recent years. Any dealings with revolutionaries were 'a positive step against the sacred principle of legitimacy' and for monarchs to sanction rebellion for any reason whatever was to invalidate all the efforts of the European Powers to restore order and the rule of law. The Portuguese had invaded Spanish territory in the River Plate and they had given at least tacit support to the rebels in Buenos Aires. Their actions, contravening all the doctrines of legitimacy, had thus greatly encouraged the revolutionary spirit and, as a consequence, they were now themselves faced with insurrection at Pernambuco. This development justified everything that Ferdinand had been saying to his fellow rulers about the dangers of not suppressing revolution wherever it occurred. Hence he now called on the Allied Powers to unite to destroy the spirit of revolution in Brazil and Spanish America and ensure the victory of legitimacy.

At first, the assembled diplomats at Paris did not appear hostile to the Spanish case and the Russian envoy, Count Pozzo di Borgo, began to intrigue on Spain's behalf.³¹ He warned his own government of the dangers of anarchy in America and he recommended that if Spain would produce a plan of reform and concessions, the Allies could act as mediators 'combining persuasion with whatever force might be available and advice with the means of making it effective'. Pozzo did not think that military reconquest alone was feasible, but he shared Spain's view that any mediation that was not supported by at least the threat of force would fail. When Fernán Núñez made it clear that Spain welcomed the prospect of an Allied mediation, Pozzo persuaded the Austrian and Prussian representatives and later Richelieu that the idea ought to be on their agenda. Sir Charles Stuart, however, quickly made the British position clear, arguing that he did not have the authority to discuss the matter and, on 20 August 1817, Castlereagh circulated to the courts of St Petersburg, Vienna, Paris and Berlin a 'Confidential Memorandum' in which he explained the British position.[32] He insisted that Britain had no desire to see the break-up of the Spanish empire, but he repeated that any international mediation to which Britain was a party could only be entertained provided Spain agreed in advance to four basic conditions: to abolish the slave trade; a general amnesty and armistice for the duration of the negotiations; equality of job opportunity for Americans; international freedom of trade with America. Finally, Britain would not take part in any mediation which entailed the threat or actual use of force.

This latest statement from London coincided with the beginning of the important debate in the Council of State starting in September 1817.[33] Although the British position had not materially changed since 1811, Pizarro remained optimistic that British support could be obtained. He admitted that mediation was not the ideal or only solution but he felt that, despite their differences, there was still a good chance of British cooperation, but their mediation should only be directed to those places such as Buenos Aires with which there was no communication. He still believed also that Britain should offer a guarantee of success and that the guarantee should consist of a commitment to help to suppress the rebels by force if the talks failed within a predetermined time limit. In return for their assistance, the British should be offered commercial benefits.

Like the British, Pizarro had not changed his views since 1811 and the differences of opinion among his colleagues remained the same. Some, for example Anselmo Rivas, the Duque del Parque, Pedro Mendinueta and the Duque de Veragua, spoke in favour of mediation, but others either wanted the matter postponed to await the results of the Paris conference or were implacably opposed to the whole idea. The most vociferous of the latter was Lozano de Torres. He blamed the British for causing the revolts and denounced their philanthropic stance as hypocritical and long since sacrificed to their mercantile ambitions. In his opinion, the best way to preserve America was to keep foreigners out and, above all, the British. Minister of War Eguía made similar points and López Araujo thought it imprudent to rely on promises made by rebels under British guarantees. Vázquez Figueroa preferred international mediation rather than exclusively British and that no approach should be made to London until all other diplomatic channels had been exhausted. Even then, mediation should only be employed as a last resort.[34]

Neither Pizarro nor the other councillors looked on mediation as the only solution. It was merely one option worth pursuing, at least as far as some of them were concerned, simultaneously with the myriad other ideas they had and much of the heated debate in the Council centred on the trading monopoly, which Pizarro and others felt must be reformed if there was to be any hope of reconciling Americans, with or without foreign intervention. Hence a range of proposals was approved of which one was that negotiations with other Powers should continue but without prejudice to the other agreed measures. Pizarro thus had the authorization he wanted and he dispatched a formal reply to the British memorandum to the Paris Conference.[35] He introduced no new ideas, simply restating the Spanish position. The revolutions were contrary to the doctrine of legitimacy, the rule of law, the dignity of nations and international trade. Europe would be the loser if the war continued because 'an indigenous barbarism' would assume power and the vast markets of the American continent would be lost. Spain had always been willing to make concessions compatible with national honour and would grant an amnesty but not an armistice. It expected the help and cooperation of its allies against the republicans and jacobins of America, but the terms of the British document were unacceptable, mainly because they offered no guarantee of success or aid if the rebels refused to agree. The Allied Powers, therefore, should present to Spain their own detailed proposals for any joint mediation which, if arranged, should take place in Madrid.

For the next few months, Pizarro continued his diplomatic effort both directly with Britain and with the European Powers but he made little or no progress. The Allied Powers were requested to mediate in the Montevideo dispute and, although some discussion did take place in Paris, it produced no firm result and negotiations with Portugal achieved nothing. The tsar floated the idea of an economic boycott of American produce, but Russia in general still favoured a joint approach and while France was sympathetic, it offered no concrete support.[36] Pizarro became increasingly frustrated. The issue, he wrote in March 1818, was 'a real chaos, leading nowhere', and despite further confirmation to London that Spain would relax the trading monopoly, the British renewed their complaints of Spanish vacillation on both the terms and place for any talks.[37] In the Council of State, Pizarro emphasized the lack of progress and warned that the situation was so critical that energetic steps independent of mediation would have to be taken as a matter of urgency if the empire was to be saved. An amnesty for Spanish exiles should be announced, free trade declared and the planned military expedition to the River Plate evaluated by the military committee. The first two of these measures, he thought, would in themselves be helpful but they would also be useful in any further attempts to get foreign support and the third would enable Spain to continue the suppression of the revolutions on its own account.[38] Much of the following discussion was again dominated by the pro- and anti- free trade factions and the destination of the military expedition provoked lengthy contoversy. Several councillors still retained their faith in British intervention although, for the most part, the mediation concept was obscured by the hopes for a military solution. Pizarro was given little firm guidance and on 9 June 1818 he presented Ferdinand with a set of recommendations and within his nineteen points, he did not include mediation.[39]

Nevertheless, despite Pizarro's disillusion with the diplomatic prospects, news had recently been received of the Allied Powers' intention of holding a conference at Aix-la-Chapelle. Ferdinand immediately instructed Cea Bermúdez at St Petersburg to impress upon the tsar that he was anxious to be represented 'for the purpose of pressing upon their consideration the urgent necessity of joint interference to effect the re-establishment of the King of Spain's authority in his colonial possessions'.[40] Pizarro was told to prepare a memorandum to the Allied Powers on the pacification of America and this was duly circulated on 17 or 18 June 1818.[41] The general points were as before – the political and economic benefits accruing to Europe from a united Spanish empire – but now Spain set out specifically the terms on which it called on the Powers to intervene. These were as follows: a general amnesty for the insurgents at the time of their submission; equal job opportunity; a rather guarded promise to liberalize the commercial code; a promise to adopt whatever measures the Allies proposed 'which shall be compatible with his dignity and the preservation of his rights'.

Whatever hopes Ferdinand had of this latest offer were soon dispelled. France and Russia were sympathetic to the idea of having America on their agenda but Austria, Prussia and, above all Britain, were opposed. Castlereagh repeated all his previous objections, emphasizing that there was as yet no agreed programme on which the Allied Powers could proceed and that his government was resolutely opposed to the use of force. Even in the face of this British opposition, however, Ferdinand continued to campaign for an invitation to the conference, warning that he would accept no decision affecting Spain taken in his absence. San Carlos and Casa Irujo were named as the Spanish representatives and their instructions once again concentrated on the harm being caused to European trade, the increase in jacobins and the threat to legitimacy.

It had all been said before and neither Britain nor Spain was willing to compromise. San Carlos knew it and he realized that no progress would be made unless a radical new approach was devised. In a series of notes to Ferdinand, he set out his own ideas.[42] The revolutions were getting worse, he said, and nothing should be expected from Britain or the other Powers because they viewed the movements for emancipation either with pleasure or with indifference. Spain could not reconquer the colonies without foreign help and that would not be forthcoming under the present conditions. It was obvious, therefore, that foreign powers must be attracted by an offer of substantial benefits. San Carlos did not at first spell out precisely what he meant by this but, in a dispatch of 25 September, he contended that the only way forward was to make major territorial concessions in the hope that by sacrificing some provinces, others could be retained. Cuba and Panama should go to Britain; the Spanish part of Santo Domingo to France; Guayana and Cumaná to Holland.

San Carlos, a close friend of the king and an experienced diplomat, shocked his colleagues in Madrid with his general pessimism and assessment that unless his radical proposals were adopted, the independence of America was virtually inevitable. In fact, his idea of territorial sacrifice was not new but it had never before been advanced by so senior a member of the régime. Luis de Onís had mentioned the possibility of transferring territory to the United States in an attempt to stop its advance into Mexico and that Santo Domingo might be given to France in exchange for naval aid.[43] Others had produced schemes for ceding the Californias to Russia, and there had also been much discussion about resolving the difficulties with Brazil by exchanging the River Plate provinces for Portugal. Fernán Núñez told Richelieu in February 1817 that Spain would cede Santo Domingo in exchange for military assistance, and there had been over the previous few years plans and projects for the exchange of most of Spanish America either for direct compensation or territories, one of which, incidentally, was Gibraltar. None of these plans, although mostly examined in the royal committees, found any significant degree of support and the same negative reaction greeted San Carlos. Ferdinand set up an *ad hoc* committee to report on his ideas and it found his pessimism unjustified, particularly in respect of getting foreign support. One member of the committee, Gómez de Liaño, agreed with San Carlos' general picture but he wanted the urgent dispatch of at least 16,000 men to the River Plate. As far as he could see, there were only two ways of persuading foreigners to help, either by granting direct trade or by ceding territory. The trading concession was regrettable but indispensable but the thought of territorial cessions was 'an infamy on the name of Spain' and he would never agree to it.[45]

Four days after Gómez de Liaño's report, the Junta de Pacificación completed its review of San Carlos' ideas. It repeated its opinion, held, it said, since 1816, that British mediation based on commercial reform was the only hope and that, despite San Carlos' advice, negotiations should be continued with the British government as well as with the Powers at Aix-la-Chapelle. At the same time, however, preparations for the expedition to the River Plate must continue to have it ready for use if any mediation failed.[46] Another respected figure, the Conde de Ofalia, added his voice in favour of seeking help at Aix-la-Chapelle. He produced a detailed programme of reforms and other measures, including Allied military aid, which he wanted presented at the conference.[47]

Pizarro received all this advice and chose to continue to explore all possible avenues. Fruitless talks were held in London with representatives of the Buenos Aires régime and Fernán Núñez was authorized to mention the possible transfer of Santo Domingo to Britain.[48] Contacts were maintained with Richelieu who had also exchanged notes with the rebel Buenos Aires authorities and he suggested that a Spanish prince should be sent there.[49] Tatischeff was encouraged to intrigue behind the scenes and, as Castlereagh told Wellesley in September 1818, 'It is quite obvious that Spain is intriguing in all quarters, and in all directions, and there are feelings connected with the old Family alliance which give her too easy an access to certain of the Powers.'[50] But, as far as Pizarro was concerned, it was all in vain and for him personally, too late, because on 15 September, Ferdinand finally lost patience and dismissed him. He was replaced by Casa Irujo who lost no time in rejecting the policies of his predecessor, especially his pursuit of foreign mediation in exchange for commercial advantages. Anyone familiar with the English, Casa Irujo told Ferdinand, should have known that such a policy would fail. They were already trading in America and it was obvious that they would not help in suppressing the movements for independence merely in return for something they already had. What, he asked, would Spain get out of mediation? What benefits were there in admitting foreigners to provinces which had not rebelled or had already been pacified by Spain's own efforts? Perhaps Buenos Aires would submit but New Spain, Guatemala, Venezuela, Peru and elsewhere would be lost. San Carlos should be instructed to stop all talks on mediation and military reconquest should be proceeded with as quickly as possible.[51] Casa Irujo's reactionary view was promptly approved by Ferdinand and instructions were sent to San Carlos and to the ambassadors in Paris and Vienna to stop all talk of mediation. A note was also sent to St Petersburg calling on the tsar to help the military effort, which was now said to be the only way left of stopping America falling into the hands of Britain and the United States.[52]

Spain did not receive an invitation to Aix-la-Chapelle, but the American issue was discussed, largely as the result of a joint Franco-Russian initiative. Castlereagh still objected to any form of military intervention and he raised various problems concerning the form and composition of any mediating body. The other powers accepted the British position and the diplomatic gulf between Spain and the rest of Europe remained as wide as ever. Subsequently there was talk, mostly promoted by Tatischeff it seems, of the Duke of Wellington being asked to lead a mediation but by then, Ferdinand and his new team of advisers were fully committed to the River Plate expedition and no longer interested in a diplomatic solution.

Throughout its three years in power, the second constitutional régime had solid reasons for not seeking foreign intervention. Many liberals were confident that the restoration of their sacred charter would bring imperial harmony if not directly and at once, at least in the sense that it provided the opportunity and atmosphere for talks with the rebels. Also, it was not long before they knew that

Ferdinand's public acceptance of the Constitution disguised his private abhorrence of it and that in secret he was trying to persuade sympathetic rulers to act on his behalf. Thus the several sources of potential foreign aid canvassed so much in the past were closed to the liberals as Ferdinand appealed to family and dynastic loyalties not for intervention in America but in the peninsula. As regards Britain, less hostile perhaps to the liberal experiment than were the absolute monarchies of Europe, it was quickly realized that no help would be forthcoming. In a policy survey of June 1820, the Minister of Foreign Affairs was told by his officials that British neutrality towards the colonies was no more than a monstrous pretence. Britain continued to assist the rebels with money, arms and volunteers and no reliance should be placed on London.[53] Finally, the constitutional authorities were confronted from the end of 1821 with the knowledge that the United States was preparing to grant diplomatic recognition to the new American nations and that other countries, notably Britain, would be unwilling to be left dragging their feet and would sooner or later follow the North American example.

For these and other reasons, therefore, the liberal governments, both moderate and radical, preferred to try direct negotiations with the insurgents. Following long and tortuous debate in the executive and in the Cortes, commissioners armed with detailed instructions set out for the various overseas provinces where they were invariably greeted with open hostility or the simple truth that the only basis for any settlement was Spanish recognition of independence, which was the one step they were forbidden to discuss. Cease-fires were arranged, talks were held with Bolívar's representatives both in America and Madrid and even with Buenos Aires where a convention was signed in June 1823. But no substantive progress was made on the real issue of independence and as each area in America consolidated its position, once again the thoughts of some turned to foreign aid. In the Council of State in October and November 1821, several councillors stated their belief that mediation or even foreign military help was still a possible option.[54] Esteban Varea wanted talks reopened with Britain and although he knew, he said, of the rumours that the British were going to recognize independence, it was worth making another approach and reminding the Powers of the treaties of Utrecht whereby they had guaranteed Spanish possession of America. Aycinena, Luyando, Flores and Anglona to some extent shared Varea's opinion. We should have persuaded Britain to help years ago, they complained, but it was not too late because the British had never wanted to conquer the New World but only to trade with it. On the other hand, the remaining Powers were not to be trusted. There was no doubt that Portugal, the United States, France and Russia 'positively want to invade America'. Portugal already controlled the southern continent; the United States wanted the eastern territories of New Spain; Russia also wanted the latter and France was seeking to establish its own colonies. Not all the councillors shared these suspicions and it was eventually decided to recommend that 'the government should ask England for whatever aid was appropriate for the pacification and conservation of the Americas' and that if those talks failed, other countries should be contacted with trading privileges again being offered as the bait. Minister of Ultramar López Pelegrín accepted the Council's advice and in his own proposals to the Cortes of January 1822, he included the idea of negotiating the active cooperation of a foreign power in exchange for commercial benefits. To advocate such a step was, he admitted, regrettable but with the kingdom weak and poor, it could not be avoided.[55]

Whatever hopes were still cherished of attracting British mediation or aid did not last long as Britain's diplomats in Madrid made it quite clear that in their view, Spain's only course of action was to accept the fact of independence and seek to negotiate an advantageous settlement. Other Powers were not so immediately discouraging. At the Congress of Verona, Metternich stated unequivocally that Austria would never recognize American independence 'so long as his Catholic Majesty shall not have freely and formally renounced the right of sovereignty which he has exercised over them'.[56] The French also offered their help and with Russia always ready with sympathy if little else, Ferdinand did not give up hope that once his allies had restored him to his legitimate pre-eminence in the peninsula, he might be able to persuade his friends to extend their assistance to the American portion of his kingdom. Ferdinand was always confronted, however, with the British refusal to sanction any external intervention in America and shortly after his return to absolute power in September 1823, Canning repeated the long-held view of his government in the so-called Polignac Memorandum that the military reconquest of America was 'utterly hopeless' and that any negotiation to reconcile Spain and America would be unsuccessful.[57] Thus Britain indicated its intention to proceed with the recognition of the former colonies and when, a few weeks later, Monroe issued his warning against European intervention in the hemisphere, it seemed that even Ferdinand would have to acknowledge that the end of the road had been reached. Yet, not unexpectedly, he did not and ignoring both the British and United States warnings, he circulated the courts of Europe inviting them to attend a conference in Paris where Allied support 'in adjusting the affairs of the revolted Colonies of America' would be discussed.[58] His case was no different to that postulated by Pizarro so many times in 1817 and 1818: the principles of order and legitimacy had to be upheld and if their subversion were countenanced, it was only a matter of time before the cancer spread to Europe. Needless to say, Canning would not agree unless Spain was willing to accept independence and he made sure that the rest of Europe was aware of his opposition.

Flying in the face of international opinion and world-wide recognition of the American republics, Ferdinand persevered and his diplomats continued to probe and encourage foreign powers to come to his aid. It was all to no avail and in 1828 the Council of State finally accepted the futility of any more diplomatic initiatives. Surveying the results of all the previous negotiations, the Council noted that initially it had seemed that Spain's allies would cooperate, but within a short time a 'certain coldness' had became evident in their responses either because they anticipated commercial benefits from the new nations or because of pressure from the court of St James. France had given positive indications of its willingness to help, but in February 1826 it had appointed agents in Mexico and admitted insurgent vessels to its ports. In Rome, the Pope had recently appointed bishops for various churches in rebel provinces and the United States had been the first to recognize independence. The Low Countries, Prussia, Württemburg, Hamburg and Switzerland had all established commercial relations with Mexico. Those governments had bowed to pressure from Britain which had betrayed its treaties and obligations to Spain. Following the death of Alexander, who had been anxious to sustain 'the imprescriptible rights of Kings', the new authorities in Russia were no longer interested. In sum, there was now no point in further diplomacy with other nations whose actions were determined by self-interest, ambition and the 'imagined wealth' they believed to be found in America. Spain must, therefore, prepare to reconquer its empire by its own efforts.[59]

Spanish hopes that other nations would come to its aid were finally extinguished. The diplomatic effort had been long and arduous and all governments had diligently pursued every opportunity but in retrospect, as Martínez de la Rosa and others understood, there had never been any real chance of success.[60] From the moment in 1810 when foreign intervention became associated with reform of the trading monopoly, powerful interest groups had campaigned against the whole idea, using economic as well as political arguments. The Cádiz *consulado* had carefully played on the traditional xenophobia of their compatriots, blaming foreigners and their smuggling as a prime cause of the revolutions and predicting that to let them anywhere near America would bring the corruption of the religious unity which held the empire together and ensure its complete disintegration. Many shared the views of the merchants, and there were those who always felt that to have to seek foreign help was humiliating and offensive to the nation's honour. They could not accept that Spain was powerless to look after its own affairs and there is no doubt that the arrogance and disdain of American capabilities was so ingrained that it was widely believed to be only a matter of time before the presumed loyal majority in the overseas provinces reasserted themselves on behalf of the Mother Country.

When it came to Britain, on which most Spanish hopes rested, there were mixed reactions. Although their invaluable ally in the peninsular war, few, if any, Spaniards trusted the British or their protestations of good faith and honest intention. They knew of British contacts with the insurgents and the ever-increasing contraband trade tacitly accepted by all British governments. They needed British help and cooperation but they feared it and, while the anti-British attitudes of Garay, Lozano de Torres and others were perhaps extreme, their general feelings were certainly shared by most of their contemporaries. The British offer to mediate of 1810–12, and all subsequent negotiations with the British government, were always suspected of ulterior motives and duplicity and British diplomats were never able to dispel the mistrust which they encountered at every stage. As the Conde de Toreno recalled, the mediation initiative put forward at Cádiz, that 'extremely arduous negotiation' as he described it, was characterized throughout by 'mutual suspicion'.[61] A decade later, Ferdinand himself wrote that 'for many years, England has been secretly working to make Spanish America independent of the metropolis'.[62]

Spain had expended a great deal of time and effort in seeking some form of international help. It had considered foreign mediation on numerous occasions; it had sought direct military intervention; it had even contemplated territorial sacrifices in the hope of preserving at least some parts of the empire. Yet at no point was any Spanish government fully confident that support from the nation's allies would provide a solution to the crisis. Ferdinand, the many ministers and advisers, despite their public pronouncements, appreciated that assistance would not come from notions of family loyalty or principles of dynastic legitimacy. It had to be bought with concessions and the price was always too high. The abolition of the trading monopoly was a possibility, but with so many dangerous implications on the domestic scene, it could not be granted except in exchange for the guarantees of success which neither Britain nor any other country could or would give. The territorial exchange or cession postulated most seriously in 1818 by San Carlos was an even higher price to pay and by the 1820s, the unthinkable, recognition of independence, was Britain's final offer. As the Cádiz merchants, Garay, Lozano de Torres, Casa Irujo and so many others concluded, the risks were too great, the price too high and the humiliation too profound.

Epilogue

It was not until 1895 when the independence of Honduras was recognized that Spain finally acknowledged the separation of all of its former colonies on the continent of America and, just three years later, the remaining island possessions of Cuba, Puerto Rico and the Philippines were lost in the humiliating war with the United States. The impact and significance of the dramatic events of 1898, and the so-called Generation of 1898 to which they gave birth, were at least in part a reflection of the fact that Spaniards throughout much of the century had never been able to accept fully that their empire had been irrevocably lost. Beset by feelings of nostalgia for past glories, they clung to their faint hopes that one day the ethnic, cultural and personal bonds with their American 'brothers' might lead to reconciliation in some form of Hispanic union. Every few years, there were ideas and projects for helping to set up new monarchies in America to be presided over by Spanish princes or of creating an economic, if not political, Hispanic confederation.[1] Whenever, as did occur from time to time, there seemed some sympathy for such schemes in one or other of the new republics, excitement and interest were aroused in Madrid where the politicians talked profoundly of fraternal union, perpetual friendship and trusted that commercial relations would be the vehicle to restore some semblance of the old imperial unity. The retention of the island colonies and, above all, Cuba which played a major role in Spanish trade throughout the nineteenth century, were crucial factors in the perpetuation of this illusion of imperial grandeur and as long as the illusion persisted, Spaniards were reluctant to accept the permanency of the loss of their empire. But they could not ignore reality. They had tried everything within their power to prevent the separation of America but the military, economic, diplomatic and all the other myriad avenues that had been explored had failed. There was only one thing left for them to do – recognition of independence had to be contemplated.

The men who first faced the dilemma of whether or not to recognize the independence of the former colonies were by and large those who, throughout the decade of revolution from 1810–20, had resolutely set their minds against it. This attitude was understandable so long as it was believed for whatever reason that independence was not inevitable, but after 1820, the evidence of Spain's impotence to change the course of events was so overwhelming that all groups and individuals were obliged to reassess the situation. Most knew that they could not prevent independence but they did not have to accept it. Instead, they needed to find reasons and arguments to justify their continued rejection of it and, of course, to sustain their hopes that the future might still bring about some form of reconciliation. The liberal dilemma of the previous decade became even more acute. Liberals had preached the virtues of popular sovereignty and self-determination and yet they had chosen to deny Americans the same natural rights to which they claimed Spaniards in the peninsula were entitled. Americans and others had not been slow to point out this inconsistency and inherent contradiction between liberal theory and practice, but the liberals had been able to reject the criticism on the grounds that the movements for colonial emancipation were the actions of a minority unrepresentative of the popular will and which would not succeed. Events had proved them wrong and with independence being consolidated across the continent during the liberal triennium, they needed to explain their continued refusal to apply their sacred political and constitutional dogma to independent America. Some liberals found their attitude difficult to justify. Writing to Lord Holland in April 1824, the liberal poet Manuel José Quintana, famed for his stirring verse in favour of liberty, declared that Ferdinand was right not to recognize independence because 'it was a loathsome contradiction to expect the king to consent to the rebellion of his subjects in America when he would not agree to the desire for constitutional rule by his vassals in Spain'.[2] In other words, if we, the Spaniards, must suffer despotism, then so must the Americans. A similar illustration of the liberal dilemma is to be seen in the views of the many liberal exiles who found themselves in London in the 1820s. Their attitude has been summarized as follows:

In a general way one can say that an event consummated in fact and accepted by themselves as inevitable, found more or less resigned approval . . . by men who considered themselves favourable, if not to independence, at least to American liberties.[3]

For the conservatives and absolutists, there was no such intellectual problem because they took their lead from Ferdinand and his response was always consistent and clear. He would quite simply never countenance recognition of independence because he chose to consider that to do so would be tantamount to breaking his oath to preserve the territorial integrity of his kingdom. He had sworn never 'to alienate, cede or divide any part of the kingdom', although he seems to have seen no inconsistency in the fact that in 1819 he had agreed to the transfer of Florida to the United States, a point to which liberal advocates of recognition were repeatedly to draw attention. Nevertheless, as Cea Bermúdez explained in 1825, 'non-recognition was with the king an article of faith. His conscience, his religion he might call it, would for ever prevent him from thinking of such an arrangement.'[4] Ferdinand never deviated from this position, believing to his dying day that his dominion in America would be restored, if not by military means, then by the spontaneous reaction of what he always thought was a loyal majority merely awaiting their opportunity to place themselves once again under his paternal protection. The fact of independence, therefore, meant nothing to him. It was not a matter for pragmatic or opportunist politics but of principle, of his inherited regal rights and his responsibilities to his overseas subjects. While an astute and flexible political opportunist on most issues, even willing publicly to humiliate himself when necessary with the hated constitutionalists in order to await developments in his favour, he could never bring himself to give way to the slightest degree on the subject of American independence. For him, and the experience of his own long and eventful career clearly explains his view, nothing was inevitable or final. Louis XVIII had, after all, he recalled, regained his throne by sheer perseverance.[5]

Ferdinand's absolute conviction and wholly unyielding attitude determined at least the public response of those devoted traditionalists among his advisers and hence there is no evidence that any of his ministers or councillors ever gave any serious thought to the possibility of recognition. Among the ministers in the several constitutional administrations, however, the possibility was certainly considered and the same conclusion was reached, although for different reasons. After 1820, some politicians and others did begin to suggest that the loss of the empire must be accepted and that negotiations should be started with the new countries to see if at least some kind of commercial advantages could be salvaged. This recognition lobby was never strong during those years but it was sufficient to force the government to seek to explain its refusal to agree. In his report of January 1822, Minister of Ultramar López Pelegrín presented the executive's official view. Should Spain, he asked, recognize the independence of those colonies in revolt, or should it accept the separation of at least some of them? The government had concluded that it should not do so for these reasons. The laws of government followed those of nature and indicated the inevitability of the emancipation of the individual, but such freedom came only when the individual had reached adulthood and maturity. The individual must have sufficiently developed physical and moral faculties to look after himself. Was America in such a condition? Manifestly not, he thought, and the impartial judgement of most observers agreed that the events of the previous decade, notably the anarchy in Buenos Aires, demonstrated that the colonies were neither prepared for nor capable of self-government. While there were talented people in America, there were not enough for self-government and the continent's backward agriculture, industry and commerce could not sustain it. Gold and silver were not enough and it was the possession of such riches which had made the region the target for the ambitions of so many other nations. If Spanish protection were removed, America would fall prey to foreign usurpers or internal chaos and it was the moral duty of the Mother Country to prevent that happening. Finally, Spain could not honourably abandon the loyal majority of Americans who wanted to remain within the imperial family.[6]

Thus López Pelegrín explained the liberal régime's case against recognition and much the same points that he used were to be made at the time and years later by other ministers. José Vadillo, for example, was also Minister of Ultramar in 1822 and, in 1830, he published a book in Paris in which he looked back on the situation which had faced him and his cabinet colleagues.[7] It was by no means clear in the years from 1820 to 1823, he insisted, that the separation of the colonies was certain and, even if it had been, recognition of independence at that point in time would not have been in the best interests of either Spain or America. Certainly, he accepted the natural right of all people to freedom but America was not ready for it. Moreover, he asked, what exactly was Spain supposed to recognize? Recognition could only be extended to properly constituted, stable régimes and it was obvious to everyone that such things did not exist in America. There the provinces were all different and wanted different things and it was no easy matter to reconcile Spain's national interests and honour with the wishes of Americans.

Vadillo's views are typical of liberal writers in the decades following Ayacucho. Their most frequent observation was that the colonies were not ready for self-government. The movements for emancipation were premature and the change from colonial status to republicanism too sudden. The liberals claimed to have understood this and convinced themselves that their refusal to grant independence was an act of altruism rather than imperial obstinacy. Martínez de la Rosa, prime minister in 1822, added another reason for the failure of his government to implement its own ideological creed. American independence was not opportune in 1822, he wrote, and recognition would have been counter-productive because of Ferdinand's known opposition but, above all, because public opinion in Spain was not prepared for it. His policy, therefore, had been to seek a cease-fire, start negotiations and allow the due process of time to enable Spaniards to become accustomed to the idea of the loss of their empire. What he wanted to achieve, he said, was 'a long truce'.[8]

Another former minister in the constitutional goverment, José Canga Argüelles, was more direct in his opposition to recognition. He changed his mind on the issue, having at one stage in the mid 1820s favoured it but, by 1829, he had become implacably opposed. Launching into a bitter attack on the 'madness, lack of thought, and intrigue' which had made Americans abandon the path of virtue, he depicted America as a continent of anarchy, dictators and factional strife, where the spread of ill-digested concepts of equality and liberty would ensure a perpetual state of war. Spain was right not to extend recognition and should on the contrary prepare for reconquest.[9]

The views of other individual ministers in the liberal triennium are not known in any detail but it may be presumed that by and large they shared those of López Pelegrín, Vadillo, Martínez de la Rosa and Canga Argüelles. Their public voice, however, may not always have reflected their private opinions. For Evaristo de San Miguel, Minister of State in 1822, according to a British diplomatic report, 'His private opinion had always been that a Recognition more or less limited was inevitable; that when the fruit was ripe, it would fall from the tree, whatever efforts were made to prevent it; it was in the natural course of things, and could not be avoided.'[10] Such also seems to have been the retrospective view of Pizarro. America, he wrote, 'must follow the fate that nature has destined for all those distant possessions separated by difficult geographical intervals from their centres; it must emancipate itself'.[11]

Like every other group involved in the search for a solution to the crisis, the Council of State after 1820 was also obliged to address the possibility of recognition. Although it voted formally never to consent to the break-up of the empire and most councillors preferred to base their assessments on that cardinal principle, some did seek to explain why they were against recognition. In a joint report, Aycinena, Luyando, Flores and Anglona emphasized that the anarchy so prevalent in Buenos Aires would be repeated elsewhere and particularly in Mexico if independence was achieved, and that it was hence the duty of the metropolis to save Americans from the consequences of their own actions. They should be told that Spain could not accept their emancipation because 'justice, politics and the very interests of Americans were against it'. After eleven years of war, it was clear that Americans did not have the necessary elements required to form governments which would be capable of maintaining public order. The experience of the recent past had proved the truth of this assertion and Spain would be failing in 'its most sacred obligation' if it placed at risk the lives, honour and property of the 15,000,000 Americans. Independence was not politic because there was no province capable of guaranteeing any pact, treaty or agreement, nor of sustaining its own existence against physical and moral attacks from other countries which sought to dominate the continent. It was not in America's interest to be free and defenceless and there was no government of any form which could offer anything like the advantages offered by that of the metropolis. Union with Spain would ensure that the internal fratricidal war which would certainly occur between independent states would be avoided; there would be complete freedom from personal taxation and reduced excise taxes; agriculture, industry and commerce would be unrestricted. Independence was thus premature at the present time and although things might be different in the future, it was probable that even then Americans would not want to separate and lose the help and support of '10,000,000, 20,000,000 or 30,000,000 of their brothers in Europe'.[12]

Although one or two of the other councillors were willing to acknowledge that it was virtually impossible to prevent the independence of some provinces, there was only one who felt able to accept that fact openly and advise recognition. Gabriel Ciscar began by saying that, in his view, it was now impossible for Spain to suppress or maintain America in its former dependent state and it was a waste of money and resources to try to do so. To beg for British military assistance was 'impolitic and indecorous', merely serving to increase American hatred of Spaniards. The continent was too distant to be governed properly from the peninsula and American complaints could not be met without inordinate delay. The moment had arrived, therefore, for America to be divided into independent nations in an Hispanic federation. To those who claimed that independence would be unconstitutional, 'absolute emancipation is more compatible with the Constitution and less transcendental than the conservation of the dependency of those countries with anti-constitutional means'.[13]

Ciscar's was a lone voice in the Council of State but his views did eventually receive rather more support in the Cortes. The deputies who assembled in 1820 from all parts of Spain and America and their successors in the subsequent sessions tried for a long time to deflect the need to face up to the question of recognition, preferring to leave any initiative to the executive. But events in America, especially in Mexico with the successful Iturbide-led revolt sanctioned by Spain's own representative, Juan O'Donojú, together with pressure from the small but vocal pro-recognition lobby, forced the congress to debate the issue. It was, of course, discussed indirectly on several occasions, but the main debate began early in 1822 when the Cabrera de Nevares proposals were introduced by deputy Golfin. He ridiculed the idea of sending more envoys to find out what Americans wanted. Everbody knew, he declared, that they wanted independence and had done so for the past eleven years. There was no agreement possible except on the basis of recognition and that must be the first step to allow talks on a new relationship to begin.

Faced with this radical assertion and in effect challenge to them, the deputies were obliged to explain their reasons for opposing it. For the Conde de Toreno, the idea of general recognition was unbecoming, impractical and impossible and rather than bringing any benefit to Spain, it would cause great harm. How, he asked, can we agree to recognize independence under certain conditions when there was no way of enforcing the conditions? Torre Marín opposed any idea of unrestricted recognition. As far as he was concerned, the American governments only wanted it in the hope that it would stop their own internal factional rivalry. Dolarea was unequivocal: any talk of recognition was treasonable and he would never agree to it because such a step would mean that at no time in the future would Spain be able to reassert its right of dominion. Also, as soon as Spain agreed to their separation, the colonies would be open to foreign aggression. For Priego, it was all rather too late to do anything other than to recognize independence subject to satisfactory treaties being negotiated. At least then, Spanish investments in America might be safeguarded. The Minister of Ultramar, speaking for the cabinet, warned that neither the executive nor the Cortes was empowered to grant independence and, in the government's view, to do so would be unconstitutional.

The debate continued with some deputies resolutely for and others just as resolutely against any move towards recognition. Those in favour tended to accept the argument of inevitability, agreeing that as a *de facto* separation now existed in most of the former colonies, it was as well to accept the situation and negotiate the best deal possible in the circumstances. For those opposed, all was not yet lost and even renewed military action had it supporters. The Mother Country could not, it was repeated, honourably abandon the many loyalists and it could not recognize governments with no semblance of stability or permanency. Just as the king had sworn to preserve his kingdom, so the members of the Cortes had undertaken not to agree to the loss of any territory and to do so would be against the constitution. Envoys could be sent to talk to the rebels about anything except independence.[14]

During the next few months, there were more committee reports and discussion, with the proposal to send envoys approved and the Treaties of Córdoba signed by O'Donojú in Mexico rejected. By June 1822 and for the remainder of the constitutional régime until the autumn of 1823, the pro- and anti-recognition supporters made their case, with two men emerging as the leading and representative spokesmen of each side. Alcalá Galiano had favoured recognition for some time and it was no surprise when he tried to persuade his colleagues in the Cortes to abandon what he thought to be their myopic obstinacy. What chance, he asked, do we have of retaining America? Regrettable and difficult though it was to admit it, the answer was none, because the nation was impotent and wholly unable by any means to prevent separation. There was no evidence to suggest any significant wish on the part of Americans to return voluntarily to Spanish rule and as a country which had adopted the principle of popular sovereignty, Spain had no right to seek to enforce its dominion. There was nothing to be gained from more conflict; commerce was being destroyed and the lives and property of thousands of Spaniards jeopardized. The independence of the empire must be recognized at once as an act of faith which would create the right conditions and atmosphere of trust in which to negotiate future arrangements. Spaniards must now accept that 'there is not the slightest hope of America being united to the Spanish empire' and 'there is not a person of sense who is not persuaded of the impossibility of forcing Americans into obedience'.

Alcalá Galiano was challenged by several deputies but none was more vehement in his opposition than Argüelles. He did not, he said, oppose freedom for their American brothers but the question was whether the present was the opportune moment for it. Any gratuitous recognition would attract not the respect but the ridicule of the world and, after all, why should Spain grant emancipation without assured recompense? There was a 300-year investment in America, obligations of family honour and reciprocal interests to be considered. There were no guarantees that Americans would respect any promises they might make to get recognition and to those who relied on good faith, 'I return to my novels of chivalry'. We must be able to command respect and if the war was to continue, then it would not rest at Spain's door. The chaos and anarchy in America were such that the Mother Country could and should not abandon its subjects to their fate. 'I do not want to insult them', he continued, 'because they are my brothers but those countries have not attained maturity or virility; they are in an inferior condition and nobody can be sure that they can resist foreign invasion.'[15]

The division of opinion in the Cortes was not resolved and the majority of the deputies could never bring themselves to recognize independence or even to talk about the possibility with the rebel régimes. Their hesitancy and fear of taking so seminal a step probably reflected public opinion, which also seems to have been unwilling to accept an admission of defeat which colonial emancipation inevitably entailed. Martínez de la Rosa had recalled that one of the reasons for his reluctance to act had been that public opinion was opposed to recognition and Alcalá Galiano had himself experienced a hostile public reaction when he advocated recognition. In 1820 he gave a speech in Cádiz in which he urged that the fact of independence be accepted. His words were greeted with polite applause by his immediate audience but when news of his opinions spread through the now decadent city and port, there was bitter resentment against him. He was challenged in a vitriolic polemic which went beyond the usual pamphlets published for and against his ideas, ending up in a duel with pistols which was only stopped at the last moment when Alcalá Galiano and his adversary were standing on the field of battle.[16]

The pamphleteers and the press in general likewise seem to have reached no consensus on the question of recognition. While the number of newspapers published during the triennium was so great that it is impossible to perceive a representative press view, there is no doubt that opinion was sharply divided. The editor of *El Censor* advised that if the separation of the overseas provinces could not be prevented, then Spain should be the first to recognize the new countries: 'there is no alternative; it must be recognized, admitted and loudly proclaimed; every colony has the right to free itself from the metropolis on the day when it believes that it will be better off emancipated than remaining united'. On the other hand, however, the colonies were not ready for independence because the necessary level of civilization, industry and commerce had not been attained. What comparison was there, the editor asked, between the state of oppression, ignorance and poverty in which Spain had maintained America for three centuries and the air of freedom that had pervaded the English colonies? America would become the playground of dictators and foreign tyrants and peace would not be seen for generations to come.[17]

Other liberal papers, for example, *Gaceta Patriótica del Ejército Nacional*, edited by Alcalá Galiano among others, *Miscelánea*, *Semanario Nacional* and *El Espectador*, all took the line that as independence could not be stopped, it might as well be recognized sooner than later.[18] In contrast, the popular and influential *El Universal* preached the virtues of unity, insisting that America did not have the maturity for self-government and that the majority of Americans still wished to be within the empire.[19] The same points were made by López Cancelada in his newspaper. He proclaimed his beliefs in the natural rights of all men to be free, but it was clear to him that most Americans did not want to lose the protection of the Mother Country which could surely not abandon 'its children'.[20]

Some papers – *El Revisor*, *Español Libre* and *Monitor Ultramarino* – supported the position of the cabinet and some deputies that recognition would be unconstitutional and that there was no body empowered to take such a step.[21] Ferdinand's return in 1823, of course, promptly stopped all press opinion in favour of recognition and propaganda in what remained of the capital and provincial press reverted to emphasizing the continued loyalty of the majority. Nevertheless, although the recognition lobby was reduced, it did not disappear and during the late 1820s and early 1830s there was renewed pressure, despite Ferdinand's known opposition. The case presented now rested largely on the commercial interests of Spain. The merchants and their spokesmen who had for so long opposed any concession began to argue that whatever the political obstacles, the needs of industry and commerce were such that some form of settlement with America was essential in order that economic relations could be restored. One newspaper put the position well when it said that commercial treaties should be negotiated as a matter of urgency 'without recognizing independence and without denying it'.[22] Even the city of Cádiz finally concluded that there was no hope of reconquest and its merchants began to press for a renewal of commercial contact. George Flinter declared that 'the day of conquest is now gone' and it was time to forget the past and look to the future. If Spain was magnanimous, America would respond generously, making large cash payments as well as granting trading privileges in return for a guaranteed peace. Americans must not be allowed to develop a taste and preference for foreign manufactures and the sooner Spanish merchants were able to send their wine, oil, cloth, silks and mercury, the sooner the peninsular economy would revive.[23] José Presas, in 1824 a fervent advocate of reconquest, changed his mind, deciding four years later that the economic benefits of recognition were paramount.[24] More and more writers made the same point and as one paper put it in 1835: 'It is a truth already recognized by those who think wisely that the commerce with our former colonies must be more advantageous for us than their possession ever was.'[25] Van Aken has expressed this change in attitude quite succinctly: 'the Spanish movement for diplomatic recognition of the daughter republics may be aptly characterized as a program for commercial reconquest of colonies which could no longer be subdued by force'.[26]

The needs of commerce thus ultimately proved stronger than the political objections to recognition and the diplomatic negotiations began in earnest in 1834, within months of Ferdinand's death, leading first to the formal recognition of Mexico on 28 December 1836. Spanish attempts to get cash settlements, preferential trade or acceptance by the new republics of at least some of the national debt by and large failed and Spain's relationship with the former colonies was to be little different to that of other countries despite the ties of tradition, customs, language, religion and all the other bonds which Spaniards had optimistically assumed would ensure substantial benefits. For subsequent generations who looked back on the years of war and the growth of the movements for emancipation, the feeling always remained that Spain was right to resist for as long as possible. Pointing to the extremes of anarchy and military dictatorship, economic stagnation and foreign intervention which did afflict much of America in the nineteenth century, Spanish writers somewhat smugly concluded that their compatriots had been correct in their assessment that the empire was not sufficiently mature for its freedom.[27] The reasons put forward in the 1820s and 1830s to justify the refusal to grant independence became part of Spanish historical tradition and, confident in their view that independence had been a mistake against the true interests and wishes of the majority of Americans, Spaniards were thus able to retain their pride in their imperial past and their faith in the possibility of eventual reunification of the empire. Historians, novelists and writers in general began to concentrate their attention, not on the events of the revolutionary era, but on the period of the conquest, and books and articles lauding the careers of Cortés, Pizarro and other *conquistadores* began to appear. The contribution made by generations of Spaniards to the culture and religion of America became a subject of national pride and also contributed to the impression that America had been better off under Spanish rule. It was not until the late 1830s that the Spanish attitude towards the American liberators began to change. As part of the process of reconciliation, under the stimulus of commercial interests, it seems to have been recognized that the standard denunciation of them as unscrupulous traitors needed to be revised. Hence articles began to appear in which Bolívar and others, while by no means depicted as heroic figures, were admitted to have been men of talent and ability.[28]

Such revisionism towards individuals did not apply to the Spanish response to the movements for independence. The analysis of causes made from 1820 onwards was rarely challenged with the Napoleonic invasion, British intrigue, the minority thesis whereby the few seduced the many, and all the other explanations, being repeated. Every policy adopted – military reconquest, reform, diplomacy – had its supporters and its critics. Liberal historians naturally tended to blame Ferdinand for the loss of the empire. Bayo, for example, condemned his use of force, ignoring the fact that the first military actions were taken by the constitutional régime.[29] Modesto Lafuente similarly believed that

Ferdinand's obstinacy was the principal cause, although he did agree that most Spaniards were opposed to any recognition of the new states.[30] Morayta wrote that it was Ferdinand's restoration of the absolutist system and his persecution of the liberals which were the vital factors in pushing Americans to independence.[31] Rico y Amat was even more convinced that history should blame Ferdinand. It was, he thought, a ridiculous idea in Madrid of 1815 that Americans could be brought to obedience merely by reminding them of the deeds of Columbus, Cortés and Pizarro. A more perspicacious monarch could have arranged a settlement of the dispute and it would not have been difficult to establish monarchies headed by Spanish princes in America, which then would have been spared all the evils of dictatorship and anarchy it had suffered. Moreover, Spaniards had never understood that they were not fighting men but ideas, 'ideas of liberty which cannot be suppressed or destroyed by force of arms; they were fighting against a memory, we were fighting for a hope'.[32] Vicente Lafuente and Menéndez Pelayo chose to blame masonic conspiracies for almost everything and, as far as they were concerned, the loss of the empire was caused by the treachery of disloyal Spaniards. Lafuente, for example, alleged that O'Donojú was a mason deliberately sent by his Rite in the peninsula to concede Mexican independence.[33]

The works of these and many other historians in the nineteenth century who participated in the post-mortem on Spain's imperial decline directly reflect the attitudes and prejudices of the generation who lived through and witnessed the loss of the empire. As in every aspect of the revolutions seen from Spain, they obviously differ in their assessment of the policies adopted and the apportionment of blame, but most tend to share the view that the several authorities in the peninsula, both constitutionalist and absolutist, did adopt the correct response in opposing the movements for emancipation. Francisco Muñoz del Monte well summarized the Spanish response when he wrote in 1853 that the independence of America had been premature and that it was 'a right, a duty, a question of honour and self-interest' for Spain to do everything it could to retain the unity of the empire. When it was evident that the process could not be stopped, he continued, Spain did what all good parents do – it absolved its emancipated children of their disobedience and the Hispanic family was divided into new families which 'are of Spanish origin, Spanish in their history and Spanish in their blood'.[34]

Notes

1 An introduction

1. M. Fernández Almagro, *La emancipación de América y su reflejo en la conciencia española* (Madrid, 1944), pp. 11ff.
2. According to one of the few extant personal diaries kept by an entirely private citizen, there was widespread public dissatisfaction at increased taxes and conscription for the military expeditions to America: J.G. del Moral, 'Memorias de la guerra de la independencia y de los sucesos políticos posteriores (1808–1825)', ed. P. Aguado Bleye, *Revista de Archivos, Bibliotecas y Museos*, XXII (1910), 132–3. A country squire, Moral lived in the province of Almería and began his memoirs in March 1815.
3. The reluctance of Spanish soldiers to serve in America and the low morale, desertion and insubordination among those who were sent are described in M.L. Woodward, 'The Spanish army and the loss of America, 1810–1824', *Hispanic American Historical Review*, 48 (1968), 586–607.
4. Fernández Almagro quotes several examples.
5. See Pérez Galdós, *Episodios Nacionales*. One of Galdós' main written sources is thought to have been E. de K. Bayo, *Historia de la vida y reinado de Fernando VII de España* (Madrid, 1842). The author of this three-volume history makes scarcely any reference to events in America nor to Spain's attempt to deal with the rebellions.
6. J.I. Ferreras, *Introducción a una sociología de la novela española del siglo XIX* (Madrid, 1973), p. 281.
7. There has been a substantial amount of research in recent years on Cádiz's colonial trade and Spanish commerce in general during the last decades of the *ancien régime*. Among several works, particularly useful for the colonial trade are: A. García-Baquero, *Comercio colonial y guerras revolucionarias* (Seville, 1972); A. Miguel Bernal and A. García-Baquero, *Tres siglos del comercio sevillano, 1598–1868: cuestiones y problemas* (Seville, 1976); J. Fontana, *La quiebra de la monarquía absoluta (1814–1820)* (Barcelona, 1971) and his 'Colapso y transformación del comercio exterior español entre 1792 y 1827', *Moneda y Crédito* (December 1970), 3–23; J. Ortíz de la Tabla, *Comercio exterior de Veracruz, 1778–1821: crisis de dependencia* (Seville, 1978); J. Fontana (ed.), *La economía española al final del Antiguo Régimen*, vol. III, *Comercio y colonias* (Madrid, 1982). These works provide mostly statistical data and analysis. For a good general explanation of the trade system, and especially the influence of the Cádiz merchants, see various section of S.J. and B.H. Stein, *The colonial heritage of Latin America* (New York, 1970).
8. R. Catalá to F. Milans, 15 March 1813. Archivo Histórico de Barcelona, Fondo Comercial (hereinafter referred to as AHB, FC), B336.

9. Lamarque y Cía., a typical company of commission agents at Barcelona, issued regular bulletins on the current price and availability of a range of colonial products. According to these bulletins, dating from 1819–21, most colonial goods were readily available with the only exception being those from the River Plate region, especially hides: AHB, FC, B687. M.J. Alvarez Pantoja, *Aspectos económicos de la Sevilla fernandina, 1800–1830* (Seville, 1970) has very useful figures on the price fluctuations of American products between 1801 and 1833.

10. One of the main centres of contraband trade in American products was Gibraltar, from where cargoes shipped from the colonies in non-Spanish vessels were smuggled into Spain; see report of Hacienda y Comercio committee in *Diario de las Cortes*, 29 January 1822 (this and all future references to the Cortes sessions of 1810–14 and 1820–3 are taken from the edition of the *Diario* published in Madrid, Impr. de J.A. García, 1871–5), and volumes published in 1858 and 1885 (see bibliography, under 'Spain').

11. *Actas del Consejo de Estado*, 11 December 1816, Archivo Histórico Nacional, Madrid (hereinafter AHN), Estado, lib. 17d. Shortly after the start of the 1822 sessions, it was pointed out in the Cortes that there were 2,200 expedientes left over from the previous session still to be settled: *Diario*, 7 March 1822.

12. Delgado notes that the government tended to ask the Cortes what to do and the Cortes asked the government; the result was inevitably delay and indecision: J. Delgado, *España y México en el siglo XIX* (Madrid, 1950–3), vol. I, p. 96.

13. J. García de León y Pizarro, *Memorias* (ed. A. Alonso Castrillo, Madrid, 1954), vol. I, pp. 249–51, 164.

14. The main members of this combined Junta de Pacificación were: Duque de Montemar, president; José Pablo Valiente, Francisco Arango; Manuel de la Bodega; Francisco Requena; Antonio Gámez; Francisco José Viaña; and Miguel de Lastarría as secretary. Several others seem to have been coopted from time to time.

15. The members of this military committee were: Infante Carlos; Francisco Javier Castaños; Enrique O'Donnell, Conde de la Bisbal; Marqués del Castelar; Juan O'Donojú; General Wimpfen; Andrés Villalba; Eugenio Palafox y Portocarrero, Conde de Montijo.

16. The members were: Jacinto Romarete; Pedro de la Cuesta; Joaquín Gómez de Liaño; Ballesteros; J Pérez; Loigorri; Francisco Requena; José Manuel Goyeneche, Conde de Guaquí; Gaspar de Vigodet; Félix María Calleja, Conde de Calderón; Marqués de la Reunión; Juan María Villavicencio; José Fernando Abascal, Marqués de la Concordia; Joaquín Blake.

17. The members were: Admiralty – José Manuel Vadillo; Sisternes; Abizu: War – Orellana; Vargas; Navarro Pingarrón: Indies – Francisco Requena; Antonio Martínez Salcedo; Manuel Junco.

18. There were several changes in this committee over the years and it is difficult to identify all the members. The following were certainly members: José de Ibarra, president; Juan Pomar represented the *consulado* of Málaga in 1816 and he was replaced by Miguel Bazo y Berri in January 1817; Francisco Durango represented Santander; Jaime Domínguez represented Barcelona in 1816 and Guillermo Oliver, also a Catalán merchant, was a member at some stage.

19. Further details of the Comisión de Reemplazos are given in chs. 3 and 4.

20. According to Comellas, many of the leading figures of the time seem to have been masons: J.L. Comellas, *Los primeros pronunciamientos en España, 1814–1820* (Madrid, 1958). Menéndez y Pelayo claimed that the independence of Spanish America was the masons' greatest achievement: *Historia de los heterodoxos españoles* (Madrid, 1956), vol. II, p. 899.

21. For example, Antonio de Ugarte, former dancing-teacher among other things and member of the camarilla, whom Ferdinand put in overall charge of preparations for the expedition to the River Plate in 1819. Accused of financial corruption before long, he fell from royal favour but soon regained it: see E. Ortíz de la Torre, 'Papeles de Ugarte: documentos para la historia de Fernando VII', *Boletín de la Biblioteca Menéndez y Pelayo*, XVI (1934), 8–32.

22. This incident became notorious and is examined or mentioned by most historians of the period. The most detailed account remains that of M. de Saralegui y Medina, *Un negocio escandaloso en tiempo de Fernando VII* (Madrid, 1904). There is a good recent outline of it in Fontana, *La quiebra*, pp. 223–5. For further details, see chapter 4.

23. The recipients of Ferdinand's generosity were the Conde de Puñonrostro, Pedro Vargas and the Duque de Alagón. The latter was the former member of the royal bodyguard, Paquito Córdoba, who was a member of the camarilla and elevated to the aristocracy by Ferdinand.

24. Notably Tomás Antonio de Lezica and Andrés Arguibel, who from 1818 onwards were working in Cádiz on behalf of the rebel government of Buenos Aires. Details of their activities and those of other American agents among the troops assembled on the outskirts of Cádiz are given in J. Torre Revello, 'El fracaso de la expedición española preparada contra el Río de la Plata (1818–1820)', *Boletín de la Academia Nacional de la Historia*, XXXIII (1962) (Buenos Aires, 1963). The Spanish authorities were warned of their activities: J. Lozano de Torres to Ferdinand, 6 July 1819, in Ortíz de la Torre, 'Ugarte', 13–18. There is an interesting file on a variety of alleged conspiracies reported to the government in 1819 in AHN, Estado, leg. 3081.

25. José Moreno Guerra, representative of Córdoba, denounced the activities of the Comisión de Reemplazos in the Cortes and promised he would reveal its 'evil manipulations' which, unfortunately, he never did: *Diario*, 4 August 1820.

26. Correspondence quoted in A. Ponce Ribadeneira, *Quito: 1809–1812* (Madrid, 1960), pp. 201–2. Montúfar was the son of the Marqués de Selva Alegre who had been president of the first rebel junta at Quito in August 1809, a fact known to the Regency.

27. C. le Brun, *Vida de Fernando Séptimo, Rey de España* (Philadelphia, 1826), pp. 68–70.

28. Le Brun, *Vida*, p. 5.

29. Comellas suggests that Ferdinand in fact treated the liberals leniently. A few leaders were jailed or exiled but most escaped with a fine or less. He points out that of the 122 deputies who voted for popular sovereignty at Cádiz, only one actually received a sentence and that was a small fine: Comellas, *Los primeros pronunciamientos*, pp. 60–5.

30. T.E. Anna, 'Institutional and political impediments to Spain's settlement of the American rebellions', *The Americas*, XXXVIII (April 1982), 483.

31. Comellas, *Los primeros pronunciamientos*, pp. 33–8, discusses the number of ministers and possible reasons for their dismissal. M. del C. Pintos Vieites, *La política de Fernando VII entre 1814 y 1820* (Pamplona, 1958), is an attempted reassessment of Ferdinand and also has various figures for the number of ministers.

32. One example was José Alvarez de Toledo. A deputy at Cádiz in 1811, sentenced to jail by the Regency, he fled to the United States and then joined and fought for the Mexican insurgents. Apparently repentant, and largely because of his schemes for pacifying the colonies, Ferdinand granted him a pardon in February 1816 and invited him back to Madrid where his ideas were given prolonged

consideration by the cabinet. He carried out diplomatic missions for Ferdinand between 1820 and 1823 and was still in royal favour in later years: Ortíz de la Torre, 'Ugarte', p. 26, n. 3.

33. Anna, 'Institutional and political impediments', 495.

2 Revolution: the view from Spain

1. Circular of Ministro Universal de las Indias, Madrid, 20 July 1814; F.M. Balmaseda (ed.), *Decretos del Rey Don Fernando VII* (Madrid, 1818), vol. 1, pp. 139–40.
2. 'Memoria de la Junta de Diputados de Consulados', 26 August 1817, Archivo del Museo Naval, Madrid (hereinafter MN), 440.
3. *El Censor*, 29 December 1821, 228–9.
4. *Semanario Patriótico*, 19 September 1811. The idea of a too-liberal colonial policy in the past became very common and was still evident years later: see, for example, J. Presas, *Juicio imparcial sobre las principales causas de la revolución de la América española* (Bordeaux, 1828), p. 12.
5. *El Redactor General*, 8 December 1811.
6. For these particular points and the more general defence of the Spanish record, see, for example, *El Observador*, 7 September 1810; *El Redactor General*, 8 December 1811; report by M. Garay, 7 December 1816, Archivo General de Indias, Seville (hereinafter AGI), Estado 87, no. 28; A.B. Gassó, *España con industria fuerte y rica* (Barcelona, 1816); Conde de Toreno in Cortes, *Diario*, 24 June 1821. Most of the Spanish historians of the nineteenth century who discuss events in America strongly defend Spain's colonization. L.F. Muro Arías has a useful summary of historians' views in 'La independencia americana vista por historiadores españoles del siglo XIX', *Estudios de Historiografía Americana* (Mexico, 1948), 297–388. For other examples, see J. Amador de los Ríos, 'Algunas reflexiones sobre la primitiva civilización de Perú', *Revista Española de Ambos Mundos* (Madrid, 1853), 1, 537–60; N. de Zamacois in *El Museo Universal*, 15 July and 30 September 1857; F. Pi y Margall, ibid., 15 May 1858.
7. Cited in M. Woodward, 'Spanish apathy and American independence' (unpublished Ph.D. thesis, University of Chicago, 1964), p. 272.
8. A. Cánovas del Castillo, 'Estudios sobre la literatura hispanoamericana. Don José María Heredia', *Revista Española de Ambos Mundos* (Madrid, 1853), 1, 303–20. The article concerns Heredia, but Cánovas inserted a digression to defend Spain's record.
9. F. Martínez de la Rosa, 'De la civilización en el siglo XIX', *Revista de Madrid* (Madrid, 1843), 3rd series, v, 107–8.
10. In a Cortes debate on 12 February 1822, deputy Torre Martín complained of the excessive use of the family metaphor. The matter was far too important, he said, for such poetic images.
11. *Semanario Patriótico*, 19 September 1811.
12. Cortes session reported in ibid., 21 February 1811.
13. *Diario*, 10 September 1811.
14. *Semanario Patriótico*, 10 October 1811.
15. M. Garay to Minister of Hacienda, 7 December 1816, AGI, Estado 87, no. 23: Garay report in Junta de Pacificación consulta, 8 February 1817, MN, 442. Ferdinand urged the clergy to use their influence to arrest 'the almost general corruption of customs': decree in *Gazeta de Madrid*, 20 October 1814.
16. Circular of Minister of Ultramar, 6 October 1812, published in *Gazeta de la Regencia*, 12 December 1812 (hereinafter referred to as *Gazeta.*)
17. *El Telégrafo Mexicano*, 30 April 1813.

18. Conde de Puñonrostro to Duque de San Carlos, 22 May 1814, AGI, Estado 87, no. 39: León y Pizarro, *Memorias*, vol. II, p. 271.
19. *Diario*, 25 June 1822.
20. *El Telégrafo Americano*, 29 January 1812.
21. M. Cabrera de Nevares, *Memoria sobre el estado actual de las Américas y modo de pacificarlas* (Madrid, 1821), pp. 4–13.
22. *Diario*, 26 June 1822.
23. *Diario*, 28 January 1822. For Rafael Sevilla, the creoles were 'bastard sons of Spain, miserable Judas to be bought with thirty pieces of silver offered to their insatiable ambition and avarice'; R. Sevilla, *Memorias de un oficial del ejército español* (Madrid, 1966), p. 283. Toreno continued to defend the Spanish record years later in J.M. Queipo de Llano, Conde de Toreno, *Historia del levantamiento, guerra y revolución de España, 1808–1814* (4 vols., Madrid, 1848, reprinted in *Biblioteca de Autores Españoles*, 64).
24. M. Torrente, *Historia de la revolución hispano-americana* (3 vols., Madrid, 1829–30).
25. Ferdinand ordered the purchase of 700 copies for circulation in the colonies: Woodward, 'Spanish apathy', p. 271.
26. The work was popular and very influential in forming Spanish opinion, according to A. Magariños Cervantes, who felt it necessary even as late as 1854 to try to refute Torrente's argument and emphasis: A. Magariños Cervantes, 'La revolución hispano-americana. Apuntes para la mejor inteligencia de la historia del Señor Don Mariano Torrente', *Revista Española de Ambos Mundos*, IV (1855), 397–417.
27. *El Telégrafo Americano*, 16 October 1811.
28. *El Redactor General*, 2 October 1811.
29. Exposition of Bishop of Guadalajara (New Spain), dated Mexico, 23 February 1811, *Diario*, 4 September 1811: Cortes Ultramar committee report, ibid., 25 June 1822.
30. Cortes Ultramar committee report, ibid.: Minister of War report to Cortes, *Diario*, 4 June 1821.
31. *El Telégrafo Americano*, 31 August 1813.
32. *La Comisión de Reemplazos representa a la Regencia del Reyno* (Cádiz, 1814), pp. 9–11.
33. *Gazeta de Madrid*, 20 June 1818.
34. Pizarro recalled in his memoirs, 'in Madrid there was nothing but hatred and a desire to punish and fight them': *Memorias*, vol. I, p. 263.
35. Probably the best account of the life and people in Cádiz at this time is R. Solís, *El Cádiz de las Cortes; La vida en la ciudad en los años 1810 a 1813* (Madrid, 1969). There are also many excellent descriptions by contemporaries; for example, J.L. Villanueva, *Mi viaje a las Cortes* (Madrid, 1860): A. Argüelles, *Examen histórico de la reforma constitucional que hicieron las Cortes* (2 vols., London, 1835).
36. The journey from the River Plate took approximately three months. On 31 August 1810, the ship *Descubierta* arrived at Cádiz from Montevideo after 83 days at sea: *Gazeta*, 31 August 1810.
37. This report is in AGI, Caracas, 437A. Alcalá Galiano said that the news was received at Cádiz on 4 July 1810: *Historia de España* (Madrid, 1844–6), vol. VII, p. 340.
38. Somewhat later, on 15 February 1811, the Regency ordered copies of the *Gazeta* and the *Diario* to be sent to all the colonies to expedite the circulation of news: E.A. Heredia, *Planes españoles para reconquistar hispanoamérica, 1810–1818* (Buenos Aires, 1974), p. 16.
39. What appears to be Cortabarría's letter of appointment, dated 16 July 1810, is in Archivo de las Cortes, Madrid (hereinafter AC), leg. 22, no. 1. Various envoys had already been sent to America.

40. Cortabarría's instructions are in AC, ibid.
41. AGI, Caracas, 437A. AC, leg. 22 contains various reports from Caracas, beginning 22 April 1810.
42. J.M. Salazar to Secretary of State, Montevideo, 6 June 1810, AC, leg. 21, no. 7.
43. AGI, Buenos Aires, 522.
44. Ibid.
45. AGI, Buenos Aires, 155, cited in Heredia, *Planes españoles*, pp. 12–13.
46. AGI, Buenos Aires, 40.
47. AGI, Buenos Aires, 155.
48. 'Informe del Marqués de Casa Irujo a Juan Ruiz de Apodaca', Rio de Janeiro, 30 September 1810, MN, 1861.
49. Salazar to Minister of Navy, Montevideo, 4 December 1810, AGI, Estado 79.
50. Letters in AGI, Buenos Aires, 156.
51. Conde de Maule to Regency, Cádiz, 26 February 1811, AGI, Buenos Aires, 317.
52. Elío to Secretary of State, Montevideo, 18 March 1811, AGI, Buenos Aires, 317.
53. For New Spain, see, for example, the reports by José Luyando and Juan Antonio Yandiola in AC, leg. 22, no. 18. Heredia, *Planes españoles*, pp. 24–8, outlines their contents.
54. *Gazeta*, 7 February, 20 July 1811.
55. For example, *El Observador*, 7 September 1810, declared: 'America will never break the bonds which unite it with Spain'; the ambitious minority would not succeed and 'their mad plans will soon be smashed and aborted before they can be implemented'. See also *El Conciso*, 25 April 1811. Delgado has examined press reaction at Cádiz in *La independencia de América en la Prensa española* (Madrid, 1949), and concluded 'There is no doubt that the independence of Spanish America, as far as the Spanish press of 1810 was concerned, was something chimerical, unattainable and harmful, not only for Spain but also for America' (p. 53). For further examples of press attitudes, not always hostile towards Americans, see Woodward, 'Spanish apathy'.
56. *Semanario Patriótico*, 17 January 1811.
57. Representation to the Cortes, dated 29 March 1811, published in *El Telégrafo Americano*, 15 January 1812.
58. *El Redactor General*, 7 September 1811. The complaint was specifically about the war in the peninsula but was equally applicable to events in America.
59. *El Telégrafo Americano*, 10 October 1811.
60. Argüelles, *Examen histórico*, vol. 1, p. 332.
61. A.J. Pérez to Duque de San Carlos, Madrid, 18 May 1814, AGI, Estado 40, no. 68.
62. *Consejo de Indias* report, 3 October 1814, AGI, Caracas, 28, no. 2.
63. J.A. Yandiola to Ferdinand VII, Madrid, 29 January 1825, AGI, Estado 87, no. 30.
64. *América Española: o observaciones sobre el estado presente de la América Española; y sobre el modo más eficaz de terminar las conmociones actuales de ella. Por un Español amante de su Patria* (London, 1817), discussed in Heredia, *Planes españoles*, pp. 360–1.
65. Report of *Junta Militar de Indias*, 8 May 1818, AGI, Estado 102, no. 47.
66. Report of Minister of Ultramar presented to Cortes and published in *Diario*, 12 July 1820.
67. *Miscelánea de Comercio*, 25 July 1820.
68. *Diario*, 6 March 1821.
69. *Consejo de Estado* report, 7 November 1821, MN, ms. 1206 and typed transcript 2254.
70. *Diario*, 14 April 1822.

71. AGI, Indiferente General, 1570, no. 52: Delgado, *España y México*, vol. 1, pp. 55–62.

72. L. Hervey to Ld. Londonderry, Madrid, 16 December 1821, in C.K. Webster (ed.), *Britain and the independence of Latin America, 1812–30* (London, 1938), vol. 11, pp. 384–5.

73. Ibid., 27 May 1822, in ibid., pp. 386–7.

74. G. Bosanquet to G. Canning, Madrid, 20 January 1825, in ibid., pp. 431–3.

75. *British and Foreign State Papers* (London, 1843), vol. xi, pp. 864–5.

76. H. Addington to Ld. Aberdeen, Madrid, 3 March 1830; Webster, *Britain*, vol. 11, pp. 475–6.

77. *Diario*, 25 October 1820. One of the envoys to the River Plate reported to the Minister of Ultramar that it was absolutely false to suggest that all the people of Buenos Aires wanted independence; the loyalist support in Montevideo, he said, was much stronger than that for the rebels: F. del Río to Minister of Ultramar, Madrid, 7 July 1821, AGI, Charcas, 587.

78. *Diario*, 12 February 1822.

79. Ibid., 25 June 1822.

80. *El Telégrafo Mexicano*, 1, 15 September, 15 November 1821. *El Universal*, one of the most successful and widely circulated newspapers of the time, echoed this general interpretation. Its editorial theme was that the insurrections were not of a popular or liberal character. They were not started by oppressed people but by ambitious creoles: L.M. Enciso Recio, *La opinión española y la independencia hispanoamericana, 1819–1820* (Valladolid, 1967), p. 155. A. Gil Novales, *Las sociedades patrióticas (1820–1823)* (Madrid, 1975) has useful details of circulation figures and titles of the 680 papers printed between 1820 and 1823.

81. *Consejo de Estado*, 3 April 1815, AHN, Estado, lib. 15d.; *Consejo de Indias* report, 16 November 1815, AGI, Estado 88, no. 9.

82. 'Memoria sobre la pacificación de las Américas de D. José Alvarez de Toledo', 1 December 1815, MN, ms. 437; León y Pizarro, *Memorias*, vol. 11, pp. 183–8.

83. 'Voto particular de Manuel de la Bodega', 9 October 1816, AGI, Estado 87, no. 41.

84. *Consejo de Indias* report, 17 May 1816, AGI, Estado 88, no. 8.

85. 'Memoria del Conde de Casa Flores', 3 December 1816, ibid., 87, no. 28.

86. 'Memoria de la Junta de diputados de Consulados', 26 August 1817. MN, ms. 440.

87. *Consejo de Estado*, 28 April 1818, 5 August 1818 AHN, Estado. lib. 21.

88. *Diario*, 25 June 1822.

89. Ibid.

90. Ibid., 26 June 1822.

91. *El Espectador*, 30 January 1822, cited in Woodward, 'Spanish apathy', p. 219.

92. *Gazeta*, 1 May 1810. The Spanish government was kept well informed of the activities of French agents, especially by the ambassador in the United States, Luis de Onís. Copies of correspondence from him in early 1810 and lists of the names of French agents are in AC, leg. 22, no. 17. Another list is in AGI, Caracas, 825. In June 1811, the government received a statement detailing French plans from a clerk formerly employed in the Madrid administration of the French king José I: AGI, Estado 87, no. 40.

93. AGI, Buenos Aires, 155: *El Redactor General*, 29 June 1811.

94. There is a signed copy of this memorandum in AC, leg. 19.

95. Cortabarría also reported in 1811 that Colonel John Robertson, a British diplomat at Curacao, was acting as a secret agent for the rebels: I. de la Pezuela to Secretary of State, 4 October 1811, AGI, Estado 63, no. 34.

96. The merchants submitted several representations to the constitutional authorities and later to Ferdinand: some of these were published, for example, *Informe dirigido a S.M. por el Consulado y Comercio de esta plaza en 24 de julio sobre los perjuicios que se originarían de la concesión del comercio libre de los extranjeros con nuestras Américas* (Cádiz, 1811). (See bibliography under Cádiz, merchant guild of.)
97. Woodward, 'Spanish apathy', pp. 27ff.
98. *Gazeta*, 9 May 1811.
99. *El Redactor General*, 19 June 1811.
100. León y Pizarro, *Memorias*, vol. i, pp. 148-9.
101. AC, leg. 21, no. 5.
102. 'Representación del Ayuntamiento de Córdoba sobre convocación de Cortes y otras varias materias' (22 September 1809), in D. Pérez Guilhou, '1809. La opinión pública peninsular y la Junta Central ante el problema americano', *Tercer Congreso Internacional de Historia de América* (Buenos Aires, 1961), vol. ii, pp. 212-13.
103. 'Informe presentado a la Comisión de Cortes por Antonio de Capmany' (17 October 1809), Pérez Guilhou, ibid., pp. 229-30.
104. A. Flórez Estrada, *Examen imparcial de las disensiones de la América con la España* (Cádiz, 1812).
105. G. Yermo to Secretary of State [?], 15 December 1810, AC, leg. 22, no. 5: F. Elío to Regency, Cádiz, 15 July 1810, AGI, Buenos Aires, 317.
106. Cited in A. de Castro, *Cortes de Cádiz. Complementos de las sesiones verificadas en la isla de León y en Cádiz* (Madrid, 1913), vol. i, pp. 319-20.
107. AC, leg. 22, no. 18.
108. J.A. Yandiola to Cortes, Mexico, 1 January 1811, AC, leg. 22, no. 18. The Cortes committee which examined Yandiola's report condemned it as inaccurate and illogical: see report of Overseas Committee in AC, leg. 22, no. 18. For Argüelles' comments, see *Diario*, 9 January 1811.
109. *Diario*, 11 January 1811.
110. Garay to Minister of Hacienda, 7 December 1816, AGI, Estado 87, no. 28 (4).
111. The Duque del Parque was an exception. In the Council of State session of 10 September 1817, he said that Spaniards had nobody to blame but themselves; their colonial administrative system and choice of officials had been notoriously bad: AHN, Estado, lib. 19d.
112. Clause 35: the full text of the manifesto is given in M.A. Diz-Lois, *El manifiesto de 1814* (Pamplona, 1967).
113. J. Baquijano y Carrillo, Conde de Vistaflorida to Duque de San Carlos, 4 June 1814 enclosing his report of 31 May 1814, AGI, Estado 87, no. 31: José de Zayas to Duque de San Carlos, 6 June 1814, ibid.
114. 'Memoria de la Junta de diputados de Consulados', 26 August 1817, MN, 440, fols, 40-1.
115. *Consejo de Estado*, 23 May 1815, AHN, Estado, lib. 15d.
116. Ibid., 17 September 1817, AHN, Estado, lib. 19d.
117. AGI, Estado 89, no. 89.
118. *Diario*, 24 June 1821.
119. P. Morillo to Minister of Ultramar, Madrid, 24 April 1821, AGI, Caracas, 55.
120. *Diario*, 12 May 1821.
121. Ibid., 23 August 1820.
122. *Consejo de Estado* report, 7 November 1821, MN, 2254, 1206.
123. 'Voto particular de Esteban Varea', 27 October 1821, MN, 2254, 1206.
124. 'Memoria del Ministro de Ultramar', 17 January 1822, AC, leg. 22.

125. After the fall of the constitutionalists in 1823, the absolutist propaganda continued to blame the liberals for events in America. For illustrations of this, see J.L. Comellas, *Los realistas en el Trienio Constitucional, 1820–1823* (Pamplona, 1958), pp. 105ff. D. Ramos neatly summarizes the liberal position: 'ideologues above everything else, they insisted on seeing everything that happened through their ideas and they thus start from the premise that the American movements are, before anything else, disagreements against the Ancien Régime': 'Las Cortes de Cádiz y America', *Revista de Estudios Políticos*, no. 126 (1962), 488–9.
126. Woodward, 'Spanish apathy', pp. 88–97.
127. *Diario*, 15 December 1821.
128. A.M. Alcalá Galiano, *Historia de España*, vol. VI, p. 407.
129. Argüelles, *Examen histórico*, vol. II, p. 39.
130. López Cancelada had persistently argued that there was some kind of conspiracy at Cádiz to achieve American independence: *El Telégrafo Americano*, October–November 1811, and, in 1822, Juan José Sánchez referred in the Cortes to 'the faction which has been protecting American independence': *Diario*, 14 April 1822.
131. Delgado, *España y México*, vol. I, pp. 18–19; Woodward, 'Spanish apathy'.
132. *Diario*, 21 March 1822.
133. Ibid., 25 June 1822.

3 The military solution

1. Representation to Cortes, 29 March 1811, published in *El Telégrafo Americano*, 15 January 1812.
2. *El Redactor General*, 7, 19 September 1811.
3. Correspondence in AGI, Buenos Aires, 156.
4. *Actas de las sesiones secretas*, 13 May 1812.
5. Heredia, *Planes españoles*, pp. 69–71.
6. Ibid., pp. 63–4; AGI, Sante Fe, 629. Heredia notes that Villavicencio's reports have been published by E. Terán and R.E. Silva in *Revista del Archivo de la Biblioteca Nacional de Quito* (1937).
7. AC, leg. 22, no. 1.
8. Minister of Hacienda to Cortes, *Diario*, 6 February 1811. The minister put the national debt at 7,194,266,839 *reales*.
9. The British and other mediation proposals are examined in chapter 8.
10. Details of the free trade controversy are given in chapter 5.
11. *Diario*, 30 August 1811.
12. Vázquez Figueroa, 'Memorias', MN, 430, fols. 72ff. Vázquez Figueroa, then the Navy Minister, states that his talks were with three merchants, Luis Gargollo, Ildefonso Ruiz del Río and Francisco Bustamante. There are other versions of how the Comisión orginated. In 1814, Antonio Joaquín Pérez stated that the initiative came from the merchants, for an expedition to New Spain: AGI, Estado 40. Writing to the Minister of State in 1818, Miguel de Lastarría said he passed on to the Regency an offer of financial help from various merchants for an expedition to the River Plate: AGI, Estado 78, no. 47. These and other versions are mentioned in Heredia, *Planes españoles*, p. 47.
13. The names of the members of the working party and its recommendations were published in *El Redactor General*, 15 September 1811.
14. *Actas de las sesiones secretas*, 8 September 1811.

15. I have described the activities of the Comisión de Reemplazos in 'Spain and the Spanish American Wars of Independence: the *Comisión de Reemplazos*, 1811–1820', *Journal of Latin American Studies*, XIII (November 1981), 223–37. Some of the detail here is taken from this article. The main source of information for the Comisión is a government report ordered by Ferdinand in 1826 and completed in 1831: 'Memoria sobre las operaciones de la Comisión de Reemplazos de América, formada de orden del Rey N.S., por la de Corte, Año de 1832'. The attached section of tables is dated 1831. The manuscript is in the library of the Ministry of Hacienda, Madrid. The date of its delivery to the king, 13 December 1831, is given by A. Matilla Tascón, 'Las expediciones o reemplazos militares enviados desde Cádiz a reprimir el movimiento de independencia de Hispano-américa', *Revista de Archivos, Bibliotecas y Museos*, 57 (Madrid, 1951), 37–52. This article provides an excellent summary of the statistical data.

16. 'Memoria de Reemplazos', fols. 26ff: *El Redactor General*, 21 September 1811.

17. *El Redactor General*, 11 October 1811.

18. *El Telégrafo Americano*, 13 November 1811.

19. All the figures given henceforth for the number of men and ships on the military expeditions are taken from the 'Memoria de Reemplazos' and from Matilla Tascón, 'Las expediciones o reemplazos militares'.

20. Heredia, *Planes españoles*, pp. 37–8.

21. It is well known that Ferdinand had extensive consultations on his journey back from France with, among others, the Duque de San Carlos, Duque del Infantado and Pedro Gómez Labrador.

22. AGI, Estado 87, no. 31.

23. Ibid., no. 39.

24. Ibid., Estado 40, no. 68.

25. Ibid., Estado 87, no. 20.

26. Heredia, *Planes españoles*, pp. 127–30, 141–2. Former American deputies at Cádiz were also asked for their views. Anna, *Spain and the loss of America*, pp. 85–93, has a detailed summary of their replies.

27. *La Comisión de Reemplazos representa a la Regencia del Reyno*, p. 20.

28. AGI, Buenos Aires 318.

29. Quoted in C. Seco, 'Tres actitudes españolas ante la independencia de América', *Boletín Americanista*, University of Barcelona (1959), no. 1, 46.

30. J.F. de Lázaro, 'La proyectada expedición de Cádiz, 1813–1820', *Apartado de Labor de los Centros de Estudios* (La Plata, 1938), XXI, no. 10, p. 115.

31. Heredia, *Planes españoles*, pp. 147–51.

32. Pintos Vieites, *La política de Fernando VII*, p. 254. There are many other estimates of the size of Spain's army at this time: for example, see P. Casado Burbano, *Las fuerzas armadas en el inicio del constitucionalismo español* (Madrid, 1982), p. 90.

33. This phrase is used by Comellas, *Los primeros pronunciamientos*, p. 46.

34. This point is made and discussed by Comellas, ibid.

35. D. de Torres y J. Gómez de Liaño to Minister of State, 3 October 1814, AGI, Estado 98, no. 6.

36. Report of 3 October 1814, AGI, Caracas 28, no. 2.

37. Royal decree of 16 October 1814 in Balmaseda, *Decretos*, vol. I, pp. 318–19.

38. AGI, Estado 98, no. 6.

39. E.A. Heredia, 'El destino de la expedición de Morillo', *Anuario de Estudios Americanos* (Seville, 1972), XXIX, 327. After some delay, Salazar left Cádiz on 31 December 1814. His first reports of February onwards were quite optimistic but the purpose of his mission was quickly discovered and he soon returned to Spain: for his instructions, reports etc., see MN, 430.

40. Balmaseda, *Decretos*, vol. i, pp. 318–19, 338–44.
41. For a detailed examination of the background to the decision to send Morillo to Venezuela, see Heredia, 'El destino de la expedición de Morillo'.
42. S.K. Stoan, *Pablo Morillo and Venezuela, 1815–1820* (Columbus, Ohio, 1974), pp. 66–8.
43. Sevilla, *Memorias*, pp. 21–4. According to the 'Memoria de Reemplazos', there were 20 warships and 59 transports and 12,254 men on the Morillo expedition.
44. Balmaseda, *Decretos*, vol. ii, pp. 312–14. The 'Memoria de Reemplazos' gives the number of men as 3,098.
45. Not all of these ships arrived. One frigate and 255 men were captured by pirates.
46. *Consejo de Estado*, 3 April, 23 May 1815, AHN, Estado, lib. 14d.
47. Correspondence in Webster, *Britain*, vol. ii, pp. 341–45.
48. L. Ullrick, 'Morillo's attempt to pacify Venezuela', *Hispanic American Historical Review*, iii (1920), 545; A.F. Zimmerman, 'Spain and its colonies, 1808–1820', ibid., xi (1931), 460; Woodard, 'The Spanish army and the loss of America', ibid., 48 (1968), 586–607.
49. Vázquez Figueroa, 'Mi representación al Rey al hacerme cargo del Ministerio de Marina sobre su estado, importancia y necesidad de su fomento', 21 February 1816, MN, 433A.
50. *Consejo de Estado*, 20 March, 17 April 1816, AHN, Estado, lib. 17d.
51. In a letter to the Conde del Abisbal of 4 June 1817, Vázquez Figueroa stated that Ferdinand decided to send the expedition to the River Plate on 25 May 1816: MN, 432.
52. *Consejo de Estado*, 6 June 1816, AHN, Estado, lib. 17d.
53. *Consejo de Indias* report, 17 May 1816, AGI, Estado 88, no. 8.
54. Abadía did not hold the post for long. He was dismissed and replaced on 1 August 1816 by Field Marshal José Ignacio Alvarez Campana. He in turn was dismissed on 13 September and the Inspección was abolished. Preparations for the expedition were then placed in the care of the Conde del Abisbal: report by Minister of War, 6 April 1820, AHN, Estado 94, no. 1.
55. Vázquez Figueroa correspondence in MN, 432.
56. Archivo Bazán, Ciudad Real (hereinafter AB), Expediciones a Indias, As. Pts, vol. i, 352.
57. *Consejo de Indias* report, 9 November 1816, AGI, Estado 88, no. 12.
58. Manuel de la Bodega, a member of the Council of the Indies and the Junta de Pacificación also opposed the use of force at this time: for example, see his reports of 9 and 24 October 1816, ibid., 87, no. 41.
59. AB, Expediciones a Indias, As. Pts, vol. i, 352.
60. *Consejo de Estado*, 20 November 1816, AHN, Estado, lib. 17d.
61. See E. Resnick, 'Spain's reaction to Portugal's invasion of the Banda Oriental in 1816', *Revista de Historia de América*, nos. 73–4 (1972), 131–43. Professor Anna postulates an interesting, if improbable, hypothesis that at least part of the River Plate expeditionary force was intended for a retaliatory attack on Portugal: T. Anna, 'The Buenos Aires expedition and Spain's secret plan to conquer Portugal', *The Americas*, xxxiv (1978), 356–80.
62. Vázquez Figueroa provided various estimates: see, for example, AB, Expediciones a Indias, As. Pts, vol. i, 352.
63. Pizarro, *Memorias*, vol. i, p. 263. Cevallos' dismissal is usually attributed to his opposition to the royal marriage to the Portuguese princesses.
64. *Consejo de Estado*, 22 January 1817, AHN, Estado, lib. 19d.
65. Campo Sagrado, brought up as a page in the court, was on close terms with the royal family and, according to Vázquez Figueroa ('Memorias', MN 432, fols.

13–14), he had considerable influence with Ferdinand. He was replaced as Minister of War in June 1817 by Francisco Eguía.

66. MN, 442.

67. *Consejo de Estado*, 19 February 1817, AHN, Estado, lib. 19d.

68. Balmaseda, *Decretos*, vol. IV, pp. 300–1. There was another, from the Spanish viewpoint, infamous expedition in 1817 when the Spaniard Francisco Mina led a force on behalf of the insurgents to New Spain. He had some success until his defeat in November 1817 and subsequent execution.

69. Heredia, *Planes españoles*, p. 348. Vázquez Figueroa said he appeared twice before the Military Committee: Vázquez Figueroa to Minister of Hacienda, 26 July 1817, MN, 432, fol. 279.

70. A copy of Enrile's report, dated 25 June 1817, is in MN, Colección Enrile, ms. 2284. It has been published in J. Friede, 'España y la independencia de América (documentos)'; *Boletín Cultural y Bibliográfico*, VIII (1965), 1678–98.

71. For example, José Alvarez de Toledo produced several reports at the request of Pizarro: they are published in Pizarro, *Memorias*, vol. II, pp. 229–46. Juan Antonio Nucio, a retired official from the Navy Ministry, submitted a detailed plan for capturing Buenos Aires, complete with street names: MN, 1622. Heredia, *Planes españoles*, pp. 341ff has details of other schemes.

72. *Consejo de Estado*, 10 September–18 October, 13 November 1817, AHN, Estado, lib. 19d.

73. A copy of Pizarro's scheme, dated 22 August 1817, is in MN, 435, fols. 341–50.

74. The full text, dated July 1817, is in AGI, Estado 88, no. 19. For Vázquez Figueroa's contribution, written in June 1817, see MN, 433A, fols. 295–320.

75. *Consejo de Estado*, 28 April 1818, AHN, Estado, lib. 21.

76. AGI, Estado 102, no. 47.

77. Pizarro, *Memorias*, vol. I, pp. 265–6.

78. *Consejo de Estado*, 22 May 1818, AHM, Estado, lib. 21d. Vázquez Figueroa's written opinion, dated 22 May 1818, is in MN, 433B.

79. Pizarro compiled his final report on the pacification issue on 9 June 1818: published in *Memorias*, vol. II, pp. 264–72. The Admiralty Board also considered the idea of a blockade of Buenos Aires. It reported on 6 July that, while desirable, there were insufficient funds to pay for it. There were also many technical problems to be overcome in the River Plate area and a blockade might not be effective: AGI, Estado 102, no. 63.

80. AGI, Estado 88, no. 66. Heredia, *Planes españoles*, pp. 376–82, has a good summary of San Carlos' ideas: see also J. Delgado, 'La pacificación de América en 1818', *Revista de Indias*, X (1950), 8–67, 263–310.

81. AGI, Estado 89, no. 91.

82. Vázquez Figueroa to viceroy of New Spain *et al.*, 24 July 1818, MN, 433B.

83. Renovales was bribed by San Carlos to desist from his plans in a deal which Pizarro, who, although he accepted it at the time, later said in his memoirs was 'essentially criminal': *Memorias*, vol. I, p. 268.

84. F. Eguía to Minister of State, 16 July 1818, AGI, Estado 89, no. 94.

85. Vázquez Figueroa correspondence in MN, 433B, fols. 530ff.

86. AGI, Estado 90, no. 122.

87. Ibid., no. 123.

88. MN, 433B, fols. 556–7.

89. Pizarro, *Memorias*, vol. I, pp. 249–51, 264: Vázquez Figueroa, 'Memorias', MN, 432, fols. 54–6, 91–8.

90. AGI, Estado 89, no. 89. Biographical details are given in E. Beerman, 'Spanish envoy to the United States (1796–1809): Marqués de Casa Irujo and his Philadelphia wife Sally McKean,' *The Americas*, 37 (1980–1), 445–6.

91. There were many secret reports in the autumn of 1818 and early months of 1819 detailing the strength of the rebel forces in Buenos Aires: several are in AGI, Estado 102.
92. Pizarro, *Memorias*, vol. I, p. 282.
93. Ortiz de la Torre 'Ugarte'.
94. Ibid., p. 10, n. 1.
95. One expedition left in 1819 for Havana with 2 warships, 12 transports and 3,123 officers and men.
96. Webster, *Britain*, vol. II, p. 374.
97. Ibid., p. 369.
98. According to Robertson, the Russian government was among those who incited Ferdinand to use force: W.S. Robertson, 'Russia and the emancipation of Spanish America, 1816–1826', *Hispanic American Historical Review*, XXI (1941), 196–221.
99. Quoted in Delgado, 'La pacificación de América', 54–5.
100. *Consejo de Estado*, 2 April 1820, AHN, Estado, lib. 22d.
101. Ibid.
102. AHN, Estado, leg. 94, no. 1.
103. *Consejo de Estado* report, ibid.
104. *El Rey a los habitantes de Ultramar*, 14 April 1820.
105. *Diario de Barcelona*, 21 May 1820, supplement.
106. M. García Venero, *Historia del parlamentarismo español, 1810–1833* (Madrid, 1946), pp. 325–7.
107. These ministerial reports were read in the Cortes on various days in July 1820 – see *Diario*. Some were also printed separately.
108. *El Censor*, 9 December 1820.
109. The Cortes did authorize on 27 October 1820 the construction of twenty warships.
110. See the *Diario* for March 1821.
111. The record of the Council's sessions for this period is in AHN, Estado 24d. The best summary of its discussions is in its general report of 7 November 1821 of which there is a manuscript and typed copy in MN, 1206 (ms), 2254 (typed). Following details of the Council's discussions are taken from both sources.
112. *Diario*, 4 June 1821.
113. Ibid., 24 June 1821. The Cádiz merchants continued to lobby congress to send expeditions to America – see ibid., secret session, 31 July 1821.
114. MN, 1206, 2254.
115. The ms text is in AC, leg. 22.
116. *Diario*, 27–30 January 1822.
117. Ibid., 6 March, 11 October 1822.
118. MN, 1206, 2254.
119. *Correo Mercantil*, 19 April 1825, quoted in Muro Arías, 'La independencia americana', 308.
120. Woodward, 'Spanish apathy', pp. 243–4.
121. Webster, *Britain*, vol. II, pp. 433–7, 454–60.
122. AGI, Estado 90, no. 161: Delgado, *España y México*, vol. III, pp. 113–19.
123. Both these schemes are described in J.M. Mariluz Urquijo, *Los proyectos españoles para reconquistar el Río de la Plata, 1820–1833* (Buenos Aires, 1958), pp. 126–9.
124. Webster, *Britain*, vol. II, p. 405.
125. Details of many of these are given by Delgado, *España y México*, vol. III and Mariluz Urquijo, *Los proyectos españoles*.
126. Mariluz Urquijo, *Los proyectos españoles*, pp. 167–74.
127. The text of the report is given in Delgado, *España y México*, vol. III, pp. 127–48.

128. Webster, *Britain*, vol. II, pp. 469–70.
129. Ibid., pp. 472–5.
130. Ibid., p. 476.
131. Torrente, *Historia de la revolución hispano-americana*, vol. III, p. 607.

4 The logistics of reconquest

1. There were also 5 postal ships. The statistics in this chapter are from the 'Memoria de Reemplazos' and the article by Matilla Tascón, 'Las expediciones o reemplazos militares'. Some paragraphs are from my article on the Comisión's activities in the *Journal of Latin American Studies* (November 1981), 223–37.
2. The 'Memoria de Reemplazos' provides a breakdown of all the costs.
3. At Cádiz, volunteers were asked to register at the home of Capt. Agustín Brun but were to remain in their employment until required to embark: *El Redactor General*, 21 September 1811.
4. José Manuel Vadillo in Cortes, *Diario*, 14 October 1821.
5. 'Memoria de Reemplazos', fol. 53.
6. Circular of Minister of Hacienda, 19 July 1816 in Balmaseda, *Decretos*, vol. III, pp. 266–7.
7. The Comisión asked for the taxes to be continued in February 1812. Although there was some opposition, both the Regency and the Cortes supported the request: *Actas de las sesiones secretas*, 29 February, 2 March 1812.
8. 'Memoria de Reemplazos', fols. 94ff.
9. Ibid., fols. 96ff.
10. Ibid., fols. 101ff; Balmaseda, *Decretos*, vol. II, pp. 494–5.
11. 'Memoria de Reemplazos', fols. 133ff; Balmaseda, *Decretos*, vol. II, pp. 533–5. The amount of each of these taxes given in the 1831 report differs slightly from the figures given in Balmaseda.
12. There was one donation in 1816 of at least 1,500,000 *reales* to be spent on getting troops to America: Matilla Tascón, 'Las expediciones o reemplazos militares', 45.
13. 'Memoria de Reemplazos', fols. 120ff. The following details of the Málaga reaction are taken from the *Actas del Consulado*. Archivo de la Cámara de Comercio, Málaga, vol. XV.
14. *Actas de las sesiones secretas*, 20 December 1821.
15. J. Carrera Pujal, *Historia política de Cataluña en el siglo XIX* (Barcelona, 1957), vol. II, pp. 17–18.
16. These merchants formed the group known as the Junta de diputados de los Consulados.
17. 'Memoria de Reemplazos', fols. 111ff.
18. Ibid., fols. 107ff.
19. Ibid., fols. 140ff.
20. Ibid., fols. 142ff; Balmaseda, *Decretos*, vol. III, pp. 413–15.
21. Following details are from 'Memoria de Reemplazos', fols. 112–37.
22. The Bilbao information is from a report on the dispute by the Council of State, dated 12 August 1820, in AHN, Estado, leg. 133, exp. 32.
23. *Actas del Consulado*, Malaga, volume for 1819.
24. On 19 June 1820 the intendant, Ramón Aldazoro, was instructed to begin disposing of the supplies: 'Memoria de Reemplazos', fol. 44.
25. *Diario*, 19 July 1820.
26. Ibid., 3, 8 January 1823.
27. The documents on this case, including the final report dated 23 August 1828, are in AHN, Estado, leg. 220, no. 19. The case was discussed several times in the Cortes; for example, see *Diario*, 14 November 1822, 19 January 1823.

28. Lázaro, 'La proyectada expedición de Cádiz', 142; Torre Revello, 'El fracaso de la expedición', 425–8.

29. D. Perkins, 'Russia and the Spanish colonies, 1817–1818', *American Historical Review*, XXVIII (1923), 657ff.

30. An alleged copy of the contract was published in the *Morning Chronicle*, 2 December 1823.

31. *Gaceta de Madrid*, 28 February 1818.

32. Vázquez Figueroa, extract of memoirs published in Pizarro, *Memorias*, vol. II, pp. 285ff.

33. *El Conservador*, 28 June 1820.

34. Saralegui, *Un negocio escandaloso*; Fontana, *La quiebra de la monarquía absoluta*, pp. 224–5. Other interesting and new detail on the Russian ships is in R.H. Bartley, *Imperial Russia and the struggle for Latin American independence, 1808–1828* (Austin, 1978), pp. 121ff.

35. In a separate contract, the tsar sold Spain three other frigates for 3,200,000 roubles. They arrived in Spain around early November 1818 and were used in America: Bartley, *Imperial Russia*, pp. 124–5; Saralegui, *Un negocio escandaloso*, pp. 56–7.

36. Memoirs in Pizarro, *Memorias*, vol. II, pp. 285ff; Vázquez Figueroa correspondence in MN, 433B.

37. Juan Antonio Yandiola in Cortes, *Diario*, 14 October 1821. The account books, correspondence etc. of the Comisión are in the recently catalogued section *Consulados* in the AGI: see A. Heredia Herrero (ed.), *AGI Inventario de los Fondos de Consulados (Sección XII) del Archivo General de Indias* (Madrid, 1979). I have not had an opportunity to study these records which perhaps will reveal in more detail the shipowners, arms manufacturers, dealers and myriad other suppliers who profited or lost from the attempt to reconquer the empire.

38. *Diario*, 20 June, 12 October 1821.

39. Ibid., 10 November 1821.

40. Ibid., 15 April 1821.

41. Ibid., 30 April, 23 May 1821.

42. Ibid., 7 May, 16 June 1821.

43. Ibid., 14 October 1821.

44. Ibid., 4 August, 26 October 1820.

45. Ibid., through October 1821.

46. Ibid., 14 January 1823.

47. Matilla Tascón, 'Las expediciones o reemplazos militares', 50–2.

48. Royal decrees of 13 August 1814 and 20 April 1815. Men who went with Morillo were to be credited with double years of service, a promise that was not kept.

49. Report of Cortes war committee, *Diario*, 8 May 1821.

50. See, for example, *Diario de Barcelona*, 31 May, 6 July, 24 September, 12 November 1819.

51. J.J. de Mora, 'Memorias históricas sobre Fernando VII, Rey de España', transl. by M.J. Quin, *Memoirs of Ferdinand VII* (London, 1824), pp. 229–30.

52. There is a good personal account of the atmosphere among the men in R. de Santillán, *Memorias (1815–1856)* (Pamplona, 1960), vol. I, pp. 8–10. Santillán was an army officer at Cádiz. He recalled that many officers chose to retire rather than join the expedition. Tatischeff told Ferdinand on 11 July 1819 that an Austrian diplomat, just back from Cádiz, reported that 'tout este superbe, point de désertion et les officiers pleins d'enthousiasme et d'espérance'; Ortiz de la Torre, 'Ugarte', 22–4.

53. Quoted in Woodward, 'Spanish apathy', p. 175.

54. *Consejo de Estado*, 20 March 1816, AHN, Estado, lib. 17d.

55. Ibid., 2 July 1825 – text in Fernández Almagro, *La emancipación de América*, p. 104.
56. *Consejo de Estado*, 7 November 1821, MN, 1206 (ms), 2254 (typed).
57. The text of Churruca's proposals is given in Delgado, *España y México*, vol. III, pp. 204–8.
58. F. Fernández de Córdova, *Memorias íntimas* (3 vols., Madrid, 1886–9, reprinted in *Biblioteca de Autores Españoles*, Madrid, 1966), I, 1–11.

5 *Economic and commercial reform*

1. *Diario*, 25 June 1822.
2. For details of the Cádiz merchants' financial contributions, see M. Lucena Salmoral, 'Los préstamos del Consulado de Cádiz a la Junta Central Suprema', *Actas I Congreso Historia de Andalucía*, vol. I, *Andalucía Contemporánea (siglos XIX y XX)* (Córdoba, 1979), pp. 147–58.
3. *El Comercio de Cádiz, representado legítimamente, recurre segunda vez a S.M. en 12 de octubre exponiéndole el resultado ruinoso que causaría al Estado el proyecto de comercio libre* (Cádiz, 1811). (See bibliography under Cádiz.)
4. Report by Garay, 1 March 1813, MN, 455.
5. *Colección de los decretos y órdenes que han expedido las Cortes generales y extraordinarias desde su instalación en 24 de setiembre de 1810 hasta igual fecha de 1811* (Cádiz, 1811), pp. 89–90.
6. T.E. Anna, *Spain and the loss of America* (Nebraska, 1983), p. 94.
7. *Diario*, 13 March 1811.
8. *Consejo de Estado*, 2 August 1813, AHN, Estado, leg. 745, no. 2.
9. Heredia, *Planes españoles*, pp. 142–5.
10. Ibid.
11. *Diario*, 9 February 1811.
12. *Gazeta de la Regencia*, 13 February 1812: Anna, *Spain and the loss of America*, p. 112.
13. *Consejo de Estado* report, February 1813, AHN, Estado, leg. 745, no. 2.
14. Ibid.
15. *El Telégrafo Americano*, 22 January 1812.
16. Ibid., 28 February 1813.
17. *Diario*, 20 November 1812.
18. Ibid., 6 June 1821.
19. AC, leg. 29.
20. *Diario*, 27 January 1822.
21. AGI, Estado 87, no. 20.
22. 'Voto particular' of Manuel de la Bodega, 9 October 1816, AGI, Estado 87, no. 41.
23. Report dated 3 December 1816, AGI, Estado 87, no. 28.
24. Alvarez de Toledo report of 8 April 1817, MN, 437 and Pizarro, *Memorias*, vol. II, pp. 229–46: Conde de Ofalia reports summarized in Delgado, 'La pacificación de América en 1818', 66ff.
25. *Consejo de Estado*, 17 September 1817, AHN, Estado, lib. 19d.
26. Ibid., 15 October 1817.
27. Heredia, *Planes españoles*, p. 236.
28. Ibid., p. 129.
29. J. Friede, *La otra verdad: la independencia americana vista por los españoles* (Bogotá, 1972), p. 31.
30. Report of J.A. Yandiola, 1 January 1811, AC, leg. 22, no. 18.
31. *Semanario Patriótico*, 19 September 1811.
32. Diz-Lois, *El manifiesto de 1814*, pp. 212–17, 229.

33. Report of J.A. Yandiola, 29 January 1815, AGI, Estado 87, no. 30: *Consejo de Indias* report, 17 May 1816, AGI, Estado 88, no. 8.
34. Garay to Minister of Hacienda, 7 December 1816, AGI, Estado 87, no. 28 (4).
35. I have examined the free trade issue in detail in Michael P. Costeloe, 'Spain and the Latin American wars of independence: the free trade controversy, 1810–20', *Hispanic American Historical Review*, 61 (May 1981), 209–34. I am grateful to Duke University Press for permission to reproduce some paragraphs from this article.
36. *Gazeta de la Regencia*, supplements 22, 29 June 1810. The best of many attempts to explain the controversy generated by this incident is in M. Lucena Salmoral, 'La orden apócrifa de 1810 sobre la "libertad de comercio" en América', *Boletín Americanista*, XXVIII, (Barcelona, 1978), 5–20.
37. AGI, Estado 86, No. 26a.
38. *Actas de las sesiones secretas*, 15, 16, 23 January 1811. The text of these proposals is given in N.L. Benson (ed.), *Mexico and the Spanish Cortes, 1810–1822* (Austin, 1966), pp. 179–82.
39. *Actas de las sesiones secretas*, 1, 2, 16, 17 June 1811.
40. The pamphlet, by López Cancelada, was entitled *Ruina de la Nueva España si se declara el comercio libre con los extranjeros*. For examples of the powerful press campaign against free trade, see *El Redactor General*, 27 June, 3, 17 August 1811.
41. *Informe dirigido a S.M. por el Consulado y Comercio de esta plaza en 24 de julio sobre los perjuicios que se originarían de la concesión del comercio libre de los extranjeros con nuestras Américas* (Cádiz, 1811). (See bibliography under Cádiz.)
42. A. Flórez Estrada to Secretary of Cortes, 28 August 1811, AC, leg. 22, no. 13. A. Flórez Estrada, *Examen imparcial de las disensiones de la América con la España* (Cádiz, 1812). Another important pro-free trade publication of the time, attributed to the Mexican deputy, J. Cayetano de Foncerrada, was *Comercio libre vindicado de la nota de ruinoso a la España y a las Américas* (Cádiz, 1811).
43. Alleged by the Cádiz guild in *El Comercio de Cádiz . . . recurre segunda vez . . . en 12 de octubre*.
44. Ibid.
45. López Cancelada continued the propaganda in his newspapers *El Telégrafo Americano* and *El Telégrafo Mexicano* and the Cádiz merchants presented a third exposition to the Cortes in February 1812: *Tercera exposición del Comercio de Cádiz a las Cortes generales y extraordinarias por medio de una diputación especial, ampliando sus ideas y observaciones sobre el proyecto de comercio libre de las Américas con las naciones extranjeras* (Cádiz, 1812).
46. See, for example, Wellesley to Castlereagh, 24 April, 24 May, 5 July 1812 in Webster, *Britain*, vol. II, pp. 321, 325, 392. A treaty was eventually signed with Britain on 5 July 1814 which included the provision that, if the American trade was opened to foreigners, Britain would be given favoured-nation status.
47. Report by Andrés García, Pedro Cevallos and Ibar Navarro, 30 April 1813, AHN, Estado, leg. 745, no. 17.
48. Report by Garay, 1 March 1813, MN 455.
49. *Consejo de Estado*, 23 May 1815, AHN, Estado, lib. 15d.
50. Cited in Heredia, *Planes españoles*, p. 193.
51. Webster, *Britain*, vol. II, pp. 341–5.
52. AGI, Estado 86A, no. 40 (3).
53. Ibid., Estado 87.
54. Ibid., Estado 88, no. 12.
55. Ibid., Estado 87, no. 28. At about this time, Casa Florez was appointed to the crucial post of ambassador to Brazil. For details of his career, see Mariluz Urquijo, *Los proyectos españoles*.

56. *Consejo de Estado*, 22 January 1817, AHN, Estado, lib. 19d.
57. *Consejo de Estado*, 19 February 1817, ibid.
58. AGI, Estado 88, no. 11: MN 442.
59. AHN, Estado, lib. 19d. Another strong attack on the monopoly was made by the Council of the Indies on 17 May 1817: AGI, Estado 88, no. 8.
60. *Consejo de Estado*, 28 April 1818, AHN, Estado, lib. 21.
61. Published in Pizarro, *Memorias*, vol. II, pp. 264-72.
62. Junta de Pacificación report on 31 July 1818, AGI, Estado 88, no. 106. For the ideas of Ofalia and Humboldt, see Heredia, *Planes españoles*, pp. 361-4, 371-4. Flórez Estrada also published another essay urging, among other things, free trade; A. Flórez Estrada, *Representación hecha a S.M.C. el señor Don Fernando VII* (London, 1818).
63. AGI, Estado 89, no. 89.
64. J. Vicens Vives, *Coyuntura económica y reformismo burgués* (4th edn, Barcelona, 1974), p. 20.
65. Yandiola's report is in AGI, Estado 87, no. 30 and Morant's in ibid., 86a, no. 40.
66. Report by Lozano de Torres, July 1817, AGI, Estado 88, no. 19.
67. Pizarro, *Memorias*, vol. I, pp. 249-51, 264.
68. 'Negociados de la primera Secretaría del Despacho de Estado al Cargo del oficial D. Diego Colón, Palacio de Madrid, 30 de junio de 1820', AHN, Estado, leg. 3024.
69. Except where indicated, details of these private deals are taken from various issues of the *Diario* from July 1820-April 1821.
70. Casa Irujo defended himself in a letter to the press, published in *Miscelánea de Comercio*, 22 August 1820.
71. The Puñonrostro case is referred to in the *Consejo de Estado*, 20 May 1820, AHN, Estado, lib. 13d.
72. *Diario*, 26 July 1820.
73. Vázquez Figueroa, 'Memorias', MN, 432, fol. 56.
74. Denouncing the proposed continuation of special privileges to Panama to trade in foreign products, the Cádiz *consulado* told newly appointed Minister of State, Casa Irujo, on 5 January 1819 that the only way to restore Spanish commerce was 'to restore everywhere the exclusive contract of the Metropolis with its Americas, with strict observance of the laws of the Indies'. Cited in García-Baquero, *Comercio colonial y guerras revolucionarias*, pp. 237-8.
75. MN, 440.
76. Apparently the United States and Britain had 100 whaling ships operating off South America. They were used to carry contraband goods which were sold before fishing began. Thus they returned, as the merchants said, filled with rich cargoes of their silver and sperm oil to the value of 180,000,000 *reales*; MN, 440, fol. 55.
77. Webster, *Britain*, vol. II, pp. 347-8.
78. The liberals did enact some changes in the commercial system, for example, the privileges of the Philippines Company were abolished; *Diario*, 17 October 1820. The Acapulco galleon had been abolished by Ferdinand on 23 April 1815.
79. *Diario*, 13, 14 July 1820.
80. Ibid., 26 July 1820.
81. Ibid., 29 July 1820.
82. The reintroduction of the convoy or fleet system had been much canvassed in earlier years. Merchants were encouraged to finance their own military escorts for their trading vessels and it seems that some did so.

83. *Diario*, 31 August 1820, *et al*. J. Hann, in his essay in Benson (ed.), *Mexico and the Spanish Cortes*, pp. 171, 183, appears to have misunderstood the complicated tariff reform. Direct foreign trade was not officially sanctioned.

84. *Memoria sobre los males que sufre el comercio español y medios de repararle. Dirigida a las Cortes por una Comisión del Comercio de Cádiz* (Cádiz, 1820). Cádiz was eventually declared a free port in 1829.

85. *Representación que . . . dirige al mismo augusto congreso la junta nacional de comercio de Cataluña manifestando la absoluta necesidad del sistema prohibitivo* (Barcelona, 1821).

86. *Consejo de Estado*, 7 November 1821, MN, 1206 (ms), 2254 (typed).

87. AC, leg. 22.

88. Webster, *Britain*, vol. II, p. 402.

89. *Actas de las sesiones secretas*, 7 January 1823.

90. *Diario*, 1–15 July 1823: de Castro, *Cortes de Cádiz*, vol. II, pp. 395–6.

91. Becker, *La independencia de América (su reconocimiento por España)* (Madrid, 1922), pp. 106–7: *British and Foreign State Papers* (London, 1843), vol. XI, pp. 864–5.

92. Cited in Becker, *Independencia*, pp. 109–10.

6 The aftermath of imperial decline

1. Fontana, 'Colapso y transformación'. Other recent detailed analyses of Spanish economy and trade are L. Prados de la Escosura, 'Comercio exterior y cambio económico en España (1792–1849)' and J. Cuenca Esteban, 'Comercio y hacienda en la caída del Imperio español, 1778–1826', both of which are in J. Fontana (ed.), *La economía española al final del Antiguo Régimen*, vol. III, *Comercio y colonias* (Madrid, 1982). The footnotes of the latter provide a good up-to-date bibliographical guide to the many recent works on Spanish trade and to the studies published in the nineteenth century by Moreau de Jonnes, Canga Argüelles *et al*. A very useful work on the trade with Mexico is Ortiz de la Tabla, *Comercio exterior de Veracruz*, and, for Cádiz, there is the seminal work of García-Baquero, *Comercio colonial y guerras revolucionarias*.

2. García-Baquero, *Comercio colonial y guerras revolucionarias*.

3. See the works by Villanueva, *Mi viaje a las Cortes*; Argüelles, *Examen histórico*; A. Alcalá Galiano, *Recuerdos de un anciano* (Madrid, 1980). For an extensive list of the many historical accounts of Cádiz, see the bibliography in the recent edition (Cádiz, 1982) of A. de Castro, *Historia de Cádiz y su provincia* (Cádiz, 1858).

4. Solís, *El Cádiz de las Cortes*, p. 152.

5. García-Baquero, *Comercio colonial y guerras revolucionarias*, p. 242; J.L. Comellas y García-Llera, 'Andalucía occidental en los informes de 1824', in *Actas I Congreso de Historia de Andalucía Contemporánea. (Siglos XIX y XX)*, vol. I, p. 47.

6. J.E. Baur, 'The evolution of a Mexican foreign trade policy (1821–1828)', *The Americas*, XIX (1962–3), p. 236.

7. Quoted in García-Baquero, *Comercio colonial y guerras revolucionarias*, p. 242.

8. Catalan economic development is the best and most studied of all regions in Spain: see the several works by J. Vicens Vives, particularly *Historia social y económica de España y América* (5 vols., Barcelona, 1957); *Industrials i politics del Segle XIX* (Barcelona, 1958); *Cataluña en el siglo XIX* (Madrid, 1961).

9. Fontana, 'Colapso y transformación', 18, n. 19.

10. *Representación que dirige al mismo augusto congreso la junta nacional de comercio de Cataluña*.

11. For these and other details of the impact on Seville, Granada, Córdoba and Andalucía in general, see Bernal and García-Baquero, *Tres siglos del comercio sevillano*; Alvarez Pantoja, *Aspectos económicos de la Sevilla fernandina*; various essays

in *Actas I Congreso Historia de Andalucía*, vol. I, *Andalucía Contemporánea*. For Málaga, see F. Bejarano, *Historia del Consulado y de la Junta de Comercio de Málaga (1785–1859)* (Madrid, 1947).

12. Bernal and García-Baquero, *Tres siglos del comercio sevillano*, p. 120.

13. Ibid., pp. 189–207.

14. S. Villalobos, *El comercio y la crisis colonial. Un mito de la independencia* (Santiago, 1968), p. 243.

15. *Diario*, 11 July 1820.

16. This manuscript collection is in the Archivo Histórico de Barcelona, entitled *Fondo Comercial* (hereinafter referred to as FC) and a catalogue of its contents has been published by P. Voltes Bou, *Catálogo del Fondo Comercial del Instituto Municipal de Historia* (Barcelona, 1961). It consists of some 1,260 volumes of the records of more than 300 commercial and industrial enterprises. I have examined the activities of some of these merchants in 'Barcelona merchants and the Latin American wars of independence,' *The Americas*, XXXIII (1982), 431–48, and some of the following paragraphs are taken from this article. Another useful article based on the same records is R.C. Fernández de Avila, 'La emancipación y el comercio catalán con América,' *Revista de Indias*, XXXV (1975), 229–60.

17. All the merchants trading with America refer to the pirate problem and certainly they seem to have suffered heavy losses to them. For example, in its issue of 22 June 1814, the *Diario de Barcelona* reported that in the previous six months, pirates had captured 16 merchant ships, including Spanish, Portuguese and English. In 1817, more than 60 ships were attacked and in 1818 a further 34 coming from America were lost together with goods to the value of 60,000,000 *reales*; García-Baquero, *Comercio colonial y guerras revolucionarias*, pp. 227–31.

18. Roig to E. de J. Picardo, 13 July 1816, FC, B785.

19. FC, B785.

20. *Diario*, 28 March, 1 April 1822.

21. FC, B785.

22. Roig to C. Toig, 26 October 1816, ibid.

23. Letters to P. Cru at Málaga (28 May 1817) and Pablo Masó (3 June 1817), FC, B786.

24. Roig to G. Oncle, 2, 7 August 1817, ibid.

25. Roig to M. Sueco y Cía, 3 July 1822, FC, B792.

26. For example, Roig to Martorell, Plá y Cía, at Veracruz, 1 February 1822, ibid.

27. Roig to J Roig, 19 November 1816, FC, B785.

28. R. Parés to D. Parés, 7 May 1814, FC, B643.

29. Accounts in FC, B395, fol. 19.

30. Riera to Bell and Watson, 24 August 1814, FC, B625. These letters were written in English.

31. Correspondence in FC, B168.

32. Riera to J. Hodge, 13, 16 March 1816, FC, B626.

33. Soler y Cía to R. de Meer, 18 October 1815, FC, B337.

34. Soler to J.F. Puig, 8 June 1816, ibid.

35. FC, B336; carpeta no. 15 contains samples of cloth, prices etc. which were to be sent to an agent in Buenos Aires, dated 3 December 1805.

36. Correspondence in FC, B336.

37. This company has been studied in two unpublished dissertations by students at the University of Barcelona: T. Timoneda, 'Estudio de la Casa Comercial "Llano y Chávarri", Barcelona, 1819–1829,' University of Barcelona, 1958, and L.C. Maleta Rodríguez, 'Comercio exterior de la casa Llano-Chávarri', University of Barcelona, 1969.

38. These details are from Timoneda, ch. III.
39. It is virtually impossible to work out the total value and volume of trade of any of these companies, not least because of the enormous confusion of currencies used in the account books and also because of participation in illicit activities; for example, slave trading was disguised in the accounts. Maleta Rodríguez 'Comercio exterior' (225) calculated that the Llano y Chávarri firm sent goods to the approximate value of 150,000 pesos per year to Veracruz and 100,000 pesos per year to Havana. Timoneda concluded that it was impossible to calculate profit margins.
40. Correspondence in FC, B541.
41. Ramón to Francisco Llano y Chávarri, 2 June 1821, ibid.
42. D. Martorell, Havana, to R. y M. Llano y Chávarri, 18 April 1822, FC, A102.
43. Letters to Tutzo y Grau and B. Mandri, 2 June 1821, FC, B541.
44. Correspondence in ibid.
45. Correspondence in ibid.
46. Ibid.
47. Comellas, *Los realistas en el Trienio Constitucional*, pp. 106, 152; Fontana, *La quiebra de la monarquía absoluta*, p. 175.
48. *Diario*, 5 March 1822.
49. Ibid., 8 October 1822. According to calculations by Treasury officials in 1814, most of the American territories by then had a deficit of income over expenditure because of the revolutions; Heredia, *Planes españoles*, pp. 116–22.
50. Ibid., 6 May, 5, 8 June 1822. Those who earned at least 1,000 pesos were granted a salary of 12,000 *reales*; those with less than 1,000 pesos were given two-thirds of their former salary.
51. *El Independiente*, 20 January 1822, cited in Woodward, 'Spanish apathy', 300.
52. *El Espectador*, 31 August 1821, 20 January 1822, ibid., 299–300.
53. G. Flinter, *Consideraciones sobre la España y sus colonias y ventajas que resultarían de su mutua reconciliación* (Madrid, 1834), pp. 1–5.
54. *Eco de Comercio*, 5 April 1835, cited in Woodward, 'Spanish apathy', 312.
55. *Revista Económica de Madrid*, 1 September 1842.
56. *El Espectador*, 31 August 1821; *El Vapor*, 27 January 1835, cited in Woodward, 'Spanish apathy', 299, 310.
57. *Disertación sobre varias cuestiones interesantes pertenecientes a los negocios de América* (Madrid, 1821), pp. 5–6.
58. *El Vapor*, 27 January 1835, cited in Woodward, 'Spanish apathy', 310.
59. *Disertación sobre . . . negocios de América*, pp. 7–9.
60. *El Espectador*, 31 August 1821, cited in Woodward, 'Spanish apathy', p. 299.
61. J. Arías de Miranda, *Examen crítico-histórico del influjo que tuvo en el comercio, industria y población de España su dominación en América* (Madrid, 1854).
62. *El Restaurador*, 11 January 1824; *El Imparcial*, 10 September 1821, cited in Woodward, 'Spanish apathy', pp. 300–1: J. de Burgos, 'Exposición dirigida al Señor D. Fernando VII desde París en 24 de enero de 1826 sobre los males que aquejaban entonces a España y los medios de remediarlos', published in *Anales del Reinado de Doña Isabel II* (Madrid, 1850–1), vol. I, pp. 47–72. In and out of exile during the Napoleonic era, Burgos became a minister and royal councillor in the 1830s and 1840s.
63. Presas, *Juicio imparcial*, p. 114.
64. *Revista de Madrid* (1838), vol. I, pp. 220–7. Van Aken described the movement for recognition as 'a program for the commercial reconquest of the colonies which could no longer be subdued by force'; M.J. Van Aken, *Pan-Hispanism. Its origin and development to 1866* (Berkeley, 1959), pp. 27ff.

65. *El Español*, 2 November 1835, cited in Woodward, 'Spanish apathy', pp. 286–7; *Consejo de Gobierno* report, 3 December 1833, text in Delgado, *España y México en el siglo XIX*, vol. III, pp. 324–5.
66. *El Comercio de Cádiz recurre segunda vez a S.M.*
67. *La Comisión de Reemplazos representa a la Regencia del Reyno*, pp. 33–7. The *Comisión* estimated that 5,000,000 Spaniards had emigrated to America.
68. *Representación que dirige . . . la junta nacional de comercio de Cataluña.*
69. Junta de Diputados de los Consulados report, 26 August 1817, MN, 440.
70. Fontana, 'Colapso y transformación'; *Cambio económico y actitudes políticas en la España del siglo XIX* (Barcelona, 1973); *La quiebra de la monarquía absoluta:* Vicens Vives, *Cataluña en el siglo XIX* and *Historia social y económica de España y América*, vol. IV.
71. Woodward, 'Spanish apathy', pp. 317–19.

7 A new relationship

1. *Junta Central* decree of 22 January 1809, cited in R.M. de Labra, *España y América, 1812–1912* (Madrid, 1912), p. 44: Regency proclamation of 14 February 1810, text in García Venero, *Historia del parlamentarismo español*, pp. 83–6.
2. Anna, *Spain and the loss of America*, pp. 59, 66ff.
3. *Colección de los decretos* (Cádiz, 1811), vol. I, p. 10; Anna, *Spain and the loss of America*, pp. 68ff; J.F. King, 'The colored castes and American representation in the Cortes of Cádiz', *Hispanic American Historical Review*, 33 (1953), 33–64.
4. *Diario*, 9 January–7 February 1811; *Semanario Patriótico*, 21 January 1811.
5. *Colección de los decretos* (Cádiz, 1811), vol. I, pp. 72–3.
6. Anna, *Spain and the loss of America*, pp. 71–2.
7. Agustín Argüelles insisted years later that Spanish motives in the equality issue were sincere and that the practical consequences inevitably needed time to be assessed; Argüelles, *Examen histórico*, p. 173.
8. *Informe . . . por el Consulado . . . 24 de julio*, pp. 14–15.
9. Report by Garay, 1 March 1813, MN 455.
10. Report dated 30 April 1813, AHN, Estado, leg. 745, no. 17.
11. Alcalá Galiano, *Historia de España*, vol. VI, p. 349.
12. *Consejo de Estado* report, 30 April 1813, AHN, Estado, leg. 745, no. 17.
13. Garay to Minister of Hacienda, 7 December 1816, AGI, Estado 87, no. 28 (4).
14. *Consejo de Indias* report, 17 May 1816, AGI, Estado 88, no. 8.
15. Anna, 'Spain and the breakdown of the imperial ethos: the problem of equality', *Hispanic American Historical Review*, 62 (1982), 258.
16. Anna, *Spain and the loss of America*, p. 80.
17. *El Telégrafo Americano*, 1 January 1812.
18. *Consejo de Estado*, September–October 1817, AHN, Estado, lib. 19d.
19. *Consejo de Estado* report, 7 November 1821 and individual opinions, MN, 2254.
20. *Disertación sobre . . . los negocios de América*, pp. 13–15.
21. Circular dated 20 July 1814, Balmaseda, *Decretos*, vol. I, pp. 129–30.
22. *Proclama a los habitantes de Ultramar*, 30 August 1812.
23. Vázquez Figueroa report of 24 September 1817 to *Consejo de Estado*, MN, 433A.
24. *Consejo de Estado* report, 7 November 1821 and individual opinions, MN, 2254.
25. *Consejo de Estado* report, 19 May 1813, AGI, Estado 88, no. 28.
26. Balmaseda, *Decretos*, vol. I, pp. 129–30.
27. *Consejo de Indias* report, 3 October 1814, AGI, Caracas 28, no. 2.
28. Balmaseda, *Decretos*, vol. IV, pp. 16–17.
29. *Consejo de Estado*, September–October 1817, AHN, Estado, lib. 19d.

30. León y Pizarro, *Memorias*, vol. II, p. 268.
31. Ferdinand's note is appended to the record of the Council's meeting of 28 April 1818, AHN, Estado, lib. 21.
32. Delgado, 'La pacificación de América', 66.
33. Report of Overseas Committee, *Diario*, 8 September 1820.
34. *Diario*, 17, 18 September 1820; García Venero, *Historia del parlamentarismo español*, pp. 358-9.
35. Heredia, *Planes españoles*, p. 90.
36. *Consejo de Estado* report, 7 November 1821 and individual opinions, MN, 2254.
37. See, for example A. Bahamondes, 'La Iglesia Católica y la independencia americana,' *Revista Católica*, 31 (1916), 329-42. For a good account of Spanish attempts to get papal support, see P. de Leturia, *Relaciones entre la Santa Sede e Hispanoamérica* (Caracas, 1959).
38. León y Pizarro, *Memorias*, vol. II, p. 270.
39. Enciso Recio, *La opinión española*, pp. 72-168.
40. Delgado, *España y México*, has a detailed account of the envoys and their various sets of instructions.
41. For a useful summary of this well-documented incident, see E.F. Resnick, 'The Council of State and Spanish America, 1814-1820' (unpublished Ph.D. dissertation, The American University, 1970), pp. 77-83.
42. Villanueva, *Mi viaje a las Cortes*, pp. 338-9.
43. Details in Heredia, *Planes españoles*, pp. 208-9.
44. Webster, *Britain*, vol. II, p. 381.
45. Delgado, *España y México*, vol. I, p. 103.
46. AHN, Estado, leg. 2579.
47. Delgado, *España y México en el siglo XIX*, vol. I, p. 103.
48. The text of the American project is given in full in Delgado, ibid., pp. 100-2.
49. L. Hervey to Marquis of Londonderry, Madrid, 5 June 1821, Webster, *Britain*, vol. II, pp. 382-4.
50. *Consejo de Estado* report, 7 November 1821 and individual opinions, MN, 2254.
51. Cabrera de Nevares, *Memoria sobre el estado actual de las Américas*.
52. *El Telégrafo Mexicano*, 15 November 1821; *El Censor*, 29 December 1821.
53. *Diario*, 24 January-13 February 1822.
54. Webster, *Britain*, vol. II, pp. 454-60, 475. Anna, *Spain and the loss of America*, pp. 174-6, makes the interesting observation that the schemes to send the infantes to America were implausible either because there were too few of them or because they did not want to go.

8 The diplomatic initiative

1. 'Extracto histórico y razonado de la negociación seguida entre el Gobierno inglés y la España, acerca de la mediación . . .', MN, 442, fols. 28-71: 'Reextracto del expediente sobre mediación,' MN, 455, fols. 334-361. Except where otherwise noted, following details of the first negotiations with Britain are taken from these contemporary surveys which include summaries of the diplomatic correspondence, Regency, Cortes, and Council of State reports. They are both undated but were prepared for Ferdinand's ministers some time after 1815. Webster, *Britain*, vol. II, also contains some of the more important diplomatic correspondence.
2. Villanueva, *Mi viaje a las Cortes*, p. 85.
3. AGI, Estado 86, no. 26a.
4. *Actas de las sesiones secretas*, 16-17 June 1811. The committee's report, dated 14 June 1811, is in AGI, Estado 87, no. 18. See also J. Rydjord, 'British mediation

between Spain and her colonies: 1811–1813', *Hispanic American Historical Review*, XXI (1941), 33–4.

5. The Prince Regent of Portugal offered to act as a co-mediator with Britain but his offer was promptly declined: *Actas de las sesiones secretas*, 4 July 1811.

6. Villa Urrutia, Marqués de, *Relaciones entre España e Inglaterra durante la guerra de la independencia. Apuntes para la historia diplomática de España de 1808 a 1814* (Madrid, 1912–14), vol. II, pp. 387–8. Villa Urrutia provides a full account of the negotiation with details not used elsewhere.

7. *Informe . . . por el consulado . . . 24 de julio*.

8. Villa Urrutia, *Relaciones*, vol. II, pp. 395–6.

9. *Actas de las sesiones secretas*, 16 July 1812.

10. Report of 30 April 1813, AHN, Estado, leg. 745, no. 17.

11. Report of 1 March 1813, MN, 455, fols. 263–333.

12. Report of 19 May 1813, AGI, Estado 88, no. 28.

13. After disagreements with Wellesley and members of the Regency over the mediation, Pizarro resigned as Minister of State after only 95 days in office in 1812: León y Pizarro, *Memorias*, vol. I, pp. 151–2.

14. *Consejo de Estado*, 3 April, 23 May 1815, AHN, Estado, lib. 15d.

15. 'Extracto histórico y razonado'.

16. Heredia, *Planes españoles*, pp. 193–8.

17. Webster, *Britain*, vol. II, pp. 341–5.

18. Ibid., pp. 345–6.

19. Montemar to Cevallos, 22 October 1816, AGI, Estado 86A, no. 40.

20. 'Voto particular' of Manuel de la Bodega, 9 October 1816, AGI, Estado 87, no. 41: *Consejo de Indias* report, 9 November 1816, AGI, Estado 88, no. 12.

21. Webster, *Britain*, vol. II, pp. 346–9.

22. Ibid., pp. 350–1.

23. Delgado, 'La pacificación de América', 16.

24. Heredia, *Planes españoles*, pp. 267–70.

25. *Consejo de Estado*, 22 January 1817, AHN, Estado. lib. 19d.

26. E.F. Resnick, 'The Council of State and Spanish America: 1814–1820', p. 149. This work contains an excellent summary of the negotiations in 1816–18.

27. León y Pizarro, *Memorias*, vol. II, pp. 259–64.

28. Delgado, 'La pacificación de América', 16.

29. W.S. Robertson, 'Russia and the emancipation of Spanish America, 1816–1826', 197–8.

30. León y Pizarro, *Memorias*, vol. II, pp. 272–4.

31. D. Perkins, 'Russia and the Spanish colonies, 1817–1818', pp. 658–60.

32. Webster, *Britain*, vol. II, pp. 352–8.

33. *Consejo de Estado* sessions, AHN, Estado, lib. 19d.

34. The full text of Vázquez Figueroa's opinion is in MN, 433A.

35. León y Pizarro, *Memorias*, vol. II, pp. 274–80.

36. Perkins, 'Russia and the Spanish colonies', 664.

37. Delgado, 'La pacificación de América', 28.

38. *Consejo de Estado*, 28 April, 6 May, 22 May 1818, AHN, Estado, lib. 21.

39. León y Pizarro, *Memorias*, vol. II, pp. 264–72.

40. Webster, *Britain*, vol. II, pp. 101–2.

41. Ibid., pp. 367–9.

42. The several notes from San Carlos are fully summarized in Heredia, *Planes españoles*, pp. 376–82 and the text of some is reproduced in Delgado, 'La pacificación de América'.

43. 'Ideas del señor don Luis de Onís', 1815, AGI, Estado 88.

44. Several of these schemes are examined in Heredia, *Planes españoles*, pp. 206–24. In 1822, the British diplomat, Lionel Hervey, reported that Spain would make any sacrifice to recover Gibraltar, including exchanging it for Cuba: Webster, *Britain*, vol. II, p. 385.
45. Report by Gómez de Liaño, 27 July 1818, AGI, Estado 89, no. 91.
46. AGI, Estado 90, no. 122.
47. Delgado, 'La pacificación de América', 66.
48. Resnick, 'The Council of State', 167.
49. Delgado, 'La pacificación de América', 58.
50. Webster, *Britain*, vol. II, pp. 369–70.
51. AGI, Estado 89, no. 89.
52. Casa Irujo to Cea Bermúdez, 17 October 1818; Delgado, 'La pacificación de América', 268–9.
53. 'Negociados de la primera Secretaría del Despacho de Estado al cargo del oficial D. Diego Colón, Palacio de Madrid, 30 de Junio de 1820', AHN, Estado, leg. 3024.
54. *Consejo de Estado* report, 7 November 1821, and individual opinions, MN, 2254.
55. AC, leg. 22.
56. W.S. Robertson, 'Metternich's attitude toward revolutions in Latin America', *Hispanic American Historical Review*, XXI (1941), 541–3.
57. Webster, *Britain*, vol. II, pp. 115–20.
58. Published in *British and Foreign State Papers* (London, 1825–41), vol. XI, pp. 54–5.
59. *Consejo de Estado* report, 29 May 1828, published in Delgado, *España y México*, vol. III, pp. 127–48.
60. F. Martínez de la Rosa, *Espíritu del Siglo* (*Biblioteca de Autores Españoles*, 155), 33–7.
61. Queipo de Llano, Conde de Toreno, *Historia del levantamiento*, p. 357.
62. AHN, Estado, leg. 2579.

Epilogue

1. Van Aken, *Pan Hispanism*, pp. 28–58, discusses some of these schemes.
2. *Biblioteca de Autores Españoles*, XIX, 586.
3. V. Lloréns, *Liberales y románticos. Una emigración española en Inglaterra* (1823–4) (2nd edn, Madrid, 1968), pp. 295–8.
4. Webster, *Britain*, vol. II, p. 443.
5. F. Soldevila, *Historia de España* (Barcelona, 1952–9), vol. VII, p. 18.
6. AC, leg. 22.
7. J.M. de Vadillo, *Apuntes sobre los principales sucesos que han influído en el estado actual de la América del Sur* (3rd edn, Cádiz, 1836), pp. 136–59.
8. F. Martínez de la Rosa, *Bosquejo histórico de la política de España desde los tiempos de los Reyes Católicos hasta nuestros días* (Madrid, 1857), vol. II, pp. 146–54.
9. J. Canga Argüelles, *Breve respuesta a la representación de los comerciantes* (London, 1829).
10. Webster, *Britain*, vol. II, p. 404.
11. León y Pizarro, *Memorias*, vol. I, p. 148.
12. *Consejo de Estado* report, 7 November 1821 and individual opinions, MN, 2254.
13. Ibid.
14. Cortes sessions in *Diario*, 24 January–14 February 1822.
15. Ibid., 22–27 June 1822, 3 August 1823.
16. Alcalá Galiano, *Memorias* (*Biblioteca de Autores Españoles*, LXXXIV), p. 74.
17. *El Censor*, 9, 29 December 1821.
18. Woodward, 'Spanish apathy', pp. 218–19; Gil Novales, *Las Sociedades Patrióticas*, vol. I, p. 20.

19. Enciso Recio, *La opinión española*, p. 155.
20. *El Telégrafo Mexicano*, 1 September, 15 November 1821.
21. Woodward, 'Spanish apathy', p. 216.
22. *El Imparcial*, 16 February 1822; Woodward, 'Spanish apathy', p. 308.
23. Flinter, *Consideraciones sobre la España*, pp. 1–31.
24. Presas, *Juicio imparcial*, pp. 114–16.
25. Van Aken, *Pan Hispanism*, p. 27.
26. Ibid.
27. Even Alcalá Galiano, in retrospect, decided that events in independent Mexico justified the Spanish view that independence had been premature: *Historia de España*, VII, 161.
28. See, for example, articles on Bolívar and Iturbide in *Revista de Madrid*, IV (1840), 3–15, 387–90.
29. Bayo, *Historia de Fernando VII*, vol. II, pp. 103–4.
30. Quoted in Muro Arías, 'La independencia americana', 374–6.
31. Ibid., 376–7.
32. J. Rico y Amat, *Historia política y parlamentaria de España desde los tiempos primitivos hasta nuestros días* (Madrid, 1860–2), vol. I, p. 492.
33. Menéndez y Pelayo, *Heterodoxos españoles*, 899–901; V. de Lafuente, *Historia de las sociedades secretas* (Lugo, 1870–1), vol. I, pp. 333–6.
34. F. Muñoz del Monte, 'España y las repúblicas hispano-americanas', *Revista de Ambos Mundos*, I (1853), 257–80.

Sources and works cited

Manuscript sources

Full details of the archival references for the manuscript sources have been given in the notes. The following archives have been used extensively:

Archivo General de Indias, Seville: sections Estado, Buenos Aires, Caracas, Charcas, Indiferente General, Lima, Santa Fe, Ultramar
Archivo Histórico Nacional, Madrid: sections Estado, Libros de actas del Consejo de Estado
Archivo de las Cortes, Madrid
Archivo del Museo Naval, Madrid
Archivo Naval 'Alvaro de Bazán', Viso del Marqués, Ciudad Real: sections Expediciones a Indias, As Parts
Archivo Histórico de Barcelona: section Fondo Comercial
Archivo de la Cámara de Comercio Málaga: section Actas del Consulado

Newspapers and periodical publications

I have consulted a large number of contemporary newspapers but for the sake of brevity the list that follows is restricted to those cited directly in the text. The studies of press reaction by Delgado, Enciso Recio and Woodward have been useful, providing information from newspapers I have not been able to see. The dates are of the years I have seen rather than the complete run of the publication:

El Censor, 1820–2
El Conciso, 1811
El Conservador, 1820
El Constitucional, 1820
El Defensor del Rey, 1823
El Diario de Barcelona, 1818–20
Gazeta del Consejo de Regencia de España e Indias, 1810–13
Gazeta de Madrid, 1814–18
Miscelánea de Comercio, Artes y Literatura, 1820
El Museo Universal, 1857–60
El Observador, 1810

El Redactor General, 1811–13
Revista de España, 1845–8
Revista Española de Ambos Mundos, 1853–5
Revista de Madrid, 1838–43
Semanario Patriótico, 1810–11
El Telégrafo Americano, 1811–12
El Telégrafo Mexicano, 1813, 1821
El Universal, 1820–1

Books and pamphlets

There is an enormous range of works on the reign of Ferdinand VII and on nineteenth-century Spanish history in general although very few indeed give due weight to the significance of the American issue. The books and articles by Artola, Arzadun, Carr, Christiansen, Herr, Suárez, and many others have been consulted but as they contain little or nothing directly relevant, they are omitted from the following list which contains only those cited in the text and a selection of others which do have some pertinent information. I have also included a small selection of contemporary pamphlets, some of which are almost book length:

Actas I Congreso Historia de Andalucía, vol. 1, *Andalucía Contemporánea (Siglos XIX y XX)*. Córdoba, 1979.
Alcalá Galiano, A.M. *Historia de España*, 7 vols. Madrid, 1844–6.
    Recuerdos de un Anciano. Biblioteca de Autores Españoles, 83.
    Memorias. Biblioteca de Autores Españoles, 83, 84.
Alvarez Pantoja, M.J. *Aspectos económicos de la Sevilla fernandina, 1800–1830*. Seville, 1970.
Anales del Reinado de Doña Isabel II, vol. 1. Madrid, 1850–1.
Anna, T.E. *Spain and the loss of America*. Nebraska, 1983.
Argüelles, A. *Examen histórico de la reforma constitucional que hicieron las Cortes generales y extraordinarias desde que se instalaron en setiembre de 1810 hasta 1813*, 2 vols. London, 1835.
    La reforma constitucional de Cádiz, ed. J. Longares, Madrid, 1970.
Arías de Miranda, J. *Examen crítico-histórico del influjo que tuvo en el comercio, industria y población de España su dominación en América*. Madrid, 1854.
Aunos, E. *Como se perdió América*. Buenos Aires, 1942.
Balanza del comercio de España con nuestras Américas y las potencias extranjeras en el año de 1827. Madrid, 1831.
Balmaseda, F.M. de (ed.) *Decretos del Rey Don Fernando VII*, 3 vols. Madrid, 1818–19.
Bartley, R.H. *Imperial Russia and the struggle for Latin American independence, 1808–1828*. Austin, 1978.
Bayo, E. de K. *Historia de la vida y reinado de Fernando VII de España*, 3 vols. Madrid, 1842.
Becker, J. *Acción de la diplomacia española durante la guerra de la independencia (1808–1814)*. Zaragoza, 1909.

La política española en las Indias. Rectificaciones históricas. Madrid, 1920.

La independencia de América (su reconocimiento por España). Madrid, 1922.

Bejarano, F. *Historia del Consulado y de la Junta de Comercio de Málaga (1785–1859).* Madrid, 1947.

Belgrano, M. *Rivadavia y sus gestiones diplomáticas con España, 1815–1820,* 3rd edn. Buenos Aires, 1945.

Benson, N.L. (ed.) *Mexico and the Spanish Cortes, 1810–1822.* Austin, 1966.

Bernal, A.M. and García-Baquero, A. *Tres siglos del comercio sevillano (1598–1868). Cuestiones y problemas.* Seville, 1976.

British and Foreign State Papers, vol. 11. London, 1843.

Brun, C. le. *Retratos políticos de la revolución de España.* Philadelphia, 1826.

Vida de Fernando Séptimo, rey de España. Philadelphia, 1826.

Cabrera de Nevares, M. *Memoria sobre el estado actual de las Américas y modo de pacificarlas.* Madrid, 1821.

Cádiz, merchant guild of. *Informe dirigido a S.M. por el Consulado y Comercio de esta plaza en 24 de julio sobre los perjuicios que se originarían de la concesión del comercio libre de los extranjeros con nuestras Américas.* Cádiz, 1811.

El Comercio de Cádiz representado legítimamente recurre la segunda vez a S.M. en 12 de octubre exponiéndole el resultado ruinoso que causaría al Estado el proyecto de comercio libre. Cádiz, 1811.

Tercera exposición del Comercio de Cádiz a las Cortes generales y extraordinarias por medio de una diputación especial, ampliando sus ideas y observaciones sobre el proyecto de comercio libre de las Américas con las naciones extranjeras. Cádiz, 1812.

Memoria sobre los males que sufre el comercio español y medios de repararlos. Cádiz, 1820.

Calderón Quijano, J.A. (ed.) *La burguesía mercantil gaditana (1650–1868).* Cádiz, 1976.

Canga Argüelles, J. *Breve respuesta a la representación de los comerciantes.* London, 1829.

Diccionario de Hacienda con aplicación a España, 2 vols. Madrid, 1833–4.

Carrera Pujal, J. *La Lonja del Mar y los Cuerpos de Comercio de Barcelona.* Barcelona, 1953.

Historia de la economía española, 3 vols. Barcelona, 1943–7.

Historia política de Cataluña en el siglo XIX, 7 vols. Barcelona, 1957.

Casado Burbano, P. *Las fuerzas armadas en el inicio del constitucionalismo español.* Madrid, 1982.

Castro, A. de. *Historia de Cádiz y su provincia.* Cádiz, 1858.

Cortes de Cádiz. Complementos de las sesiones verificadas en la isla de León y en Cádiz, 2 vols. Madrid, 1913.

Colección de los decretos y órdenes que han expedido las Cortes generales y extraordinarias desde su instalación en 24 de setiembre de 1810 hasta igual fecha de 1811. Cádiz, 1811.

Colección de los decretos y órdenes que han expedido las Cortes generales extraordinarias desde su instalación de 24 setiembre de 1810 hasta 19 de febrero de 1823, 10 vols. Madrid. 1820–3.

Comellas, J.L. *Los primeros pronunciamientos en España, 1814–1820.* Madrid, 1958.

Los realistas en el Trienio Constitucional, 1820–1823. Pamplona, 1958.

El Trienio Constitucional. Madrid, 1963.

(La) Comisión de Reemplazos representa a la Regencia del Reyno, el estado de insurrección en que se hallan algunas provincias de Ultramar, la urgente necesidad de enérgicas medidas para la pacificación, clase y extensión de las que deben adoptarse con este objeto, y males que amenazan a la Nación Española si el gobierno no remite los auxilios que se reclaman. Cádiz, 1814.

Condiciones y semblanzas de los diputados a Cortes para la legislatura de 1820–1821. Madrid, 1821.

Cordero Torres, J.M. *El Consejo de Estado. Su trayectoria y perspectivas en España.* Madrid, 1944.

Cuenca Toribio, J.M. *Estudios sobre la Sevilla liberal (1812–1814).* Seville, 1973.

Delgado, J. *España y México en el siglo XIX,* 3 vols. Madrid, 1950–3.

La independencia de América en la Prensa española. Madrid, 1949.

Disertación sobre varias cuestiones interesantes pertenecientes a los negocios de América. Madrid, 1821.

Diz-Lois, M.C. *El Manifiesto de 1814.* Pamplona, 1967.

Domínguez, J.I. *Insurrection or loyalty: the breakdown of the Spanish American empire.* Harvard University Press, 1980.

Enciso Recio, L.M. *La opinión española y la independencia hispanoamericana, 1819–1820.* Valladolid, 1967.

Fernández Almagro, M. *La emancipación de América y su reflejo en la conciencia española.* Madrid, 1944.

Fernández de Córdova, F. *Memorias íntimas,* 3 vols. Madrid, 1886–9, reprinted *Biblioteca de Autores Españoles,* 192, 193.

Ferreras, J.I. *Introducción a una sociología de la novela española del siglo XIX.* Madrid, 1973.

Flinter, G. *Consideraciones sobre la España y sus colonias y ventajas que resultarían de su mutua reconciliación.* Madrid, 1834.

Flórez Estrada, A. *Examen imparcial de las disensiones de la América con la España.* Cádiz, 1812, reprinted *Biblioteca de Autores Españoles,* 113.

Representación hecha a S.M.C. el señor Don Fernando VII. London, 1818, reprinted *Biblioteca de Autores Españoles,* 113.

Foncerrada, J.C. de. *Comercio libre vindicado de la nota de ruinoso a la España y a las Américas.* Cádiz, 1811.

Fontana, J. *La quiebra de la monarquía absoluta (1814–1820).* Barcelona, 1971.

Hacienda y Estado en la crisis final del Antiguo régimen español: 1823–1833. Madrid, 1973.

Cambio económico y actitudes políticas en la España del Siglo XIX. Barcelona, 1973.

(ed.) *La economía española al final del Antiguo Régimen,* vol. III, *Comercio y Colonias.* Madrid, 1982.

Friede, Juan. *La otra verdad: la independencia americana vista por los españoles,* 2nd edn. Bogota, 1972.

García-Baquero, A. *Comercio colonial y guerras revolucionarias. La decadencia económica de Cádiz a raíz de la emancipación americana.* Seville, 1972.

García de León y Pizarro, J. *Memorias de la vida del Excelentísimo señor don José*

García de León y Pizarro, escritos por él mismo, ed. Alvaro Alonso Castrillo, 2 vols. Madrid, 1953.

García Montero, C. *Málaga en los comienzos de la industrialización: Manuel Agustín Heredia (1786–1846)*. Córdoba, 1978.

García Venero, M. *Historia del parlamentarismo español, 1810–1835*. Madrid, 1946.

Gassó, A.B. *España con industria fuerte y rica*. Barcelona, 1816.

Gil Novales. A. (ed.) *Las Sociedades Patrióticas (1820–1823)*, 2 vols. Madrid, 1975.

Ilustración española e independencia de América. Barcelona, 1979.

Guiard y Larrauri, T. *Historia del Consulado y Casa de Contratación de Bilbao*, 3 vols. Bilbao, 1972.

Heredia, E.A. *Planes españoles para reconquistar Hispanoamérica, 1810–1818*. Buenos Aires, 1974.

España y la independencia del Río de la Plata: capítulos de su historia. Córdoba, 1977.

Heredia, N. de, Conde de Ofalia. *Escritos del Conde de Ofalia*. Bilbao, 1894.

Kaufmann, W. *British policy and the independence of Latin America, 1804–1821*. Yale, 1967.

Labra, R.M. *España y América, 1812–1912. Estudios políticos, históricos y de derecho internacional*. Madrid, 1913.

América y la constitución española de 1812. Madrid, 1914.

Lafuente, V. de. *Historia de las sociedades secretas*, 3 vols. Lugo, 1870–1.

Leturia, P. de. *Relaciones entre la Santa Sede e Hispanoamérica*. Caracas, 1959.

Llorens, V. *Liberales y románticos; una emigración en Inglaterra (1823–1824)*, 2nd edn. Madrid, 1968.

López Cancelada, J. *Ruina de la Nueva España si se declara el comercio libre con los extranjeros*. Cádiz, 1811.

López Guedez, H. *Un aspecto de la pacificación de América (1810–1814)*. Mérida, Venezuela, 1964.

Dos informes sobre la pacificación de América en 1824. Mérida, Venezuela, 1967.

Lovett, G. *Napoleon and the birth of modern Spain*, 2 vols. New York, 1965.

Luli, F. *Refutación contra la memoria presentada por D. Miguel Cabrera sobre las Américas*. Madrid, 1821.

Maleta Rodríguez, L.C. 'Comercio exterior de la casa Llano-Chávarri.' Unpublished dissertation, University of Barcelona, 1969.

Mariluz Urquijo, J.M. *Los proyectos españoles para reconquistar el Río de la Plata, 1820–1833*. Buenos Aires, 1958.

Martínez Quinteiro, E. *Los grupos liberales antes de las Cortes de Cádiz*. Madrid, 1977.

Martínez de la Rosa, F. *Bosquejo histórico de la política de España desde los tiempos de los Reyes Católicos hasta nuestros días*, 2 vols. Madrid, 1857.

Espíritu del Siglo. Biblioteca de Autores Españoles, 155.

Menéndez Pelayo, M. *Historia de los heterodoxos españoles*. Buenos Aires, 1945.

Mesonero Romanos, R. de. *Memorias de un setentón. Biblioteca de Autores Españoles* 203.

Mora, J.J. de. 'Memorias históricas sobre Fernando VII, Rey de España', transl. M.J. Quin, *Memoirs of Ferdinand VII*. London, 1824.

Nadal, J. *El fracaso de la revolución industrial en España, 1814–1933*. Barcelona, 1975.

Ortiz de la Tabla, J. *Comercio exterior de Veracruz, 1778–1821: crisis de dependencia*. Seville, 1978.

Pérez Guilhou, D. *La opinión pública española y las Cortes de Cádiz frente a la emancipación hispanoamericana, 1808–1814*. Buenos Aires, 1981.

Pintos Vieites, M. del C. *La política de Fernando VII entre 1814 y 1820*. Pamplona, 1958.

Ponce Ribadeneira, A. *Quito: 1809–1812. Según los documentos del Archivo Nacional de Madrid*. Madrid, 1960.

Presas, J. *Juicio imparcial sobre las principales causas de la revolución de la América española*. Bordeaux, 1828.

Queipo de Llano, J.M., Conde de Toreno. *Historia del levantamiento, guerra y revolución de España, 1808–1814*, 4 vols. Madrid, 1848, reprinted *Biblioteca de Autores Españoles*, 64.

Quintana, M.J. *Obras completas. Biblioteca de Autores Españoles*, 19.

Representación que en contestación a la que han dirigido a las Cortes las corporaciones de Cádiz en 23 de marzo de este año dirige al mismo augusto congreso la Junta Nacional de Comercio de Cataluña manifestando la absoluta necesidad del sistema prohibitivo. Barcelona, 1821.

Resnick, E.F. 'The Council of State and Spanish America, 1814–1820'. Unpublished Ph.D. dissertation, The American University, 1970.

Rhodes, A.M. 'The Argentine policy of Ferdinand VII'. Unpublished Ph.D dissertation, University of North Carolina, 1973.

Rico y Amat, J. *Historia política y parlamentaria de España desde los tiempos primitivos hasta nuestros días*, 3 vols. Madrid, 1860–2.

Rodríguez, M. *The Cádiz experiment in Central America, 1808–1826*. Berkeley, 1978.

Rubio y Esteban, J.M. *La infanta Carlota Joaquina y la política de España en América (1808–1812)*. Madrid, 1920.

Ruíz y Pablo, A. *Historia de la Real Junta Particular de Comercio de Barcelona (1758–1847)*. Barcelona, 1919.

Santillán, R. de *Memorias (1815–1856)*, 2 vols. Pamplona, 1960.

Saralegui y Medina, M. de. *Un negocio escandaloso en tiempo de Fernando VII*. Madrid, 1904.

Sevilla, R. *Memorias de un oficial del ejército español*. Madrid, 1916.

Soldevila, F. *Historia de España*, vol. VII. Barcelona, 1952–9.

Solís, R. *El Cádiz de las Cortes*. Barcelona, 1978.

Spain. Cortes, 1810–13. *Diario de sesiones de las Cortes generales y extraordinarias*, 9 vols. Madrid, 1870–4.

1810–14. *Actas de las sesiones secretas de las Cortes generales y extraordinarias*. Madrid, 1874.

1820–3. *Diario de las sesiones de Cortes*, 14 vols. Madrid, 1871–5.

1823. *Diario de las sesiones de Cortes celebradas en Madrid*. Madrid, 1885.

1823. *Diario de las sesiones de Cortes celebradas en Sevilla y Cádiz*. Madrid, 1858.

1820–3. *Actas de las sesiones secretas de las Cortes ordinarias y extraordinarias*. Madrid, 1874.

Stein, S.J. and B.H. *The colonial heritage of Latin America*. New York, 1970.

Stoan, S.K. *Pablo Morillo and Venezuela, 1815–1820*. Columbus, Ohio, 1974.

Timoneda, T.M. 'Estudio de la casa comercial "Llano y Chávarri", Barcelona, 1819–1829'. Unpublished Ph.D. dissertation, University of Barcelona, 1958.

Torrente, M. *Historia de la revolución hispano-americana*, 3 vols. Madrid, 1829–30.

Vadillo, J.M. de. *Apuntes sobre los principales sucesos que han influído en el estado actual de la América del Sur*, 3rd edn. Cádiz, 1836.

Van Aken, M.J. *Pan-Hispanism. Its origin and development to 1866*. Berkeley, 1959.

Vicens Vives, J. *Historia social y económica de España y América*, 5 vols. Barcelona, 1957.

Industrials i politics del Segle XIX. Barcelona, 1958.

Cataluña en el siglo XIX. Madrid, 1961.

Coyuntura económica y reformismo burgués, 4th edn. Barcelona, 1974.

Villalobos, S. *El comercio y la crisis colonial. Un mito de la independencia*. Santiago, 1968.

Villanueva, J.L. *Mi viaje a las Cortes. Biblioteca de Autores Españoles*, 97.

Villa-Urrutia, Marqués de. *Relaciones entre España e Inglaterra durante la guerra de la independencia*, 3 vols. Madrid, 1912–14.

Webster, C.K. (ed.) *Britain and the independence of Latin America*, 2 vols. Oxford, 1938.

Woodward, M. 'Spanish apathy and American independence (1810–1843)'. Unpublished Ph.D dissertation, University of Chicago, 1964.

Articles

Alvarez Rubiano, P. 'El espíritu de reforma en las colonias españolas en el siglo XIX: proposición de Tabasco a las Cortes de Cádiz'. *Revista de Indias*, 11 (1951).

Anna, T. 'The Buenos Aires expedition and Spain's secret plan to conquer Portugal'. *The Americas*, 34 (1978), 356–80.

'Institutional and political impediments to Spain's settlement of the American rebellions.' *The Americas*, 38 (1982), 481–95.

'Spain and the breakdown of the imperial ethos: the problem of equality'. *Hispanic American Historical Review*, 62 (1982), 254–72.

Bahamondes, A. 'La Iglesia católica y la independencia americana'. *Revista Católica*, 31 (1916), 329–42.

Baur, J.E. 'The evolution of a Mexican foreign trade policy (1821–1828)'. *The Americas*, 19 (1962–3), 225–61.

Beerman, E. 'Spanish envoy to the United States (1796–1809): Marqués de Casa Irujo and his Philadelphia wife Sally McKean'. *The Americas*, 37 (1980–1), 445–6.

Bender de Díaz Sola, N. 'Memorandum ruso del 17 de noviembre de 1817 relativo al Río de la Plata y su repercusión en el gobierno español', in *Academia Nacional de la Historia, Cuarto Congreso Internacional de Historia de América*, Buenos Aires, 1966, 4, 343–62.

Brown, V.L. 'Contraband trade: a factor in the decline of Spain's empire in America'. *Hispanic American Historical Review*, 8 (1928), 178–89.

Caillet-Bois. R. 'Miguel Lastarría; Memoria sobre la representación y plan de seguridad de las provincias del Río de la Plata'. *Boletín del Instituto de Historia Argentina 'Dr Emilio Ravignani'*, 1:1, Buenos Aires, 1956, 269–96.

Cánovas del Castillo, A. 'Estudios sobre la literatura hispanoamericana. Don José María Heredia'. *Revista Española de Ambos Mundos*, 1 (1853), 303–20.

Costeloe, M.P. 'Spain and the Latin American wars of independence: the free trade controversy, 1810–1820'. *Hispanic American Historical Review*, 61 (1981), 209–34.

'Spain and the Spanish American wars of independence: the Comisión de Reemplazos, 1811–1820'. *Journal of Latin American Studies*, 13 (1981), 223–37.

'Barcelona merchants and the Latin American wars of independence'. *The Americas*, XXXVIII (1982), 431–48.

Delgado, J. 'La política americanista de España el el siglo XIX'. *Cuadernos Hispanoamericanos*, 2 (1948), 29–49.

'La "pacificación de América" en 1818'. *Revista de Indias*, 10 (1950), 7–67, 263–310.

Destefani, L.H. 'La real armada española y la guerra naval de la emancipación hispanoamericana', in *Academia Nacional de Historia, Cuarto Congreso Internacional de Historia de América*, Buenos Aires, 1966, 4, 285–405.

Fehrenback, C.W. 'Moderados and exaltados: the liberal opposition to Ferdinand VII, 1814–1823'. *Hispanic American Historical Review*, 50 (1970), 52–69.

Fernández de Avila, R.C. 'La emancipación y el comercio catalán con América'. *Revista de Indias*, 35 (1975), 229–60.

Fontana, Lázaro, J. 'Colapso y transformación del comercio exterior español entre 1792 y 1827'. *Moneda y Crédito*, 115 (1970), 3–23.

Friede, J. 'España y la independencia de América (documentos)'. *Boletín Cultural y Bibliográfico*, 8 (1965), 1678–98, 1814–23: 9 (1966), 50–9, 261–8.

González Sabariegos, R. 'Pedro de Urquinaona y Pardo (un colombiano al servicio de España'. *Revista de Indias*, 19 (1959), 435–48.

Guerrero Balfagón, E. 'La política americanista del Consejo de Estado y la proyectada expedición española al Río de la Plata', in *Academia Nacional de Historia, Cuarto Congreso Internacional de Historia de América*, Buenos Aires, 1966, 7.

Heredia, E.A. 'José Fernández de Castro y la independencia del Río de la Plata'. *Historiografía y Bibliografía Americanistas*, Seville, 1971, 15, 183–.

'El destino de la expedición de Morillo'. *Anuario de Estudios Americanos*, XXIX (1972), 315–42.

Izard, M. 'Comercio libre, guerras coloniales y mercado americano', in *Actas del Primer Coloquio de Historia Económica de España*, 1972, 295–321.

King, J.F. 'The colored castes and American representation in the Cortes of Cádiz'. *Hispanic American Historical Review*, XXXIII (1953), 33–64.

Lázaro, J.F. de. 'La proyectada expedición de Cádiz, 1813–1820'. *Apartado de Labor de los Centros de Estudios*, La Plata, 1938, 21, 114–61.

Lohmann Villena, G. 'Propuesta de don Mariano Tramarria para la designación de informantes sobre la situación de América (1816)'. *Anuario de Estudios Americanos*, 3 (1946).

López Guedez, H. 'La mediación de Inglaterra en la independencia de América durante el gobierno del Consejo de Regencia'. *Humanidades*, 2 (1960), 61–6.

'La pacificación de América, 1810–1836'. *Anuario*, Mérida, Venezuela, 5–6 (1964), 109–84.

Lucena Salmoral, M. 'La orden apócrifa de 1810 sobre la "libertad de comercio" en América'. *Boletín Americanista*. 28, University of Barcelona, 1978, 5–21.

Magariños Cervantes, A. 'La revolución hispanoamericana. Apuntes para la mejor inteligencia de la historia del Señor Don Mariano Torrente'. *Revista Española de Ambos Mundos*, 4 (1855), 397–417.

Martínez de la Rosa, F. 'De la civilización en el siglo XIX'. *Revista de Madrid*, 5 (Madrid, 1843), 107–24.

Matilla Tascón, A. 'Las expediciones o reemplazos militares enviados desde Cádiz a reprimir el movimiento de independencia de Hispanoamérica'. *Revista de Archivos, Bibliotecas y Museos*, 57 (1951), 37–52.

'La ayuda económica inglesa en la guerra de independencia'. *Revista de Archivos, Bibliotecas y Museos*, 68 (1960), 451–75.

Molinari, D.L. 'Fernando VII y la emancipación de America, 1814–1819', in *Segundo Congreso Internacional de Historia*, Buenos Aires, 1939, 4, 256–319.

Moral, J.C. del. 'Memorias de la guerra de la independencia y de los sucesos políticos posteriores (1808–1825)', ed. P. Aguado Bleye. *Revista de archivos, bibliotecas y museos*, 18 (1908), 416–37; 19 (1908), 111–24; 22 (1910), 124–33, 284–301.

Muro Arías, L.F. 'La independencia americana vista por historiadores españoles del siglo XIX', in *Estudios de Historiografía Americana*, Mexico, 1948, 297–388.

Nadal, J., and Tortella, G. 'Agricultura, comercio colonial y crecimiento económico en la España contemporánea', in *Actas del Primer Coloquio de Historia Económica de España*, 1972.

Ortiz de la Torre, E. 'Papeles de Ugarte: documentos para la historia de Fernando VII'. *Boletín de la Biblioteca Menéndez y Pelayo*, 16 (1934), 8–32.

Pérez-Bustamente, C. 'Martínez de la Rosa y la independencia de América'. *Revista de Indias*, 21 (1961), 385–404.

Pérez Guilhou, D. '1809. La opinión pública peninsular y la Junta Central ante el problema americano', in *Tercer Congreso Internacional de Historia de América*, Buenos Aires, 1961, 2, 191–232.

Perkins, D. 'Russia and the Spanish colonies, 1817–1818'. *American Historical Review*, xxviii (1923), 656–72.

Ramos, D. 'Las Cortes de Cádiz y América'. *Revista de Estudios Políticos*, 126 (1962), 433–639.

Resnick, E. 'Spain's reaction to Portugal's invasion of the Banda Oriental in 1816'. *Revista de Historia de América*, 73–4 (1972), 131–44.

Ríos, A. de los. 'Algunas reflexiones sobre la primitiva civilización de Perú'. *Revista Española de Ambos Mundos*, 1 (1853), 537–60.

Robertson, W.S. 'Juntas of 1808 and the Spanish colonies'. *English Historical Review*, 21 (1916), 573–85.

  'Russia and the emancipation of Spanish America, 1816–1826'. *Hispanic American Historical Review*, 21 (1941), 196–221.

  'Metternich's attitude toward revolutions in Latin America'. *Hispanic American Historical Review*, 21 (1941), 538–58.

  'The policy of Spain towards its revolted colonies, 1820–1823'. *Hispanic American Historical Review*, 6 (1926), 21–46.

Rodríguez, M. 'The "American question" at the Cortes of Madrid'. *The Americas*, 38 (1982), 293–314.

Rydjord, J. 'British Mediation between Spain and her colonies, 1811–1813'. *Hispanic American Historical Review*, 21 (1941), 29–50.

Seco, C. 'Tres actitudes españolas ante la independencia de América'. *Boletín Americanista*, University of Barcelona, 1 (1959), 43–50.

Suste, J.A. 'Las primeras noticias de nuestra emancipación de 1821 recibidas en la Corte española'. *Lotería*, 9:108 (1964), 16–19.

Torre Revello, J. 'El fracaso de la expedición española preparada contra el Río de la Plata (1818–1820)'. *Boletín de la Academia Nacional de Historia*, Buenos Aires, 33 (1962), 421–38.

Ullrick, L. 'Morillo's attempt to pacify Venezuela'. *Hispanic American Historical Review*, 3 (1920), 535–65.

Vital-Hawell, V. 'La cuestión de las colonias españolas y Europa en vísperas del congreso de Aquisgrán (1811–1818)'. *Revista de Indias*, 21 (1961), 459–84.

Woodward, M.L. 'The Spanish army and the loss of America, 1810–1824'. *Hispanic American Historical Review*, 48 (1968), 586–607.

Zimmerman, A.F. 'Spain and its colonies, 1808–1820'. *Hispanic American Historical Review*, 11 (1931), 439–63.

Index

Abad y Queipo, Manuel, 87
Abadía, Francisco Xavier, 15–16, 68
Aberdeen, Lord, 37, 100
Addington, Henry, 37, 100
Aguado, Alejandro, 109
Aix-la-Chapelle, congress, 78, 126, 183,
  209, 211–12
Alagón, Duque de, 140
Alaix, I., 165
Alamán, Lucas, 125
Alcalá Galiano, Antonio, 40, 49–51, 177,
  225–7
Alcántara de Toledo, Pedro, see Infantado,
  Duque del
Altamira, 99
Alvarez de Toledo, José, 38, 126, 180
Amarillas, Marqués de las, 86, 89
America: agents, 14–15, 50, 84; reform
  demands, 54, 120, 122, 129, 145, 173–8,
  189; representatives, 49–50, 54, 57
Amnesty, 77, 86, 182–4
Andalucía, 41, 153
Aner de Esteve, Felipe, 56
Anglona, Prince of, 93, 146, 179, 213–14,
  223
Angoulême, Duke of, 98
Anna, T., 19, 178
Aranda, Conde de, 187
Arenas, Alfonso, 158
Argüelles, Agustín, 34, 44, 50, 117, 122,
  226–7
Arías, José, 167
Artigas, José, 201
Ayacucho, battle of, 1, 2, 96
Ayacuchos, 165
Aycinena, José, 87, 93, 146, 179, 213–14,
  223

Balguerie, Sarget et Cie., 109
Banda Oriental, 30, 70–1, 94, 97–8, 202
Baquícano y Carrillo, José, see Vistaflorida,
  Conde de
Barcelona: bankruptcies 155–64; effects of

loss of empire, 152–3; Junta de Comercio,
  153; loans, 103; see also Catalonia;
  Consulados; Merchants; Trade
Bardají, Eusebio, 36, 57, 189, 195–6
Barradas, Isidro, 99–100
Barrell, George, 139
Basadre, Vicente, 28
Bayo, E. de K., 229
Belgrano, Manuel, 78, 186
Bell, J., 158
Bernal, A.M., 153
Blake, Joaquín, 68, 77, 87
Bodega, Manuel de la, 39, 126, 134, 141,
  187, 202
Bolívar, Simón, 26–7, 62, 229
Bouyon, Honorato, 111
Brazil, 30, 63, 70–1, 94, 127
Bringas, Francisco, 140
Britain: diplomatic reports, 36–7, 66, 99;
  mediation, 6, 45, 55, 57–8, 73, 75–7,
  130–49 passim, 194–202, 203–17 passim;
  Spanish mistrust of, 30, 41–2, 45–6, 82,
  132, 138, 199–200, 297–8, 212–13, 216–
  17; treaties with, 156, 200
Brun, Carlos le, 16
Buenos Aires: reports on, 29–33, 35, 37, 39,
  41, 49; representatives, 37, 41, 67; see also
  River Plate expedition
Burgos, 111, 145
Burgos, J. de, 168

Cabral de Noruña, Miguel, 186
Cabrera de Nevares, Miguel, 24, 40, 190–1,
  224
Cádiz: anti-British feeling, 42; consulado, 35,
  55, 104, 131, 141, 145, 177, 216; decline
  of, 4, 151–2; importance of, 4, 119;
  opposition to mediation, 55, 130, 196–7,
  216; representations, 35, 131; see also
  Cortes; Economy; Merchants; Political
  reforms; Spaniards; Trade
Calleja, Félix, 61
Campo Sagrado, Marqués de, 69, 73

Campuzano, Joaquín Francisco, 78
Canaleta, Cayetano, 160–1
Canga Argüelles, José 143, 155, 166, 222
Canning, George, 147, 214
Cánovas del Castillo, Antonio, 22
Capmany, Antonio, 43
Carlos, Infante, 12, 61, 70
Carlota Joaquina (sister of Ferdinand VII),
   53, 61, 187–8
Carr, Raymond, 165
Carrasco, Antonio, 97
Caruana, Ciappino y Cía, 158
Carvajal y Manrique, José de, see San
   Carlos, Duque de
Casa Flores, Conde de, 39, 126–8, 134, 180
Casa Irujo, Marqués de, 42, 46, 82, 136,
   138–9, 186, 210, 212, 217
Castaños, Xavier, 15, 66, 88
Castlereagh, Lord, 84, 133, 143, 188, 198,
   202–3, 205–12 passim
Catalá, Juan, 159–60
Catalá, Rafael, 4
Catalonia: economy, 120, 153, 161, 170; see
   also Barcelona; Economy; Merchants;
   Trade
Cea Bermúdez, Francisco, 36, 204–5, 209,
   220
Cevallos, Pedro, 38, 45, 65–7, 70–2, 132–3,
   177, 186, 199, 201–2
Chile, 1, 25, 38–9, 45, 78–9, 88, 92, 96, 154
Churruca, Pasqual, 116
Ciscar, Gabriel de, 88, 94, 190, 223–4
Cisneros, Baltasar Hidalgo de, 83, 110–11
Clergy, use of, 184; see also Papacy
Clouet, Luis, 140
Cochrane, Thomas, 79
Comisión de Reemplazos: agents, 61, 63;
   creditors, 111–14; discussed in Cortes,
   112–13; finances, 56, 66; liquidation,
   112–14; operations, 59, 64, 66, 68, 81,
   101–11 passim; origins, 13, 56, 131;
   representations, 26, 60–3, 169; see also
   Military; River Plate expedition
Commonwealth idea, 187–92
Constitution (1812), 7, 16, 21, 57–8, 84–5,
   121, 180
Consulados: Barcelona, 106, 145; Bilbao, 108;
   (La)Coruña, 145; Guadalajara (New
   Spain), 107; Málaga, 105–6, 108, 112,
   145; Mexico City, 107, 145; Santander,
   112; Veracruz, 107, 145; see also Cádiz
Córdoba, 43, 46
Córdoba (New Spain), Treaties of, 49, 163,
   191, 225
Cortabarría, Antonio Ignacio de, 28–9, 41–
   2, 53–4
Cortes: attitude to revolutions, 34, 37, 90;
   committee reports, 37, 54, 112, 125, 143,

197–8; debates, 9, 23, 37–8, 40, 46, 47,
   55, 88–9, 92, 94–5, 112–13, 122, 125,
   130, 140, 173–5, 195–6, 224–6; see also
   America: representatives
Cortés, Hernán, 166, 229
Costa Firme, 59, 61, 101
Council of Government, 168
Council of the Indies: reports on Buenos
   Aires, 31, 41; reports on Caracas, 27–8, 41,
   180; reports on America, 34–5, 38–9, 63–
   4, 67–9, 97, 128, 133–4, 148, 178, 182–3,
   201–2
Council of State: debates, 39–40, 45, 69–78
   passim, 86–7, 92, 115–16, 120, 133–8,
   189–90, 201, 207, 213–14; decisions, 73,
   126, 134; membership, 87; reports, 38–
   40, 53, 65–8, 91–4, 99, 121, 123, 132,
   146, 177, 183, 185, 199–200, 204, 215,
   223–4
Creus, Jaime, 23, 122
Cuba, 1, 35, 91–2, 99, 113, 139, 141, 150

Delgado, Jaime, 50
Dolares, Alejandro, 95
Domingo Parés y Cía, 157
Dotres, Juan Bautista, 160
Dou, Ramón Lázaro, 122
Downie, Juan, 139

Echandia, Marqués de, 140
Economy: Cádiz influence, 118–19; criteria
   of reforms, 117–20, 127–9; difficulty of
   change, 117–20; domestic impact, 117–
   20; effects of loss of empire, 150–70
   passim; manufacturers, 120; merchant
   interests, 118–20; reforms, 120 passim;
   relationship with America, 117;
   retrospective views, 168–9; see also
   Merchants; Trade
Eguía, Francisco, 76, 79–82, 85, 110, 138,
   140, 183, 208
Elío, Francisco, 30, 32, 53
Enrile, Pascual, 62, 74–5
Envoys, 6, 36–7, 48, 53, 61, 125, 147, 186,
   213
Eros, Felipe de los, 111
Erro, Juan de, 148
Espartero, Baldomero, 165
Estrada, Bernardo, 156
Extremadura, 87, 103

Federation proposal, 187–92, 218, 224
Feliú, Ramón, 187
Ferdinand VII: camarilla, 14, 81; policy,
   59, 62, 84–5, 97; views, 10, 71–2, 81–2,
   84–5, 97, 100, 137–8, 188 191, 220
Fernán Núñez, Conde de, 143, 203–5, 207,
   211

Fernández Almagro, Melchor, 1
Fernández de Castro, José, 30
Fernández de Córdova, Luis, 116
Fernández Golfín, Francisco, 190, 224
Ferrer, Joaquín, 25, 40
Flinter, George, 166, 228
Flores, Luis Antonio, 93, 146, 179, 213–14, 223
Flórez Estrada, Alvaro, 43, 46, 131, 140
Fontana, Josep, 110, 150, 170
Freire, Juan, 47, 145

Galicia, 87, 103, 120
Gámez, Francisco, 162
Garay, Martín: appointment, 72; dismissal, 82; views on free trade, 119, 132, 137–8; views on Americans, 24; views on policy, 58, 80, 117, 128, 177–9, 183, 199–200, 204, 216–17
García, Andrés, 132, 177, 199
García Herreros, Manuel, 122
García de León y Pizarro, José: appointment, 11, 72; diplomacy, 76–7, 204–12; dismissal, 46, 82; reports, 75–8; views, 11, 24, 39, 43, 74, 80–1, 89, 134–49 passim, 179, 182–3, 185–7, 222–3
García de la Torre, José, 148
Gayoso, Miguel, 92
Gibraltar, 211
Gil de la Cuadra, Ramón, 35
Girón, Pedro Agustín, see Amarillas, Marqués de las
Godoy, Manuel, 187
Gómez de Liaño, Joaquín, 63, 78, 211
Gómez de Navarrete, Juan Nepomuceno, 189
González Salmón, Antonio, 86
Gordon y Murphy, 139
Goyeneche, José Manuel, Conde de Guaquí, 98
Guadalquivir Navigation Company, 107
Guaira, La 80, 101
Guatemala, 35, 91
Guayana, 27, 61
Guayaquil 91
Guerra, José Moreno, 46
Guitart, Salvador, 161
Gutiérrez de la Huerta, Francisco, 56

Havana, 29, 57, 72, 79, 80, 95–6, 99–101, 111, 142
Heredia, Manuel Agustín de, 140
Heredia, Narciso de, see Ofalia, Conde de
Hervey, Lionel, 36–7
Hidalgo, Miguel, 26, 33, 184
Hodge, John, 159
Holland, 79, 142
Holland, Lord, 219

Hualde, Guillermo, 76–7
Huancavelica, 43
Humboldt, W. von, 136

Ibar Navarro, Justo María, 132, 177, 199
Ibarra, José, 71, 76, 126, 179, 183
Iguala, Plan of, 189
Imaz, José, 83
Indian tribute, 120–2
Indies, Laws of, 21, 128, 178
Infantado, Duque del, 77, 138, 197
Iturbide, Agustín de, 26, 36, 91–2, 163

Jabat, Juan, 89
João VI, 53, 70
Junta Central, 15, 41, 43, 45, 47–8, 173
Junta de diputados de los Consulados: origins, 13, 106; members, 109; reports, 39, 45, 112, 128, 141–2, 169
Junta de Generales, 12, 61
Junta de Pacificación: membership, 98; origins, 12; reports, 38, 73–4, 80, 133–5, 204, 211

Kolly, Baron de, 140

Lafuente, Modesto, 229–30
Lafuente, V., 230
Land distribution, 124–5
Lardizábal y Uribe, Miguel de, 15–16, 21, 87, 180, 182
Larra, Mariano, 2
Las Casas, Bartolomé de, 21, 25
Lastarria, Miguel de, 98, 126
Lequerica, Agustín Antonio, 108
Leyenda negra: Spanish refutation, 21, 44
Liberal triennium: attitude to independence, 5, 7, 46, 54; policy, 85–96; reforms, 124–5, 138, 143–8; see also Cortes; Political reforms; Trade; Spain
Lima, 38, 53, 59, 65, 79–80, 89, 94, 96, 101
Liñán, Pascual de, 63, 69, 91
Liniers, Santiago, 31, 45
Liverpool, 110
Lizana, Archbishop, 43
Llano y Chávarri, Francisco, 160–3, 170
Llano y Chávarri, Manuel, 160–3, 170
Llano y Chávarri, Ramón, 160–3, 170
Londonderry, Lord, 36
López, Marcial Antonio, 95
López Araujo, Manuel, 72, 77, 138, 204, 208
López Cancelada, Juan, 24, 33–4, 38, 53, 57–8, 114, 124, 130, 179, 190, 227
López Lisperguer, Francisco, 127
López Pelegrín, Ramón, 47, 94, 125, 147, 214, 221–2
López de Santa Anna, Antonio, 99–100

Lozano de Torres, Juan, 45, 75–6, 81–2, 85, 126, 138, 140, 179, 207, 216–17
Luyando, José, 93, 146, 179, 213–14, 223

Magariños, Francisco, 37
Maipú, battle of, 78
Mallorca, 158
Mandri, Buenaventura, 160
Maracaibo, 59, 91, 101
Maroto, Rafael, 165
Martínez, P., 168
Martínez de Irujo y Tacón, Carlos, see Casa Irujo, Marqués de
Martínez de la Rosa, Francisco, 22, 36, 216, 222, 226
Martorell, Domingo, 160–2
Masonic influence, 14–15, 50, 84
Mataró, 146
Matilla Tascón, Antonio, 102
Maule, Conde de, 31
Maurell, Francisco, 81
Mediation: European, 146–7, 203–17 passim; see also Britain; Cádiz; Cortes; Council of State; Merchants
Mendinueta, Pedro, 77, 137, 207
Menéndez y Pelayo, M., 230
Merchants; aid to military policy, 55–6, 58, 103–12 passim; attitude to insurgents, 21, 160–2; attitude to loss of empire, 168–9, 228; attitude to recognition of independence 228; case histories, 154–63; financial contributions, 56, 103–12 passim; opposition to free trade, 45, 55, 119–49 passim; opposition to mediation, 45, 55; see also Barcelona; Cádiz; Comisión de Reemplazos; Consulados; Trade
Mérida, 49
Mesonero Romanos, Ramón de, 2
Metternich, Prince of, 214
Mexico: military expeditions, 6, 53, 56–7, 59, 61–4, 77, 95, 97–100; reports on, 32–4, 35–6, 38, 41, 44, 47, 89; see also Iturbide, Agustín de; Iguala, Plan of: Córdoba, Treaties of
Military: attitudes of, 2, 64–5, 84, 95, 114–16 passim; doubts of success, 59, 67–9, 70, 72, 93–4; expeditions, 53, 57–9, 60–1, 63, 65, 69–70, 72, 74, 80, 91, 95, 101–10 passim; funding, 55–6, 101–14 passim; importance of navy, 59, 67, 71, 74, 79, 87, 89, 93–4, 96; logistics, 57, 74, 88, 101–14 passim; policy, 6, 38, 52, 59, 62, 67, 72–3, 78–80, 86–8, 90, 92–7; post-Ayacucho, 116; recruitment, 56, 87, 103; supplies, 101–11 passim; see also comisión de Reemplazos; Morillo expedition; River Plate expedition

Ministerio Universal de las Indias, 10, 15, 182
Ministry of Ultramar, 10, 181
Miranda, Francisco, 26, 29, 33, 199
Monopolies, 122–23
Montemar, Duque de, 12, 133, 136, 148, 202
Montevideo, 29–31, 37, 42, 53, 57–65 passim, 74, 101, 116
Montúfar, Carlos, 15
Morales Gallego, José, 197
Morant, Rafael, 137
Morayta, M., 230
Morelos, José María, 26, 34, 184
Moreno Guerra, José, 112–13, 140, 144
Morillo, Pablo, see Morillo expedition
Morillo expedition: departure, 64–5; financing, 66, 103–11 passim; impact, 65–8, 72, 74, 79–80, 86, 89, 91; origins, 12, 62–5
Moscoso, José María, 37
Muñoz del Monte, Francisco, 230

Navarre, 107, 146
Navarrete, Félix, 49
New Granada, 37–8, 53, 64
New Spain, see Mexico
Noriega, Francisco de, 44

O'Donnell, Enrique, Conde de la Bisbal, 81, 114
O'Donojú, Juan, 163, 191, 224–5, 230
Ofalia, Conde de, 126, 136, 183, 211
O'Higgins, Bernardo, 79
Oliver y Salvá, Guillermo, 109, 145
Onís, Luis de, 188, 210
Ouvrard, Gabriel, 98

Palarea, 95
Palma, 158
Panama, 35, 65, 123, 139, 141
Papacy: encyclicals, 185; talks with, 185
Paraguay, 33, 63, 99
Paris: Peace of, 203, 206; Ambassadorial Conference, 208
Parque, Duque del, 76–7, 207
Patagonia, 141
Patrón, Benito, 140, 191
Pérez, Antonio Joaquín, 34, 47, 60, 115
Pérez de Castro, Evaristo, 89
Pérez Galdós, Benito, 2, 165
Pérez Villamil, Juan, 66
Pernambuco revolt, 206
Persas, manifesto, 44, 47, 128, 177
Peru, 25, 32–3, 36, 38, 53, 64, 77–9, 89, 91, 95–6
Pezuela, Ignacio, 87, 92–3
Philippines, 1, 150
Philippines Company, 14, 107

Piedra, Blanca, Marqués de, 87, 93, 179, 189

Pino, Pedro Bautista, 124

Political reforms: American representation, 173–8; colonial officials, 180; constraints on, 170–73; equality, 173–8; equality of job opportunity, 178–81; negotiations, 186; see also commonwealth idea; Federation proposal

Popham, Sir Home, 204

Porcel, Antonio, 35, 85, 89–90, 92–3, 182

Portobelo, 72, 80, 101

Portugal: attitude to revolutions, 49; diplomacy with, 70–1; fear of, 42, 45; invasion of banda Oriental, 70–1

Posada, Ramón de, 121–2

Pozzo di Borgo, Count, 206–7

Presas, José, 168, 228

Press: censorship, 48, 96, 114; opinion on recognition, 96, 165–6, 227–8; opinion on revolutions, 32–4, 38, 42, 53, 88, 90, 165–6; use of, 32–3, 114, 185–6

Priego, Pedro Juan de, 225

Pueblo Viejo, 99

Puerto Rico, 1, 29, 35, 57, 72, 91, 101, 113, 150

Puñonrostro, Conde de, 24, 60, 139

Queipo de Llano, José María, see Toreno, Conde de,

Quintana, Juan Climaco, 122

Quintana, Manuel José, 219

Quiroga, Antonio, 115

Quito, 15, 44

Ramírez, José Miguel, 189

Ranz Romanillos, Antonio, 87, 92

Recognition of independence: conservatives' views, 220; Cortes debates, 40, 224–6; Council of State, 94, 223–4; Ferdinand's position, 220; liberals' views, 219–22; merchants, 228; retrospective views, 2–3, 7, 8, 20, 222–30

Reconquest propaganda, 116; schemes, 97–9

Regency (Cádiz): decrees, 129; policies, 9, 28; proclamations, 32, 41; reports, 129–30 see Britain; Mediation; Trade

Renovales, Mariano, 79

Requena, Francisco, 87, 185

Richelieu, Duque de, 207, 211

Rico, Juan, 24

Rico y Amat, J., 230

Riego, Rafael del, 84

Riera, Valentín, 158–9

Rio de Janeiro, 31, 42, 53, 61, 63–4, 70, 82

Rivadavia, Bernardo, 67, 186

Rivas, Anselmo, 183, 207

River Plate expedition: destination, 77–8; financing, 81, 103–11, passim, 185; origins, 12, 67–8; preparations, 68–77 passim, 80–1, 83–4; postponement, 69, 80; result, 83–4 see also Comisión de Reemplazos; Military

Roa, Bernardo, see Piedra Blanca, Marqués de

Rodil, Ramón, 165

Rodríguez del Monte, Luis, 56

Roig y Vidal, Cristóbal, 155–6

Roig, Juan, 157

Rudol, Federico, 111

Ruíz de Alzedo, Joaquín, 160

Russia 12, 206–17 passim

Russian ships, purchase of, 14, 83, 110–15 passim, 206

Sacasa, José de, 144

Sagristá, Juan, 161

Salas y Quiroga, Jacinto, 168

Salazar, José María, 29, 31, 42, 53, 63–4

Salcedo, José, 43

Salvá, Vicente, 165

San Carlos, Bank of, 107

San Carlos, Duque de, 78–9, 82, 180–1, 186, 210–12, 217

San Fernando, Duque de, 138

San Martín, José, 78–9

San Miguel, Evaristo de, 147, 222

San Sebastián, 103

Sancho, Vicente, 87

Santa Fe, 29, 45, 122

Santa Marta, 59, 91, 101

Santo Domingo, 35

Saralegui y Medina, M. de, 110

Serna, La, 93, 182

Serra y Soler, Mariano, 156

Sevilla, Rafael 64–5, 114

Seville junta, 43

Seville, industry, 153–4

Shepeler, Bertold, 140

Soler, Gaspar, 159

Spain: analysis of revolutions, 7, 8, 20 passim, 27, 29, 41 passim, 50–1; assessment of rebel support, 29–38, 96; attitudes towards Indians, creoles, castes, 22–5; attitudes towards rebels, 26–7; attitude to recognition, 5, 22, 35–7, 40, 95–6, 218–30 passim, general attitudes, 2, 4–5, 8, 17–18, 20, 50–2, 95, 100, 118, 171–3, 193

Stuart, Sir Charles, 207

Tamaulipas, 99

Tampico, 99

Tattischef, Dimitri, 83, 110, 205, 211–12

Taxation, 2, 56, 103–14 passim, 121, 164–5

Toreno, Conde de, 25, 37, 46, 92, 94, 117, 140, 144, 216, 224

Torre, Miguel de la, 91
Torre Marín, Francisco de, 224
Torrente, Mariano, 25, 100, 116
Torres, Domingo de, 63
Trade: concessions, 9; free trade issue, 55, 65–6, 75–7, 94, 119–20, 129–49 *passim*, 194–217 *passim*, impact of loss of empire, 119–20, 150–70 *passim*; insurance, 157; monopoly, defence of, 132–49 *passim*; privileged contracts, 138–9; tariff reform, 144–6; taxation, 142; *see also* Britain; Mediation, Economy; Merchants

Ugarte y Larrazabal, Antonio de, 83, 110, 140

Vadillo, José Manuel, 112–13, 221–2
Valcárcel y Dato, José, 44
Valdés, Cayetano, 87
Valiente, José, 23
Valle, Juan del, 145
Van Aken, M.J., 228
Varea, Esteban, 47, 87, 92–3, 179, 189, 213
Vargas, Pedro, 140
Vargas Laguna, Antonio, 185
Vargas Ponce, José, 144
Vaughan, Charles, 66, 133, 202
Vázquez Figueroa, José: appointment, 66; dismissal, 82; reports, 66–8, 79; views, 8, 50, 69–74 *passim*, 77–81, 93, 110–11, 137–8, 140, 182, 208
Venezuela, 28, 33, 35, 37–9, 59, 64–5, 79, 89–92, 95, 111, 139

Veracruz, 69, 72, 79–80, 92–3, 95, 101, 139
Veragua, Duque de, 183, 207
Verona, congress of, 214
Vich, 146
Victorica, Miguel, 140
Vienna, 82; congress of, 203, 206
Vigodet, Gaspar, 53
Vilar, P., 4
Vilardaga, Juliá y Reinals, 156
Villalba, Andrés, 70
Villalobos, Rafael de, 161
Villalva, Joaquín, 156
Villar, Francisco de Paula, 98
Villavicencio, Antonio de, 53
Viniegra, Leandro José, 111
Vistaflorida, Conde de, 45, 60
Vives, V., 137
Vizcaya, 103

Watson J., 158
Wellesley, Sir Henry, 55, 57, 83, 130, 132, 188, 195–205 *passim*, 211; *see also* Britain: mediation
Wellington, Duke of, 198, 212
Wilson, Robert, 79

Ximeno, Antonio, 154

Yandiola, Juan Antonio, 35, 44, 112, 127–8, 137
Yermo, Gabriel, 43

Zayas, José de, 45, 60, 126